Health and the National Health Service

CHANGE IN BRITAIN SERIES – A NEW AUDIT

Series Editors Paul Rock and David Downes (London School of Economics)

Britain is evidently undergoing rapid social and political change, and the press, academics and others strive to make sense of its principal features. All too often, the language of crisis and conflict is employed to describe what is afoot. It is clear that crises and dissensions do exist, but it is also clear that it is often difficult to gain a proper appreciation of their significance. There are fashions in reporting that can over-simplify or bypass problems of interpretation and analysis; observers sometimes have a political or journalistic stake in writing in a dramatic, exciting and perturbing way; and the uneventful does not often receive attention merely because it is unremarkable. The outcome has been notably few dispassionate attempts to ascertain quite how change is occurring in particular areas of social life; what problems, if any, it presents and to whom; how those problems should be gauged; how recent or unusual they are; and their probable future course.

A New Audit reports on areas of British life conceived conventionally to be changng fast. It assesses the scale and character of that change and the problems which may accompany it, considering new or little heeded evidence, balancing the claims of different commentators, and placing them in their historical and social context, allowing intelligent judgements to be made. It provides prognoses about their likely development, ascertaining what means have been taken to manage them, and what success they have met with, drawing on international experience where helpful.

CHANGE IN BRITAIN SERIES
– A NEW AUDIT

5

Health and the
National Health Service

JOHN CARRIER AND IAN KENDALL

THE ATHLONE PRESS
London & Atlantic Highlands, NJ

First published 1998 by
THE ATHLONE PRESS
1 Park Drive, London NW11 7SG
and 165 First Avenue,
Atlantic Highlands, NJ 07716

British Library Cataloguing in Publication Data
*A Catalogue record for this book is available
from the British Library*

ISBN 0 485 80007 1 hb
ISBN 0 485 80107 8 pb

Library of Congress Cataloging-in-Publication Data

Carrier, John.
    Health and the National Health Service / John Carrier and Ian
Kendall.
        p.   cm. — (Conflict and change in Britain series ; 5)
    Includes bibliographical references and index.
    ISBN 0–485–80007–1 (hb). — ISBN 0–485–80107–8 (pb)
    1. National Health Service (Great Britain)   2. Medical care—Great
Britain.   I. Kendall, Ian.   II. Title.   III. Series.
RA395.G6C38   1997
362.1′0941—dc21
                                                                97–18611
                                                                    CIP

Typeset by Ensystems, Saffron Walden

Printed and bound in Great Britain by
Cambridge University Press

For our grandchildren

In memory of
Brian Abel-Smith
(November 6, 1926 – April 4, 1996)
Scholar, teacher and friend

Contents

Series Editors' Preface

The British National Health Service is the most enduring monument to the surge of postwar idealism that created the 'Welfare State'. Its popular appeal rests on a practical idea that is stunningly simple and easily grasped. Serious illness strikes most people at some point in their lives, often at several points and, for a minority, almost continuously. Yet despite advances in epidemiology and actuarial statistics, we never know when, on whom, where and under what circumstances the blow may fall. Treatment is correspondingly difficult to prepare for: the healthiest pregnancy may develop complications; the most robust athlete fall prey to some dire condition; the most sickly child may survive but need constant medical attention. Each individual faces something of a lottery in the health stakes, which are an awesome amalgam of genetic endowment, the nature of the environment, social location, personal habits, exposure to infection and sheer accident. The individual can of course insure against ill-health, both financially and by sensible living. But to insure against the most serious and rare conditions is astronomically expensive. How much more convenient and prudent, living behind this veil of ignorance, to pool small amounts of income which, collectively, covers the risks of illness wherever they happen to strike. Free access to full treatment is then guaranteed for all. That is the core of the immense sway the NHS has exerted for half a century since its inception in 1948 under the aegis of Aneurin Bevan, Minister of Health in the Labour Government of Clement Attlee.

Has it worked? The answer to this question is vital because, however potent the ideal, if it is not matched by hard experience, it will duly founder. Two sets of statistics suggest that it has indeed paid off, both in health terms and as value for money. In the UK and the USA, life expectancy at birth in 1989 was virtually identical: respectively, for males, 72.4 and 71.9 years; and for females 78.1 and 79.0 years (CSO, 1991, p. 33). Yet health care expenditure in the USA, as a proportion of Gross Domestic Product, is *double* that in the UK, 12 per cent compared to 6 per cent in 1989 (Hills, 1993, p. 56). Both countries spend roughly the same proportion of GDP on public health care services, about 5 per cent. The huge difference arises from the much greater expenditure in the USA on private health care: some 7 per cent of GDP, compared with 1 per cent in Britain. If the acid test of health care systems is longevity, despite the array of complex issues involved, then the NHS delivers the same goods at half the price and with far less anxiety about how to pay for it. The issue is seemingly settled. Why bother with an audit?

One reason is that the NHS is under siege as never before – though, as the authors of this book make abundantly clear, it has *never* basked in some roseate steady state. Its critics are diverse and usually seek to improve its effectiveness and efficiency rather than wind it up. They have mounted such fundamental questions about the NHS as:

1. Could it not do more and better with the same resources?
2. Could it not do more and better with *fewer* resources?
3. Are its resources fairly distributed?
4. Would it not do better if more private resources were tapped to supplement those provided from public funding out of taxation?

These questions have built up to a crisis pitch, especially so in the context of a politics of enduring fiscal crisis, whereby both major parties now equate any hint of increased taxation with nemesis. The mismatch between rising expectations and same-level funding has led to endless bouts of re-organisation to bridge the gap. But these 'reforms' have led to such absurdities as hospital and bed closures being traded off for more attractive doctors' waiting rooms. August institutions such as St Bartholomew's Hospital have been effectively closed by amalgamation. There are widespread fears that the medical profession is demoralised, 'managed to death' and that the core principles of the NHS are being eroded by the 'quasi-marketeers'. All this has especial poignancy because, as Peter Hennessey conveyed so well in the title of his history of the 1945–51 period of social reconstruction, *Never Again* (1992) are we likely to have the historic opportunity to pull off so gigantic an accomplishment as the creation of the National Health Service.

For these reasons among others, this audit could not have been more timely. By placing these and other issues in a detailed historical context, the authors have avoided the narrow, distorting focus on the immediate present. The range and dispassionate quality of their analysis allows us to take stock of health care in Britain in a sober and freshly informed way.

David Downes
Paul Rock

Acknowledgements

As this book neared completion, our long time mentor, Professor Brian Abel-Smith died. As will be apparent we rely heavily upon his scholarship, especially his 1964 publication *The Hospitals 1800–1948* for the early chapters of this book. Unfortunately the manuscript was not completed before we might have benefitted from his always generous wisdom.

We are also indebted to other scholars especially Bob Pinkers, Jeanne Brand, Harry Eckstein, Bentley Gilbert, Howard Glennerster, Ruth Hodgkinson, Rudolf Klein, Julian Le Grand, Almont Lindsey, Rosemary Stevens, Richard Titmuss and Charles Webster for their interpretation of events which we have drawn upon for this work. In trying to understand how a professional medical service has been delivered to the British population through a state funded and administered system, these references have been invaluable. They have helped us develop our main theme – that it has been possible to guarantee a comprehensive health service to the population of a modern society within a state system, despite the inevitable conflicts that sociological predictions suggest should arise from the clash between the authority of the state and the independence of professional practitioners of health care. The above references have helped to illuminate this theme, and we willingly acknowledge our own intellectual debt to these scholars.

We also wish to acknowledge a debt to the Editors of this series, Professors David Downes and Paul Rock for their continued support, encouragement and tolerance, especially during the period of the writing of this book when it looked as if changes in the NHS were so continuous, that we could never complete the final manuscript, and to our publishers, The Athlone Press, for their patience and support.

John Carrier
Ian Kendall

Preface

The term audit is familiar to the language of accountancy so its appearance in a book on health care may seem to be out of place. Traditionally, audit has been concerned with accounting for resources used, whereas health and medical care has used the language of science and ethics without consideration of a financial 'bottom-line'. But certainly since the 1980s the term audit has been used by groups other than accountants in contexts other than financial balance sheets. This is particularly true in Britain where the language of market principles has entered social service areas, encouraged by Conservative governments since 1979, and exemplified by the establishment of the National Audit Office (NAO).

In the context of medical care, audit is likely to mean the relationship between the resources used and a successful outcome for a patient who has undergone a medical procedure; a surgical intervention; the treatment by drug therapy of an acute episode; or the care of a patient with a chronic condition. Often benefit is immediately obvious, with a dramatic medical or surgical intervention saving life or stabilising an acute condition. But if the benefit from a particular procedure is neither immediate nor obvious then an audit raises the most sensitive question of how to justify using scarce resources in a particular way. This has been a particular concern of economists because scarcity involves selecting priorities with a proven beneficial outcome.

A combination of scarcity, scepticism of biomedical approaches in health care, and a more challenging public, have raised the question of the benefits and returns that should be derived from the use of health care resources. In this sense audit might be interpreted by those trusted with these resources, as a check upon their professional judgement and therefore a challenge to their therapeutic and economic use. The position of government funding agencies towards this issue will be that of *accountability* for public money. Politically, this becomes interpreted as *value*-for-money. Given this context, it is almost impossible to believe that audit can be considered in a value-free and non-contentious atmosphere. Checks and accountability are bound to question the technical judgements and ethical positions of those responsible for matching these resources to meet professionally defined needs. This atmosphere has become dominant in the field of medical care in the last fifteen to twenty years and has coincided with an increased public awareness of the benefits and costs of medical and surgical interventions, parallel to concerns about cost containment.

Thus audit has a two-edged purpose; to assess once unchallenge-able medical and surgical professional judgements and to raise value-for-money concerns. In this context the National Health Service (NHS) might be seen to be caught in a set of conflicting and contradictory expectations – the assumption of the highest possible standards resting alongside a distrust of the use of resources in situations which do not appear to have an immedi-ately obvious beneficial outcome.

For our purposes the idea of audit is not concerned with medical or clinical audit but rather with addressing the question how well is the NHS doing in the context of current administrative, pro-fessional and economic criteria on the one hand and public awareness and expectations on the other. The period since the early 1970s, especially in the more affluent countries of the world, has been one in which there has been an increasing use of financial criteria in measuring the contribution of medical care to health status. This will not surprise economists, whose concerns with effectiveness and efficiency have long been used to measure costs and benefits in public programmes. However, the centre-stage taken by auditing, performance indicators, effectiveness and effi-ciency since the mid-1970s is related to the dominant concerns of scarcity and cost-containment. Cost-containment, while a phrase of the late 1970s and 1980s, has a lengthy history for those concerned with providing resources for health care systems; it summarises a major fear, that of a medical care system which is out of financial control, with spiralling costs. The worst examples are usually taken from market-based systems of which the USA is a prime candidate, but the idea of controlling resources going into the system and expecting 'value-for-money' has also become common to State-supported systems and mixed-economy arrangements.

The United Kingdom has long been held up as an example of a well-established state system based upon the non-market criteria of universal access, comprehensive coverage, professional freedom to treat and prescribe, and the equitable distribution of medical care resources. All this has taken place within the context of the accountability of government for a NHS funded through general taxation. Cost-containment questions, however, have forced the idea of audit into the debate about the provision of medical care. At the same time it has been suggested that the legal changes in the administration and organization of the NHS since 1990 have raised questions about the level and standard of medical care which patients can expect from the service, and the responsibilities of professionals in providing these levels and standards (see Newdick, 1995)

These developments can be seen as contributing to more conflict – 'within' health care systems between different participants (eg managers, clinicians and patients) and in the relationship between health care providers, health care users, and the rest of society (eg taxpayers and insurance premium payers). The aim of our audit is to locate health care in a series of contexts – both historical and contemporary – by which the nature and significance of these conflicts may be assessed. For example, are new attitudes and approaches engendering new forms of conflict or are contemporary conflicts merely the most recent variants of deep-seated and long-standing conflicts inherent in matters of health and health care? To what extent can current changes and conflicts be set against evidence of continuities in and consensus about health and health care?

It is not in the nature of social science enquiries to produce one true account that will answer these questions with the precision that an auditor seeks to balance the books. Balancing the books in a social audit of this sort may be more concerned to warn against, rather than to enable, precise conclusions to be drawn. With this in mind we offer *one* new audit of conflict and change in health and health care in Britain. In so doing we deliberately adopt a more conceptual and historical approach than is found in some other texts on the National Health Service. This means that references to specific policies and administrative arrangements may be made in passing rather than in detail, since it is our view that students have a wealth of literature on the current policy debates in the NHS to draw upon, whereas this text seeks to place those debates in a broader context. This is necessary in order to emphasise our major theme, that the development of health care in the UK has not been an uncontested series of changes but instead has been characterised by conflicts about the purpose, funding, organization, distribution and quality of the care it provides. Our book is but one contribution to an analysis of this development.

Part One:
An Historical Audit

The majority of the population in England consider it ... the most natural thing in the world, when they fall ill, to ... receive free treatment without question or delay

Americans hold ... that no person is entitled to occupy a free bed unless or until he can prove beyond dispute that he is unable to pay something for the treatment he received in the hospital ward. (H.C. Burdett, *Hospitals and Asylums of the World*, 1893, p. 56)

In the early nineteenth century many of the voluntary hospitals ... moved into a prolonged crisis. (Harris, 1979, p. 287)

There is no new thing under the sun. (Ecclesiastes 1: 8)

Introduction

Issues of health and health care are usually considered in the separate disciplines of medicine and health administration. They have also been the subject of political and philosophical debate in Britain for over a century and have found their way into textbooks of political science and ethics, the former focusing on pressure groups and histories of the development of the NHS, the latter on justifications for medical intervention. All these texts have treated health and health care as areas of potential conflict. Pressure groups have always had their own purposes in arguing for change in medical care. Those concerned with the ethics of providing medical care have usually been concerned with rights to such care, including the questions of consent and redress for medical mishaps, the duties of professionals to provide such care, the obligations of government to fund such care, and the accountability of government to the public for guaranteeing the existence, quantum and standard of medical care. Each of the above is fraught with conflict.

Such conflicts have never been absent from both the discussion and practical administration of health care although they have taken different forms and have varied in intensity for over a century. For these reasons, Part One of this book aims to locate current disputes and conflicts within and about the NHS in the context of historical developments in the British welfare state. These clearly have their origin in nineteenth century concerns including the appropriate role of the state in relation to problems identified with both industrialisation and urbanisation (see Chapter 1). These 'social problems' included perceived needs for health care and it was these needs which brought politicians and state officials into a relationship with those professionals whose task it was to define and alleviate these needs. How this relationship was stabilised and changed has been a major cause of the conflict which has appeared to surround the provision of medical care in Britain, even though this provision represented for many years one of the most reliable and high quality services in the industrial world.

It will become clear that few of the conflicts identified in contemporary debates are entirely new and that some have a long-established history. Basic questions about individual and collective responsibility and the role of the state were posed by the public health debate in the nineteenth century (see Chapter 1). If we can identify, in the first forty years of the twentieth century, elements of health care which would be incorporated in the NHS (compulsory health insurance and municipal health services), we can, in that same period, identify origins of later conflicts about costs, remuneration, clinical freedom and (again) the role of the state (see Chapter 2). Also to be observed are the seemingly conflicting roles of the medical profession. The profession has been a major source of innovatory ideas about health care reforms and could be categorised as 'progressive' rather than 'conservative'. Where governments have been reluctant to provide medical care on a continuing and open basis, the role of the medical profession has been critical, as for example, the contribution of Poor Law medical officers in the nineteenth century (see Chapter 1); Lord Dawson's Report in 1920, the role of the British Medical Association (BMA) and the Socialist Medical Association (SMA) in the 1930s (see Chapter 2); and the influences of the Royal Colleges in the late 1980s and early 1990s (see Chapter 7), are further examples of professional persuasion, influence and pressure on British governments with respect to providing a national health service. At the same time the profession has also been a major source of opposition to health care reforms, regardless of the political party forming the government, but especially in battles to influence and delay the establishment of National Health Insurance (NHI) before 1913 and the NHS before 1948. As recently as 1990 the BMA took a strong stand against the introduction of the so-called 'internal market' thus providing an example of a so-called 'conservative' profession in direct opposition to a Conservative government.

There is perhaps a conflict of conventional 'expectations' with 'reality' when health care histories indicate that wartime priorities afforded a greater significance to health care reforms in practice and in theory, than had ever been recognised by peacetime governments (see Chapter 3). This was the immediate background for the well-documented dispute between an incoming radical Labour government in the 1940s and a conservative medical profession – often interpreted as an episode in which it looked as if the medical profession would hold out against a state-financed, delivered and regulated service (see Chapter 4).

The NHS subsequently assumed a central role in 'the establishment of the welfare state', the latter seen as an expression of, and a contributor to, a 'post-war consensus'. Whether events felt as consensual for those within the Service is an interesting question. The period between 1948 and 1979 was not trouble-free but was constantly beset by problems concerning funding, administration and management, the payment of general practitioners, the degree of private practice allowed in NHS hospitals, concerns about equality of resources between social groups and regions of the country; the balance between acute, chronic and preventive medicine; the competing needs of priority groups (elderly people, people with mental health problems) and those acutely sick people who require technological intervention (dialysis, transplants) (see Chapter 5). Along with this there was a growing realisation by patients that they were part of a consumer-conscious society, the values of which began to be applied to the judgment of professional services.

There was plenty of scope for conflict between concepts of professional autonomy, democratic accountability and rational planning (Chapters 5, 6 and 14); and between commitments to meeting identified needs and to cost containment in accord with what the public purse could afford. Current commentators who see controversy *and* novelty in questions of whether the state can afford a comprehensive health service (and incidentally universal pensions) may conclude they are right only on the first count when they revisit the Guillebaud and Phillips Reports (Guillebaud Report, 1956; Phillips Report, 1954; see Chapters 4 and 5).

Regardless of how we divide up and compartmentalise the history of health care in the UK, most periods seem to contain within themselves major differences of opinion about the rationale, the methods and the outcomes of providing and judging medical care in a national health service. All were contentious in their time and all have in common the uneasy relationship between professional definitions of adequate health care, government funding and organization of such care, and the expectations of patients (actual and potential).

The concentration on continuing episodes of conflict, whether between government and the profession, or between government and organised pressure groups, runs the danger of ignoring or forgetting what to a non-British visitor has been a remarkable consensus surrounding the delivery of health care through the NHS. Overseas visitors still comment on the simplicity of funding arrangements and the guarantee of medical care based upon need not purchasing power (despite well publicised cases of scarcity, see, for example, Newdick, 1995, pp. 120–35). The NHS is well-established within British social and political arrangements, perhaps because some of its characteristics (for example, health care that is largely free at the point of consumption) were present in the arrangements for health care before the Service was established (see Chapters 1 and 2). The taken for granted presence of a medical care response to a whole range of health-threatening episodes, from the most minor visit to an Accident and Emergency department to major transplant surgery or long-term care, seemed to preclude even the relatively radical, post-1979 Conservative governments from dramatically recasting the basic relationship between the state and the citizenship right to adequate health care. The most prominent member of these governments was to declare that the National Health Service was safe in the hands of her government, despite the willingness of that government to contemplate conflicts with the medical profession and other health service personnel reaching an apparent climax with the imposition of a quasi-market system (Bartlett and Harrison, 1993) in the face of considerable professional opposition (see Chapter 7). The London case-study we discuss later raises a question over whether a Conservative government determined to rationalise health care in London could keep this promise. It should be noted that it was London-based Conservative MPs who were to become most critical when the hospitals and accident and emergency departments in their London constituencies were threatened with abolition as part of a 'rationalisation' of services (see Chapter 9).

In preparing our historical account we have been guided by the aims of our audit. Given the seemingly universal predilection to construct peaceful and serene 'golden ages' to set against contemporary 'crises' we have placed some emphasis on the conflict-laden history of health and medical care in the UK. The identification of this continuing and lengthy history of conflict is of more than academic interest. Long-running conflicts that successive generations have failed to resolve, may involve irreconcilable aims and interests. This may seem a rather obvious point, but has been often ignored in the not infrequent pursuit of 'single-best solutions' to the organization and delivery of health care in the UK.

We have sought also to balance this awareness of enduring and long-running conflicts with the evidence of continuity and consensus. For example, we have made a conscious effort in constructing our historical audit to re-visit classic texts on the history of health care in the UK, especially Abel-Smith (1964), Brand (1965), Eckstein (1958), Gilbert (1966), Klein (1983), Stevens (1966), Titmuss (1950, 1963, 1968) and Willcocks (1967). This is partly in recognition of their intrinsic quality but also to ensure we identify some of the continuities in the analysis and evaluation of health care in the UK. It is one of our key themes that there are some long-standing conflicts about health care which need to be recognised as a backdrop to contemporary disputes about for example, GP fund-holders and internal markets. There are also some long-standing themes in analysis and evaluation which should not be re-presented as new simply because the terminology has changed and quasi-autonomous teaching hospitals are now quasi-autonomous NHS Trusts. We have no doubt that it is possible to construct a range of plausible accounts of the history of health care in the UK (Carrier and Kendall, 1977). What follows is *one* such plausible account.

1
Social assistance and voluntarism

Introduction

We begin our evaluation of conflict not only before the twentieth century, but also before the full impact of industrialisation and urbanisation was discernible. The reason for taking this longer term historical perspective is that these conflicts and divisions have influenced a number of subsequent developments in health and health care in the UK, at least in part because 'most of the basic characteristics of British medical practice were ... clearly in existence by 1900' (Stevens, 1966, p. 11). The major state interventions of the twentieth century – National Health Insurance (NHI, 1911) and the National Health Service (NHS, 1946) – were constructed around the divisions within the medical profession and the voluntary sector which existed in the nineteenth century. Furthermore the conflicts identifiable within late nineteenth century health care played a part in how the interventions of the state were structured (see especially Chapters 2 and 4).

Old Poor Law to New Poor Law

The new Poor Law was thrust on England in an age of economic and social dislocation. The grave consequences of this upheaval were the mass of actual pauperism engendered and the migratory army of poor who were turned adrift to find livelihood and shelter in the new urban slums. Action for this chaotic flotsam and jetsam was inevitable, but fear was its conditioning agent; and national unrest made immediate legislation in the early thirties imperative. (Hodgkinson, 1967, p. 1)

The origins of contemporary conflicts relating to issues associated with health and health care might plausibly be located in the development of the nation state rather than the establishment of a National Health Service. With the emergence of nation states and national economies, issues of poverty and destitution became matters of concern for governments – a concern, it has been suggested, connected as much with repression as with compassion (see Bruce, 1961, p. 23). In the UK we can identify the Elizabethan Poor Laws as indicators of this concern. In so far as ill-health was either a cause, or a consequence, of poverty and destitution, the activities of the Poor Law included some degree of care and support for sick paupers (Abel-Smith, 1964, pp. 3–4). The availability of even rudimentary health care was therefore an indirect consequence of a very limited form of public assistance; this meant also that such health care would be part of whatever conflicts would be associated with the subsequent development of this public assistance.

Some of the most well-documented and enduring of these conflicts were those between parishes (as Poor Law authorities), concerning the locality responsible for particular paupers (Bruce, 1961, p. 37). The contemporary echo of this issue concerns newspaper stories of dying and distressed patients being moved from one hospital to another in the mid-1990s to receive the appropriate medical care. The disputes between parishes were one indication that this system of public assistance was intended to expend minimal sums of public money to achieve broader social and political goals. It was also an enduring theme, and it was unsurprising that the entire framework of parish-based relief should be the subject of particular interest and conflict in the early part of the nineteenth century when escalating expenditure generated concerns about its economic effects.

The resulting 'New Poor Law' followed a Royal Commission and an Act of Parliament (Poor Law Amendment Act, 1834) and has been widely identified with the liberal 'laissez-faire' ideology and the concept of 'The Liberal Break' (see for example, Doyal, 1979, p. 142; Fraser, 1973, Ch.5; Gilbert, 1966, 13–14, and Thane, 1982, p. 11). The core ideas of the latter included notions of individualistic freedom and self-help, and were essentially antithetical to anything more than minimal state intervention in areas broadly encompassed by the categories of economic and social policy. From this perspective the final decades of the 'Old Poor Law' had been an exercise in misplaced compassion involving excessive state expenditure on public assistance and excessive state intervention in social and economic affairs through the mechanism of 'outdoor relief'. The latter involved a situation in which many parishes had been party to the establishment of a range of 'allowance systems' supporting families in the community beyond the confines of the poorhouse.

The new order ushered in by the 1834 legislation was intended to proscribe the role of public assistance by a more precise delineation of who might be in receipt of such assistance. The principles underpinning the 'New Poor Law' were not new, but were clearly intended to be more rigorously adhered to than had apparently been the case in the final years of the 'Old Poor Law'. The Poor Law had never sought to provide aid to all the poor, but its function of assisting only those who were completely destitute was now set down with greater clarity. The means by which such a minimal role could be maintained, whilst causing no offence to work incentives and the value of self-help, was the 'less-eligibility' or 'workhouse test'. Conditions within the workhouses of the Boards of Guardians (the new Poor Law authorities) were to be made less eligible than that of the lowest paid worker in the community and there was to be no poor relief offered beyond the confines of the workhouse. The framers of the Poor Law 'had assumed the individual to be poor because he was evil, and as such might be treated with a generous helping of salutary harshness' (Gilbert, 1966, p. 26). The Act of 1834 was 'conceived for the welfare of the wealthy' (Hodgkinson, 1967, p. 695)

The outcome was health care for the poor 'marked by a chilling and pervasive atmosphere of deterrence' (Brand, 1965, p. 86), the intention being the maintenance of an ideal-type of minimal state intervention in health and welfare – an institution-based / 'less eligibility' residual model. 'Almost the only thought from officials high and low was, "reduce expenditure and save the rates". Year after year the Annual Reports congratulated the country that the cost of relief was diminishing when compared with the wealth and population of the nation' (Hodgkinson, 1967, p. 65). Within twenty five years at least one medical practitioner would develop plans for a state medical service on an insurance basis (see Rumsey, 1856, 265–9) and within fifty years a President of the Poor Law Board would write that:

the economical and social advantages of free medicine to the poorer classes generally, as distinguished from actual paupers, and perfect accessibility to medical advice at all times under a thorough organization, may be considered as so important in themselves, as to render it necessary to weight with the greatest care all the reasons which may be adduced in their favour. (Quoted in Hodgkinson, 1967, pp. 332–3).

Thus, subsequent developments and the trend away from the model embodied in the new Poor Law, were anticipated by professionals and managers in the nineteenth century – although this trend would be accompanied by continuing conflicts about its desirability (see in particular Chapters 11 and 12).

The 'New Poor Law' was intended also to provide a more efficient system of administration. A smaller number of larger poor law authorities were established – Boards of Guardians replaced parishes – and there was to be more central control through the Poor Law Commission. This may represent one of the earlier examples in British social policy of the tendency 'to seek administrative solutions to problems that are basically economic or technological' (Brown, 1972, p. 132). It would certainly not be the last occasion on which larger units of administration and more central control were seen as the most appropriate reform (see Chapters 6, 7 and 14).

If one of the intentions of the new Poor Law was to limit what medical assistance it might offer in terms of quantity and quality, then it might be said to have done a service to those sick paupers for whom it was providing relief! The limitations of contemporary medical education, medical practice, and hospital care, in the first half of the nineteenth century, have been well-documented. For hospitals the 'most notorious and persistent of ... controversies centred upon the question of whether ... (they) ... actually killed more people than they cured' (Harris, 1979, p. 287). Medical education was rudimentary, although improving through the adoption of scientific findings into the curriculum; practice was commercial not social in orientation, and therefore not rationally distributed to match needs; and hospital care varied in quality, distribution, and successful outcome for the patient (see for example, Eckstein, 1958, pp. 15–16 and Stevens, 1966, p. 23).

The operation of the 'New Poor Law' did not altogether accord with the aims of its advocates. There is evidence of a considerable continuity of personnel and practices between the pre-1834 and post-1834 situations with the relatively limited powers of the central Poor Law Commission providing ample opportunity for local variations in the scale and standard of provision (see for example, Brand, 1965, p. 82, Thane, 1982, p. 12 and Abel-Smith, 1964, p. 47 and p. 50). After twenty years of operation the vast majority of paupers were on outdoor relief (Fraser, 1973, p. 48); one indication that the new Poor Law might have constituted some sort of response to rural destitution but could hardly be made to work at all for the poverties of industrialism.

The 'New Poor Law' was coming under pressure from two closely related factors. The first was the doubling of the population of Great Britain between 1801 and 1851, and again between 1851 and the outbreak of World War One; alongside this there was the movement of the population from rural to urban settings. The second factor was the social conditions in these urban settings – the new industrial towns and cities – dramatically demonstrated by Chadwick and others (see for example, Brand, 1965, pp. 2–21 and Hodgkinson, 1967, Ch.17). These factors formed the basis of the initial case for specific state intervention in health care made by the 'public health movement' – an intervention that could claim some support from those who favoured policies to minimise public expenditure on health and welfare.

> (Sickness) ... destroys a man's capacity for labour, and if he has failed to make timely provisions (or if wages are too low to do so) he is at once prostrated, when sickness overtakes him, and has therefore of necessity to look for help to others, Whilst therefore adhering in their entirety to the principles of the Poor Law Amendment Act, *we may yet admit that medical relief is in its nature, not only the least objectionable of all modes of relief, but it is within reasonable limits admissible and in the existing state of society, even necessary.* (Nicholls, 1854, quoted in Hodgkinson, 1967, p. 59)

Public health

(A) ... hell of depression and misery and hopeless degradation. Foul odors, vermin, vile food, drunkenness and promiscuity were the chief by-products of its depauperate and crowded existence: crime and disease were but the inevitable psychological and physiological responses. (Mumford, 1940, p. 12, on the industrial slums of Victorian England)

With the steadily mounting population came the new sanitary problems and mounting urban deaths. 'Laissez-faire', still the favourite nineteenth century watchword, provided no solution (Brand, 1965, p. 1)

To apply the prevention principle to the new social problems necessitated a new type of activity . . . departure from 'laissez-faire' was inevitable. (Hodgkinson, 1967, p. 621)

The Vaccination Act of 1840 was an indicator of a potential conflict between the ideology that was intended to underpin the social policies in the first half of the nineteenth century and the social problems of the period. This piece of legislation provided for free vaccination to all who applied for it without reference to their circumstances.

Vaccination was the first of the free health services provided by the legislature on a national scale. A beginning in positive health measures had been made, and it was administered through the channels of the Poor Law. (Hodgkinson, 1967, p. 31).

However, this identification of a social problem with a forthcoming administrative response can suggest that health reforms of the time logically followed the identification of 'public concerns' (see Paulus, 1974). What can easily be forgotten in describing this identification and response to the 'social problem of public health' was the extent to which this expansion of state intervention was extremely contentious at the time. Cholera scares seem to have been 'of great service to the advancement of English sanitation' – reformers being well aware that this fear of cholera could be used to good effect to enact changes that had more impact on other threats to the public health (Brand, 1965, p. 45). But support for reform 'waned with the passing of . . . (each) . . . epidemic' (Brand, 1965, p. 2) and was anyway not sufficient to convince the leader writer in *The Times* who argued that the population might wish to take their 'chance of cholera and the rest' rather than be 'bullied into health' (see *The Times*, Leading Article, 1/8/1854). As one commentator was to observe subsequently, it was not until a considerable time after the passage of the Public Health Act of 1848 'that there was a general conviction that it might be better to suffer the compulsion of being kept alive than to enjoy the privilege of being allowed to die in an epidemic of fever' (Wilson, 1938, p. 21). Such attitudes are one explanation of the delay in getting effective public health legislation on the statute book.

The marked differences between death rates in urban and rural areas was being documented by the Registrar-General in the 1830s, yet it was 1848 before the first Public Health Act was passed. This has been identified as one of the earliest examples of state control over the lives of individuals in a predominantly laissez-faire society (Doyal, 1979, p. 142) although it was permissive legislation and had a limited impact. Almost a quarter of century would pass until a comprehensive and mandatory piece of legislation was placed on the statute book (see Thane, 1982, p. 40); and there would be graphic evidence after its enactment of a failure to use the resulting statutory powers effectively (see Gilbert, 1966, pp. 28–9). If there was a necessary logic to public health legislation, it was a logic that took many years to be accepted by the government. The 'public health problem' of Britain's industrial cities had claimed many victims between the emergence of the 'objective evidence' collected by Government civil servants and the acceptance of the need for action by the politicians in government. To identify a problem did not necessarily mean that a state-supported solution to eliminate that problem would be the 'rational response'. This is a further indication that the wide-ranging consensus around the necessity of this form of state intervention, which we take-for-granted today, was the subject of considerable conflict at the time.

In the period over which the Government edged painfully slowly towards putting effective public health legislation on the statute book, the modern medical profession emerged – at least in so far as its legal status is concerned. The latter was confirmed by the 1858 Medical Act, the passing of which can be seen as the culmination of another conflict – that between the members and supporters of 'traditional professional groups' – the apothecaries, physicians, surgeons and their professional associations – and those other individuals who aspired to the status of medical practitioner. The latter were a significant group in numbers at least. There were 30,000 individuals who recorded their occupation as 'doctor' which can be set against the 11,000 qualified physicians listed in the 1845 Medical Directory. Following the Act of 1858 the Poor Law Board would demand that all poor law medical officers should be registered and should possess a legal qualification to practice both medicine and surgery – actually requiring them to obtain better professional training than some practitioners in private practice (Brand, 1965, p. 88).

The success of 'personal health care practitioners' (surgeons, physicians and apothecaries) in attaining a professional status legitimated by the state makes an interesting contrast with the long drawn out and controversial battle to place effective public health legislation on the statute book. The UK had effective 'professionalisation of health' legislation before it had effective 'public health' legislation – although health professionals were significant campaigners for public health reform (Brand, 1965, pp. 2, 10). In terms of 'functions' for society – that is, meeting 'the needs of an industrial society' – the potential of public health reform was demonstratable when that of personal health professionals was dubious. Indeed the relative significance of public health and environmental measures by comparison with personal health services has been a continuing theme in much subsequent epidemiological literature (see for example, McKeown, 1976). Whilst being active advocates of continuing public health reform from the country-wide requirement for their appointment in 1872 (see Brand, 1965, Ch.6), public health professionals have continued to experience a status that appears to be inversely (and some would say perversely) related to the contribution they have made to the health and well-being of the urban populations of industrial societies (see Chapter 10 for a further discussion of these issues)

There always has been a widely held distinction between meeting individual medical need, and protecting society at large from the indivisible costs of large-scale disease (eg: cholera, typhoid) through public health services. This distinction may reflect the difference between the perceptions of medical care and health held by the lay public on the one hand and the public health professions on the other. The former may be unaware of the invisible public health base of individual health status and may see only personal health services as responsible for their freedom from sickness, illness, and disease.

If public health issues had become somewhat less contentious in the latter half of the nineteenth century, it should not be presumed that this situation applied to state provision of personal health services. Nonetheless by 1900 the British state was an important source of health care. Public health issues made a contribution to this change; local authorities were first empowered to build their own hospitals under Section 37 of the Sanitary Act, 1866.

> These powers were further consolidated with the passing of Disraeli's Public Health Act in 1875 which permitted local authorities to build 'hospitals or temporary places for the reception of the sick'. (Pinker, 1966, p. 78)

By 1900 there would be nearly one thousand isolation hospitals and other institutions under the public health service, although only two local authorities had used their statutory powers to open their own general hospitals (see Stevens, 1966, pp. 34–5; Pinker, 1966, p. 78; and Parker, 1965, p. 29). Another dimension of state intervention in health care in the first half of the nineteenth century was the building of asylums following the County Asylums Act, 1808. However this was 'permissive' legislation allowing, but not requiring, Justices of the Peace to raise rates to build such asylums. By 1827 only 9 such asylums were in operation (see Jones, 1972, pp. 88–9).

That local authority hospitals and county asylums might be deemed necessary at all, given the existence of an extensive network of voluntary hospitals, is indicative of one reason for the changing role of the British state in health care provision. That the state should get drawn into a more central role in the direct provision of personal health services might be attributable to a conflict between *the reality* of the scope of health care that could be provided through voluntary institutions, and *the aspirations* of those who would continue to argue for the health and welfare functions of the state to be constrained within a residual, deterrent system of public assistance represented by the new Poor Law.

Hospital care

The voluntary hospital found its origin in medieval piety, and grew in later centuries through the philanthropy of laymen and doctors. The eighteenth century particularly saw the establishment of hospitals to give medical relief to the sick poor, but unlike developments on the Continent they depended on charity and not on public provision (Hodgkinson, 1967, p. 195)

In nineteenth century Britain, voluntary institutions appeared well-placed to meet the health care needs of the nation with limited recourse to state intervention. The predominantly middle-class and upper-class tradition of philanthropic, charitable activity was represented by the voluntary hospitals (Abel-Smith, 1964, pp. 4–5). A small number of these hospitals were well-endowed with historical tradition and resources. Others were of more recent origins, forming part of the extensive establishment of new hospitals that had taken place in Britain between 1700 and 1825 when 'one hundred and fifty-four new hospitals and dispensaries were established as charitable institutions' (Stevens, 1966, p. 14; see also Eckstein, 1958, p. 15 and Woodward, 1974, Chs. 2, 3 and p. 36). Similar developments took place in other European countries (see Abel-Smith, 1976, pp. 3–8).

Whilst these philanthropic institutions were not always held in the highest esteem (viz. the hospital riots at Manchester and Paisley, see Eckstein, 1958, p. 16) there was the apparent potential within the voluntary hospital system to meet a wide range of health care needs for a broad spectrum of the population. Throughout Europe the voluntary hospital tradition involved providing care largely free of charge to the poorer sections of the community. This was partly attributable to the charitable origins and aims of these institutions, but was also linked to the position of many of them as institutions for teaching and research – for example, 85 per cent of London's general hospital beds were in teaching hospitals in 1861 (Abel-Smith, 1964, p. 41). Interesting cases for teaching and research are as likely to be found amongst the poor as the rich, and the former are not well placed to object to their status as teaching subjects. The costs of the institutions were also minimised by having to pay nothing more than a modest honorarium for medical services. Appointments in such institutions were sought after as the basis for a reputation; the latter serving to obtain remuneration from a private practice that might well be conducted elsewhere (eg: Harley Street in London) – 'charitable work became the key to fame and fortune' (Abel-Smith, 1964, p. 19; see also pp. 6–7 and Baggott, 1994, p. 75, Stevens, 1966, pp. 14,15,17; and Woodward, 1974, p. 23).

But there were limitations to the scale and scope of voluntary hospital provision. The principal source of finance for these hospitals came from the subscriptions paid by individuals, parishes, or towns. This provided a sound resource base for the hospitals even if did lead to concerns that some institutions were less than accurate with their statistics, as competing institutions sought to attract subscribers – an early example of the limitations of simple, crude statistically-based league tables (see Woodward, 1974, pp. 139–42 and Abel-Smith, 1964, pp. 39–40). But this system also meant that the sick person had to find a subscriber who was willing to certify that the person in question was a proper object of charity (see Woodward, 1974, pp. 18, 38, 39).

> This was the only way of gaining admittance to a hospital unless the prospective patient had been involved in an accident or had symptoms which needed immediate relief. (Woodward, 1974, p. 39)

The scope of philanthropy also fell some way short of the 'universal stranger' (Titmuss, 1970, p. 238) since worthy objects of charity frequently excluded servants, apprentices, and of course paupers. The net result was that entry into hospital 'was bounded with many restrictions, which narrowed the section of the population for which the medical facilities were available' (Woodward, 1974, p. 43; see also p. 40 and Abel-Smith, 1964, pp. 14–15 and pp. 36–40).

Furthermore, whilst the need for 'interesting cases' and alternative sources of medical remuneration provided a rationale and a means to maintain the tradition of free hospital care for the poor, they also limited the contribution made by voluntary hospitals to identifiable needs for health care. It was a general feature of charity in nineteenth century Britain that it was highly localised (see Thane, 1982, p. 21) and this was true of the voluntary hospitals. The range and scope of their provision was linked to the range and scope of private practice (see Stevens, 1966, Ch.4). Voluntary hospitals could only lay claim to be adequate providers of the nation's hospital care in the more affluent or the densely populated parts of the country; they were established 'principally in the capital and in the main provincial centres of population' (Woodward, 1974, p. 144); 'the voluntary hospitals, due to their geographical distribution, were available only to a small portion of the working population' (Gilbert, 1966, p. 304).

As well as this significant spatial limitation, 'the voluntary movement never became more than marginally involved in the needs of the chronically sick' (Pinker, 1966, p. 72). This was in part a consequence of the focus on 'interesting cases'. This was linked to teaching needs and professional prestige (Abel-Smith, 1964, p. 45). It was also linked to fund-raising, for example,

> the more acute the cases admitted, the greater were the number of inpatients that could be treated in a given number of beds during the year. Such statistics were valuable for appeal purposes. (Abel-Smith, 1964, p. 39)

It appears that the rules of admission to the voluntary hospitals 'were generally designed to exclude the chronic sick and the cases which might prove troublesome in one way or another' (Woodward, 1974, p. 45). These exclusions link to the already mentioned public health problems of industrialisation and urbanization.

> As more epidemics raged across Britain's large and growing cities, more and more hospitals were excluding the victims. (Abel-Smith, 1964, p. 45)

The beginnings of state education in Britain can also be related to the limitations of voluntary institutions. Pilot surveys in four large cities ordered by Forster, Vice-President of the Board of Education in Gladstone's first Ministry, found less than 10 per cent of their population in schools and one advocate of voluntarism was forced to write:

> I confess to a strong distress of government action, a passionate love for voluntary action and self-reliance but now as a practical man I am compelled to abandon the purely

voluntary system. (Edward Baines quoted in D. Fraser, 1973, p. 80).

In what seems like an almost inevitable parallel with the development of state intervention in education, the public authorities assumed a responsibility for 'what was left undone by charity' and private enterprise (see Abel-Smith, 1964, p. 45 and Thane, 1982, p. 41).

The epidemics associated with urbanisation, the restricted scope of voluntary hospital activity, and a combination of parsimony and permissive mental health legislation, all had an impact on the health care activities of the poor law authorities. The Poor Law Amendment Act of 1834 was intended to ensure that state intervention in health and welfare would be minimal. Alongside the failure to control outdoor relief (see p. 13, above) can be recorded a failure to distance the state from any form of personal health services. Against the 14,722 beds in voluntary hospitals in 1861 can be set the 50,000 beds in the workhouses as recorded by the poor law authorities (see Pinker, 1966 pp. 73 and 75).

By 1891 the public sector was providing 2.88 beds per thousand of the population . . . .1.02 beds per thousand of the population were in voluntary hospitals. (Pinker, 1966, p. 70)

It was the poor law authorities which accommodated 'the bulk of the sick children, the mental cases, the skin conditions, those with epilepsy, tuberculosis and venereal diseases and the unexplored mass of the chronic sick' (Abel-Smith, 1964, p. 49). Medical care therefore began to be provided as an addendum to economic deprivation. Paupers 'housed' for reasons of destitution, turned Poor Law institutions into Poor Law infirmaries catering for the poor and the sick. A different set of institutions, administered by men not of the social elite which ran the voluntary hospitals (Abel-Smith, 1964, p. 63) and employing a separate group of doctors, were becoming 'the real hospitals of the land' (The Lancet Commission Report, p. ix quoted in Abel-Smith, 1964, p. 64). 'The Poor Law institutions had become the first public hospitals' (Hodgkinson, 1967, p. 451) and an important precedent had been set – 'the poor had gained the right to institutional care when they were sick' (Abel-Smith, 1964, p. 65)

The consequent duty of the state to provide hospitals for the poor received its first formal acknowledgement in the Metropolitan Poor Act of 1867 (Ayers, 1971, p. 1). The scene was set for 'the development of a poor law hospital service' (Pinker, 1966, p. 75) in so far as an increasing proportion of 'sick paupers' were located in workhouse sick wards and more significantly in separate poor law infirmaries. In 1904, new hospitals were accounting for 44 per cent of total expenditure on new Poor Law building (Abel-Smith, 1964, p. 204). Between 1891 and 1911 the number of beds in separate infirmaries rose by 338 per cent (see Pinker, 1966, p. 76). The trend towards 'specialist' provision was also discernible in the building of asylums and the subsequent re-location of 'pauper lunatics' which was given a financial incentive with changes introduced in 1874 through 'Grant in Aid' made available to encourage the transfer of those paupers identified as mentally ill and mentally handicapped from the workhouse to specialist institutions (Jones, 1972, pp. 160–1).

Much of the separate provision within the Poor Law remained of variable and often minimal quality – especially in rural areas – and the majority of the sick paupers remained in unclassified institutions, nursed by aged convalescent and feeble-minded paupers (see Brand, 1965, pp. 96–8 and Abel-Smith, 1964, pp. 212–15). But in some parts of the country, notably in London through the Metropolitan Asylums Board, a publicly-funded hospital system was emerging under the aegis of the New Poor Law. When the Public Health (London) Act of 1891 removed the power of poor law authorities in London to charge patients with infectious diseases 'every citizen in London had become entitled to free treatment from the Metropolitan Asylum Board'. This developed into 'one of the largest and most effective hospital systems in the world – while operating nominally as a branch of the Poor Law' (Abel-Smith, 1964, pp. 126–7; see also Brand, 1965, p. 95).

As Poor Law infirmaries improved in quality they became effectively the general hospital for the community – notably where voluntary hospital provision was limited (Abel-Smith, 1964, p. 206); they also began to acquire some other characteristics of the voluntary hospitals. Some were potentially problematic, for example, a preference for the acute sick over the chronic sick; others were an integral part of the emergence of 'modern health care' in Britain, with the Poor Law infirmaries making a substantial contribution to the development of nurse education and training (see Abel-Smith, 1964, pp. 154, 206–11 and Hodgkinson, 1967, pp. 556–72). Thus,

> the whole character of the Poor Law infirmaries was beginning to change ... (the) development was in complete contrast to the whole philosophy upon which the Poor Laws were based. (Abel-Smith, 1964, p. 132).

If changes largely within the Poor Law were leading to the establishment of a public hospital system, there was also, at the end of the nineteenth century, a rapid expansion of beds in private nursing homes. This expansion was associated with public and professional concerns about the costs and standards of care within this new private sector, with demands being made for its regulation (see Abel-Smith, 1964, pp. 189, 192–4)

Community health care

If the expansion of the charitable/philanthropic voluntary hospital sector could in the end meet only some of the nation's need for hospital provision, this was equally true of the community health services made available through the voluntary associations of the working-class mutual-aid tradition – the Friendly Societies. As with voluntary hospitals a similar growth in voluntary health insurance institutions took place in other European countries (Abel-Smith, 1976, pp. 8–11). In Britain membership of Friendly Societies was already 10 per cent of the population in 1804 (Abel-Smith, 1994, p. 68) and it continued to grow throughout the nineteenth century. By the turn of the century Friendly Societies had at least seven million members, over four times that of trade unions, and they were the largest exclusively working-class organizations in Britain, estimated to include half the adult male population (see Abel-Smith, 1994, p. 68; Gilbert, 1966, p. 166, and Thane, 1982, p. 29). Most of these societies provided medical benefit – principally the payment of sickness benefit and the services of general practitioners under contract to provide medical services to their members (see Thane, 1982, pp. 28–9). As with the voluntary hospitals, the Friendly Societies appeared to have considerable potential to meet at least the non-hospital health care needs of the working-classes. But like the voluntary hospitals, the reality was less encouraging for those who wished to see significant state provision of health care rendered unnecessary by the scale of provision by voluntary associations.

> Never ... were the weaker and more helpless elements of the working class successful in effecting a system of lasting consolidated societies. For generally, weak physical constitutions resulting from low wages, malnutrition, bad housing and squalid and filthy environments entailed an increase in disease, and therefore multiplied the claims for sickness benefits on a society which would obviously be impecunious. (Hodgkinson, 1967, p. 236).

Thus the Friendly Societies made 'no appeal whatever to the grey, faceless lower third of the working class' and 'Friendly society membership was not for the crossing sweeper, the dock labourer, the railroad navvy' (Gilbert, 1966, pp. 166–7). Instead membership was 'the badge of the skilled artisan' – 'the elite of the working-class' (Honigsbaum, 1989, p. 4); furthermore few societies admitted both men and women. Most women earned too little to pay their own contributions and few working-class families could afford double contributions (see Thane, 1982, pp. 29,30). If the health care needs of those unable to afford Friendly Society membership were met at all it might be through the outpatient department of a voluntary hospital – if location and circumstances permitted. More often it would be the Poor Law infirmaries and dispensaries that were the major providers of health care for women and children. More dispensaries appeared after the Metropolitan Poor Act of 1867 (Brand, 1965, pp. 87, 98–9 and Hodgkinson, 1967, Chapter 7) and indeed

> elaborate systematisation of outdoor medical relief ... put within reach of sick paupers medical attendance far superior to that accessible to the lowest grade of independent labourers, but even placed sick paupers in the Metropolis, without loss of liberty, in a position equal to that of the superior artisan subscribing to a good provident dispensary. (Webb, 1910; quoted by Hodgkinson, 1967, pp. 426–7)

Neither the personal nor the public health problems of an industrial and urban society seemed to be satisfactorily resolved by activities and institutions embodied in the 'Liberal Break' philosophy of 'laissez faire' – personal initiative, voluntary associations and an institution-based, less-eligibility model of minimal state welfare.

Conflicts

It was apparent in the last thirty years of the nineteenth century that the concept of a 'less eligibility' Poor Law was being compromised; firstly, by substantial variation in provision, especially between larger cities and elsewhere (Brand, 1965, p. 106); secondly, by the principles applied by Poor Law medical officers in granting medical relief (Abel-Smith, 1964, pp. 64, 206); and thirdly, by the standards attained by the best Poor Law infirmaries. Given the latter, the problem, as the framers of the 'less eligibility' principle might have predicted, had become one of moderating the use of nominally Poor Law institutions by the 'non-poor' (see Abel-Smith, 1964, p. 218).

If there was a conflict between the Poor Law ideology and at least some Poor Law provision, there was potentially another one between that ideology and demands for even better provision; the argument that a 'system of public relief deliberately made hideous for its recipients could not long outlast the grant of universal franchise' (Gilbert, 1966, p. 15). But if there was a conflict between the ideology formally underpinning the Poor Law, the reality of what the poor law authorities were making available in their areas, and the demands that might follow an extension of the franchise, they were not the only, even if the most significant, points of conflict within the pattern of health care provision in late nineteenth century Britain.

There was the continuing significance of the long-standing divisions and related conflicts within the medical profession (see Brand, 1965, pp. 147–8; Stevens, 1966, pp. 11–33, Woodward, 1974, pp. 4, 27–8, and Abel-Smith, 1964, pp. 2–3, 116). The training and registration of the medical practitioners had been formally unified and their professional status legitimated by the Medical Act, 1858. Nonetheless the separate traditions of physicians, surgeons and apothecaries were still clearly represented in the division between community-based general practitioners and hospital based specialist practitioners (GPs and consultants). This division was reflected in the different voluntary associations, with Friendly Societies employing general practitioners, and the specialist hospital doctors working in the voluntary hospitals. It remained a potential source of conflict within the profession because of the differential financial rewards favouring private practice (see Abel-Smith, 1964, pp. 108–17, 143–7); and indeed this division can be seen as one contributory factor in the maintenance of free voluntary hospital care in Britain at a time when 'pay hospitals' were developed in many other countries (Abel-Smith, 1964, p. 137). The emergence of the referral system, by which the general practitioners had the patients and the specialists had the hospital beds, ameliorated the potential for conflict over remuneration by ensuring that the former played a role in the process of access to hospital care (Stevens, 1966, pp. 32–3 and Honigsbaum, 1979, Ch.1).

There were potential sources of conflict between the medical profession, the state and the voluntary sector. Both the growing involvement of the state (through the poor law medical services) and the voluntary associations (through the Friendly Societies) were seen as threats to notions of professional autonomy and clinical freedom. Both poor law authorities and Friendly Societies sought to exercise detailed control over those medical practitioners under contract to them, raising the spectre of lay control over the profession (see Brand, 1965, pp. 85–7, 94, 102; Abel-Smith, 1964, pp. 60–2, 71, 91; and Honigsbaum, 1989, p. 5). In addition both the medical and emerging nursing profession found themselves in conflict with the poor law authorities over what they perceived as inadequate standards of care – the Poor Law medical officers becoming 'increasingly vocal on the need for reform in Poor Law medical care' (Brand, 1965, p. 85; see also Abel-Smith, 1964, pp. 71–3). The level of remuneration was also a cause of complaint (Brand, 1965, p. 88). On the other hand, contractual work undertaken on behalf of the poor law authorities and the Friendly Societies provided a relatively secure source of income for many members of the medical profession not linked with eminent voluntary hospitals and the more lucrative forms of private practice (see Abel-Smith, 1964, pp. 214–15 and Titmuss,

1968, pp. 233–8). The threats and merits of poor law and Friendly Society were inextricably linked. It was the employment and other (eg: prescribing) costs of their medical practitioners that led the poor law authorities and Friendly Societies to seek to exercise such close control over them. By contrast, the management environment of the voluntary hospitals was altogether more amenable to notions of professionalism; Governors were

> careful not to question the clinical judgement or examine the quality of the work of any of the doctors ... unless they were forced to do so. (Abel-Smith, 1964, p. 33).

An altogether lighter touch was deemed appropriate for the eminent specialists working for mere honoraria!

Whilst the relationship between voluntary hospitals and their medical practitioners appeared relatively harmonious, the former's activities – in terms of the provision of largely free hospital services – brought that sector into conflict with both general practitioners in private practice and the poor law authorities. The general practitioners saw the outpatient departments of the voluntary hospitals as a threat to their livelihood in so far as the referral system was not universally applied at this time (Abel-Smith, 1964, pp. 104–8). The poor law authorities also found these outpatient departments conflicting with their attempts to restrict access to free treatment within the poor law, as one Guardian explained,

> when the attempt was made to extract a contribution from a patient with a broken arm before treatment 'the man might use some very coarse expression to us and walk out of the room. He goes straight to the London Hospital, where he gets treated for nothing'. (Abel-Smith, 1964, p. 131).

We should note that even in the nineteenth century there were disputes about costs and the need for cost containment (Abel-Smith, 1964, p. 35) and that by the end of the century the voluntary hospitals were finding it difficult to maintain the hospitals at the standard to which they aspired – in particular the cost of providing nursing care was rising (Abel-Smith, 1964, p. 134). The establishment of the Hospital Sunday Fund and Hospital Saturday Fund –

two national organizations to raise money for the voluntary hospitals was a further early but clear indicator of the association between 'modern medicine' and 'escalating costs' – one of the most enduring conflicts within twentieth century health care.

Finally more fundamental conflicts can be discerned at this time by which new ideas might threaten the future of existing political parties or perhaps of the political system itself.

> In the Trafalgar Square riot of February 8, 1886, the old humanitarianism died in a spasm of terror. The poor were no longer to be pitied and to be helped from Christian generosity. They were now a menace to be bought off ... what, it was asked, can the governors of the nation do to prevent the poor from using their franchise to overturn a society based on capitalist wealth? (Gilbert, 1966, p. 32 and p. 19)

The response to these conflicts would be a significant factor in further changes in health care for 'as it turned out the defence against socialism was social legislation' (Gilbert, 1966, p. 19).

Conclusions

> The National Health Service had its direct roots in the medical services of the Poor Law (Hodgkinson, 1967, p. 696)

Our brief review of health care provision in the UK before the twentieth century provides clear evidence on the following. Firstly, that conflicts involving the state, its agencies and the medical profession existed long before there was any significant discussion of a national health service. Secondly, that the earliest signs of contemporary conflicts (eg: between cost containment and professional autonomy) are also discernible in this period (eg: contracted medical practice for the Friendly Societies). Thirdly, unless the state and the organizations representing the professionals could agree upon the role of each in defining and meeting health care needs, with their subsequent administrative, economic and ethical consequences, then any relationship between them was bound to be conflictual rather than complementary and consensual.

2
Social insurance and local government

Introduction

The preceding chapter outlined the struggles involved in providing health care for a growing population living in unsatisfactory urban conditions. It was suggested that the compromises arrived at were solutions to the health care problems of the time, but not necessarily resilient enough to cope with changing ideas on medical care and its administration. This is particularly so when examining the significant events that were to structure health care in the present century.

The period immediately before the First World War is typically characterised as one of quite dynamic and extensive social policy reform. This is principally associated with the Liberal governments of 1905–1914 and involved changing policies and provision in areas of child care, special needs education, employment services, income benefits for the sick and unemployed, maternity services, mental handicap, old age pensions and especially health care. The latter included the introduction of school health services identified as one of two innovations that marked the beginning of the welfare state in Britain (Gilbert, 1966, p. 102). The health care changes in this period both extended local government involvement in matters of health and at the same time introduced the concept of social insurance. The legislation introducing the latter has been described as one of the 'most expensive, the most ambitious, and the most controversial' of the social welfare reforms associated with the 1905–1914 Liberal governments (Gilbert, 1966, p. 289).

Conflict and the Liberal reforms

> Steps had to be taken to lighten the load of the poor lest the poor take violent steps to lighten the load of the rich. (Abel-Smith, 1959, p. 351)

> As a working-class revolution resulting from poverty and unemployment had appeared to threaten the social structure in the eighties, so national physical deterioration became a clear danger after the Boer War, not only to the structure of domestic society, but to the very existence of Great Britain as a world power. (Gilbert, 1966, p. 85)

The 'Liberal welfare reforms' and their broader context can be related to a number of conflicts. Firstly, there was the potential conflict between the government and interest groups whose circumstances, especially financial circumstances, might be adversely affected by the Liberal welfare reforms. This was most obvious in relation to the proposed introduction of a state regulated system of compulsory health insurance which developed into a classic exercise in pressure group politics.

Secondly, there was the potential for conflict on party political lines. In particular what was the political motivation of the 'Liberal welfare reforms'; for example, were the social reformist aspirations of the 'New Liberalism' associated with a concern to head off the political threat of the newly emergent Labour Party whose first MPs sat in the House of Commons following the General Election of 1905?

Thirdly, the reforms became the focus of debates which pointed up potential conflicts (and perhaps contradictions) within the dominant ideologies of the time – especially those which combined a commitment to imperialist ideals abroad and a minimal state at home. Over the period 1893 to 1902 the official rate of Army rejections was of one in every three men examined by a recruiting officer and at least one Army general 'estimated that 60 per cent of men who volunteered were unfit for military service' (Brand, 1965, p. 138). The latter statistic, relating specifically to Manchester in 1899, was publicised in White's book *Efficiency and Empire* (1901). Of a similar order was the conclusion in Rowntree's study of living conditions among the working classes in York which could indicate that at least one-half of the manpower in

England would be unavailable for military duty (*Poverty, A Study of Town Life*, 1901). These concerns gained a wider currency with the contemporaneous experience of the South African (Boer) War when 'rumours of . . . widespread weakness and positive physical disability' (Gilbert, 1966, p. 60) combined with revelations about ill-educated officers to generate an interest in 'national efficiency'.

> The noun 'efficiency' could take many qualifying adjectives. There could be political, educational, commercial, industrial, and above all, physical efficiency . . . the quest for national efficiency, therefore, gave social reform what it has not had before – the status of a respectable political question. Imperialism and the 'condition of the people question' became linked. (Gilbert, 1966, pp. 60–1);

and the particular interest in physical efficiency gave a special emphasis to the *physical* condition of the people and a particular resonance to social reforms relating to matters of health and health care.

Fourthly, the Liberal welfare reforms can be set in the context of class conflict and the potential – real or imagined – for social unrest and even revolution. Socialist ideas could be perceived as dangerous to the political system as a whole, rather than just one identified political party within the system. Indeed the whole social, economic and political order of capitalist, industrial societies might well have been seen to be threatened by the arrival of a 'workers' party whose social and economic demands bridged the gap between the workplace and the home through the collectivist ideals. From this perspective, social insurance and the other social reforms of this period become not so much the means of saving the Liberal Party from the threat of the Labour Party, but of 'delivering Britain from the socialist solution to poverty' (Gilbert, 1966, p. 451).

Finally, and perhaps most fundamentally, the Liberal welfare reforms can be seen as part of a long-running conflict between individualist and collectivist ideas and associated themes relating to the relative roles of the state, professionals and voluntary institutions.

Against this backcloth of interrelated conflicts linked to ideologies, interests and power, we can trace the particular conflicts of the health care reforms. Although hardly seen as the stuff of revolutionary politics, the school health services, health visiting and social insurance were to become important precursors of the National Health Service. The first two shared a focus on the perceived health needs of children and were to be provided through local government. They were introduced in a relatively uncontentious manner. The third involved a new form of taxation and a new principle of entitlement – a service partially financed by and accessed through what were termed insurance contributions. To implement this concept of social insurance a new set of administrative arrangement would be put in place and the latter in particular can now be seen as providing a foretaste of the conflicts that would be engendered around the involvement of the state in bringing health care to a wider population.

Health services for children
The introduction of a school health service was a rather muted affair; a surprising outcome for a new personal health service given the conflicts surrounding the establishment of public health legislation. This may be attributed to its origins in the Education (Administrative Provision) Act of 1907 which authorised the introduction of school medical *inspections* rather than a school medical *service*.

> Even this authorization was buried among more than a dozen other clauses dealing with uninteresting and involved house-keeping details of State school administration ... (thus) ... the medical service grew unnoticed and quietly from ministerial order. (Gilbert, 1966, p. 117)

The wording of the relevant clause allowed local education authorities 'to make such arrangements as may be sanctioned by the Board of Education for attending to the health and physical condition of children educated in public elementary schools' but the entire debate on this clause occupied less than twenty pages in Hansard (see Gilbert, 1966, pp. 130–1).

What at least some advocates of inspection anticipated, and hoped for, was that medical inspection would reveal such a volume of ill-health that subsequent advocacy of a school medical service would be difficult to resist. The recent Report of the Committee on Physical Deterioration indicated that the former was a possible outcome; its recommendations noted the importance of both environmental health reforms and a system of school medical inspection. But the attitude of the Conservative Government to this Report was significantly influenced by considerations of money:

> Prime Minister Balfour had told Anson curtly that so far as children's welfare was concerned he 'could be as sympathetic as he liked, but there would no increase in the rates'. (Gilbert, 1966, p. 95).

After the election of the Liberal government in 1905 there were still issues to be resolved given disagreements about how such treatment should be administered and paid for, without making incursions into the income of private medical practice, replicating the stigmatising means testing of the poor law, or imperilling the financial and administrative independence of the voluntary hospitals. In the end medical treatment provided by local education authorities became the norm with over 75 per cent of authorities making such provision by 1914 (Gilbert, 1966, p. 156).

Health Visiting

In the same year that local government acquired the powers to develop school medical services, the development of health visiting services was facilitated under the Notification of Births Act, 1907 (Parker, 1965, p. 27). Local authorities were acquiring health service powers and duties beyond those most directly linked with the 'public health question', a trend that would continue such that a local government health service would be reasonably seen as the cornerstone of a national health service when the format of the latter became the subject of serious discussion (see Chapters 3 and 4).

Social insurance

Meanwhile another model of health service administration was established; its introduction generating significantly more conflict than the issues surrounding the school health services and health visiting. This was the concept of social insurance – to be inevitably linked with the concept of socialism – and which was embodied in a scheme to which the label National Health Insurance (NHI) was attached as part of National Insurance legislation which also introduced unemployment benefits.

Under Part One of the National Insurance Act, 1911, manual workers and all others with incomes under £160 per annum were required to pay contributions to an approved society. Contributions were also required from their employers and there was a contribution to the scheme from other forms of taxation. In return for these contributions, insured persons became entitled to a limited cash benefit in sickness, to the services of a general practitioner and to a pharmaceutical benefit. There were optional additional benefits which approved societies were entitled to provide and the principle of free choice of doctor was enshrined in the Act. The Act did not directly affect the hospitals except through the provision for the care of tuberculosis patients. The latter operated partly through the new national insurance scheme – a sum being made available for expenditure on sanatorium benefit – and partly through central government grants for the construction of new accommodation (Abel-Smith, 1964, pp. 238–9; see also Brand, 1965 and Honigsbaum, 1989).

The establishment of NHI in the UK can be seen as part of a trend apparent in a number of European countries in which voluntary health insurance, offering extensive but partial provision of community general practitioner-based health care for working-class men, was supplanted by compulsory health insurance in which the services of general practitioners were extended to most working-class men. However whilst discernible as a common trend in a number of industrial societies, and indeed coming some considerable time after similar developments in other European countries, this introduction of a social insurance based, limited health service (it excluded hospital care) for a limited section of the population (it excluded all children, most working-class women, and men in non-manual occupations) generated considerable conflict. This related particularly to the position of potentially powerful interest groups whose circumstances – especially financial circumstances – might be adversely affected by the introduction of NHI.

These groups included the doctors – another common factor with the establishment of the National Health Service. Another group – to be of limited political consequence thirty-five years later – has been described as 'the single most powerful vested interest encountered by the social reformers of the New Liberalism' (Gilbert, 1966, p. 165). This vested interest was the Friendly Societies, whose membership and activities had grown significantly during the latter half of the nineteenth century, and which had a long tradition of political conservatism and hostility to all government activity – despite its predominantly working-class membership. A state social insurance scheme appeared to pose a very real threat to their continued existence as providers of voluntary health insurance.

This opposition of the Friendly Societies was contained by enabling them to administer the Government's scheme as Approved Societies, a device employed in other countries and which significantly reduced the administrative costs of establishing a new state scheme. But the political and administrative advantages of this manoeuvre merely brought the Government into conflict with the medical profession and the industrial insurance companies. The former were opposed to being permanently consigned to the control of Friendly Societies in a government health scheme. The latter saw their lucrative insurance business threatened by the potential expansion of their competitors as part of a government scheme. In the end the conflict was contained by two administrative devices.

Firstly, the requirements for the 'Approved Societies', which were responsible for the day-to-day management of NHI, were constructed in such a way that industrial insurance companies, in addition to Friendly Societies, could qualify to administer the scheme on behalf of the government. The industrial insurance companies had forced 'a virtual remodelling of national health insurance to permit their entry into the scheme' and achieved a 'great ... victory over the Government and over their colleagues in the friendly societies' (Gilbert, 1970, p. 108). This arrangement lasted until Beveridge destroyed the veil of 'administrative rationality' that had eased the establishment of NHI. Secondly, a system for contracting with and paying the general practitioners was devised that avoided direct control by the Approved Societies. The latter solution was to survive the establishment of the

National Health Service and several reorganizations of that service becoming one of the more durable political compromises in British social policy (see Klein, 1973, Chs.3 and 4). Neither for the first nor last time, opposition to government commitment to a health care programme in the UK was contained by political manoeuvring.

One impact of the NHI scheme was to reinforce the existing referral system when some voluntary hospitals refused to treat NHI patients unless they were referred by their NHI doctors. Hospital out-patient departments also began to turn away 'trivial cases' on the grounds that treatment could be obtained through NHI. Whilst this approach was beneficial to hospital budgets, it was a factor in diminishing the value of the hospital setting as the sole location for medical education and training. But perhaps the major impact was on those members of the medical profession who joined the new scheme. Given the publicly stated fears of state control, it is ironical that NHI doctors found their remuneration guaranteed (and for most of them increased); their autonomy preserved and their professional status enhanced (see for example, Klein, 1973, pp. 60–3). They were at last freed from what they had seen as the petty administrative control and scrutiny of the Friendly Societies. Indeed the argument has been advanced that NHI in the UK 'saved the GP' and 'reinforced general practice at the very time that specialisation was threatening it' (Stevens, 1966, p. 53). The NHI scheme was responsible for locating general practice in a secure and central position in British health care. The outcome was to become a point of principle with the British Medical Association (BMA) in subsequent conflicts with government, the right to an independent contractor status within state health services.

The result of the conflicts engendered by NHI, and the actions taken to accommodate and ameliorate these conflicts, was that the social insurance scheme that became law in 1911 'bore practically no resemblance to the plan originally conceived in meetings with the friendly society representatives in October 1908' (Gilbert, 1966, p. 290). This serves as perhaps the first example of a recurrent theme by which the detailed arrangements of health care reforms are significantly restructured to accommodate the perceived interests of key groups (see also Chapters 4 and 6).

The introduction of NHI can serve to demonstrate not only the potential of professional power, but also its limitations. The NHI

Act found its way on to the statute book not by accident, but by determined government action. The detailed administrative arrangements of NHI were significantly modified to accommodate key interest groups. But the government's major commitment was to introduce a system of compulsory health insurance. This was established and the BMA's attempt to continue its boycott of the new system ended with a large-scale desertion of its members to the new NHI 'panels' (see Eckstein, 1955, p. 347 and Lindsey, 1962, p. 9) – a trend to be repeated in 1948 and the early 1990s. The establishment of NHI marked another stage in a long-term trend in the UK and other industrialising societies by which significant changes were taking place in the relative roles of voluntary institutions and institutions of the state (approved societies, local government and poor law authorities) in the provision of health care.

The availability of general practitioner services under NHI was subsequently extended. In 1919 the scheme was expanded to cover workers earning up to £250 p.a. 'bringing to 14 million the total of people within its orbit' (Hennessey, 1992, p. 123). By 1940 it was estimated that 40 per cent of the population were covered by the scheme (Stevens, 1966, p. 53; see also, Fraser, 1973, p. 184). But the latter figure concealed a major gender variation; for those aged between fourteen and sixty four years, the scheme covered 77 per cent of all men but only 39 per cent of women (see Titmuss, 1963, p. 213). Thus despite this extension, NHI remained true to its origins in providing a GP service primarily for working-class men. It continued to exclude most women and most forms of hospital care. At the same time it bestowed the status of 'panel patient' on its recipients which whilst being some way removed from the overtly stigmatising status of 'sick pauper' could embody a discriminatory and divisive approach when general practitioners also had private patients (see Webster, 1988, p. 27 and Timmins, 1995, p. 107). Finally 'the absence of integration and co-ordination among the thousands of participating units made the scheme expensive, inefficient and unwieldy' (Lindsey, 1962, pp. 10–11)

Drawing more of the population into the NHI scheme was one of two modest extensions of state welfare activity in the nation's health care between the wars. The other strand of growing state intervention was the embryonic local government health service, the framework of which was certainly discernible by the 1930s.

Municipal health services

In 1913 the Mental Deficiency Act required local authorities to appoint Mental Deficiency Committees whose responsibilities included the provision and maintenance of suitable institutions. The Maternity and Child Welfare Act of 1918 made grants available to local authorities to improve their maternity services, infant welfare clinics and health visiting (Parker, 1965, p. 28). In 1920 Tuberculosis sanatoria became a responsibility of local authorities to enable the Approved Societies to meet the cost of increased capitation fees payable to NHI doctors (Gilbert, 1970, pp. 269–70). There was continued expansion of provision in local authority institutions which by 1921 provided nearly 22 per cent of the beds in England and Wales (Pinker, 1966, p. 65). By 1936 local authorities had an obligation to provide, or at least finance, an adequate midwifery service and the power to provide a home help service (Parker, 1965, p. 32). This was in addition to their other powers and obligations to employ health visitors, to provide a school health service and to undertake their long-standing public health responsibilities.

In addition, local government was a major provider of hospital care. Local authorities had inherited hospitals built by the nineteenth century sanitary authorities (see Chapter 1). There were further piecemeal additions to this stock of fever hospitals and other sanatoria, and following the Mental Treatment Act, 1930 the local authority asylums had been redesignated as mental hospitals; they were also responsible for institutions for those classified as 'mentally deficient'. But the most significant change had been the Local Government Act, 1929 which implemented a proposal of the Reconstruction Committee (Haldane) set up by Lloyd-George in 1917. The Act left the Poor Law on the statute book, but abolished the poor law authorities (Boards of Guardians) and transferred all powers, duties, buildings, personnel and paupers to county councils and county boroughs. The result was the potential for the establishment of a general municipal hospital service. By 1935 local authority health services 'accounted for about 60 per cent of expenditure in organised health care in Britain' (Webster, 1995, p. 1584). By 1938:

> from being a largely unorganised group of institutions mainly used by the infectious sick, the local authority hospital service

had become a reasonably well organised and diversified system based on county and county borough authorities. (Pinker, 1966, p. 108).

Even more significantly there was in place not only extensive local government *hospital services*, but a broad range of municipal *health services* (see for example, Webster, 1988, pp. 5–10). There was considerable scope for the development of a more comprehensive and co-ordinated set of health services located within the framework of local government.

The circumstances were a model scenario for further modest, incremental extensions of state intervention in health care via both National Health Insurance and local government in line with any perceived pressure in that direction from the electorate (see for example, Timmins, 1995, p. 109). Furthermore, these developments appeared to provide two potentially complementary means by which the state could intervene whilst leaving intact the established traditions of voluntary hospitals and substantial private medical practice.

The voluntary hospitals

the voluntary hospitals ... were drifting into ... a profound economic crisis. (Webster, 1990, p. 144)

There was certainly pressure from some quarters to do something at this time about the organization and finance of health care in the UK. This may be partly attributable to an emerging conflict within the voluntary hospital sector between the principles of voluntarism and the perceived need for modern hospital services. Whilst further expansion of poor law hospital services and their incorporation into local government complemented the acute focus of the voluntary hospitals, the latter were finding it increasingly difficult to meet needs even within their own narrowly defined sphere of competence.

Medical advances were increasingly associated with escalating medical costs indicating a seemingly inevitable conflict between the scope of voluntary contributions and charitable bequests on the one hand and the needs of modern hospital services on the other. Between 1913 and 1920 contributions to the funds of voluntary hospitals rose by 67 per cent; but their expenditure rose by 138 per cent (Lindsey, 1962, p. 14). The medical advances are illustrated by the account of a well-known provincial hospital which undertook less than 600 X-ray examinations in 1918 and was undertaking approximately 20,000 per annum in the 1940s. In the same hospital, pathological examinations multiplied by a factor of 33 and blood counts by a factor of 50 between 1927 and 1947. One source estimated that voluntary hospital spending was six hundred and forty times greater in 1947 than it had been in 1900 (Lindsey, 1962, pp. 24–5). These escalating costs associated with advances in medical technology were taking the voluntary hospitals up to and beyond the limits of philanthropy. It was no longer possible to sustain the standards of hospital work associated with the most eminent institutions without recourse to a much more substantial reliance on patient charges, some form of government funding or a combination of the two (Abel-Smith, 1964, p. 303).

Payments by patients had formed 5 per cent of the income of London's voluntary hospital income in 1890, this became 10 per cent just before World War One, 40 per cent by 1931 and 50 per cent by 1938 (see Abel-Smith, 1964, p. 149 and p. 404; see, Webster, 1988, p. 4 for similar figures for England and Wales).

> Between 1921 and 1938, total income from charitable dona-
> tions doubled, and investment income also doubled, but
> income from fees and patient contributions increased four-
> fold. (Harris, 1979, p. 290).

The Hospital Saving Association by which individuals sought to meet some of these new costs associated with hospital care, was set up in London in 1922, had 62,000 members by 1924 and 650,000 members by 1929. There were 300 similar schemes in place across the country by 1930.

The character of the voluntary hospital sector was changing dramatically; they remained non-profit making but were losing some of their philanthropic features. With these changes another potential conflict loomed as the medical profession sought to change the terms under which they worked for these institutions. If the hospitals were charging fees for services should not some of this income accrue to their doctors?

Alongside the incremental changes in National Health Insurance and local government, and the crises in the costs and character of the voluntary hospital sector, there is clear evidence that the issue of health care reform was now firmly on the political agenda and not just a matter of private debate between the profession and the existing health care institutions. A series of reports and associated recommendations emerged from a variety of sources throughout the inter-war period.

Recommendations for change

The Reconstruction Committee set up by Lloyd-George in 1917 recommended the abolition of the Board of Guardians – with all arrangements for the sick and infirm to be met through Public Health Committees. By 1918 the Labour Party was committed to the concept of a free national health service under democratic control centrally and locally. The voluntary hospitals would be merged into this system which would embody the principle of free choice of doctors. In the light of subsequent conflicts between the profession and a subsequent Labour government, it is interesting that a spokesman for the BMA was reported to have expressed gratification at how much the Labour Party and the BMA were in agreement (see Abel-Smith, 1964, pp. 285–7).

An early case for extending state intervention was made in the Dawson Report (1920). This can be seen as a precursor to the debate about rational management and arrangements for the equal distribution of health care which were to be an enduring point of discussion and conflict once the NHS was established. The Report is important for what it had to say about the organization of health services. It recommended insurance as a sound policy in view of the rising costs of medical care and recommended the establishment of primary level GP-serviced district hospitals for general cases and secondary level general hospitals serviced by medical specialists for more complicated cases. The Commission concluded that:

the changes which we advise are rendered necessary because the organization of medicine has become insufficient and because it fails to bring the advantages of medical knowledge adequately within reach of people. This insufficiency of organization has become more apparent with the growth of knowledge and with the increasing conviction that the best means of maintaining health and curing disease should be made available to all citizens. (Dawson Report, 1920)

The Dawson Report received favourable press coverage and the medical profession, in the form of the BMA, was said to have 'no fundamental criticism' of its proposals (Abel-Smith, 1964, pp. 292–3). The issue that Dawson raised was one which pointed out the conflict between delivering medical care to the population through essentially nineteenth century administrative means, protected by nineteenth century guild-like professional concerns, and the twentieth century growth in scientific knowledge. This mismatch between a delivery system and the content of health care was to produce a long drawn-out debate about whether or not a centralised service with decisions made in the Ministry should affect all parts of the UK. This insight of Dawson's retains its general validity. A mismatch between scientific medical advance, public expectations and a well-funded and rationally administered system remains an enduring source of potential conflict.

The Cave Committee (1920–21) anticipated the increasing role of patient contributions in the finances of the voluntary hospital sector but also recommended temporary support from public funds. Parliament responded with a grant half of that recommended by the Committee (Ministry of Health, 1921). In 1924 Lord Knutsford recommended that all voluntary hospitals and Poor Law infirmaries should be placed under one local management arrangement with financial support in the form of large grants from the Ministry of Health (see Abel-Smith, 1964, p. 321).

The Royal Commission on National Health Insurance reported in 1926 and concluded that the scheme was working reasonably well. Both majority and minority reports recommended extending the coverage of NHI in terms of population (dependents) and health care (eg: dental care). However the minority report not only identified the limitations of NHI already referred to, but judged the insurance principle to be an unsound method of financing medical services, concluding that ultimately medical benefits would have to be financed from public funds (see Gilbert, 1970, pp. 276, 281).

A professional view was represented by the British Medical Association's proposals for a *General Medical Service for the*

Nation published in 1930 and reissued in a revised form in 1938. Key recommendations included the extension of NHI to dependents of insured persons but the emphasis was on the provision of more health care (eg: maternity services) rather than extending those sections of the population eligible to receive such health care (an income limit of £250 per annum would be retained) (BMA, 1930). This would have the desirable effect, from the point of view of the profession, of maintaining the clinical autonomy associated with voluntary hospital work, whilst introducing remuneration for doctors in these institutions. It was intriguing if somewhat prophetic that the medical profession anticipated that the remuneration of voluntary hospital staff would introduce no more supervision over their activities than was the norm when they were practising as essentially unpaid professionals. Under this proposal, private practice would of course remain extensive for the more affluent members of society whose incomes took them beyond the upper limits of NHI (see Abel-Smith, 1964, pp. 348–51).

The revised 1938 report continued to emphasise the need to pay all hospital staff and also contended that there should be no GP services in hospital outpatient departments, the latter being the latest expression of the GP's fear of any system that enabled their prospective patients to seek out an alternative service to their own or an alternative mode of access (other than GP referral) to more specialist services (BMA, 1938).

In between the two versions of the BMA's report, a Voluntary Hospitals Commission (British Hospital Associations, 1937) sought to draw public attention to both the value of the existing voluntary hospital system and for the need for co-operation between competing voluntary and local government hospitals. This identifies one theme in the developing debate about health care reform – the need for a rationalisation of the fragmented and somewhat haphazard assemblage of health care institutions that constituted pre-NHS health care in the UK. A partial National Health Insurance scheme that excluded children, non-earning wives, the self-employed, many old people and higher paid employees, operated alongside other services whose scope and effectiveness depended on the wealth of each area, the political initiative of different local authorities, the 'provincial patriotism and parochial jealousies' (Eckstein, 1958, p. 71) of a 'system' whose finances depended on 'the donations of the living and the legacies of the dead' (Abel-Smith, 1990, p. 11). There was 'no hospital system' but rather a collection of individual hospitals 'criss-crossed, separated and enclosed by local government boundary barriers, legal, residential and occupational barriers, medical category and financial barriers' (Titmuss, 1963, p. 143). Outcomes included a 'disjunction between municipal and voluntary hospital sectors . . . (and) . . . unevenness of provision, especially of hospital resources' (Webster, 1988, pp. 20, 12; see also Lindsey, 1962, pp. 14, 17).

Arguments for change were given added weight for some commentators since the arrangements gave ample opportunity for enormous variations in service provision in different parts of the country. Whilst there is some evidence that public sector hospital provision did compensate to some extent for the vagaries in the voluntary hospital sector (see Powell, 1992a, 1992b), the overall effect was of profound regional disparities as indicated by per capita measurements of GPs, consultants and hospital beds (see Eckstein, 1958 and Lindsey, 1962, pp. 7, 15). The NHI system compounded this problem through the system which allowed the approved societies to make available additional medical benefits (eg: home nursing) subject to their finances being in a satisfactory state. But many urban societies were in a parlous financial situation attributable to variations in the incidence of industrial diseases and unemployment; these societies were not in a position to provide any additional benefits (see Eckstein, 1958, p. 29).

This was paralleled by significant variations in indices of health status. For example, infant mortality rates (IMR) in places like Glasgow and Jarrow were much higher than those for Surrey and Oxford – Jarrow's IMR was four times the rate in Oxford in 1936 (Briggs, 1978, p. 448 and Fraser, 1973, pp. 185–6). A rather dramatic inverse care law appeared to be in operation by which those parts of the country which appeared to have the greatest need were also most deficient in health care facilities.

Around the twin and related themes of efficiency and equity it was possible to construct a powerful case for health care reform for Britain's 'remarkably inefficient and inadequate set of services' (Eckstein, 1958, p. viii) and there is evidence that the profession, the voluntary hospitals and successive governments recognised this case. In an obvious parallel with early debates about NHI and school health services, it was less clear whether any degree of consensus about the need to 'do something' could be carried over into the more detailed discussion of what form that 'something' should take. There were disagreements on the roles of local government, voluntary hospitals and contributory insurance (see, Webster, 1988 pp. 391–2).

Conflicts

The period covered by this chapter provides further evidence of the conflicts actual and potential which have characterised health care developments in the UK. Firstly, and perhaps most readily identified and understood, there are the conflicts associated with the broad macro-debates about the role of the state in health and welfare. NHI represented a commitment to guaranteed access for a substantial proportion of the population to a state regulated form of health care based upon a stable system of finance, and without a means test. Any proposal or action, like NHI, which takes the role of the state beyond a less-eligibility model of minimal state welfare has the capacity to generate conflicting opinions – for whom should the state provide, on what conditions and at what standard – and to encounter opposing interests – especially those of non-state welfare institutions (eg: Friendly Societies and private insurance companies).

Secondly, emerging particularly from the more detailed social and political histories of state health and welfare developments, there are the conflicts engendered by the micro-debates about administrative details. Any outcome that leaves the state with a significant role in providing health care is likely to provoke ongoing and quite fierce conflicts over the organizational and financial arrangements of these state-provided health services. Once the relationship between the state and the medical profession is formalised, this encourages debates on resources, remuneration and redistribution (see for example, Chs.5, 6 and 14). It is impossible to avoid conflict in discussions of these areas.

Thirdly, there was the conflict between the past successes and contemporary roles of the poor law authorities. As we noted in Chapter 1, the latter had become important providers of health care at least in part through the limitations of the voluntary institutions. But despite the standard of its better health care facilities, the Poor Law could not escape the success of past legislators and administrators in creating its indelible association with the stigmatising status of pauper;

> when the welfare state began to grow, practically all the vast nineteenth century apparatus of parochial relief had to be abandoned lest it taint the new reform measures. (Gilbert, 1966, p. 22; see also Lindsey, 1962, p. 10))

If governments were to take seriously the concept of extending and improving the public provision of health services they would have to look to some administrative arrangement clearly differentiated from the poor law authorities. The transfer of poor law health care to local government in 1929 represented one such administrative arrangement. However both the unsuitable nature of many old Poor Law institutions, and the continuity of individuals and ideologies between the old Poor Law Boards of Guardians and the new local authority Public Assistance Committees, restricted the potential of the new arrangements (see Abel-Smith, 1964, p. 369–70).

Fourthly, the quite wide-ranging consensus about the need for health care reform yielded limited action in part because there was less agreement about the details of reform, but also because successive inter-war governments 'practised ruthlessly the dogma of traditional public finance and were meeting the economic crisis with rigid economy on public expenditure' (Abel-Smith, 1964, p. 298; see, also Gilbert, 1970, pp. 302–3).

Finally, we can note the enduring theme of the conflict between traditional concepts of voluntarism – voluntary organizations financed by voluntary contributions – and the generally accepted needs of a modern health care system. By the inter-war period it was apparent that the voluntary tradition could not be maintained even in the context of significant but narrowly defined forms of hospital care. 'The voluntary hospitals had become primarily trading concerns and only secondarily charitable institutions' (Abel-Smith, 1964, p. 402).

Conclusions

> By the end of the 1930s, after a long period of discussion, a number of ideas had crystallised on the need for reform and redefinition of medical services. (Stevens, 1966, p. 53)

Taken together our first two chapters provide considerable evidence of wide-ranging conflicts relating to health care and its provision before any government had made any commitment towards anything resembling a national health service. By this time we can note also a further source of conflict concerning the interpretation of the events of the period. For some the introduction of social insurance was an antidote to more radical socialist ideas. For others it represented a further step in the direction of socialism. For Dicey social insurance would represent another in the 'line of Acts' influenced by Benthamite ideas representing 'an almost unconscious change in legislative opinion ... .in the direction of socialism' (Dicey, 1930, p. 68). This is further evidence that health care was a source of conflicting ideas and interests some time before the National Health Service.

The inter-war years can also be the subject of differing interpretations. As well as the material on health inequalities linked to class and geography, there were major scandals relating to infant mortality, maternal mortality and child health. On the other hand there was evidence of increased public expenditure on health (see Webster, 1990, p. 142). There was certainly considerable interest in health care reforms as we have noted; but this was understandable when inter-war health policy could be characterised as follows.

> Strict Treasury discipline, an inclination to evade problems until public outcry made further evasion impossible, the use of investigative committees and commissioners to delay action, a minimum legislative response with maximum reliance on permissive powers, strict control of new services to give the impression of adequate response to need while actually providing services only on a token basis, a failure to distribute services according to need, and finally a preference for services maximising the growth of medical bureaucracies, even when this involved inefficient use of resources. (Webster, 1990, p. 143).

However by the end of 1939 there may have been a sense that any resolution of the problems of British health care would not form part of a political agenda since the nation was involved in an altogether more significant conflict. In the event quite the opposite occurred, and questions of the quality, distribution and responsibility for health care were to form part of the wartime political agenda – in particular the purposes for which the war was being fought. As a result, the nation's health services became the core of the reconstruction of civil society during and in the immediate aftermath of the Second World War.

3
War and welfare

We reach a ... (further) ... stage in our ascending scale of interest. Not only was it necessary for the State to take positive steps in all spheres of the national economy to safeguard the physical health of the people; it was also imperative for war strategy for the authorities to concern themselves with that elusive concept 'civilian morale'. (Titmuss, 1963, pp. 81–2)

War-time commitment to planning and inter-war crisis exposed the instability and inappropriateness of the ramshackle edifice of medical services. (Webster, 1988, p. 16)

Statement of a reconstruction policy by a nation at war is a statement of the uses to which that nation means to put victory, when victory is achieved. In a war which many nations must wage together as whole-hearted allies, if they are to win victory, such a statement of the uses of victory may be vital. (Beveridge Report, 1942, p. 171, para.459)

Introduction

An initial and understandable judgement might be that total war in Europe would consign the conflicts over health care reform to a forgotten corner of the political agenda for the duration of an altogether more substantial and dramatic set of conflicts. But governments who wage war are forced to consider the implications for the health of combatant troops, veteran services and the health care of the civilian population – a lesson demonstrated in the American Civil War, the Franco-Prussian war, the Boer War, World War One, but above all World War Two. It is no surprise that many of the descriptions and analysis of the modern National Health Service (NHS) raise the intriguing question of the relationship between total war and the development of universal health care.

The impact of war

The connection between military conflict and changes in health care can be traced back at least as far as the Crimean War, including the changes in the nursing profession that flowed from Florence Nightingale's experiences of military hospitals. Public concern was generated by publicising the primary role of preventable disease rather than battle as the major cause of military mortality (Brand, 1965, p. 137). Subsequently, the experience of the Boer War confirmed again the potential threat to the armed forces posed by preventable conditions such as enteric fever and dysentery (Brand, 1965, p. 140; see, also Trombley, 1989, Chs.7 and 8). In addition, problems of military recruitment during the Boer War provided a focus for the concerns about 'national efficiency' that underpinned some of the Liberal welfare reforms – particularly the development of the medical inspection of children in schools (see Chapter 2). This concern re-emerged with the continuing rejection of recruits on health grounds during World War One. A parallel inter-relationship between war and welfare was the inflation associated with World War One – subsequently identified as one factor in pricing the least well-off out of the housing market, precipitating rent control and contributing to the ending of working-class house building as a profitable enterprise (see for example, Fraser, 1973, p. 168). Finally we can note the significant impact of war on the financial fortunes of the key voluntary institutions involved in health care – both the voluntary hospitals and the approved societies emerged from World War One in a significantly improved financial situation (see Abel-Smith, 1964, p. 282 and Gilbert, 1970, pp. 263–5).

This theme of linking war and social policy was explored in a well-known essay by Richard Titmuss (from which the opening quotation of this chapter is taken) and in his classic *Problems of Social Policy* (1950). Both texts include the argument that the growing scale and intensity of war had stimulated a growing concern about the quantity and quality of the population. As the nature of warfare changed so the scope of public concern broadened to include 'the health and well-being of the whole population and, in particular, of children, the next generation of recruits' (Titmuss, 1963, p. 78). With the Second World War, a war in which Britain depended on the contribution of nearly all its citizens, we arrive at the situation where 'the war could not be won unless millions of ordinary people were convinced that we had something better to offer than had our enemies – not only during, but after the war' (Titmuss, 1963, p. 82).

The significance of this was recognised in the famous leader in *The Times* – a compelling contrast with the comments from the same source on public health (see p. 15).

> If we speak of democracy, we do not mean a democracy which maintains the right to vote but forgets the right to work and the right to live. If we speak of freedom, we do not mean a rugged individualism which excludes social organization and economic planning. If we speak of equality, we do not mean a political equality nullified by social and economic privilege. If we speak of economic reconstruction, we think less of maximum production (though this too will be required) than of equitable distribution. (Leader, *The Times*, 1/7/1940)

In these circumstances the relevance of pre-war debates about health care was not only retained but enhanced. Health care reforms would be in line with *The Times*'s clarion call of objectives, even if past experience of conflict between the government of the day and the medical profession would suggest they might be difficult to achieve.

Even without these broader concerns, the perceived inefficiencies of the hospital sector of the health services were of immediate concern in planning for the likelihood of significant civilian air raid casualties (see Eckstein, 1958, pp. 86–7). The solution to the haphazard and extremely variable quality of existing hospital services was a significant degree of central government control and expenditure through the Emergency Medical Services (EMS) – 'in a sense the hospitals were temporarily nationalised' (Lindsey, 1962, p. 19; see also, Abel-Smith, 1964, Ch.26 and Eckstein, 1958, Ch.4). The effects of the EMS have been characterised as 'almost the proportions of a revolution' (Webster, 1988, p. 24). Extensive investment was needed to bring the poorest quality institutions up to a reasonable standard involving the addition of at least 50,000 beds, the installation of one thousand completely new operating theatres and the ordering of forty-eight million bandages, dressings and fitments (the estimated number of artery forceps now required represented over thirty years previous demand for the whole country); specialised treatment centres were also established; and the ambulance service was improved (see Eckstein, 1958, p. 48; Abel-Smith, 1964, p. 426; Titmuss, 1950, p. 83; Lindsey, 1962, p. 19). The experience of the EMS added weight to the arguments that existing provision was both inefficient and inequitable, and made credible the concept of a national plan for health by demonstrating 'what the central government could accomplish through planning and financial assistance' (Lindsey, 1962, p. 19). The deficiencies of many hospitals also became 'visible' for the first time to London-based doctors redeployed to the provinces (Abel-Smith, 1964, p. 436 and Harris, 1979, p. 290) and middle-class patients who had not used certain services before (Eckstein, 1958, p. 98). Furthermore the poor physical state of many urban children also became 'more visible' with the evacuation of children (Packman, 1975, p. 21). The public expenditure on health services and the public and professional experiences of using and providing such services, added considerably to existing arguments that the patchwork quilt of local government and voluntary provision which constituted the British hospital services was far from adequate to meet the health care needs of the population.

More recommendations for change
Meanwhile reports on the future of Britain's health services continued to be issued in war-time Britain. In 1939 *The Lancet* appointed Dr.Taylor to produce a plan. This recommended a National Hospital Corporation to take over all hospitals and run them on a regional basis with full-time salaried staff but minimal lay control (see Abel-Smith, 1964, Ch.27). The following year the Socialist Medical Association's plan was for a unified medical service organised on a regional basis with a salaried service. In the same year the BMA set up a Medical Planning Commission (see Honigsbaum, 1989, pp. 36–7) and in 1941 a group of younger doctors and health service workers created Medical Planning

Research through the columns of *The Lancet* fearing that the age and background of the members of the Medical Planning Commission would lead to reactionary and unrepresentative conclusions (see Abel-Smith, 1964, Ch.27).

This activity was one indication that a state of total war was not considered inconsistent with a concern for the issues associated with health care reform. A most dramatic example of this continuing concern was the announcement in October 1941 by the Ministry of Health that the government was committed to establishing a comprehensive *hospital* service after the war, including the intention that appropriate treatment would be available to all who needed it (Honigsbaum, 1989, pp. 28–9 and Hennessey, 1992, p. 134). This announcement did not stem the flow of reports and recommendations.

In 1942 the BMA published the report of its Medical Planning Commission. The Commission was against local government control and a full-time salaried service, and in favour of forms of organization with strong medical leadership and representation. A regional hospital service was favoured with health centres as the focal point for general practice. The Commission also favoured the retention and expansion of NHI to cover approximately 90 per cent of the population (see Lindsey, 1962, pp. 28–30); but in September 1942 the annual representative meeting of the BMA decided that provision should be made for the 'whole of the community'. Two months later the report of the Medical Planning Research group also supported a health service available to the whole community. They recommended a free health service as part of a comprehensive social security scheme with generous cash benefits, to be run by a national corporation operating through eleven regions. However the espousal of the principle of universality by the BMA and the Medical Planning Research group was to be overshadowed by a more widely publicised advocacy of universality, including health services for the whole of the community (Lindsey, 1962, pp. 30–1).

The Beveridge Report

Provision for most of the many varieties of need through interruption of earnings and other causes that may arise in modern industrial communities had already been made in

Britain on a scale not surpassed and hardly rivalled in any other country of the world. In one respect only of the first importance, namely limitation of medical service, both in the range of treatment that is provided as of right and in respect of the classes of persons for whom it is provided as of right, does Britain's achievement fall seriously short of what has been accomplished elsewhere. (Beveridge Report, 1942, para.3).

A comprehensive national health service will ensure that for every citizen there is available whatever medical treatment he requires, in whatever form that he requires it, domiciliary or institutional, general, specialist or consultant, and nursing and midwifery and rehabilitation after accidents ... the service itself should ... be provided where needed without contribution conditions in any individual case. (Beveridge Report, 1942, paras. 426/427).

The Battle of Alamein began 23rd October and finished 10th November 1942. A week before the Battle began questions were being asked, as usual, in the House of Commons. On the 15th October 1942 the Prime Minister was asked about the possibility of transferring the Elgin Marbles to the Greek government for restoration to their original site after the war. A question was also asked about placing disabled ex-service men poultry keepers in the same category as the blind respecting supplementary rations for their flocks. Sandwiched between these was an innocuous sounding question. 'Is the Postmaster General in a position to say when the Beveridge Report on Social Insurance will be made available to the House?' (see House of Commons, 1942, Cols.805, 1229, 1633, 1762).

Beveridge was sixty years old when he was asked to chair the Manpower Requirements Committee of the Production Council in July 1940. As with so many others of the day, he never got on with Ernest Bevin and was moved sideways to an innocuous, almost soporific sounding inter-departmental committee on social security and allied services (Honigsbaum, 1989, p. 35). His brief was to tidy up the fragmented social security system of the day, disentangle Victorian and Edwardian social security legislation and administrative rules in preparation for post-war reconstruction and make recommendations to the wartime coalition government.

What Beveridge found was a haphazard piecemeal social security system in which seven government departments administered cash benefits. For example, he found that cash benefits were administered by the following central departments: Workmens Compensation by the Home Office; unemployment insurance by the Ministry of Labour; National Health Insurance by the Ministry of Health; non-contributory old age pensions by Customs and Excise; contributory old age pensions by the Ministry of Health; Supplementary Pensions by the Unemployment Assistance Board; war victims benefits by the Ministry of Pensions and the civilian widows, disabled and orphans benefits by the Ministry of Health. In addition, all benefits were funded differently. Workman's Compensation by the employer; war pensions, non-contributory old age pensions, and unemployment assistance by the tax payer; public assistance by the rate payer; health, unemployment, old age insurance split between employee, employer and the State. Furthermore the size and scope of the benefits varied. The whole system was characterized by overlap and duplication. Children and the aged were missed out; inequalities and anomalies abounded. As for medical benefit, this was provided by a panel system, excluding dependants and open to those only below a certain income limit.

> Again and again witnesses pressed spontaneously and independently for measures which became the main policy proposals of the Beveridge Report – namely, family allowances, full-employment, universal health services. (Harris, 1977, p. 414)

The main idea behind the report was that there would be a single national insurance scheme, administered by a single department, and which would be 'universal' its coverage – meaning that all members of the population would be potential contributors (via national insurance contributions) and potential beneficiaries (via national insurance benefits) for the contingencies identified as the major causes of poverty. Three principles underpinned the Report's recommendations. These were that firstly, proposals for the future should not be restricted by the consideration of sectional interests; secondly, that social insurance should be seen as one part of an attack upon Want – 'in some ways the easiest to attack' (Beveridge Report, 1942, p. 6, para 8) whilst still leaving the giants of Disease, Ignorance, Squalor and Idleness to be addressed; and thirdly, that social security must be achieved by co-operation between the state and the individual. The principles underpinning the Beveridge Report were to be supported by three assumptions – that 'no satisfactory scheme of social security can be devised' without childrens allowances, policies for maintenance of employment and 'Assumption B' – comprehensive health and rehabilitation services for prevention and cure of disease and restoration of capacity for work, available to all members of the community (Beveridge Report, 1942, p. 120, para.301). It is this latter, a comprehensive health service in the language of Beveridge's report, which was both the great promise of what the British population could expect and the 'Achilles Heel' of the health service depending as it did on finance, politics and the law. The history of the health service has been one of attempting to meet this high ideal constrained by financial and other socio-political and legal factors.

Beveridge and health care

(Beveridge assumed) ... that the reform of social security must be accompanied by the setting up of a health service for prevention and comprehensive treatment available to all members of the community ... The Report re-iterated the ambitious series of proposals that he had outlined in numerous memoranda over the previous nine months – a free NHS. (Harris, 1977, pp. 390, 413).

Six key concerns can be identified in reading the Beveridge Report. There are concerns with the relationship between social security and the health of individuals, families and communities; with administrative rationality; with comprehensive coverage; with services free at the point of consumption; with future demand and cost; and with the philosophy of a national health service.

On the relationship between social security and health, Beveridge was particularly critical of the existing scheme of Workmen's Compensation which he regarded as especially ineffective provision for the rehabilitation of injured workers (Beveridge Report, 1942, para.80, p. 38). This serves as a particular example of the role of comprehensive health and rehabilitation services in the prevention and cure of disease and restoration of capacity for work – the extent to which expenditure on effective health care contributes to containing the costs of the social security system, by minimising expenditure on unmet needs for health care.

The Report was critical of the 'the anomalies and overlapping, the multiplicity of agencies and the needless administrative cost' of existing administrative arrangements; Beveridge's preference was for 'co-ordination, simplicity and economy' (Beveridge Report, 1942, p. 15, para.29) and accordingly he recommended the ending of that seemingly essential element of the political settlement which had established National Health Insurance – the Approved Societies (see Chapter 2). 'Experience and evidence together points the way to making a single Approved Society for the nation' (Beveridge Report, 1942, p. 15, para.29). Beveridge was also to recommend the 'separation of medical treatment from the administration of cash benefits and the setting up of a comprehensive medical service for every citizen, covering all treatment and every form of disability' under the supervision of the Health Departments' (Beveridge Report, 1942, p. 15, para.30 and para.106). For all practical purposes the social insurance principle, which was to be retained as a key principle of the social security reforms, was abandoned so that 'all classes will be covered for comprehensive medical treatment and rehabilitation and for funeral expenses' (Beveridge Report, 1942, p. 10, para.19, iii).

This advocacy of comprehensive coverage was clearly an important element in the Report given the degree of popular support it seemed to command. Although with hindsight it can be readily identified as a continuation of existing trends, government acceptance of this proposal would constitute a significant shift beyond the stated commitment to some sort of national hospital service. In addition the 'separation of medical treatment from the administration of cash benefits and setting up of a comprehensive medical service for every citizen, covering all treatment and every form of disability (Beveridge Report, 1942, p. 48, para.105) might have implications for the organization of health care that could not be accommodated by incremental changes to the resourcing of, and relationships between, existing health care providers.

The recommendation that there will be 'comprehensive medical treatment, both domiciliary and institutional for all citizens and their dependants which ... will be without charge on treatment at any point' (Beveridge Report, 1942, p. 14, para.28) can also be represented as continuing a well-established British tradition (see Chapter 1) but also as a challenge to the emerging pattern of financing hospital care in the voluntary sector (see Chapter 2).

A comprehensive health service largely free at the point of consumption has potentially profound implications for the demands that might be placed on such a service and the resulting costs of maintaining the service. This potentially explosive problem was to be at least partially ameliorated by developing 'a health service which will diminish disease by prevention and cure' (Beveridge Report, 1942, para.437). This accords with a subsequent comment by Titmuss that

> among all the ideas of the 1930s and 1940s which led to the creation of the Health Service the one which increasingly dominated the mind of the public and the profession alike was the idea of prevention. (Titmuss, 1963, p. 140)

Thus the outcome of a better health service could be a healthier population that would have less need for health services and make fewer demands on social security benefits available for sickness and disability. This assumption can be related to both the existing evidence of an inverse care law – areas with the worst health services had the worst health (see Chapter 2) and to a widely held view that improved personal health services have a simple and explicit relationship with improved health status (see Chapter 10)

Philosophically, Beveridge's plan for social security was in his words 'first and foremost a method of redistributing income, so as to put the first and most urgent needs first, so as to make the best possible use of whatever resources are available' (Beveridge Report, 1942, p. 170, para.457). It was also about 'balancing arguments and equities, comparing desires and resources' and devising 'methods of making all the immense good that has been accomplished into something better still' (Beveridge Report, 1942, p. 20, para.40).

The Politics of Beveridge

The greatest public acclaim was given to the proposal which was outside the report's field (Calder, 1971, p. 611).

Probably few members of the Government, least of all Churchill, guessed the impact which the Beveridge Report would make on the public mind (Foot, 1975, p. 407).

Beveridge's Report had been generating considerable controversy before its publication. One MP had been critical of the 'powerful interests who are already trying to prejudge and sabotage the report in advance'. He was referring to the Approved Societies who administered sickness benefit under the existing NHI scheme. Industrial insurance companies were responsible for one hundred million policies a year in 1941, bringing in a total of £74,000,000 per year; forty per cent of this went in management expenses. These policies were sold to the poor who often got into arrears, and once in arrears, the possibility that their benefits might lapse and their investment be lost (see for example, Gilbert, 1966, pp. 319–26). Parliamentary grumbles continued over the Report until the Parliamentary debate in the House of Commons on 17th February 1943. The flavour of these grumbles gives us some idea of how potentially contentious the Report was. For example, *The Daily Telegraph* reported Beveridge as saying his Report 'would take us half way to Moscow'. Beveridge made a short and mild disclaimer in the newspaper. Other MPs were more concerned with leaked proposals to abolish 'free doctoring'. Others insisted that what was required in addition to Beveridge's proposals, was 'a statutory minimum wage'. Large numbers of Labour members pressed the Postmaster-General continuously from September to November (1942) about the Report and all raised their own particular topics of importance. For example, would it contain proposals to reform old age pensions? A further series of Parliamentary skirmishes took place concerning the leak of the Report to the press before it was considered by Parliament and the question was raised as to whether the BBC were using it as propaganda by broadcasting its contents to 'all parts of the world'. Bevan and Shinwell were furious with Anthony Eden for the press leak – 'if this practice goes much further, debates in this House will be rigged by private interests'. Eden gave an undertaking that in future the House would receive its policy papers before the press (House of Commons, 1943, Cols.1613–1694).

The Report, with the somewhat uninspiring title of 'Social Insurance and Allied Services', was made available to the general public in December 1942 (Beveridge Report, 1942). People lined up outside the shops of His Majesty's Stationery Office to buy the Report, forming what one commentator has termed 'the most significant queues of the war' (Calder, 1971, p. 609). A brief official summary of the Beveridge Report was issued and the combined sales of the full report and the summary reached 650,000.

> Within two weeks of its publication, Gallup Poll discovered that 19 out of 20 people had heard of the report and 9 out of 10 believed that its proposals should be adopted. (Calder, 1971, p. 609; see also Barnett, 1986, p. 29).

There was little doubt that the proposal that after the war Britain should have not just a comprehensive *hospital* service, but a comprehensive *health* service was quite firmly on the political agenda, despite the other pressing concerns of wartime Britain. A head of steam had built up politically to force the Coalition government to accept the recommendations of the report almost before they were published. In February, 1943, the House of Commons debated the Beveridge Report (House of Commons, 1943, Cols.1613–2050). The government announced that it welcomed the conception of a reorganised and comprehensive health service which would cover the people as a whole and include institutional treatment. The debate included some unequivocal statements of support for Beveridge's proposals, especially as they related to a national health service.

> Freedom from want when people suffer adversity whether through lack of work, sickness, accident, disablement, loss of breadwinner or old age, seem to me to be our first human task ... a further step to be taken along the road to prosperity to ensure the fulfilment of freedom from want means there

must be hospital rehabilitation and medical services. I do not regard charges for these services crippling, but as an invest- ment which will yield a rich return in human life ... efficiency and happiness. We must pay a price for such desirable ends ... state medical services should be expanded and brought within the reach of a wider public, even though the financial cost of such services is not yet calculable ... the poor demand that in health services they have the right to the best that is possible, therefore it comes to a question of finance. (House of Commons, 1943, Cols.1613–1694).

Replying for the government the Lord President of the Council, Sir John Anderson described the report as one of 'great ingenuity', 'high idealism' and 'practical realities' promising that the Govern- ment would follow general lines of development laid down in the report. He went on to describe the expenditure involved as 'formidable', but also said the Government would not be deterred by doubts as to finance. He recognised that a comprehensive health service 'implies a reorganization of existing services ... (into) ... 'one unified and comprehensive service'. And by com- prehensive he meant

a service covering the people as a whole, no one left out and inclusion of institutional treatment to be administered by the Health Department not the Ministry of Social Security ... the object is to secure through a publicly organized and regulated service that any man woman and child who wants it, can obtain easily and readily a whole range of medical advice and attention through the general practitioner, the consultant, the hospital and every related branch of the profession up to date methods. The cooperation of public authorities, voluntary hospitals, voluntary agencies and the profession towards one common end.

Before concluding he also noted the need to ensure that 'pro- fessional interests must be amply and properly safeguarded and most important of all a free choice of doctor' (House of Commons, 1943, Cols.1655–1678).

The subsequent debate generated a range of comments and observations – that for example, 'a large sum on income tax would be acceptable – if people want a scheme, they should pay for it during their lifetime'. Others used the opportunity to draw attention to TB in Scotland, bringing forward old age pensions, and the fear of destroying the livelihood of the insurance companies. It was left to the Chancellor of the Exchequer, Sir Kingsley Wood, to remind everyone of the financial consequences of implementing Beveridge. In stating the government's priorities after the war – housing, education, and civil aviation – the Chancellor, while in favour of Beveridge, also made the following comments:

> generous hearts do not foot bills ... the financial aspect should be considered and weighted ... we should not hold out hopes that we are not able to fulfil.

On the question of a comprehensive health service, he said, 'before we come to a final conclusion we must obviously have regard to the costs and other claims that will be made upon us' (House of Commons, 1943, Cols.1825–1838). Others in the debate made the same point, referring constantly to costs against high ideals. Some attacked the Government for placing implementation of the Report above other priorities -'our national defence are more important than this report' and 'housing must occupy a leading position in our post war considerations'.

Commander King Hall of the Brains Trust, an MP, detected a deliberate lukewarm attitude by the Government towards the Report because of the financial implications which he described as follows.

> He, the Chancellor of the Exchequer, reminded me of a man who says to you – I hope you will spend a weekend with me, but of course my wife may die before you come, or the trains may not be running, or we may be invaded, or a tree may fall down and block the road – after all those provisos you come to the conclusion that, after all, the man is not very keen on your spending the weekend with him. (House of Commons, 1943, Cols.1765–1916).

On the third day of the debate, 18th February 1943, Bevan, Griffiths and Shinwell moved an amendment to challenge the implementation of the Report in its current form, mainly because the Government of the day would not give an undertaking to create a Ministry of Social Security (see Campbell, 1987, p. 127). The Home Secretary thought there would be a serious constitutional and parliamentary issue if the amendment was carried. The Lord President of the Council committed the government of the day, broadly speaking, to the principles of the Report. The amendment was defeated and the Report was supported in the House of Commons being described as a 'landmark document' and a 'great state paper' (House of Commons, 1943, Cols.1964–2050).

A somewhat literary millenarian language summarized the philosophy of this 'great state paper'. No less than to slay five giants – want, squalor, idleness, ignorance and disease. The programmes for this would be: national insurance; a housing policy relying on council housing; full employment; secondary education for all (the 1944 Act) and a health service. A modernised social security system was Beveridge's main concern and this was to be the decisive break with nineteenth century methods of relieving poverty and twentieth century struggles with the consequences of unemployment. A health service was seen by Beveridge as being a necessary partner in supporting a modernised social security system.

With the House of Commons debate and the government's announcement of support for a comprehensive health service, the final stages of the policy-making process leading to the establishment of the NHS had begun. In this process the impact of the wider military conflict would be moderated and the conflicts which had been manifested in previous debates about extending state intervention in health care would assume a new significance. Beveridge's proposals for a comprehensive health service reflected current thinking in the medical profession and the Ministry of Health (see for example, Harris, 1977, p. 429 and Stark-Murray, 1971, p. 56). There was professional support for reform, but within parameters set by the profession. In moving the discussion towards the details of a comprehensive health service the government might wish to redefine these parameters.

Establishing a National Health Service 1

What happened in 1942 ... (was) ... very simple; up to that time, planning for medical reform had been predominantly a professional enterprise and a paper enterprise. Now the government had shown its willingness to act on paper schemes, the possibility of reform became more concrete and imminent. Moreover the responsibility for reform was about to pass into the hands of the laymen, and worse into the hands of politicians and bureaucrats. Anxiety now gripped Tavistock Square. (Eckstein, 1958, p. 132)

In reviewing the final stages of the processes leading to the establishment of the NHS, we are entering a particularly well-documented phase in its history – and one in which issues of conflict and consensus have perhaps been most widely discussed. Most commentators agree that at this time the emphasis of professional interests changed. The medical profession had contributed to placing health care reform on the pre-war agenda and the profession's own wartime activities (eg: Medical Planning Commission) and experience (eg: EMS) reinforced a considerable professional commitment to reform. But with the publication of the Beveridge Report and the wartime government's commitment to a NHS, the BMA 'lost its passion for reform' (Lindsey, 1962, pp. 39–40) and 'began to act as a trade union ... in the hope of obtaining the most favourable terms of service' (Abel-Smith, 1964, p. 459; see, also Campbell, 1987, p. 166). This meant that the conflict with the medical profession followed a rather predictable pattern in which support for general principles is replaced by concerns about, and often outright opposition to, the detailed proposals (see for example, Brand, 1965, p. 15 on the medical profession and sanitary reform in the nineteenth century). The final outcome seems often to have been the passing of the legislation despite professional opposition – for example, the Public Health Act of 1872 (see Brand, 1965, p. 18) and the National Insurance Act, 1911 (see Chapter 2). One interesting outcome was the growing unpopularity of Beveridge amongst members of the medical profession, despite Beveridge's clearly stated view that both the medical profession and the voluntary hospitals should be involved in discussions relating to the detailed arrangements for the new Service (see Beveridge Report, 1942, p. 169, para.453)

A month after the Beveridge Report was published, the Ministry of Health drew up its own outline of possible legislation. Charles Webster's authoritative book, *Health Services since the War Volume 1*, shows this outline to have contained the key principle, a service free at the point of use, evidence that senior civil servants in the Ministry had already accepted the idea (Webster, 1988). They had also considered the idea that charges for the hotel costs associated with hospital care might be necessary, along with National Insurance and Exchequer 'support' as the main source of finance. With reference to the organization of the NHS, the 'Ministry view' was that representation of local authority and the key medical interests would be essential in discussions concerning the implementation of the scheme, as well as its future administration.

The Coalition Government's first attempt to take forward the process of reform was the never officially published 'Brown Plan' – named after the then Minister of Health (March 1943). These proposals resembled earlier plans produced by the National Association of Local Government Officers (NALGO) and the Society of Medical Officers (Willcocks, 1967, p. 24). It was influenced by a local government perspective, but perhaps also by a relatively apolitical 'civil service perspective' in which the pre-war significance of municipal health services (see Chapter 2) led to a proposal for a unified health service based on regional local government units, despite predictions that this could generate considerable professional opposition (see Webster, 1990, p. 202). The voluntary hospitals would be utilised (and therefore at least partially financed) by the new service, but would not be nationalised. General practitioners would be employed in a full-time salaried service. The Plan was discussed with interested parties and was clearly opposed by the British Medical Association (BMA) both in principle and in detail. For the BMA, a universal scheme would destroy the private income of doctors; both voluntary hospitals and doctors refused point blank to consider being run by local authorities; and for GPs to work for government funded health centres would restrict professional freedom. Only the Socialist Medical Association approved. These were but opening shots in 'the war' to come and the Minister spent the rest of the year listening to the conflicting views of various pressure groups before being replaced in December 1943 by a new Minister of Health – Henry Willink.

In February 1944 the first official publication emerged. This was the White Paper – *A National Health Service* – it included a commitment to 'divorce the care of health from questions of personal means or other factors irrelevant to it' (Ministry of Health, 1944, p. 47) and the idea of a comprehensive Health Service (Ministry of Health, 1944, pp. 9, 47). In other respects, its proposals were simple and conservative; and included only a passing reference to the Beveridge Report (see Webster, 1988, p. 55). The White Paper proposed a local organization for the new service based on joint local authority areas. The new organization would take over municipal hospitals and lay down the conditions under which voluntary hospitals would contribute – in return for which they would receive grants towards part of the cost of patient care. Financial support for voluntary hospitals was uncertain. It marked

> the first detailed attempt to achieve a marriage of what was probably two incompatibles – the independence of the voluntary hospitals and a co-ordinated hospital service. (Willcocks, 1967, p. 63; see also, Abel-Smith, 1964, Ch.27).

Under this scheme the GPs would be under contract to a Central Medical Board – with remuneration in the same format as National Health Insurance (NHI). However doctors working in health centres would be salaried, and the Central Medical Board was to have the power to refuse doctors the right to practice in over-doctored areas and to compel new doctors to work in poorly-served areas. Speaking in the House of Commons, Willink identified four principles of the proposed NHS – it would be comprehensive; there would be complete freedom for doctors and patients to use the service; there would be democratic responsibility through Parliament and local government; and there would be the use of expert and professional guidance to ensure the best performance of the new service (see Lindsey, 1962, p. 36).

The White Paper received an 'enthusiastic parliamentary reception' (Eckstein, 1958, p. 139) but Dr. Charles Hill, the popular

Radio Doctor, used the *Daily Express* to suggest such a plan would stop people getting advice from their own doctors. The BMA was still not satisfied with the government proposals, especially any form of salaried service for GPs, the location where doctors could or could not practice and the significant role for local government. Two weeks after the White Paper was published the Secretary of the BMA was reported as regretting both the absence of a corporate body at the top of the service and that the government had been unwilling to dilute a democratic principle by including, in the public interest, some non-elected professional expert members in the joint authorities. A subsequent BMA poll recorded that 53 per cent of those polled were against the White Paper and 78 per cent against the control of hospitals by the proposed joint authorities (see Eckstein, 1958, p. 148; see also, Honigsbaum, 1989, Chapter 7). The medical profession's antagonism towards local government was proving a major impediment to reaching agreement. A leader in *The Times* commented that the medical profession appeared to have 'willed almost all the ends and rejected almost all the means'. A Political and Economic Planning Report was to characterise the doctors' approach as 'an evasion of the responsibilities of democratic citizenship' (quoted in Abel-Smith, 1964, p. 467). Webster concludes that because the White Paper was 'neither a declaration of firm policy, nor a presentation of alternatives for adjudication by interested parties' it resulted in 'further destabilising negotiations' (Webster, 1988, p. 44) rather than a swift transition to legislation.

By the early summer of 1945 the Minister had assembled the elements of an alternative plan (The Willink Plan) of 'nightmarish complexity embracing elements from all previous plans' (Webster, 1990, p. 130). This introduced a two tier system of regional and area planning authorities made up of equal local authority and voluntary hospital representation. Municipal hospitals would remain under local government control. Health centres were relegated to 'experimental status' and the powers of direction previously proposed for the Central Medical Board would disappear. Local administration of GP services would be undertaken by a modified version of the existing NHI committees. The right to 'sell practices' – taken away by the White Paper – was reinstated. The major medical organizations were now happier.

But the Willink Plan was never officially published. With the surrender of Germany, the Second World War was coming to an end and a General Election was to take place in August 1945. The result was an overwhelming victory for the Labour Party – the Party with the most unequivocal commitment to a range of social policy reforms – including the implementation of the recommendations set down in the Beveridge Report (see Morgan, 1984b, p. 183). Britain had its first Labour Government to hold an absolute majority in the House of Commons and there was a new Minister of Health – Aneurin Bevan.

Conclusions

> The war ... inevitably brought about the end of the old medical system, both by the shortcomings it revealed in it and the attitudes towards medical reform which it engendered. (Eckstein, 1958, p. 83)

> Catalysed by the disruption of the war years, but built on ideas that had crystallised in the 1930s (Stevens, 1966, p. 67)

> (One) ... of the lessons of the war, as a citizens' war, was the popular demand for the abolition of the poor law; of ineligible citizens; of personally merited disease; of inequality before 'the best ascertained laws of health'. (Titmuss, 1968, p. 241)

The hesitant steps towards a more comprehensive and accessible health service in the first half of the century were epitomised by the passing of the NHI Act and the subsequent concerns published in successive reports in the 1920s and 1930s – the latter indicating a broad if somewhat ill-defined consensus around the need for further reforms in the organization of health care. The experience of war appeared to confirm and reinforce that consensus. The 'efficiency' arguments were even clearer as the demands of wartime exposed even more clearly the deficiencies of the pre-war system. The 'equity' arguments were also strengthened by concerns about social justice associated with the 'levelling effect' of war (Lindsey, 1962, p. 23). Political pressures on government intensified when the public reaction to the Beveridge Report confirmed the strength of public opinion in support of social policy reform, including health service reform and key interest groups (especially the medical profession) remained in favour of reform – at least until the government made a tangible response to the arguments and interests in favour of reform.

Once the consensus had culminated in a tangible government commitment to establish a universal, comprehensive health service, there were indications that the consensus around generalities concealed conflicts about details – especially where the interests of the medical profession were concerned. This emphasises a constant theme of this book; that few conflicts spring from original and unconsidered concerns. Often they are adaptations, amendments, and attempts to address the unresolved problems of earlier periods. In some cases these were perceived or conceptualised as problems that would reappear to challenge the claim of the UK to be providing the modern comprehensive, adequate and universally available health services in which its legislators, professionals and public believed.

Beveridge was 'embarrassed when people referred to him as the creator of the NHS, insisting this term could only be applied to the Labour Minister of Health – Aneurin Bevan' (Harris, 1977, p. 459). Nonetheless it is difficult to consider the state of affairs in the current British National Health Service without assessing the significance of the Beveridge Report upon the development of the NHS. This significance relates to the values, the administration and structure, and the financing of today's NHS. Beveridge's chief concern was to rationalise the social security system; the right to medical care of those defined in need by qualified professionals was a crucial, but supplementary, concern. At no time was Beveridge involved in the policy discussions of the wartime Coalition or the post-war Labour government; and at no stage can he be seen as personally responsible for any great social policy statutes of this period – the Family Allowances Act of 1945, the National Insurance and NHS Acts of 1946 and the National Assistance Act of 1948 – but:

> the main structure and many of the principles of the welfare legislation of 1945–48 were those which Beveridge had laid down in 1942. In devising these principles Beveridge's role has been mainly that of a synthesizer and publicist rather than that of an innovator and it is difficult to claim that he had made any inherently original contribution to subsequent

social policy. But, nevertheless, it was Beveridge who interpreted the main stream of public opinion and transformed an
incoherent mass of popular feeling into a blueprint for social
reform. (Harris, 1977, p. 448)

The importance of the Beveridge Report for a future NHS lay
in its refusal to restrict itself to a simple tidying-up of the Poor
Law legacy of cash benefits. Instead Beveridge's biographer
describes the scope of his enquiry as a 'radical interpretation' of
his terms of references, going beyond a concern with cash benefits
to other policy areas,especially medical treatment. He adopted a
comprehensive conception of medical treatment – that is comprehensive in scope and universally available to all (see Harris, 1977,
p. 387). The philosophical issue of providing a service to meet
health care needs without a test of means and free at the point of
use was the final significant break with Poor Law thinking, and
can be seen as completing the changes set in motion by the Liberal
welfare reforms earlier in the century.

But this conception of a universal, comprehensive national
health service was to bring open conflict when the attempts to
operationalise Beveridge's ideas for a health service in the immediate aftermath of the Second World War were undertaken. Some
would also say that Beveridge laid the basis for expectations of
health care for all citizens, but in the face of growing financial
restraints and reluctant Treasury support. Such expectations in the
face of budgetary concerns, let alone professional views of problems of equity, was bound to produce conflicts, even if the
protagonists protested that they shared the same purposes.

4

Political parties and pressure groups

Discussing the new social measures, Mr.Bevan said that the
'slight conflict over the National Health Service never
worried him very much because – as a credulous idealist – he
knew the truth would survive, and that as the medical
profession came to know its provisions they would support it.
The Act was not based upon contributions, and every individual had equal rights to the scheme, whether insured or
not. He paid sincere tribute to the voluntary work of hospitals, but said that private charity could never be a substitute
for organised justice' (4 July 1948). (Webster (ed), 1991,
pp. 123–4)

Establishing a National Health Service 2
The context for the remainder of this policy-making process were
the struggles of the 1945–51 Labour government to carry out its
reconstruction policy for post-war Britain. The NHS moved to
centre-stage in this, it having become the most popular of these
reforms (Calder, 1971, p. 611), ahead of nationalising the commanding heights of the economy. To move from Beveridge's
recommendation for a comprehensive and universally available
service to an administratively practicable service was the task
facing the Labour government with an inheritance of pre-1945
thinking on the structure, philosophy and funding of medical care.

The first major obstacle in the way of turning the ideal into the
feasible was the power of the deeply entrenched professional
interest groups – especially the doctors who were able, until the
Act, to control the size of patient lists, the sale of practices and
where doctors would be allowed to practice (see Willcocks, 1967;
Webster, 1988). The administrative problem related to the tra-

ditional points of conflict between bureaucracy and professionalism and between democracy and professionalism – represented by the doctors' fear of the loss of clinical freedom (see Chapter 14). The administrative compromises of National Health Insurance (NHI) had resolved the former with regard to the Friendly societies and the doctors (see Chapter 2). The poor law authorities, in the form of the Boards of Guardians, and then (after 1929) local government, represented elements of both these conflicts and neither had been resolved to the satisfaction of the medical profession prior to 1945 (see Chapters 1 and 2). This was a particular dilemma given the crucial role of local government in existing health care (see Chapter 2). A means had to be found to integrate professionals into a governmental bureaucracy without raising professional opposition whilst at the same time making the health care system accountable to the political process. Bevan's mission – as the new Minister of Health – was subsequently described as persuading 'the most conservative and respected profession in the country to accept and operate the Labour Government's most intrinsically socialist proposition' (Foot, 1975, p. 104). The economic problem was the potential conflict between the aim of providing a universalist, comprehensive health service of a good standard and that of containing health costs to a reasonable level – how to finance the system in such a way that certainty and sufficiency of funds could be guaranteed.

There were three related sets of debates, discussions and negotiations; between Bevan, the Labour cabinet and the doctors; between Bevan, the Parliamentary Labour Party and the Conservatives; and between Bevan and the teaching hospitals. Each was characterised by two sorts of conflict, one over ideology – the role of the state in potentially dominating a free profession – and the second over the administrative procedures that would be tight enough to guarantee an equitable distribution of scarce and valued medical care, yet loose enough to allow a professional discretion to remain unfettered within financial boundaries set by Parliament – the minimum administrative regulations necessary to assure medical care to the population based upon Beveridge's aspiration in paragraph 426 of his report (Beveridge Report, 1942).

Bevan's solution was to rationalise the Health Service by using the political tool of the day, nationalising 'the commanding heights' of health care, the hospital (Campbell, 1987, p. 167). The operation of the Emergency Medical Service (EMS) having exposed both the problems of a non-planned system and the potential for state planning. Herbert Morrison opposed this in Cabinet, seeing it as an attack on local government hospitals, especially the London County Council (see Morgan, 1984b, pp. 154–5; Hennessey, 1992, p. 139, and Campbell, 1987, pp. 169–70). The voluntary hospitals also opposed the idea but were weakened by the underlying frailty of their financial circumstances with 80 per cent of their income already being provided by the state. The Conservative Party also opposed it, led by the ex-Minister of Health responsible for the original White Paper.

A new White Paper (Ministry of Health, 1946) and Bill were both published in March 1946. The Second and Third Readings of the Bill were in April and July of the same year. Bevan made an hour and a quarter speech including his famous comment in support of the 'rational planning' of hospital provision:

> I would rather be kept alive in the efficient if cold altruism of a large hospital than expire in a gush of warm sympathy in a small one. (Webster (ed), 1991, p. 62)

Although the Bill adopted most of the proposals of the Willink Plan (see Willcocks, 1967, p. 57) the Conservative opposition actually divided the House on the third reading – a division at this stage of parliamentary proceedings traditionally being one of opposition based upon objections to the principles of a Bill. The BMA tried to wreck the whole Bill, although there was support from 'medical peers' in the House of Lords (Lords Moran and Horder) because the future of the major voluntary hospitals was assured within the new NHS. This was indicative of the way Bevan had exploited old conflicts and divisions within the medical profession – that between specialist hospital doctors and general practitioners working in the community (see Chapter 1; Honigsbaum, 1989, Ch.13; and Jenkins, 1963, pp. 240–1). The BMA was in these circumstances more effective at representing the views of certain sections of the medical profession – especially GPs. Bevan's proposals for the NHS offered considerable gains to hospital doctors and this weakened the position of the BMA.

The BMA then balloted its members; 41,000 were against, 4,000 in favour. Bevan proceeded as planned but put forward a compromise in the Bill that a salaried service for GPs would not be introduced without further specific legislation. The BMA balloted again; this time there was a smaller majority against the Bill, and a fear of a debacle like that which followed the NHI legislation with doctors rushing to join the new service (see Chapter 2).

There were two key reasons for the approach that Bevan had taken; one was political, the other administrative. Politically he did it 'to universalise the best'; there had to be equal rights of access to the best medical care regardless of income and residence; this was the 'egalitarian socialist' at work. Administratively, the existing 'system' was not a system; it was a hotchpotch of hospitals and community services; sources of finance were neither sufficient nor certain; a national health service required national administration.

The resulting characteristics of the new NHS were as follows. Firstly, income guaranteed by national government with revenue derived from predominantly national rather than local taxation; within the former, social insurance contributions (National Insurance) would play only a limited role and would in no way determine entitlements to use the NHS. Secondly, and related to the financial arrangements, there would be only a limited role for local government in providing health care (eg: community nursing services) and employing doctors (eg: Medical Officers of Health). Thirdly, for doctors and their patients there would be the doctor of choice, free treatment at the point of use, and referral to the hospital by general practitioners. Fourthly, GPs remained self-employed independent contractors (continuing the political compromise developed for NHI, see Chapter 2) although they could work in groups and partnerships, owning their own premises, receiving capitation fees, giving primary care, diagnosis and the rights of referral. Fifthly, GP services would be administered by appointed bodies, Executive Councils, which would hold the contracts of GPs, dentists, and pharmacists; half the membership of these Councils being nominated by professional bodies. Sixthly, for the hospitals there would be a predominantly two tier system. Regional Hospital Boards, covering populations of approximately five million people, would employ the senior hospital doctors (the consultants) and aim to establish an equal distribution of this scarce professional medical manpower. Hospital Management Committees would run hospitals on a day to day basis and employ

Figure 1: The Administrative Structure of the NHS, 1948

TEACHING HOSPITALS	NON-TEACHING HOSPITALS	COMMUNITY AND PUBLIC HEALTH SERVICES	THE FAMILY PRACTITIONER SERVICES
	15 Regional Hospital Boards		
36 Boards of Governors	330 Hospital Management Committees	175 Local Health Authorities (counties and county boroughs)	134 Executive Councils

all other hospital staff. Not only local authority mental hospitals but also local authority mental deficiency institutions were to become NHS hospitals; the latter was perhaps particularly inappropriate in terms of the needs of the individuals in those institutions (see for example, Ryan and Thomas, 1980, pp. 14–18, and Townsend, 1973, pp. 208–9). The two tier arrangement did not apply to a group of special hospitals which were to be directly administered by the Ministry, whilst teaching hospitals would retain considerable independence from both the Ministry and the RHBs and would be managed by their own Boards of Governors (see Figure One).

Later commentators would be largely in agreement that the 1946 Act was 'a rationalisation and redistribution rather than a great advance' (Willcocks, 1967, p. 20; see also Eckstein, 1958, p. 3) with an 'odd administrative structure, especially when viewed against early attempts at a simplified but comprehensive administration' (Willcocks, 1967, pp. 19–20). The medical profession is also sometimes portrayed as 'a winner' from the associated pressure group politics especially by contrast with those with administrative skills and those with property to offer – the latter losing their influence once the decision was taken to nationalise the hospitals (Willcocks, 1967, pp. 30–3, 71; Honigsbaum, 1989, p. 183).

However whilst it can be argued that the post-war Labour government paid relatively dearly for the settlements that drew the profession into the NHS, two points can be made. Firstly that the doctors were 'formidable obstacles to anything other than incremental change' (Webster, 1988, p. 16). Secondly that the limitations of the resulting compromise can be compared not only with more 'desirable' and 'radical' alternatives, but also with the widely recognised limitations of pre-war health care in the UK which was characterised by 'anachronism, administrative complexity, duplication, parochialism, inertia, stagnation' (Webster, 1988, p. 1; see also Willcocks, 1967, p. 21). Set against this, the potential of the NHS was considerable, even when handicapped by financial and organizational arrangements which owed so much to the demands of political expediency.

Professional power and influence

On 5 July 1948, most of Britain's hospitals were taken into national ownership. Only three years earlier there had been hardly any advocate of such an extreme solution to the problems of hospital planning and hospital administration. The processes which led to this development came not from any doctrines of the Labour Party, which by 1945 was confining its proposals for nationalisation to the industrial sector, but from aspirations of parts of the medical profession. Nationalisation seemed the only way by which consultants and specialists, could achieve their principal objectives – adequate financial support for the hospitals in which they worked, the retention of private practice and an effective 'say' in the running of all hospital services. (Abel-Smith, 1964, p. 488)

There is clearly a prima facie case for seeing the establishment of the NHS as a location for a conflict between the state and an established professional group (see Doyal, 1979, p. 180). Furthermore, it is possible to suggest that the professional group gained greatly from that conflict; hence comments that the NHS Act was 'a doctors' measure rather than a patients measure' (Eckstein, 1958, p. 3). Evidence of the power of the medical profession in the establishment of NHI (see Chapter Two) and in other countries (see, for example, Alford, 1975) lend weight to a perspective that emphasises the significance of professional power in 'welfare state developments'. The prestige of the medical profession, the private market for their skills outside the NHS, and indeed an international marketplace for medical expertise, can all provide plausible explanations for this example of professional power and influence.

We know sections of the medical profession were active as pressure groups and we know the plans for the health service changed with regard to administrative and financial arrangements. Indeed it has been suggested that the 'NHS which was created in 1948 was very different from that which has been originally proposed in 1943' (Doyal, 1979, p. 180) – an exact parallel of observations made about the establishment of NHI (see Chapter 2 and Gilbert, 1966, p. 290). We know also that the plans changed in ways which can be seen to benefit sections of the medical profession and on which the profession campaigned. As Willcocks notes

It is quite clear that the original Government aims like those of the victorious Labour Party of 1945 had to be progressively modified or eroded to meet the conflicting views of the groups most concerned. (Willcocks, 1967, p. 105).

This is perhaps most obvious with the role of local government in health care which was significantly diminished when both voluntary and municipal hospitals were nationalised. The democratic and bureaucratic challenge to professional autonomy represented by local government was eliminated – at least for most of the medical profession (Honigsbaum, 1989, Chs.5 and 12). The nationalised system would inherit a management system much more like that of the voluntary than the municipal hospital system – one that placed considerable emphasis on clinical freedom (see for example, Abel-Smith, 1964, p. 281 and Gilbert, 1970, p. 234). This was of course indicative of the long-standing sensitivities surrounding professional / managerial relations, elements of which were obvious in voluntary hospital management in the nineteenth century (see Chapter 1) and which would remain controversial in the future (see Chapter 7). The system of merit awards to supplement salaries and the ability, not only to continue with private practice, but also to undertake this work in NHS hospitals via the pay-beds system, were further benefits accruing to hospital doctors under the NHS. It was this combination of attractive financial arrangements that would cause Bevan to make his famous remark with regard to the hospital doctors that he 'stuffed their mouths with gold' (see Webster (ed), 1991, pp. 219–22). Thus the hospital doctors gained a good deal – voluntary hospital doctors gained pay with little diminution in autonomy; local government hospital doctors gained more pay with more autonomy. The introduction of the NHS improved the circumstances of hospital doctors significantly, in much the same way as the introduction of NHI improved the position of most GPs (see Chapter 2; Abel-Smith, 1964, Ch.29; Campbell, 1987, pp. 168–9).

In addition, the most prestigious hospitals – the teaching hospitals – were afforded a special administrative and financial status within the NHS. They were to be financed directly by the Ministry, enabled to retain their pre-NHS endowments and given considerable managerial autonomy – a situation they would lose in subsequent NHS reorganizations but be enabled to regain with the introduction of an 'internal market' including the opportunity to seek NHS trust status (see Chapter 7). Perhaps less surprisingly the financial and administrative arrangements introduced for the NHI general practitioner system were carried forward into the NHS general practitioner system. Nonetheless a case could be made both for a salaried GP service and for more consumer and/ or community representation within these organizational arrangements – the latter would be significantly diminished by comparison with arrangements for NHI (see p. 308).

The tripartite structure of the new NHS was constructed around long-established divisions within the medical profession – retaining elements of the NHI arrangements for GPs in the NHS; continuing the employment of Medical Officers of Health by local government; and making separate arrangements for hospital doctors. In so doing the new Service replicated, within a state health service, the organizational divisions of Victorian Britain – the Friendly Societies, the sanitary authorities and the voluntary hospitals. The tripartite structure can also be seen as part of a broader trend of the demunicipalisation of state welfare (local government involvement in social security was ended at this time) (see Chapter 14).

The Coalition and Labour governments – especially the latter – were committed to a universalist and comprehensive health service. There was substantial support from sections of the medical profession for the '90 per cent solution' proposed by the Medical Planning Commission in 1942 (see Chapter 3). This envisaged a national health insurance system extended to cover hospital care for approximately 90 per cent of the population – the richest 10 per cent remaining outside state schemes to sustain private practice (Willcocks, 1967, pp. 34, 45–48). As with NHI the government of the day may have made significant adjustments to professional interests on administrative matters, but it retained and enacted the key principles of the proposed reform. Furthermore, whilst the diminution of local government involvement in health care may have suited professional interests, it also served the interests of those in central government who wished to keep a close control over public expenditure on health and welfare.

The establishment of the NHS, like the establishment of NHI (see Chapter 2), was part of a wider set of social policy reforms introduced by the war-time Coalition, but principally by the postwar Labour, governments. These included secondary education for all, universalist social security policies (following the Beveridge Report, 1942), housing and town planning legislation and a new Childrens Act. These reforms have attracted a range of descriptions from the 'creation of the welfare state' to the 'final shaping of the welfare state'. Many of the reforms, including the health care reforms, attracted considerable support – reflecting a wartime and sometimes pre-war 'political consensus or near-consensus' (Briggs, 1978, p. 448; see also Barnett, 1986, p. 33). It has been suggested that the particular achievement of the Labour government was to put the wartime plans into effect 'with none of the qualifications about 'attractive schemes which turn out to be economically impossible' (to quote a 1942 memorandum of Winston Churchill)' (Bruce, 1961, p. 26).

An Age of Austerity
Financing the NHS was an instant and persistent headache. (Hennessey, 1992. p. 143)

The NHS came on stream during what has become known as 'the age of austerity', in which raw materials were rationed, there was competition for infrastructure schemes for council house and school building, and the pound sterling was devalued. Indeed without a loan negotiated with the USA 'the welfare state ... would not have been possible' (Morgan, 1984b, p. 151). In 1949 and 1950, the Service was hit by the backlog of pent up demand, following years in which many in the population had ignored and neglected their own health needs when faced with services 'marred by the taint of charity, less eligibility, minimum standards ... heavy handed bureaucracy ... social discrimination and the indignities of the poor law' (Webster, 1988, p. 15 and Titmuss, 1950, p. 514). In addition,

> the NHS was hit simultaneously by increases both in staff numbers and pay levels, the inevitable result being unforeseen escalation in staff costs in the hospital sector. This was merely one, although the greatest of indications for the Treasury that NHS expenditure was out of control. (Webster, 1988, p. 137)

When the Korean war led to increased defence spending, the Treasury sought economies in housing and the NHS. Charges were suggested for spectacles, dentures and prescriptions – the Treasury view being that such charges were merely the first steps towards tighter financial control within the health service (Webster, 1988, p. 182). Aneurin Bevan and Harold Wilson resigned from the Government over this issue. The Labour Government in its final days reduced public expenditure on all the social policy areas and the new Conservative Chancellor of the Exchequer (Butler) carried on where they had begun. Churchill with his 'Set the People Free' slogan, pursued tax cuts in 1952, 1953 and 1954; reduced public expenditure to be the means by which this was achieved. There were recommendations for charging fees in secondary schools, charges for school meals and health service charges. By late 1951 the number of posts in health management had been frozen, especially clerical and administrative posts, following Treasury demands for 5 per cent reduction in non-medical and nursing staff. By June 1952 prescription charges were introduced and hospital building capital expenditure reduced. By December 1952 Ministerial control was absolute; senior medical staff establishment had to be approved by the Minister himself (see Glennerster, 1995, pp. 75–7). The issue of financing the NHS 'was never to be unimportant again' (Briggs, 1978, p. 448).

For a nation 'struggling with the economic consequences of the war' the post-war social policy reforms have been described as 'little short of breathtaking' (Townsend, 1973, p. 3). Perhaps we overreached ourselves as a nation; with the 'welfare state' in general, and the NHS in particular, being unaffordable. This point was made often enough at the time and it is perhaps unsurprising to see it revived more recently with the thesis that:

> the post-war fulfilment by the Labour Government of the wartime dream loaded a ... crushing burden on the economy ... (and leading to) ... a segregated, sub-literate, unskilled, unhealthy and institutionalized proletariat hanging on the nipple of State materialism. (Barnett, 1995, p. xiii and Barnett, 1986, p. 304).

However comparative data offer little support for the thesis that the post-war Labour government committed the UK to relatively excessive state welfare expenditure. Indeed West Germany, Austria and Belgium were already spending a larger percentage of their gross domestic products on social security by 1950. During the 1950s France, Denmark, Italy, Sweden and the Netherlands moved above the UK in this particular league table so that from 1970 onwards 'Britain consistently devoted a lower proportion of national income to social security purposes than any other European country, with the sole exception of Switzerland' (Harris, 1990, p. 180). By 1980 Britain would be grouped with other 'lean-spending democracies' (see Wilensky, 1981)

For the NHS the 'age of austerity' would continue throughout the 1950s, sustained as much by an ideological preference for the 'public burden model of state welfare' (Titmuss, 1968, pp. 124–5) as by pressing economic circumstances. The Guillebaud Report (1956) into the cost of the NHS gave the NHS an 'economic clean bill of health'; there was no evidence of waste or extravagance (Guillebaud Committee, 1956) and the cost of the service as a percentage of GDP 'fell from 3.51 per cent to 3.24 per cent in the mid-1950s' (Briggs, 1978, p. 449). The analysis suggested by Guillebaud and undertaken by Abel-Smith and Titmuss concluded that 'capital expenditure in 1952/3 was at a third of the rate of 1938/9' (Abel-Smith and Titmuss, 1956, p. 138) and the Committee recommendation was that a major capital programme was required immediately.

Conflicts, consensus and continuity

> The National Health Service has been easily the most widely publicised and the most widely criticised of all the projects undertaken by the postwar Labour governments. (Eckstein, 1958, p. 1)

> The whole attitude of the Leader of the House, seconded by the *Minister of Health* ... is to offend, wound, injure and provoke those over whom they have got so great a Parliamentary majority ... the treatment which has been meted out to us, and which has already produced party antagonism, bitter as anything I have seen in my long life of political conflict (Winston Churchill, 6 December, 1945, speaking in the House of Commons in support of a Motion of Censure in which His Majesty's Government are said to be 'neglecting their first duty ... (including) ... the drastic curtailment of our swollen national expenditure'. (See House of Commons, 1946, Cols.2530, 2531 and 2534)

> I have examined the ... (NHS) ... Bill and it looks to me uncommonly like the first step, and a big one, towards National Socialism as practised in Germany. (Dr.Alfred Cox, former Secretary of the BMA, quoted in Timmins, 1995, p. 119)

The NHS came into existence in an atmosphere of conflict. This conflict was generated by the strong ideological commitment of the post-Second World War Labour Government, and the opposition of the Conservative Party and some sections of the medical profession, to what was perceived as a thoroughly socialist aspiration; a health service, universally available, comprehensive, centrally-planned and free at the time of need. In addition, there were some long standing and deep-seated grievances within sections of the medical profession resulting in the new Labour government being 'exposed to the full blast of a campaign which had been gathering momentum since 1911' (Webster, 1990, p. 199).

Nonetheless despite these well-documented conflicts, especially around administrative details, the establishment of the NHS owed something to an emerging pre-war and subsequent war-time consensus or near-consensus about the need for health care reform (see for example, Klein, 1983, pp. 2–7; Briggs, 1978, p. 448). Furthermore, the establishment of the NHS cannot be disaggregated from a wider range of social policy reforms enacted by the war-time Coalition and post-war Labour governments; these reforms being in part a product of, and a means by which, the Second World War was conducted in Britain (see Eckstein, 1958, p. 133). It can also be seen as 'an important part of the post-war settlement between capital and labour' (Doyal, 1979, p. 179) and thus a further episode in the class and ideological conflicts which prefigured the Liberal welfare reforms (see Chapter 2).

Finally there is the case that 'in many respects the National Health Service extended and developed practices which had been built up over many generations'; that it could be viewed as 'no more than a stage in the evolution of the nation's social services' and in particular that:

> for a century or more, medical care in Britain had been regarded ... as a responsibility for which the community should in some form provide. It was this heritage of shared opinion which was responsible for the widespread acceptance in Britain of what others chose to call 'socialised medicine'. (Abel-Smith, 1964, pp. 500, 502)

There seems little doubt that what was put in place by the post-war Labour government was influenced in its administrative detail by professional interests; and that the process by which this influence was exercised represents a classic example of both pressure group politics and interest group conflicts. The outcome has been described as a 'victory of tactical considerations over administrative and political logic, coherence and consistency' (Klein, 1983, p. 22). However the resulting organizational compromise would endure for a quarter of a century (see Chapter 6) and might therefore claim to be an effective one – although it was to pose significant problems for a co-ordinated approach to community care and the development of non-medical approaches to the needs of people with learning difficulties (see Chapter 13). However it was acceptable to key groups, especially the more influential and powerful sections of the medical profession. But if professionally-based pressure groups disputed the detail, there is also little doubt that the principles of the NHS were 'accepted by the vast majority of the British people' and the profession 'could not deny public opinion' (Abel-Smith, 1964, p. 500). It may be this considerable and consistent degree of public support which explains why the NHS would retain at least ostensible governmental support until the present day.

Therefore the well-documented conflicts associated with the establishment of the NHS can be set in a contemporary and recent historical context of a wide-ranging and well-established consensus as well as the broader historical contexts of class conflict and cultural continuity. It serves as a classic example of the interrelationship between the themes of conflict, consensus and continuity in the provision of health care in Britain.

Conclusions

The Service has scored considerable popular success – to the point indeed, where, ten years after its inception, it seems to be accepted as an altogether natural feature of the British landscape, almost a part of the Constitution – so that it is now good politics not to let the Labour Party take all the credit for it. (Eckstein, 1958, p. 2)

The establishment of the NHS was one of a number of post-war social policy reforms based on the political notion of equal shares and which structured the 'establishment of the welfare state' and the 'post-war settlement between capital and labour' in which labour receives its social wage through state welfare services. Whilst this intense period of social policy initiatives seems to justify some general use of the label 'welfare state', the constituent elements of the 'post-war settlement' were not of equal status or lasting effect, and the NHS can be conceived as more radical in its implications than other changes implemented at the time. For some, the NHS Act was 'one of the most unsordid and civilised actions in the history of health and welfare policy' (Titmuss, 1968, p. 208), although for others, it may be 'misleading to think of the NHS as a social welfare measure at all' – rather more an organizational rationalisation to combat inefficiencies and inadequacies (Eckstein, 1958, p. viii).

Certain aspects of the new service proved to be controversial right from the start, especially those concerned with the professional issues of doctor/patient relations, state regulation, remuneration of doctors and the relationships between the centre and local administration of the service. The role of the medical profession and the setting up of the National Health Service has served as a classic example of pressure group politics and most commentators agree that they played a leading role in shaping at least some of the decisions about the organization of the new NHS (Eckstein, 1958, p. 4). There seems a rather obvious link between the observation that 'the only person not represented round the Minister's table was the patient' (Willcocks, 1967, p. 33) and an outcome in which the nationalisation of the hospitals is identified with 'the aspirations of parts of the medical profession' (Abel-Smith, 1964, p. 488); the doctors emerge as perhaps the major beneficiaries of the introduction of the new Service (Titmuss, 1968, p. 241) and an organizational structure which owed 'more to the opinion of the doctors than to political and public opinion' (Titmuss, 1968, p. 235).

Most of the medical profession were committed to some kind of health care reform. In particular it is worth noting that the most powerful and influential section of the profession worked in those hospitals that were most involved in the 'voluntary health care crisis'. Given recognition of what they saw as important factors – the maintenance of clinical freedom within hospitals and the ability to sustain private practice – these doctors (in the voluntary hospitals) were quite likely to be supportive of increased state intervention in health care, if that intervention could resolve the 'health care crisis' that most concerned them without compromising their 'clinical freedom'.

Despite the heated debates surrounding the 1946 NHS Act, the original objectives of the Service as contained in the White Paper (Ministry of Health, 1944) nevertheless appeared, in the longer run at least, to command a large measure of support from the public, politicians, and the professionals so that,

> by the mid-50s the NHS was protected by a broad consensus embracing all social classes, both political parties, all but an eccentric fringe of the medical profession and all others employed by the Service. (Webster, 1988, pp. 389–90)

These objectives were to bring health care to the entire population of the UK and to provide preventive, curative and rehabilitation services paid for out of general taxation so that they would be free at the time of need. The passage of the legislation is of more than symbolic importance, it institutionalised for the first time a 'free' health care service, publicly funded with unrestricted access providing a comprehensive range of services. At 'the time of its creation it was a unique example of the collective provision of health care in a market society' (Klein, 1983, p. 1), and despite

> the many compromises involved in the course of converting the plan devised in 1943 into the Service inaugurated in 1948 the NHS was at that time and has remained the most ambitious, publicly provided health service to be established by a major Western democracy. (Webster, 1988, p. 397)

There is a continuity between Beveridge's analysis and values and the political commitment and initiative which translated Beveridge into policy. From 1948 onwards the policy was being translated into action but with the change of government in 1951 with a potential conflict of, rather than continuity of, values. However, political expediency, if nothing else, would require successive Conservative governments to persist with the concept of a national health service. The difficulties were to be 'the finance and funding' or how to provide an economically effective and efficient service, (see Chapter 5) and 'the delivery system', how to administer and manage such a Service (see Chapter 6).

In his capacity as Minister of Health in the new Labour Government, Bevan had no doubt about the social and integrating purpose as against the political and economic value of the National Health Service:

> Society becomes more wholesome, more serene, and spiritually healthier, if it knows that its citizen have at the back of their consciousness the knowledge that not only themselves, but all their fellows have access, when ill, to the best that medical skill can provide. But private charity and endowment, although inescapably essential at one time, cannot meet the cost of all this. If the job is to be done, the state must accept financial responsibility. (Bevan, 1978, p. 100)

The fifth of July 1948 was one of *the* great days in British history ... it was a day that transformed like no other before or since the lives and life chances of the British people. (Hennessey, 1992, p. 143)

5
Efficiency and equity

Introduction

The history of the provision of health services from the establishment of National Health Insurance (NHI) in 1913 until the establishment of the National Health Service (NHS) in 1948 was one of state financed and regulated medical care being supplied to limited, clearly designated groups of the population. The historians of the pre-1948 period suggest that services were deficient in coverage and that provision was unequal, when judged by the criteria of social class and geographical distribution. Accordingly, the health needs of the population were met more by the chance of living in an area well endowed with public health services, voluntary teaching hospitals, or enough panel doctors per head of population than by any rational planning criteria of matching population health care needs to available medical care resources.

It was these circumstances that underpinned what we have labelled the 'efficiency' and 'equity' arguments for the health care reforms that became the NHS (see Chapter 2). The former focused on the role of 'national and rational' planning as the means by which we would get a more effective and efficient allocation of resources to replace the haphazard nature of pre-NHS health care. The latter concerned the manifest inequalities in health and the distribution of health care resources between different groups within the population (the 'inverse care law'). Here again 'rational planning' would play a role, although the basic principles of the service – an optimum standard service available to all citizens (universalist) funded by taxation rather than user-charges (free) – were seen as making a crucial contribution to minimising these inequalities. To what extent did the National Health Service achieve the goals of a more efficient and equitable health service in its first thirty years of operation?

Efficiency and planning

Comprehensive planning of health services which is population-based and priority-led has existed in the NHS *only since the mid-1970s*. (Kings Fund, 1987, p. 1, our emphasis)

There is certainly evidence of 'more efficient' use of hospitals since the establishment of the NHS. Associated with the closure of smaller hospitals and the concentration of beds in larger units, the number of patients treated increased. This was accommodated by an increase in the number of cases treated per available bed (or throughout) reflecting a shorter average length of stay in hospital (see for example, Allsop, 1984, p. 83); part of a wide-ranging trend towards the de-institutionalisation of a range of health and social care activities (see Chapter 13).

These changes indicated an increasingly intensive use of expensive hospital resources. They could certainly be taken as evidence of greater efficiency in the use of health care facilities. In particular they appear to serve as evidence of the benefits of a national *health* service. Obviously, more efficient use of hospital resources is facilitated by the effective use of community-based health care (GPs, community nurses) – for example where continuing care is required, but not continuing care in a hospital bed.

One means of getting a more efficient health service was through planning – for example by planning community health care developments to facilitate the more efficient use of hospital-based health care. There was a notable lack of planning in the pre-war health services but the wartime experience strongly indicated the potential for national and regional planning as a means of remedying perceived deficiencies in service provision. Peacetime planning was to prove more difficult at least in part for political reasons.

There was evidence of peace-time planning – most obviously with the publication of the Hospital Plan in 1962. The Plan recognised that with increased capital sums being allocated to hospital building these allocations should be based on the principles of priorities in bed usage for particular patients groups, coupled with an overall pattern of development of services throughout the Regions. It aimed to establish bed norm provision in the main specialities and ensure that all Regions met these norms. It also introduced the concept of the District General

Hospital of 600–800 beds serving a population of 100–150,000 and proposed extensive investment in new hospitals. It was intended to provide 'a *rational* basis for the development of the hospital services' (Allsop, 1984, p. 55, our emphasis). However, despite this evidence of efficiency and planning, it was apparent that the NHS was not the paragon of 'rational planning' hoped for by its advocates at the time of its inception.

Firstly and most obviously, fourteen years had elapsed between the establishment of the NHS and the publication of the first major NHS plan. Secondly, it was a *hospital service* plan not a *health service* plan. There was a community care plan published the following year but close inspection revealed that to be little more than a collection of rather disparate local plans rather than a genuinely complementary exercise to the Hospital Plan (see for example, Mittler, 1965). It is from this point in time that the origins of some of the more recent concerns about community care can be traced. It was the Hospital Plan that contained the first official projection of a reduction of mental hospital in-patients, but it was far from clear that the projected increases in community mental health services contained in the local authority health and welfare plans were sufficient to offset the effects of the projected decreases in in-patient services contained in the hospital plan (see Chapter 13). Since these rival plans were the products of different parts of the 'tripartite' organizational structure they could be taken as further evidence of the limitations of this structure – especially for the development of effective health service planning (see Chapter 6). This failure to bring together hospital and community health service planning was perplexing given the potential contribution of the latter to supporting the existing trend towards a more efficient use of hospital resources. From a community health perspective the Plan could be viewed as evidence of the continuing dominance of the hospital sector and of acute medicine in the NHS (Allsop, 1984, p. 55).

Thirdly, a detailed reading of the Plan revealed a significant investment in London, and especially the London teaching hospitals. This investment was the 'cheapest' way, in the short run, to remedy deficiencies in medical education (see Abel-Smith, 1990, p. 13), despite the by now well established concerns about regional disparities in health service provision (see below and Chapter 9). Despite the hopes and aspirations of its founders, 'rational planning' was a late arrival in the NHS and when it came it was with a partial (hospital-based) and flawed (London teaching hospitals) plan. The sort of 'rational planning' (eg population-based and priority-led) for which advocates of a national health service might have hoped was not in place until 1974 (see Kings Fund, 1987, p. 1) What happened to NHS planning – the vision of an efficient, rationally, nationally planned service?

Planning and conflicts

The historical inheritance of the NHS was not conducive to the swift implementation of effective planning – there was virtually no tradition of planning or planning expertise to draw upon. But this hardly explains a delay of over a quarter of century before the introduction of the first effective forms of comprehensive planning, especially given the quite successful wartime planning (see Chapter 3). However there was a potential conflict between planning and political ideology as this model (of wartime planning) was not attractive to the Conservative governments which were in power from 1951 onwards. They held state planning to be anathema, given their avowed aim of 'liberating the economy' from those wartime controls that had been retained by the post-war Labour governments (see Chapter 4).

The limitations and problems of planning might also be explained by the political conflicts involved in establishing the NHS (see Chapters 3 and 4) and especially the tripartite organizational structure of the Service that emerged from that conflict. This political compromise gave every appearance of hindering rather than helping the planning process (see Chapter 6). Of course, that compromise was in part a function of professional power and influence, and planning may be seen as at least partially a victim of that same power and influence

> Vested interests of the medical profession certainly have an effect. The medical profession, particularly GPs, have always fought against anything smacking of direction of labour. (Buxton, 1976, p. 35).

The ideals of planning can be seen as conflicting with both political and professional ideologies.

If sections of the medical profession were not inclined to lend their whole-hearted support to planning, they were likely to find allies elsewhere, perhaps most noticeably in HM Treasury where the concerns most likely to be expressed were less those of 'can we afford an *unplanned* NHS?' and rather more those of 'can we afford *any sort of* NHS?'. These concerns had some basis in the discrepancy between widely held expectations of the costs of the new NHS and the reality of its actual costs.

In the period leading up to the establishment of the NHS the hope was expressed that an efficient and effective national health service could be developed that would diminish the incidence of disease and disability (Beveridge Report, 1942, p. 105, para.270(3); p. 158, para.426; and p. 162, para.437). The resulting lower demand on health care resources held out the possibility of stable, or even decreasing, costs for the new service (see for example, Campbell, 1987, pp. 180–1). The reality was well-represented by Titmuss's reference to

> the backlog of needs, accumulated during the war and its uneasy aftermath ... most vividly depicted by the demand for spectacles, dentures, hearing aids and other postponable adjuncts to better health. (Titmuss, 1963, p. 153).

The reality seemed to be one of higher demand and increasing costs (see Chapter 4).

The outcome was predictable. Within twenty-one months the first cash-limit was introduced into the NHS; charges were introduced for dentures in 1951 and for spectacles and prescriptions in 1952 (Abel-Smith, 1990, p. 12). The first major report into the new service commissioned by the new Conservative government was concerned about its 'present and prospective cost'; how to limit 'the burden on the Exchequer' through the 'effective control and efficient use of ... Exchequer funds'. It was a report on *the cost* of the NHS; it was apparent that containing the costs of the new NHS was firmly on the political agenda (see Guillebaud Report, 1956). Indeed Aneurin Bevan was said to have seen the establishment of the committee as a 'partisan resort to expose and isolate the service as the most extravagant feature of the welfare state and one which any prudent government must curb or curtail' (Foot, 1975, p. 212). It seemed that not only did the concept of a national health service contain an inevitable conflict between notions of professional autonomy and planning, but also between the reflective, research-based and lengthy time-scales needed for effective planning, and the reactive, resource-based approach within limited time scales seen as appropriate to the goal of cost containment.

Of course the issue of cost containment was not merely a result of the divorce between expectations and reality in post-war Britain. In some respects this problem reflected the growing significance of the factors that had begun to undermine the finances of voluntary hospitals towards the end of the nineteenth century (see Chapter 1), indicating that the pre-war financial crises of the voluntary hospitals were the result of something fundamental about health care in industrial societies – a seemingly endless escalator of rising costs. The political implications of this fundamental dilemma were acknowledged in 1948 by Bevan when he observed that 'we will never have all we need ... expectations will always exceed capacity' (Foot, 1975, p. 209). Indeed rising expectations were one of the factors leading to increasing costs, the others being demographic trends and medical advances.

Demographic trends
It is an established demographic fact that most industrial societies are characterised by increasing numbers of elderly people – the greying of the population. Amongst this group there exists a greater number then ever before of frail, elderly people whose need for health care is markedly higher than not only the rest of the population, but also of younger groups of older people in the 65 to 75 years age group.

The main cause of this demographic trend has been identified as declining mortality among all age groups, testimony to both medical and non-medical interventions (see Chapter 10) as well as a long-term downward trend in fertility (see for example, Kings Fund, 1992a, p. 71). The implications for health care are dramatic. Since the end of World War Two, there has been a doubling of people aged 65 years and over. Given more significant and more chronic health care problems for this age group they constitute a significantly greater proportion of hospital discharges and hospital in-patient days. Furthermore the 'older old' (those aged seventy-five years and over) have an even more significant impact on the demand for and organization of health care, there being marked increases in chronic illness and disability in this age group compared to those aged 65 to 74 years, including significantly greater use of domiciliary, GP and community nursing services (see for example, Phillipson, 1990, pp. 57–9).

Armed with these statistics, demographic trends can be extrapolated to a scenario when existing hospital resources are largely taken up with the health care needs of the older members of society! Such projections tend to discount other factors – including medical advances (see below). Nonetheless there is no doubt that the demographic profile of industrial societies has changed and there are an associated set of changes in the disease profile as 'chronic degenerative diseases and cancers have replaced acute infectious diseases as the primary causes of disability and death in Britain' (Kings Fund, 1992a, p. 70). This linked combination of demographic trends and the changing spectrum of disease can be seen as key factors in pushing up the costs not only of the NHS, but of health care systems throughout the industrialised world.

Medical advances
The post-war period saw a continuing growth in new forms of medical intervention and the development of new therapeutic methods of which most involved additional expenditure. For example, during this period medical technology dramatically improved with the introduction of procedures that could be life-saving and/or improve the quality of life (dialysis, CAT scanners, and transplantation are three obvious examples). At the same time the development of new therapeutic methods for treating and preventing infection with antibiotics as well as stabilising people with long-term chronic illness (eg chlorpromazine for those with mental health problems) became commonplace and no longer novel and innovative procedures.

Rising expectations
The publicity surrounding advances in medical technology was almost certainly a contributory factor to rising expectations about what the service can and should deliver. An assumption of

optimum standards was built into the aims and expectations of the Service and certainly by 1969 one Secretary of State for Social Services was identifying a 'revolution of rising expectations' that extends from physical goods to education and health (see Crossman, 1969, pp. 5–7). Subsequent evidence has indeed suggested that 'public attitudes to health and health care are changing … people are becoming more discriminating about what health care offers' (Kings Fund, 1992a, p. 70).

A combination of demographic trends, medical advances and rising expectations increased the potential volume of treatable illness confronting the NHS – indeed any one of these factors could have that effect. Successive governments found themselves confronting a situation in which additional expenditure was necessary merely to enable the Service to maintain its current level of provision. In common with other public services the NHS also afforded few opportunities for productivity gains. Indeed making more efficient use of its most expensive service – hospital in-patient care – required more, rather than fewer, hospital-based medical, nursing and other health professionals. In so far as the conflict between the desirability of obtaining modern health care and the desirability of containing costs was most marked in the area of acute medicine, the nationalisation of the voluntary hospitals had brought that conflict into the public sector, and into the context of an even longer running conflict about the scale and scope of state welfare. Some commentators were quick to make this connection – an indication that at least in the immediate post-war period any 'professional consensus' around the 'welfare state' and the NHS was somewhat fragile.

> The National Health Service is heading for the bankruptcy court … and we are facing bankruptcy because of the Utopian finances of the Welfare State. (British Medical Journal, Editorial, December 2, 1950)

Equity

The pursuit of a more equitable allocation of health care resources was one of the more clearly stated goals of the Service (Klein, 1983, p. 25). As Aneurin Bevan explained in the House of

Commons when presenting his bill, the intention was to 'universalise the best' by removing financial barriers and distributing resources equally across the country.

The key inequalities concerned the allocation of, access to, and the utilisation of the resources and facilities of the NHS. The Service's inheritance was of profound spatial inequalities with a set of associated inequalities linked to social class. Also part of the inheritance, especially linked to the different histories of the voluntary and local government (Poor Law) hospitals was the different provision for different types of care, different groups of patient and different sorts of need (see Chapter 1).

It was hoped that the elimination of explicit financial barriers (user charges) to the utilisation of health care would have a profound impact on social class inequalities in utilisation, and by implication social class inequalities in health. However by the mid-1960s there was a growing recognition that the 'higher income groups know how to make better use of the Service' (Titmuss, 1968, p. 196). The 'free play of market forces' may have been significantly moderated with the introduction of a largely 'free at the point of consumption' universalist health service but the 'free play of social forces' (Pinker, 1971, p. 188) generated persistent evidence of the ability of some social groups to make more effective use of the NHS. This could be turned into an argument asserting the 'failure' of the NHS. However a recognition of the limitations of universalism is quite compatible with the idea that a universalist approach might represent the most effective approach to ameliorating inequalities in access and utilisation (see Chapters 11 and 15). Indeed there was evidence in the early years of the operation of the service that it had significantly improved the access of elderly people to services in ophthalmology which subsequent policies on charges for eye tests may have reversed (see Titmuss, 1968, p. 78).

Social class inequalities in access to health care remained an issue in part because of the persistence of spatial inequalities. The 'inverse care law' evident before the NHS, was still apparent twenty years after its establishment; 'the availability of good medical care tends to vary inversely with the need of the population served' (Tudor Hart, 1971). Some of these differences between different types of care, different groups of patients and different sorts of needs are represented in Figure 2 below.

Figure 2: Status and health care

HIGH STATUS	LOW STATUS
physical health problems	mental health problems
hospital-based	community-based
curative	caring
curative	preventive
curative	health-promotion
acute health problems	chronic health problems
life-saving interventions	terminal care
disease	disability

Generally speaking professional prestige and resources seemed to be attached to the left-hand column rather than the right hand column. The diagram can be used to identify contrasting sectors of the health services. It suggests that community-based care for people with chronic mental health problems will be relatively less well resourced than hospital-based services for people with acute physical health problems and indeed there appeared to be growing evidence of these inequalities continuing under the NHS – especially from the late 1960s onwards as a series of scandals and crises (Martin, J.P. 1984) drew attention particularly to the provision for elderly people and people with mental health problems and learning disabilities. The label 'Cinderella services' was attached to this part of the NHS. The particular focus for concern was the long-stay institutions which seemed to be providing poor quality care in settings that were increasingly felt to be expensive, unnecessary and stigmatising. The perceived failings of these institutions gave a further boost to policies for community care (see Chapter 13).

Why did the problems of inequalities persist despite the clearly stated commitment to ameliorate this problem? One answer lies in the past, and the profound inequalities inherited by the NHS. Whilst this does not excuse or explain subsequent inaction, it is important to assert that a more active post-war policy would have been unlikely to completely 'solve' this problem.

Secondly, the limitations of post-war planning provide us with another factor. A pattern of resource allocation based on historic cost-budgeting ensured that all areas benefitted from increasing resources, but simply underwrote and perpetuated the inherited pattern of inequalities. The ratio of resources going to hospitals, primary and community care, and local authority services altered only marginally between 1948 and 1976 (Carrier, 1978, p. 119). In addition, there was now evidence that variations within regions were even more significant than those between regions (Buxton and Klein, 1975). However it must also be noted that 'planning for territorial justice' is difficult. The NHS has had an abundance of *quantitative* measures of health care *inputs* and it seems likely that the more significant variations in such inputs (eg: numbers of health professionals employed by a service) represents some variation in service quantity and quality. However the pursuit of a finer degree of territorial justice requires 'worthwhile' measures of spatial variations in health care needs to be set against *qualitative* measures of health care *outputs*. This argument would be deployed with particular force following the RAWP initiative (see below) with calls for more research into the relationship between revenue inputs and patient care outputs (see for example, Barr and Logan, 1977). The issue would remain relevant in the 1980s when more systematic use would be made of performance indicators which would provide some information on outputs but 'none about outcomes' and which would remain 'silent about the question of quality' (Klein, 1995a, p. 145).

Thirdly, professional power and influence may have played a part; and not only in relation to the professional opposition to planning. The types of care and patient who were eventually identified as the 'cinderella areas' of the NHS represented those areas of medical and nursing activity to which the professions attached the lowest status and prestige. These distinctions were long-established and were clear before the twentieth century when prestige and status were associated with the doctors working in the voluntary hospitals (see Chapter 1). In addition there was also evidence of the 'unwillingness of trained nurses to care for cases of chronic sickness' (Abel-Smith, 1964, p. 210); of the Poor Law doctors seeking to refer elsewhere their 'burdensome' patients; and of the superintendents of the infirmaries in London being:

> remarkably successful in keeping out the 'aged and infirm' patients. (Abel-Smith, 1964, p. 206)

The potential for health professionals to restrict resource allocation to areas of the service that they consider to be 'less interesting' may be considerable. Thus the perceived biases of the NHS in favour of hospital-based intervention in episodes of acute health problems and the relative neglect of preventive measures, may both be at least partially attributable to these forms of health care being defined as respectively 'interesting' and 'uninteresting' by a range of health professionals. Services for elderly people with chronic health problems and for people with mental health problems, are justifiably labelled 'cinderella services'; and this can be at least partially attributed to the interests of a range of health and social care professions (see for example, Royal Commission on NHS, 1979, Ch.6)

Finally, it was becoming increasingly apparent – as noted above – that the relationship between social and economic factors and the utilisation of health care and between health care and health status was a complex one. Seeking to provide good quality health care on a universalist basis at little or no cost to service users did not translate simply into either equitable utilisation of that health care or a diminution in ill-health. From this it followed that the relationship between the NHS and inequalities in health would be even less simple. Breaking the 'inverse care law' might be significantly more achievable in terms of outcomes for inequalities in access to health care, rather than inequalities in health (see Chapter 10 for a further discussion of these issues).

Planning and priorities
After 1974, the NHS had a new organizational structure which was somewhat more amenable to effective planning (see Chapter 6) and a formal planning system was in place by 1976 (DHSS, 1976c; see Butler and Vaile, 1984, p. 109). At the same time more active policies were pursued by the 1974–79 Labour government to redress spatial disparities and to redirect the balance of resources in favour of the 'cinderella areas'.

Between 1975 and 1977 the government published five important policy documents which proposed to alter the traditional pattern of resource allocation. Whilst the public expenditure White Papers (Treasury, 1976; Treasury, 1977) laid down a pattern of future expenditure that would stabilise capital investment and contain the rising revenue costs in the NHS, the Priorities documents (DHSS, 1976a; DHSS, 1977) faced the question of redistri-

buting resources in favour of neglected client groups – elderly
people, people with mental health problems, people with learning
difficulties and children. The Report of the Resource Allocation
Working Party (RAWP) began the process of equalising resources
going to similar client groups in different regions throughout
England (DHSS, 1976b). Both the RAWP and Priorities documents can be seen as outcomes of a long process of discussion
about the planning, organization and administration and ultimately the justification of the NHS as the major means of
providing health care to meet the needs of the population.

Subsequently the Secretary of State for Social Services was to
endorse a commitment to what he called 'positive discrimination'
and to follow it up in circulars related to the Court Report on
child health services (see Carrier, 1978, p. 119). The terms of
reference for RAWP involved a commitment to 'a pattern of
distribution responsive objectively, equitably and efficiently to
relative need'. The Working Party identified their underlying
objective as securing 'through resource allocation that there would
eventually be equal opportunity of access to health care for people
at equal risk' and to this end identified criteria for need which
they suggested had been largely ignored in existing resource
allocations. These criteria included population size and composition, morbidity, and relative cost (DHSS, 1976b, paras.1.6 to 1.9).

The problems faced by the Working Party related especially to
the quality, complexity and sources of information; this included
finding reliable indicators of unhealthiness. For the latter, RAWP's
formula involved using the Standardised Mortality Ratio (SMR)
as a measure of morbidity; this, and other aspects of their
approach, attracted a good deal of criticism (see Carrier, 1978,
pp. 124–35). The policy implications of RAWP were clear – a
significant redistribution of resources away from Oxford RHA,
South-Western RHA and London, with the latter attracting particular criticism (see Chapter 9).

The 1976/7 allocations to Regional Health Authorities (RHAs)
were based on the first RAWP report (DHSS, 1975a). The
Secretary of State would subsequently claim that he was taking a
'middle course' in his response to the Final RAWP report in which
all regions would receive 'real increases' in their allocations with
the equalisation of resources recommended by RAWP being
phased in over a ten year period. In addition to the proposed

reallocation of resources between regions it was proposed that similar principles of re-distribution should, as far as possible, be applied to allocations at area and district levels (see Treasury, 1976).

The 'Priorities' documents acknowledged the RAWP principles and some of the difficulties that might flow from operating them alongside their own projections for increased spending on the 'cinderella services'. Of course it was the RAWP principles that had the most direct impact on resource allocation – even if intended to work over a full decade. The Priorities principles had less tangible outcomes leading to the understandable observation that 'in practice the language of norms and objectives turned out to be merely the vocabulary of exhortation'; although even critics had to note that there was evidence of the priorities being incorporated in the allocation of resources (Klein, 1983, p. 128). The second Priorities document – *The Way Forward* – also noted the issue of social class inequalities, reporting that a Working Group on Inequalities in Health had been set up by the DHSS (DHSS, 1977, p. 29). The report that emerged two years later was to become politically contentious. Work was completed as the Conservative Government took office in 1979 and few copies were published. The interpretations used by the Report were disputed by the then Secretary of State, Patrick Jenkin (see Chapter 7). One outcome was a resurgence of interest in the whole area of social divisions, social inequalities and health (see Chapter 10).

Priorities and conflicts

The attempt to plan the allocation of NHS resources to reflect identified priorities illustrated some old and new conflicts. We have already noted the potential conflict between the concepts of 'rational planning' and 'professional autonomy'. This would inevitably be heightened when the priorities involved a reallocation of resources away from the more professionally prestigious locations and types of health care. The resulting professional opposition may be assuaged by moderating the policies (eg introducing them over a lengthy time period) or providing the resources to limit the impact on the 'non-priority' areas.

Concerns about cost containment seem likely to rule out the latter leaving a potential conflict between, in this instance, the

Priorities documents and the RAWP principle of a more equitable distribution of resources. A conflict of this nature might only be resolved through 'a massive reduction in acute services' (Klein, 1976, p. 983) which would exacerbate professional opposition.

In the context of these seemingly inevitable conflicts it is not that easy to evaluate the greater commitment to planning and priorities evidenced in the 1970s. Key initiatives were introduced in 1976 – notably the NHS planning system with its strategic and operational framework; but this was the same year that the cuts were imposed on public expenditure in the UK (see Glennerster, 1995, p. 167). It was not an auspicious moment to attempt a more active pursuit of some of the original goals of the NHS. Within three years a Conservative government was elected which seemed likely to be more interested in questioning those original goals, than the failure of previous (and notably Conservative) governments to enable those goals to be effectively pursued, and whose search for savings in the use of resources might extend some way beyond the closure of a few hospitals and units (see Chapter 7).

Conclusions

> When the Service began to operate in 1948 it … inherited the debts of a decade of sacrifice and neglect, financial poverty and disorganization. (Titmuss, 1963, p. 153)

Following the Appointed Day it appeared that the administrative and political compromise struck with the profession had overcome the most dangerous opposition to the new Service – the potential of the doctors non-co-operation. However the underestimation of unmet medical care need coupled with popular aspirations about the new Service combined to create a new danger, placing the Service under increasing financial pressure from Day One, forcing the Minister to ask for Supplementary Estimates so that in the early years of the Service the pattern of increasing demand up against reluctant supply became a characteristic feature of all NHS discussions.

The NHS did not prove to be the model of rational planning and organization for which many of its founders may have hoped. There was clear enough evidence of more efficient use of resources, especially in the hospital sector. But formal planning was delayed, partial and compromised by political concerns about the shortages of doctors. It seems likely that professional power and influence played its part both in limiting the scope of NHS planning and in influencing its content – the focus on hospitals and in particular the need of the London teaching hospitals. If one political concern was to continue to placate the concerns of the most prestigious members of the medical profession, another of equal force was that of controlling public expenditure. The problems of cost-containment, rather than the problems of planning, dominated the political agenda of the NHS from its early years.

One of the most profound changes affecting the work of the NHS and the financial responsibilities now assumed by the state, was the growth of medical technology and the development of new therapeutic methods. The publicity surrounding such developments has almost certainly contributed to rising expectations about what the service can and should deliver, whilst an assumption of optimum standards was built into the aims and expectations of the Service. The Service has also had to contend with increasing demands associated with demographic changes. In these circumstances increases in costs have been inevitable. The idea that an improved health service might diminish the need for health care by producing a healthier population has proved to be an illusion. Both medical advances and the provision of more accessible and acceptable services increase the potential volume of treatable illness confronting the NHS, and expectations rise in terms of both what the Service can achieve and the manner of its delivery.

That technological, demographic and attitudinal changes have demanded ever more of the NHS, may explain why the twin goals of efficiency and equity were not pursued with the vigour that some may have hoped and anticipated. The resources for the Service appear to be destined never to be able to cover the demands made by the public and the profession. The seeds of conflict were therefore inherent in scarcity at the inception of the Service.

6
Reorganizations and rationality

Introduction

The organizational structuring of the state's involvement in health care has been the subject of conflict at least since the introduction of National Health Insurance (Chapter 2). With the establishment of the NHS it became a major focus for political debate in which a considerable degree of political consensus around the general case for reform dissolved into conflicting views about the details of the reform – especially the organizational details (see Chapters 3 and 4).

The outcome, as virtually all commentators seem to agree, was a political compromise in the form of the so-called tripartite organizational structure of the NHS (Chapter 4). In fact whilst 'tripartism' did appear to be a key concept in the organizational structure established in 1948, the major three way division into GP, hospital and local community health services was further complicated, firstly, by slightly different organizational arrangements in England and Wales, Northern Ireland and Scotland; and secondly, by different organizational arrangements for non-teaching, special and teaching hospitals (see Figure One, p. 75). Finally three other health services – the school health service, port health and other environmental health services and occupational health services were formally separate from the NHS and from each other.

Under these arrangements, the NHS was administered by more than 500 separate administrative units, based both inside and outside local government, servicing areas which were not necessarily co-terminous one with another. The situation was especially complex in London where the boundaries of four regional hospital boards converged on a point in central London and there were a large number of teaching hospitals operating independently of those Boards (see Chapter 9).

Organizational problems

We have noted the evidence for the more efficient use of hospital resources from the inception of the NHS (Chapter 5). One potentially significant contributory factor to such 'efficiency gains' was the effective use of community health services; for example, enabling the earlier discharge of patients who no longer need 24 hours a day in-patient care. But the 'tripartite' structure separated hospital and community health services.

Another potentially significant contributory factor to the more effective use of community health resources was better communications and co-operation between medical and nursing services; for example, enabling general practitioners to work as a team with district nurses. But the 'tripartite' structure separated community-based medical practitioners (GPs) from the community-based nurses (domiciliary midwives, district nurses and health visitors) working for local authority health departments.

This organizational structure was problematic at all levels of health care delivery. It was a hindrance to basic day-to-day administration and the management of a range of theoretically complementary services (see for example, J Parker, 1965, pp. 86–93). It was a threat to continuity of care, especially for the many patients who would become the responsibility of more than one branch of the service, an area that assumed greater and greater significance with the trends towards more efficient use of hospital resources and the development of community care. Finally it made the concept of health service planning very difficult to realise even without the other issues identified in Chapter 5.

The division between those services inside and outside of local government was especially problematic. There were at least four areas of difficulty. Firstly, different financial bases – most obviously the separate system of local government taxation (rates, community charge and council tax); secondly, different cultural contexts – the NHS had two main professions while local government had many professions and a bargaining environment with political control (elections); thirdly, different structural arrangements – the NHS was hierarchical and was controlled by one central government department while local government was not hierarchial (county and district councils are independent of one another) and was responsible to several central government departments; and finally, different procedures and time planning systems (see for example, Thomas and Stoten, 1974, pp. 65–9).

These problems were recognised from the inception of the service. One possible solution was the development of health centres. Health centres had the potential to promote liaison and co-operation between key health professionals. They could be a work-base for GPs, community nurses and some hospital-based doctors whose outpatient clinics could be relocated to the centres. They certainly afforded the opportunity to give some patients a less fragmentary experience of health care delivery by providing a single, major location for much of their health care (see Figure 3).

Figure 3: Health services and Health Centres

Hospital outpatient services	Community nursing services	General medical practitioner services

these services might all be located in

HEALTH CENTRES

In the event, very few health centres were built until the mid-1960s. The reasons are familiar and relate to some of our enduring themes of conflict. Firstly, investment in health centres required capital expenditure and hence a conflict with concerns for cost-containment. Secondly, health centres were to be built and managed by local government and hence a conflict with concerns about professional autonomy – and the perceived threat of local government to that autonomy (see Chapters 3 and 4) (see Hall, 1975, p. 285; Campbell, 1987, p. 179; and Webster, 1988, p. 393).

Given the latter, it was unsurprising that the government did not respond positively to the suggestion made in 1951 in the Association of Municipal Corporation memoranda to the Select Committee on Estimates (enquiring into the Hospital Service) that the organizational problems of the NHS would be ameliorated by making the whole service a local government responsibility (see J Parker, 1965, p.78). Organizational problems were recognised by the Guillebaud Committee (1956), especially with regard to services for elderly people and the maternity services. However the Committee suggested that it would be too disruptive to attempt any major changes at that time and emphasised the need for greater co-operation between the different parts of the Service. Subsequently, a separate committee was established to look at the maternity services identifying the need for greater clarity about the respective roles of different parts of the service (Cranbrook Report, 1959).

Proposals for reform
That circumstances might be more amenable to organizational reform was signalled by the publication of the Porritt Report (1962). This was a report from a non-governmental, predominantly professional committee, and it recommended the unification of most of the NHS under Area Health Boards – although the teaching hospitals would retain their separate status (see Watkin, 1978, pp. 134–6).

Certainly by 1962 the case for reform could be based on identifiable trends and policy initiatives; these included early discharge schemes in the maternity services, the attachment of nursing staff to general practice, and the commitment to develop community-based mental health services (see for example, Abel-Smith, 1978, pp. 35–7). In the event twelve years would pass before the service was reorganised – a time-scale that was at least partly indicative of the continuing political sensitivity surrounding organizational issues in health care. This organizational restructuring of health care was also part of a broader agenda of organizational change in state welfare.

In particular, the case for organizational changes in health care was paralleled by similar debates relating to the personal social services. These services had a similarly fragmented structure, although in this case mostly within local government. Once again the move away from traditional institutionally based services (childrens homes, residential care for elderly people) to community-based services (day-care for under-fives, home helps) was seen to be hindered by the division of service responsibilities between different departments. The Seebohm Committee was established in 1965 to review the personal social services. At the same time, concerns were expressed about the overall structure of local government which consisted (outside of London) of unitary authorities based on cities and large towns (county boroughs) and a two-tier system in the more rural areas (county and district councils). In response to these concerns a Royal Commission on Local Government in England (1969) was established.

Thus when the government made its first pronouncements on a possible organizational restructuring in health care in what became known as the First Green Paper (Ministry of Health, 1968), it had already set in train parallel reviews to restructure the personal social services and local government. The potential for discontinuities and contradictions in this situation were all too obvious. They were made more so with the publication of this First Green Paper, since its central proposal for unifying the NHS under 40 to 50 Area Health Boards mooted the possibility of these Boards taking responsibility for local authority port health and public health responsibilities; and more significantly that the Boards might be incorporated in the new local authorities to be established following the publication of the Redcliffe-Maud Commission. But the Redcliffe Maud Commission had not been required to examine the implications for the NHS of any recommendations they might make (Abel-Smith, 1978, p. 38).

We did not have to wait long for the first tangible contradiction to emerge from this process. The Seebohm Committee reported soon after the publication of The First Green Paper and recommended a different division between health and social care to that contained in the latter. Seebohm proposed that key services located in the local authority health departments would move to a new local authority social services department rather than the new Area Health Boards (see Seebohm Report, 1968)

Between the first and second Green Papers the Government reassured the medical profession that the 'new NHS' would not be part of the 'new local government' and took steps to implement most of the recommendations of the Seebohm Committee to the evident satisfaction of most of the social work profession. The Second Green Paper (DHSS, 1970) confirmed that new Area Health Authorities (of which there would now be about 90) would be outside of local government, but there would be enhanced potential for NHS/local government co-operation through coterminosity – the new AHAs would match the new local authorities proposed by the Redcliffe-Maud Commission (Royal Commission on Local Government in England, 1969).

The simplicity of the First Green Paper was also modified. Whilst the chain of authority would run directly from the Secretary of State to the AHAs, there would be regional health councils with a mainly advisory role and there would be Family Practitioner Committees to administer the family practitioner committees on behalf of the AHA. Given the key role of regional authorities for hospital consultants – in the non-teaching hospitals their contracts were held at the regional level (see Chapter 4) – and the long-term commitment of general practitioners to their own distinctive organizational arrangements, these additions to the simple Area Health Board model seemed like the beginning of a re-assertion of the priorities and interests that had shaped the original 'tripartite' compromise of 1948.

Finally, the Second Green Paper contained a commitment to what we might call 'the professional principle' (see DHSS, 1970, p. 10, para.31). All that was social work related would remain in local government as part of the new Social Services Department. All that was medical and nursing-related was to move outside of local government into the reorganised NHS. As aspects of the old tripartite division disappeared – most obviously between hospital and community-based nursing services – a new and even clearer health and social care division was being established. Indeed the outcome of the 1974 reorganization was a more clearly delineated administrative, financial and professional division than at any previous stage in the history of post-war health and community care policies (Carrier and Kendall, 1995, p. 17). For some writers this signalled the end of, for example, specialised mental health services (see Jones, 1972, p. 34; Jones, 1983, pp. 218–34; see also Chapter 13).

Before the 1974 reorganizations were implemented three further documents were published by the new Conservative government. A Consultative Document (DHSS, 1971a) and a White Paper (DHSS, 1972b) set out the Government's proposals for England, with separate documents setting out the similar proposals for Wales and Scotland. Crucially a set of regional health authorities (RHAs) were re-introduced in a direct line relationship between the Secretary of State and the Area Health Authorities

(AHAs) leading to a concern that 'RHAs based on RHB areas and staff will perpetuate the hospital orientation of these authorities' (Draper, Grenholm and Best, 1976; see also Abel-Smith, 1971).

The AHAs were to be coterminous with the new county councils and metropolitan districts introduced by the 1974 local government reorganization. A statutory duty to co-operate via Joint Consultative Committees was incorporated in the relevant legislation and there were to be joint consultative committees to facilitate this local government/NHS co-operation. But the new pattern of local government was not suitable for aspects of health services (especially hospital) management and planning. The result was that most AHAs created a sub-tier of health service management in the form of District Management Teams. Districts also formed the focus of Community Health Councils (CHCs) intended to represent the views of consumers.

A further document specified aspects of the internal management arrangements (The Grey Book, DHSS, 1972c) notably the concept of the District Management Team (DMT) as a consensus forming team of equals – a model that was to attract subsequent criticism in the first Griffiths Report (DHSS 1983; see Chapter 7). The 'management team' approach had some basis in previous arrangements. More novel was that in England there would be no line management between the DMT and their area counterparts, but instead they would be directly accountable to the AHA.

> This sophisticated and many felt unworkable relationship was peculiar to England. In Wales, Scotland, Northern Ireland, things were arranged in a more straightforward manner, with a line relationship between area officers and their district counterparts. (Watkin, 1978, p. 147)

Following the NHS Reorganization Act, 1973, the new restructured NHS came into effect on April 1st, 1974, the same day as the new restructured local government. Of course the latter generated significant upheaval for many of the new local authority Social Services Department which had been operational for only three years at the time of this restructuring.

1974 NHS Restructuring – an evaluation

We have already identified some of the major concerns expressed at the time about this restructuring, notably the separation of related NHS, personal social services and local government changes with their particular impact on a new health and social care divide and the management and organizational problems of AHAs (eg: divisions into districts). However the changes introduced in 1974 generated an even wider range of criticisms which can be categorised under four main headings and at least some of which were to be repeated with regard to subsequent major managerial and organizational reforms (see Chapter 7). They were to question firstly, the way the reorganization was carried out (the way it was done); secondly, the value of the substantive content of the reorganization (what was done); thirdly, the costs and benefits of this particular reorganization (was it worth doing?); fourthly and finally, the costs and benefits of this sort of reorganization (the value of organizational change).

The way it was done Here we are not concerned with what might be seen as substantive points regarding the basic principles of the reorganisation, but the manner or style in which the reorganisation was carried out. However this is not to be regarded as a peripheral issue. The quality of care provided by the NHS rests on the skills of its personnel and such matters as their commitment to the service. If a reorganisation is carried out in such a way as to seriously undermine staff morale, it may well have an effect on the quality of service the staff give, and its effect might be quite substantial and quite long lasting.

One comment was that the restructuring was carried out too quickly. This seems rather strange; the reorganisation took place in 1974, the first government document on reorganisation (First Green Paper) had appeared in 1968. How could the reorganisation have been undertaken too quickly? The problem arose because of conflicts. The First Green Paper was not acceptable, especially to the medical profession and the combination of medical politics and party politics (in the form of a change of government) meant that the reorganisation actually took place only about 18 months after the relevant legislation. If the reorganisation had been 'introduced in stages starting with a fairly leisurely pilot demonstration' perhaps some of the associated problems would have been avoided since 'paper planning tends to be over-optimistic, and is no substitute for actual experimentation' (Brown, 1979, pp. 184, 200). Subsequently, the research team working for the Royal Commission on the NHS would suggest that health authorities

> should begin to make a *careful, slow* and *reflective* attempt to enhance delegation, to remove levels of administration, many of which are known to fail to contribute towards efficient working. (Royal Commission on the NHS Research Paper 1, 1978, p. 231, our emphasis)

The role of the NHS Staff Commission, set up in April 1972 to supervise and transfer staff to new NHS authorities was also the subject of critical comment (see Watkin 1978, pp 147–51; Brown, 1979, p. 188) in particular the Commission was seen to have contributed 'a substantial degree ... (to) ... the widespread demoralisation of the NHS in the early months after reorganisation' (Watkin, 1978, p. 148).

'That there was so little public involvement in shaping the details of a structure' (Brown, 1979, p. 60) was also the subject of comment with suggestions that the implementation of the restructuring 'was largely carried out 'behind the scenes' and with a minimum of public participation' (Draper, Grenholm and Best, 1976, p. 273).

What was done? Was too much expected of a reorganisation which was intended to be much more than an amalgamation of different types of health authorities? In particular the restructuring aimed for a more co-ordinated management and operation of interlocking services, particularly those requiring interaction between hospital and community; more critical evaluation of current resource-use; clearer lines of managerial accountability, with responsibilities decentralised as far as possible, subject to guidelines from higher levels and performance monitoring; more clearly articulated arrangements for participation by the professions in management and planning; more sensitivity to user interests, particularly as institutionalised in Community Health Councils (see for example, Brown, 1979, pp. 161–2).

But at the same time as being too ambitious, perhaps the

changes were insufficiently ambitious in terms of some long-standing concerns about the old 'tripartite structure'. As one of the best examples of this we can note the English health authorities where the

> main part of the primary care budget (doctors and dentists fees and drug costs) is allocated direct to the Family Practitioner Committee by the DHSS. It is impossible to transfer resources from this to the main AHA budget. An AHA that is short of GPs or dentists does not get the cash saved to spend on substitutable services. Conversely, the AHA is not directly affected by GPs' prescribing costs and cannot therefore offer the incentive of, say, better diagnostic facilities as a reward for more economical prescribing. Nor, given the separation of budgets, is there much point in considering the effective way of dividing responsibility for, say, family planning or the dental health of school children. (Brown, 1979, p. 208)

In addition there was the more general problem of the new health and social care divide – between the NHS and the personal social services. This particularly affected the 'Cinderella services' which were concurrently being identified as priorities (see Chapter 5). They all suffered a 'double handicap because responsibility is divided and both sides have more attractive uses for their money' (Brown, 1979, p. 207). Of course there were the Joint Consultative Committees and Exchequer money was made available for schemes to be jointly financed by health and local authorities (see Abel-Smith, 1978, p. 49). But understandably local authorities were not always willing to support schemes whose long-term implications were greater expenditure for them and reduced expenditure by the NHS. Furthermore it was noted that machinery to facilitate co-operation between the NHS and local government,

> cannot overcome the basic problem – that two separate organisations have been established upon different principles of administration. The areas over which collaboration *must* occur are sensitive ones for both sides and will inevitably highlight the inherent weaknesses of this organisational dichotomy. (Thomas and Stoten, 1974, p. 69)

We have already noted the broader implications of the 'professional principle' whereby the previous Labour Government decided that the services should be organised 'according to the main skills required to provide them rather than by any categorisation of primary user' (DHSS, 1970, p. 10). Apart from exacerbating the administrative and financial division between local government and the NHS already mentioned, the principle was anyway not fully applied. Within the personal social services in England and Wales, the Probation Service remained outside of local government whereas in Scotland it was incorporated in the new local authority social work departments. In addition the incorporation of educational welfare work within the new social services/social work departments was left to local authority discretion and rarely occurred. All these decisions have been attributed primarily to reasons of political expediency. Finally any thorough debate of the implications of this 'professional principle' would surely have led to a fuller debate about the future of services for people with learning difficulties – the incorporation of which into the NHS hospital services had been anomalous in 1948 and was even more so by 1974 (see Chapter 12).

Was it worth doing?

For the most part, the aims of reorganisation have not been achieved three or four years after it, and where they have been achieved it has been costly in terms of additional work, uncertainty and frustration. (Royal Commission on the NHS Research Paper, 1, 1978 p. 223).

In summary, the health service reorganisation was too ambitious, was in some ways misconceived, and created an undesirable number of side effects. (Brown, 1979, p. 198).

There is little doubt, as the previous section and the above quotations indicate, that a sufficient body of criticism can be identified that calls into question whether the 1974 restructuring of the NHS was worth the considerable effort expended on it. Researchers certainly found a degree of uncertainty and confusion amongst NHS staff (see for example, Brown, 1979, p. 196).

There is also little doubt that the gains from the changes were more modest than might have been anticipated and hoped for at the time of the publication of the Porritt Report or the First Green Paper. This was in part due to the limited achievements of the restructuring in eliminating the organizational and financial divisions that were seen as hindering the development of community care. But it was also due to changes that had taken place not only since the Porritt Report, but also since the First Green Paper. These changes had lessened the significance of some of the concerns that provided the rationale for organizational change. These included the growth of group practice and more especially Health Centre practice amongst GPs and the emergence of the 'community health team' of GP / district nurse / health visitor / domiciliary midwife. The latter was further facilitated by the Health Services and Public Health Act (1968) which enabled local authorities to arrange for cross-boundary visiting to patients on the list of general practitioners working in their area. By 1972, 70 per cent of health visitors and 68 per cent of home nurses were working in association with general practitioners (see Mays, Forder, Keidan (eds), 1975, p 191). The amelioration of administrative divisions between GPs and community nursing staff – one of the few tangible achievements of the 1974 restructuring – had been rendered largely irrelevant before the restructured service came into operation. Furthermore researchers were identifying administrative structures as only part of the problem. Differences in professional perspectives allied to a lack of resources were perhaps the more significant barriers to identified desirable service objectives (see for example, Brown, 1972, p. 132; see also, Scammells, 1971).

Was the whole restructuring a totally worthless exercise? To be set against the criticisms, there were a number of advantages which could be identified. The new arrangements did afford the opportunity for more integrated management and co-ordination with other services. Perhaps most significantly in terms of issues of equity and efficiency there was now more scope for 'rational planning' as it became more feasible to look coherently at problems of allocation (Brown, 1979, pp. 162–3, 196). The implication was that a more rational (or less irrational) structure has been established that did offer more scope for comprehensive planning than the previous system (see Chapter 5).

The Value of Organizational Change
> The lesson of this study is perhaps that it is often better to live with some disadvantages than to incur costs of major change to secure improvements that may turn out to be illusory. (Brown, 1979, p. 202)

This leads up to the final, more general question – is such organisational change ever worth taking? What is the significance of organisational structure for the quality of health and community care services? Perhaps the crucial observation is that 'even if some restructuring . . . is a necessary condition for better management and planning, it is by no means a sufficient condition' (Brown, 1979, p. 163). This places a value on organizational restructuring but implies there is a danger of presuming that too much can be achieved through these means. Commentators on the 1974 restructuring were able to identify a series of fallacies associated with organizational change. These fallacies overlap one with another but are worth identifying separately. They have a resonance going well beyond the 1974 restructuring.

Firstly, and perhaps most specifically, there is the 'unitary fallacy' defined as 'the belief that conflicts of objectives will be resolved by bringing all together in one system' (Royal Commission on NHS Research Paper No.1, 1978, p. 223). The independence of GPs remained an issue in Scotland and Northern Ireland where the Family Practitioner Committees were not created (Royal Commission on the NHS Research Paper 1, 1978, p.14) and coterminosity did not necessarily bring benefits that were obvious to all.

> A surprisingly large number of respondents, and in all disciplines, positively expressed the view that the principle of coterminosity was irrelevant or worse, to the running of the health services and its relationship with cognate local authority services . . . where work is highly technical and specialist, or is based on particular philosophies, as is true in the whole range of health and welfare services, working together may not be easily assured by the simple application of solutions such as coterminosity or organisational integration. (Royal Commission on NHS, Research Paper No.1, 1978, pp. 50, 54)

Secondly, we might perhaps subsume the 'unitary fallacy' as part of a broader 'organizational fallacy':

> the assumption that institutional change will, of itself, cause good working together of professional groups with different expertise, social values and traditions of relations with clients. (Royal Commission on NHS Research Paper No.1, 1978, p. 229).

Thirdly, there are the even broader assumptions of the 'technocratic fallacy' – the hope that better information or improved administrative machinery can prevent the emergence of policy dilemmas. That organizational change can effect not just inter-professional collaboration but a much wider range of problems has also been labelled the 'administrative solution' fallacy – a tendency to 'seek administrative solutions to problems that are basically economic or technological' (Brown, 1972, p 132).

Finally, and perhaps most significant of all, we can detect in the 1974 attempts to restructure health care the 'single best solution fallacy' – 'the idea that there is one best way of doing something if only we were clever enough to find it' (Draper, Grenholm and Best, 1976, p. 269).

> There will not be a 'right' policy for the most part, but only policies that are seen to be the result of careful thought and reasonable process, and acknowledged as such. It is difficult to see how any of this can be changed by administrative or structural reorganisation. It may be well-meaning but fallacious optimism to assume that the redefinition of the boundaries of health care can be made other than through professional interaction. (Royal Commission on NHS Research Paper No.1, 1978, p. 227)

Reorganising the reorganisation 1

Given the controversy surrounding the changes introduced in 1974 it is unsurprising that attempts were soon made to modify structures, especially given the further change in government in 1974. The new Labour government was quick to do something about their criticism of the undemocratic nature of the new NHS with the publication of *Democracy in NHS* (DHSS, 1974). This proposed changes in the composition of AHAs and RHAs, plus a number of changes relating to CHCs. The Secretary of State's decisions on these proposals, following submissions by interested parties, was made in July 1975.

In the following year joint financing money was made available after the initial failure of the statutory requirements for local government and the NHS to co-operate with one another. However the sums involved were modest (1976–7: £8m; 1978–9: £32m) and the new scheme ran into similar difficulties.

> No scheme was ever better intentioned, but joint funding demonstrates the difficulty of creating inter-organizational working when the contributing organizations have different objectives, political environments and modes of working to reconcile. (Royal Commission on NHS Research Paper No 1, 1978, p. 59; see also Booth, 1981)

Conclusions

> What eventually emerged was inevitably a compromise between conflicting interests. (Abel-Smith, 1978, p. 41)

This quotation relates to the 1974 NHS reorganization. It can also stand for the initial organizational structure of the NHS in 1948. The limitations of the latter were a product of accommodating conflicts; action to ameliorate these limitations (eg: development of health centres) was delayed because of similar and additional conflicts. Meanwhile the subsequent delay in tackling these organizational shortcomings would hinder policies for a more equitable and efficient health service (see Chapter 5) and would exacerbate the inevitable difficulties of recasting the balance between institution-based and community-based health and social care (see Chapter 13).

Twenty years would elapse before a government published a consultation document on this issue (First Green Paper) initiating a five year period of debate and discussion culminating in the NHS Reorganization Act, 1973 and the introduction of a new organizational structure in 1974. This new structure was soon to attract as much criticism as the previous system, this time for being over-bureaucratic and top-heavy with managerial hierarchies. It was also seen as affording rather limited gains in terms of organizational change. One part of the previous organizational division between hospital and community care went, with the virtual elimination of local government health responsibilities and the transfer of community health hospital services to Area and Regional Health Authorities – an outcome predicted by Herbert Morrison (Honigsbaum, 1979, p. 176). But the administration of GPs remained largely separate via Family Practitioner Committees. Finally an earlier reorganization of personal social services within local government had created (in 1971) Social Services Departments with major responsibilities for developing community-based services for elderly people and people with mental health problems and learning disabilities. The result was that policies for community care were still hampered by what was to become known as the health / social care divide. Health care services (eg: home nursing and day-hospitals) were to remain the responsibility of the NHS; social care services (eg: home helps and day-centres) were to remain the responsibility of local authority social services departments.

If the 1974 reorganization failed to meet the needs of patients and service-users, it could be seen to have served several political purposes. One radical but simple organizational solution to perceived problems would have been to unify the NHS under the control of local government. Not only would this have bridged the divisions between hospital and community health care, but it would also have afforded the opportunity for a consistent and co-ordinated approach to health and related social care services (see Chapter 14). But central government did not want to transfer the NHS to local government for fear of losing control of public expenditure on health (the cost containment issue) whilst the medical profession did not want local government to control the NHS for rather similar reasons to those expressed before 1948 (the professional autonomy issue). In addition, the social workers did not want social care services to become part of the NHS for fear of being controlled by another profession (another professional autonomy issue). The long term consequences of this were to be quite profound. The new arrangements would be the subject of several critical reports in the 1980s culminating in a major reform of the organizational and financial basis of community care (see Chapter 7). Subsequent to those reforms the issue of Government's guidelines on long-stay hospital and residential care for the elderly and the associated discussion was evidence of the continuing significance of this issue (see Chapter 9).

Nonetheless the 1974 reorganization of the NHS taken with the Priorities and RAWP documents (Chapter 5) can be seen as having a major impact on the management of the NHS. The emphasis of the latter on the geographical and functional (ie: between services) redistribution of resources could not have been countenanced without more integration of policy-making, planning, funding and operational activities for complementary services to the same or similar population than was feasible under the tripartite format. The organizational gains from the 1974 changes were in some respects modest but were sufficient to support a more sustained and systematic pursuit of the goals of equity and efficiency (Kings Fund,1987, p. 1).

7
Managers and markets

Let me make one thing absolutely clear. The National
Health Service is safe with us. (Margaret Thatcher in a
speech to the Conservative Party Conference, 8 October
1982, reported in *The Times*, 9 October 1982)

The 1980s were indeed a period of relative deprivation for
the NHS. (Klein, 1995a, p. 141)

Introduction

Changes in government have been associated with significant
changes in social policies including policies on health, often based
on manifesto promises. Major changes – the introduction of NHI
and the NHS – were associated with reformist, 'left of centre'
governments. However it has been suggested that alternate
periods of Labour and Conservative government in post-war
Britain did not herald major changes in policy. The period has
been categorised as one of 'post-war consensus'.

The election of a Conservative government in 1979, with
Mrs.Thatcher as Prime Minister, has been identified as signalling
the demise of this 'post-war consensus'. This is because the new
government was identified with a particular political ideology
sometimes labelled the 'New Right' or 'radical right'. Two important themes have been identified with that 1979 government.
Firstly, there was a belief in the virtues of the market – that the
market is the best mechanism for producing and distributing
resources. In particular the market is seen as more efficient and
more responsive to people's needs than the state provision.
Secondly, there was an emphasis on individualism – the belief that
the individual is to be seen as self-reliant and responsible for her

or his own actions (see for example, Savage and Robins, 1990, pp. 5–6).

Although these themes have been identified with the 'New Right' they can be seen as very similar to the 'laissez-faire' ideology that was particularly influential during the nineteenth century (see Chapter 1). A belief in the virtues of the market and individualism implies a very limited role for state intervention in economic and social affairs. Commitment to this political ideology would seem to raise serious questions about the future of the NHS. These questions and their answers were to dominate the period 1979–91 and the subsequent reforms would constitute the controversial policies of the 1990s. This is unsurprising because despite the idea of a 'post-war consensus', there had always been politicians and commentators who had questioned the concept of a National Health Service on the basis that health care needs of the population could best be met by the operation of a private market system rather than a government financed and regulated health care system (see Chapter 11). Now there was a government in power which seemed to share this view.

The Royal Commission

The first major Government publication on health care in 1979 was that of the Royal Commission. Although set up in the mid-1970s to buy 'breathing space' for the Labour government of the time, it reported to a Conservative government in 1979 (Royal Commission on the NHS, 1979). The Commission endorsed the general criticism of the 1974 reorganization concluding that they could recommend 'no simple, universal panaceas for the cure of the administrative ills of the NHS' (Royal Commission on the NHS, 1979, p 325); they also observed that:

> it seems to us obvious that the way health care should be brought to the people of Wester Ross and to the people of Tower Hamlets will be entirely different: and that there is no reason other than the false god of administrative tidiness, why the service management arrangements should be the same, or indeed why they should even resemble each other to any great degree. (Royal Commission on the NHS, 1979, p. 313)

In other respects the Commission lent considerable support to the concept of a national health service and to the basic priorities of the Service. The Commission's brief had included the examination of the possibility of a greater reliance on insurance and charges as a means of financing the NHS. It rejected both, emphasising a point which was to be made with considerable force over the next decade, that by comparison with the health care systems of other advanced industrial societies, the NHS was remarkably cheap and by implication probably quite efficient.

Despite this endorsement of the NHS and its basic principles, the incoming Conservative Government commissioned its own review of the financing of health care. This still officially unpublished 1981 review was intended to reduce the extent to which health services are financed by the taxpayer and involved examining a number of alternatives including an almost total switch to private spending (see Carrier and Kendall, 1990a, p. 89). It seems likely that the Government was deterred from publishing the report because of its growing awareness of the enduring popularity of the NHS amongst the general public. Certainly official Government policy made no mention of a dramatic retreat from the concept of a National Health Service. The future of the NHS seemed reasonably secure and previous commitments to reduce inequalities in resource allocations to regions and to the 'Cinderella areas' were continued. On the other hand, the Foreword to the Black Report (1980) written by the Conservative Secretary of State Patrick Jenkin, noted that the policy recommendations contained in the report could not be considered because they were too expensive. This was a clear indication that whilst the government had abandoned the notion of eliminating the 'burden' of taxation associated with the provision of the NHS, it was very keen to moderate that 'burden' in various respects. One means of doing this would be to make the service more efficient.

Reorganising the reorganization 2
The initial attempt to make a more efficient service took a relatively conventional approach. The organizational structure established in 1974 was subject to a further reorganization (see DHSS, 1979). This was unsurprising given the considerable body of criticism which had been directed at the 1974 reorganization

(see Chapter 6). That structure was widely characterised as a top-heavy bureaucracy and some simplification had been supported by the Royal Commission; the latter also made a series of detailed recommendations for organizational reform. These included enabling Community Health Councils (CHCs) to have right of access to Family Practitioner Committee (FPC) meetings; the transfer of DHSS accountability to Regional Health Authorities; recommending the establishment of a Select Committee on the NHS and more generally a flexible approach to administration. The Commission also recommended the abolition of FPCs and concluded that there was one tier too many in the NHS and thought there should only be one management tier below the region (see Royal Commission on the NHS, 1979, pp. 149, 307–9, 313, 325, 327 and 324).

The Consultative Document *Patients First* (DHSS, 1979) was published in December 1979. In that document the Government rejected the Royal Commission's proposal that RHAs should become accountable to Parliament saying it was inconsistent with statutory responsibility and accountability to Parliament which the Secretary of State must retain. There was agreement regarding only one management tier below RHAs, and the Consultative Document included the proposal to establish District Health Authorities (DHAs) serving areas similar to existing 'health districts'. These DHAs would have boundaries coterminous with social services, housing and education and there would be management teams like those for the existing AHAs. Members of the DHAs would continue the NHS tradition of being appointed (by RHAs) and with only one quarter local government nominees. Statutory joint consultative committees and the present arrangements for FPCs would continue but it was suggested that CHCs might be unnecessary in the new structure (see DHSS, 1979, pp. 5, 6,para.10, 7, 9, 12–14).

The following July a circular (HC (80) 8) was issued confirming the proposals set out in *Patients First*. RHAs were to make recommendations on the new NHS structure to the Secretary of State by February 1981 (ie: on the boundaries of the new DHAs) with the process of structural change to be completed by April 1983. It was anticipated that most DHAs would be in existence on or before 1 April, 1982. CHCs were to be retained. The new administrative structure came into effect in 1982, with subsequent confirmation that the Family Practitioner Committees would be reconstituted as separate health authorities in their own right. The result was the abandonment of any attempt to maintain some sort of geographical relationship between local government and health authorities in favour of coterminosity where social service and health care needs required assessing.

This process of organizational change was less contentious than those associated with the establishment of the NHS and the changes introduced in 1974. This may reflect the degree of consensus about the need for change, but also the absence of the ideas most likely to generate conflict – changing the independent contractor status of GPs or enhancing the role of local government in health service provision. The most controversial aspect of the new organizational structure was the extent to which, after many years of debate and considerable investment of resources, another 'tripartite' organizational structure had been established with a major division between social care (responsibility of local author- ity Social Services Departments) and health care (responsibility of the NHS), with the latter divided into two by the continuing separate organizational and budgetary arrangements for GPs.

The potential to develop effective policies for community care for elderly people, people with mental health problems and people with learning disabilities would continue to be restricted by these continuing administrative, budgetary and professional divisions between health and social care. The failure of the 1974 and 1982 reorganizations in this respect, was to be the subject of a series of critical reports in the 1980s. These criticisms and the burgeoning social security budget for private sector nursing and residential care were key factors in drawing the government into a set of community care reforms that clearly parallel the changes intro- duced in the NHS (see below and Chapter 13).

This rather traditional administrative reform can be seen as evidence that the government did not altogether intend to follow through the implications of its own 'radical right' ideology and undertake some dramatic retreat from state involvement in health care. On the other hand it could be seen as taking some steps to lessen the 'burden' on the taxpayers of a universalist health service. As we have noted these steps might include conventional organizational reforms aiming to making the service more efficient. It could also pursue an option almost as old as the NHS itself, and review the potential for increased and additional user charges. Attempts could be made to encourage greater use of non-state welfare institutions – private medicine, the voluntary sector, families and communities. Finally, it could examine the potential for bringing the virtues of private sector management to bear on the presumed 'inefficiencies' of public sector bureaucracy.

A less free service – user charges

Perhaps the most obvious means by which the burden on the taxpayer could be diminished is by increasing the burden on the service user. Of course charges were not a new element in the 'free' NHS (see Chapter 4). Nonetheless new charges were introduced (eg: for eye tests) and well-established charges (eg: dental and prescription charges) were increased by significantly more than the rate of inflation. Indeed prescription charges, which had remained unchanged throughout most of the 1970s, were increased by '40 times the rate of inflation' between 1979 and 1994 (Timmins, 1995, p. 505). Despite these changes the NHS remained the most prominent health care system in the industrial world that was least reliant on direct service-user charges as a source of finance -and less reliant than it had been in the 1950s and early 1960s (see Klein, 1995a, p. 162 and Timmins, 1995, p. 505).

A role for non-state health care

The views of the Conservative administrations from 1979 was that the NHS would cost less if people turned to non-state institutions for their health and social care, and accordingly the government sought to encourage and emphasise the virtues of these alternatives to the NHS. Significantly steps were taken to reduce sharply the role of the NHS in the provision of ophthalmic services. The result of this was High Street 'shop front' ophthalmic services. In a similar vein the White Paper on services for elderly people contained an unequivocal statement that the advancement of community care would rely less on public provision and more on the community itself (see DHSS, 1981a) and the voluntary sector found itself drawn back into mainstream provision in areas such as day care.

Previous attempts by Labour governments to limit pay beds in

NHS hospitals and control private hospital development were both abandoned. Supportive comments were made regarding private hospitals and nursing homes as alternatives to the NHS. In addition, the latter were to receive dramatically increased indirect support via the social security budget during the 1980s. This had the paradoxical effect of increasing government intervention in traditional forms of residential care whilst financial restrictions were placed on local government which had significant responsibilities for developing the social care dimension of community care. The escalating costs of this 'policy accident' (Klein, 1995a, p. 158) may have been one of the factors influencing the government's commitment to reform policies for community care. It was certainly subject to criticism in the report of the Audit Commission (1986) along with organizational and other divisions identified above.

Cost-containment and contracting out

The old theme of cost containment was pursued by requiring health authorities to produce efficiency savings; drug budgets were cash limited; generic prescribing was proposed but after much heated discussion between representatives of general practitioners and the government, agreement was reached on a 'limited list' of drugs which could and those which could not be prescribed; finally, forms of resource management were introduced. The perceived advantages of the market were to be obtained by the introduction of contracting-out. Ancillary services were the main target (see Klein, 1995a, p. 160). Private sector firms would be given the opportunity to tender for contracts to provide catering, cleaning and laundry services. The theory was that the most efficient contractor would provide the cheapest tender and the NHS would benefit from cheaper and more efficient services. This was seen as an effective way of containing costs and bringing the virtues of private sector management into a large public sector organization. However it also led to a resurgence of trade union militancy in hospitals, reminiscent of the conflicts over 'pay-beds'; understandable given that the 'price of successfully defending in-house contracts tended to be lower earnings and redundancies' (Klein, 1995a, p. 161).

However this approach had its limitations. How could the

virtues of private sector management be brought to those parts of the NHS that 'contracting out' could not reach? The answer lay in a more fundamental reform of management arrangements within the Service.

Managerial changes

Prior to the 1980s the NHS had embodied a range of management traditions. The self-employed general practitioners were largely left to manage their own workloads. Community and public health services were, until the 1974 NHS reorganization, managed in a manner similar to other profession-based departments in local government. Within the hospital sector there had emerged a form of shared management by doctors, nurses and administrators based on a perceived need and demand for considerable professional autonomy – especially for the hospital consultants – and having its origins in the management style of the leading voluntary hospitals at the end of the nineteenth century (see Chapter 4 and Abel-Smith, 1964, p. 68). This shared management approach was most obviously and formally recognised in the 1970–74 Conservative Government's White Paper on NHS reorganization (see DHSS, 1972b, p. 57). At regional, area and district levels, the NHS was to be managed by consensus forming management teams including doctors, nurses, treasurers and administrators (see Chapter 6).

The document outlining the 1982 proposals for administrative restructuring also indicated that the government was additionally interested in managerial reform within the Service (DHSS, 1979), although it also restated the commitment to the appointment of consensus forming teams of equals to co-ordinate activities in the new district health authorities (DHAs). In addition the DHAs were required to organise their hospital and other services in consensus management units.

At this stage it seemed that this managerial reform was to be left to the health authorities themselves to take forward. But at a time when the new management units were still coping with the impact of this most recent reorganization, and some DHAs were still in the process of appointing staff to their new unit management teams, the Secretary of State announced the establishment of an independent NHS management inquiry headed by Roy Griffiths.

The inquiry team's key observation was that there was a 'lack of a clearly defined general management function throughout the NHS' (DHSS, 1983, p. 11). To remedy this situation they recommended the introduction of a single general manager acting as a chief executive and final decision-taker to replace the consensus management teams. This commitment to general management was to be extended above and below the level of health authorities. As well as a District General Manager for each DHA, there would be a general manager for every unit of management within the DHA. Each Regional Health Authority (RHA) would have a Regional General Manager and there would be a small management board at the centre, the Chair of which would have the general management function at a national level.

The government's commitment to the appointment of general managers regardless of discipline involved a significant move away from the previously stated principles (1972 White Paper and 1979 Consultative Document) that some NHS professionals should be exempted from managerial hierarchies and others should be managed by their fellow professionals. It implied that health care managers should manage efficiently, using management skills which might be applied with equal effectiveness in public or private sector organizations. It might also be seen as a vindication of the view expressed by the medical superintendents of the old London County Council that in every government hospital, clinicians must be answerable to someone (Honigsbaum, 1979, p. 171).

Reservations were expressed on this occasion by professional groups, health authorities and the House of Commons Social Services Committee, associated in many instances by requests for pilot schemes to evaluate the costs and benefits of the new ideas (see Carrier and Kendall, 1986, pp. 206–13). The latter approach would probably receive the support of many of the critics of the 1974 reorganization (see Chapter 6).

Such reservations and requests were ignored as the new general managers were appointed with great speed. The Government may have abandoned any notion of significantly diminishing a major social policy programme of government expenditure on health care but it appeared to have a growing commitment to displacing the traditional modes of public service administration and professionalism by a form of private sector managerialism. However although general management was accepted, there was little evidence of a substantial change in organizational culture during its first five years of operation (see Pollitt, Harrison, Hunter and Marnoch, 1991) and the NHS was still being criticised for poor management, including inadequate recruiting and training policies, and failures of communication, a full decade later (see Audit Commisson, 1994).

Government policies towards the NHS were assuming a pattern recognisable in some other social policy programmes. The broad parameters of government responsibilities for health services remained unchanged. Some, possibly increasing, relief on the problem of costs (for the taxpayer) was to be gained from an expanding private sector and increased charges. The potential role of the voluntary sector and informal carers was also highlighted in the area of community care. Cost-containment within the NHS was to be achieved by refusing to enter into any new major policy commitments like those advocated by the Black Report or which might have been anticipated in the White Paper on services for elderly people. In addition, there was a more rigorous application of cash limits, and health authorities were required to produce efficiency savings. Finally the system of administration and management was to be changed – not so much by the sort of restructuring undertaken in 1982, but rather through the application of 'private sector efficiency' by 'contracting out' services and bringing in a system of management modelled on the private sector. In terms of the original aims of the Service the emphasis seemed to be largely on efficiency. But it was also a particular form of efficiency. The traditional ideals of coherent planning towards meeting aims defined in terms of needs, seemed to be displaced by the ideal of remaining within budgets defined in terms of cash-limits.

The government went into the next General Election (May 1987) seemingly confident that the reforms it had put in place, culminating in the introduction of general management, had provided the basis for a more efficient NHS and that no new major reforms were required. However there was evidence of pressure building up for further reforms in the NHS before the

General Election. In April 1987 it was reported that some teaching hospitals were refusing to accept patients from outside their boundaries without some form of payment from the patients's health authority (Carrier and Kendall, 1990a, p. 90).

Whilst the Government may have claimed that its focus on efficiency was intended to benefit the patients, the latter seemed increasingly sceptical of the outcome. The view seemed to be gaining ground that the Government's cash limits were leading to 'real cuts' in services. The results in some cases appeared to be inefficiencies – consultants apparently told not to work to prevent their Units from overspending their cash-limited budget. The needs-led approach, for which there was certainly widespread support, seemed to be clearly at risk when hospitals were closing specialist units for seriously ill children (eg: Guys Special Care Baby Unit). By September 1987, it was reported in the press that health authorities might be making their biggest round of ward closures and deferred developments for at least four years. By mid-November, many hundreds of beds been taken out of service. The growing perception that the Service was in serious financial difficulties was given further confirmation in December 1987 when the Presidents of the three senior Royal Colleges – the surgeons, the physicians and the obstetricians and gynaecologists – issued a statement warning that the NHS had 'almost reached breaking point'.

It was at this rather inauspicious time that the Government published their White Paper on primary care. This proposed more spending on family doctor services, paid for in part by new and higher charges. It included measures to introduce more competition between GPs, tougher monitoring of their work, more preventive and health promotion, and more information and consumer choice for patients (see DHSS, 1987).

The mounting public and professional concern in the latter half of 1987 eventually drew a response from the government. Mrs. Thatcher in a TV interview announced the creation of a Ministerial Working Group to review the NHS, mainly composed of Treasury Ministers. A year-long review took place. During this time, the RAWP formula was modified to take account of social deprivation in the inner cities; the Griffiths Report on Community Care was published but seemingly ignored by the government. It included recommendations for a Minister for Community Care, ring fencing funds for community care, and a lead role for Local Authorities (see Griffiths, 1988).

Throughout 1988 speculation was rife about the future financial, managerial and administrative structure of the NHS with rumours circulating with regard to the likely content of the eventual document (see Timmins, 1988). During this period much was written on the state of the Service by professional pressure groups and academics. The House of Commons Social Services Committee also produced three reports while the review was in progress. The First Report recommended that the government should make good the acknowledged (by the DHSS) shortfall in the funding of pay and price inflation for 1987–88 (see Social Services Committee, 1988, p. xix). The majority of the submissions received by the Committee were in favour of retaining the NHS in its existing form. The Committee's own recommendations included no basic changes in the funding of the NHS and some limited experimentation with internal markets (see Carrier and Kendall, 1990a, p. 91). The Review was eventually published in January 1989 as the White Paper, *Working for Patients* (Cm.555); it was billed by the Prime Minister as the most far reaching reform of the NHS in its forty-year history (DoH, 1989a).

The internal market: the end of the 1948 compromise?

Mrs. Thatcher in *The Downing Street Years* (1993) said that 'the NHS had become a bottomless financial pit' (Thatcher, 1993). Nigel Lawson claimed in *The View from No.11: Memoirs of a Tory Radical* that at a private dinner with Mrs. Thatcher in January 1988 to discuss the Budget, a review of the NHS was raised. The basic way the NHS was financed was thought to be correct, it was thought to be working well, the object was to make it better. Private finance was ruled out and the question was, should you float off hospitals as independent privatised units (Lawson, 1993; quoted in Glennerster, 1995, p. 204)?

Some three years earlier, an American health economist, Alan Enthoven, reviewing the NHS while on a six month sabbatical stay with the Nuffield Provincial Hospital Trust, described the Service as approaching the New York traffic grid lock; the solution was to 'free it up' as a market of purchasers and providers

(Enthoven, 1985). Enthoven's model was accepted by the government, with the 'internal market' as a basis for the reform. Purchasers would be separated from providers, and capital charging on assets introduced to stimulate competition between NHS and private sector providers. The White Paper proposed self-managing NHS Trusts to run the larger hospitals as one such group of providers – almost a re-discovery of the autonomous management status of teaching hospitals within the NHS between 1948 and 1974 (see Chapter 4) or perhaps the pre-NHS voluntary hospitals. General practitioner services were to be brought into the internal market through direct allocation of budgets on a voluntary basis to larger general practices to enable the buying of certain hospital services. The DHAs would hold a budget to ensure the health of a defined population, identifying health needs, planning ways to satisfy them and ensuring the quality of the service. The 'ideal model' was of the DHAs (and the GPs) buying care from semi-independent hospitals, thereby creating a purchaser/provider split, retaining a public system of responsibilities, resources and regulation but disciplined by the operation of an 'internal market'.

In organizational terms the Review recommended the replacement of the existing resource allocation system (ie: RAWP, see Chapter 5) with one based on population weighted for age and the relative cost of providing services. The White Paper also contained proposals for the local governance of the NHS through management boards with no local authority representation and a restructuring of the DoH into a NHS Policy Board and a NHS Management Executive taking, respectively, strategic and day-to-day decisions. The separate Family Practitioner Authorities would become more managerially oriented and, for the first time, be subject to overall control by Regional Health Authorities. A series of ten Working Papers were issued subsequently to the publication of the White Paper, filling in some of the detail absent from the latter. The proposed autonomous Trusts could take responsibility for both groupings of smaller hospitals and community-based NHS services. Similarly smaller GP practices would be allowed to co-operate over budget-holding.

Enthoven's comment on the White Paper was that he was 'very surprised by the lack of detail' in the proposals. Echoing the Research Reports on the 1974 reorganization and many of the comments on the implementation of the Griffiths Report, Enthoven also considered the lack of pilot studies to be a mistake.

> I cannot understand why the Government did not choose to test their very promising ideas in a series of pilot projects. (Smith, 1989).

This comment was repeated by the House of Commons Social Services Committee in May 1989. They had

> attempted to find out more about the details of the proposals in three sessions of oral evidence with the Secretary of State. Those sessions, like the working papers, have raised more questions than they have answered. (Social Services Committee, 1989, p. vii)

The House of Commons Social Services Committee noted the generally hostile reception given to the White Paper, both inside and outside of the NHS (Social Services Committee, 1989, p. vi). The BMA warned of the dangers of fragmenting the NHS; claimed that concerns with costs might override the need for treatment; rejected moves to involve managers in appointing consultants; and condemned GP budgets and hospital trusts. The Association of Community Health Councils deplored the disappearance of local authority representation from the smaller, management-orientated health authorities, criticising the change as a distancing of the service from the service-users (see Carrier and Kendall, 1990a, pp. 95–6).

Doubts about the wisdom of either the basic principles of the White Paper and/or the manner of its implementation were further compounded and confused by its coincidence with negotiations over a new contract for GPs which followed on the publication of the White Paper on primary care (DHSS, 1987).

In 1990 the NHS and Community Care Act received Royal Assent and was implemented from April 1991. This Act implemented not only the reforms derived from *Working for Patients* (see above) but also those set down in a White Paper on community care *Caring for People* (see below).

Community care

The extensive post-war efficiency gains recorded in the use of expensive hospital resources (patient throughput) were certainly facilitated by the contribution of community health care services (see Chapter 5). For many patients, community social care services (eg: home helps) also made an important contribution and government policy documents noted the impossibility of drawing a clear line between the role of NHS day hospitals and local authority day care facilities (see Chapter 6).

Successive reorganizations of health and social care between 1971 and 1985 made limited contributions to creating a framework which would facilitate, rather than hinder, the effective co-operation and co-ordination between health and social care agencies and professionals. Basic organizational and budgetary divisions were compounded by differences in professional and managerial cultures (see Chapter 6).

The Royal Commission on the NHS had recognised the attraction and logic of the transfer of NHS to local government, but advised against it at the time (there being no regional tier of local government); the Commission considered the transfer of the personal social services to NHS an insufficient reform (if health, why not education and housing?); but also offered the slightly contradictory opinion that the system in Northern Ireland (where health and personal social services are combined in one agency) should be encouraged and further developed. They also rejected the transfer of client groups on the grounds that this would lead to intra-professional divisions (see Royal Commission on the NHS, 1979, pp. 265–6, 266–7).

Care in Action (DHSS, 1981b) stressed the need for accessibility, non-separateness, and co-ordinated and complementary community care services. In June of that year a Government minister noted that 32 local authorities were still making no provision for people with mental health problems and 7 provided no residential accommodation. In 1981 the Government also published *Care in the Community*; this referred to four means by which resources might be moved from traditional hospital-based to community-based services. These were firstly, extending joint finance arrangements; secondly, pooling funds for client groups and planning services jointly; thirdly, transferring funds centrally from NHS to personal social services; and finally, concentrating responsibility for a client group on a single agency (DHSS, 1981c). If nothing else, *Care in the Community* involved a recognition that the shift of the balance of care from the NHS to local authorities, and of resources to priority groups was happening far more slowly than had been hoped. Perhaps the most effective critique of community care policies, in terms of political impact, came with the Second Report of the Social Services Committee; Community Care, 1984–5 which included the following comment:

> We do not wish to slow down the exodus from mental illness or mental handicap hospitals for its own sake. but we do look to see the same degree of Ministerial pressure, and the provision of the necessary resources, devoted to the creation of alternative services. Any fool can close a long stay hospital: it takes more time and trouble to do it properly and compassionately. (Social Services Committee, 1985, para. 40).

The Committee went on to say:

> the Minister must ensure that mental illness or mental handicap hospital provision is not reduced without demonstrably adequate alternative services being provided beforehand for those discharged from hospital and for those who would otherwise seek admission. (Social Services Committee, 1985).

In November 1985 the Government published its response to the House of Commons Community Care Report. It confirmed governmental commitment to the development of the integrated network of central policies and local services necessary for community care. The following year the Audit Commission published a report – *Making A Reality of Community Care* -which reviewed a variety of community care schemes. This concluded that all the successful schemes known to them involved 'a radical departure from the generally accepted ways of doing things'. In particular they were characterised by six features:

> The presence of strong and committed local 'champions' of change;

a focus on action not bureaucratic machinery;
locally integrated machinery for service planning purposes;
a focus on the local neighbourhood;
a multi-professional team approach; and
a partnership between statutory services and voluntary organisations. (see Audit Commission, 1986).

At the same time the Government announced the appointment
of Sir Roy Griffiths to undertake another review – this time of
community care. This announcement following the Audit Commission's remarks, was a response, not to the good practices
highlighted by the Commission, but to the Commission's criticism
that the substantial sum of money spent on services for the care of
people with mental health problems, people with learning difficulties and elderly people (estimated at £6 billion) was not being
effectively deployed. Sir Roy Griffiths was also charged with
investigating whether or not the structure of social security payments was having the effect of forcing people into residential care,
instead of keeping them in their own homes supported by professional staff – an indication that its attempts to favour the private
sector and relieve the 'burden' of the NHS was in one case simply
shifting that 'burden' to another budget heading – in the end it
was the budget of a governmental bureaucracy (social security)
not private enterprise that was 'really providing' for those in long-
stay nursing and residential care.

The Griffiths Report was published in March 1988 and re-stated
many of the themes of the Social Services Committee and the
Audit Commission – 'community care is a poor relation, everybody's distant relative but no-body's baby' (Griffiths, 1988, p. iv).
His answer was to identify a key role for local government (in the
form of Social Services Departments) as:

the designers, organisers and purchasers of non-health care
services. (Griffiths, 1988, p. 1)

To some extent he was advocating an 'internal market' in community care; certainly a purchaser / provider split in which local
authorities would be major purchasers rather than direct providers; as purchasers they would make:

maximum possible use of voluntary and private sector bodies to widen consumer choice, stimulate innovation and encourage efficiency. (Griffiths, 1988, p. 1)

Griffiths also advocated a 'Minister for Community Care' and a ring-fenced specific grant for community care services.

Despite building on a degree of consensus about what was wrong about the organizational infrastructure for community care policies, the Government was slow to respond to Griffiths' recommendations – usually attributed to the important role he assigned to local government (see for example, Evans, 1994, p. 225). It was not until November 1989 that the White Paper, *Caring for People*, was published.

The White Paper followed closely the Griffiths proposals. The role of local authority social services departments would be crucial in enabling people to live in their own homes wherever feasible and sensible; this to be achieved by promoting the development of domiciliary, day and respite services. The social security budget for private institutional care would be redirected to local authorities to enable them to fulfil this role. Services would include a 'flourishing independent sector alongside good quality public services' (DoH, 1989b, p. 5). Significantly as a later government publication was to note:

if implementation is to be effective, there must be close working links between all agencies – social services departments, NHS bodies, housing authorities and associations, voluntary organizations and social services providers. (DoH, 1990)

Even after *Caring for People* the long standing division remained between health authorities as purchasers of health care and local government as the lead agency for social care. The proposals were incorporated in the same legislation that introduced the 'internal market' into the NHS – the NHS and Community Care Act, 1991 – but full implementation was delayed until April 1993 by which time it was hoped that the problems of local government (ie: the poll tax) would be resolved.

Conflicts, consensus, crisis and costs

The election of the first Thatcher government in 1979 introduced a government whose ideological position involved a commitment to reduce 'burdensome public expenditure on welfare'. However, there is some evidence to support the contention that the government soon discovered that blanket condemnations of the 'welfare state', of the sort favoured by its supporters from the radical right, did not strike a uniform chord amongst the general public. A disinclination to vote for restrictions on private health care was not the same as a vote for abandoning the National Health Service. Reservations about public expenditure in support of unemployed people in times of fuller employment, were not necessarily associated with similar reservations about public expenditure on sick children in hospital. The White Paper which introduced the internal market was prefaced with a personal statement unequivocal in its support for a tax-funded universalist health service.

Whilst the government may have abandoned any notion of significantly diminishing a major social policy programme of public expenditure on health care, it did appear to have a growing commitment to displacing the traditional modes of public service administration and professionalism by a form of private sector managerialism. Whilst the emphasis on efficiency was far from new, it did seem to be taking a particular form. The traditional ideal of 'rational' coherent planning to meet needs (see for example, the Priorities documents, see Chapter 5), seemed to be displaced by a new idea of 'strong' managerial control to remain within cash limits. On the other hand, in its impact on the Service, this retreat from 'rational planning' was more rhetorical than real. As we have noted in Chapter 5, the first effective NHS planning system had not been introduced until 1976.

Finally, there is the political background to the NHS Review. This would seem to be fairly represented as an exercise in crisis management. Its establishment was announced within eight weeks of a general election in which the Conservative Party's manifesto had contained no indication that such a review would take place and within a fortnight of John Moore (Secretary of State for Social Services) dismissing rumours that any such action was intended. Government action – setting up the Review – was a response to a perceived resource crisis in the NHS. For a major public service which operated for all of twenty-one months before its first cash-limit was introduced, the scenario was depressing if somewhat familiar.

Conclusions

The publication of *Working for Patients* provoked a number of concerns about the operation of the internal market. Would hospital trusts specialise in areas of greatest 'economic gain' and would the market ensure that these were appropriate to the needs of local communities? Might hospital trusts tend to discharge patients to the community before it would otherwise be appropriate? Would budget holding GPs have an incentive to get their patients admitted to hospitals as emergencies rather than straightforward referrals? Would people with costly problems of ill-health find themselves being treated by reference to the size of a general practitioner's budget and the accessibility of specialist hospital care, rather than by reference to their real care needs? These questions would not be easy to answer. Any definitive evaluation of the internal market, NHS trusts and GP fundholders would be difficult given the Government's predilection (see also grant-maintained schools) for encouraging, rather than requiring, the adoption of trust and fund-holder status. The first trusts and fund-holders probably constituted a distinctly biased sample – representing those who considered they or their patients had most to benefit from the new arrangements. Furthermore some of the identified benefits – especially of fundholding – might not be sustained if the status is more widely adopted. Whatever its political or other merits, this approach to organizational change did not lend itself to systematic or swift policy evaluation!

For collaboration in health and social care another range of possibilities emerged including on the one hand, community nurses, occupational therapists and social workers in cut-throat competition with one another for scarce and sought after contracts to provide services; to, on the other hand, the development of new, innovative and collaborative inter-professional service providers, released from the artificial constraints of the previous budgetary and organizational divisions between health (NHS) and social care (Social Services Departments). There were indications that primary health care providers (GPs) were beginning to develop much closer working relationships with other community health services, indicating the potential for more effectively integrated care management systems and the possibility that the internal market might facilitate the emergence of organizational arrangements for health and social care that had eluded the more conventional forms of restructuring previously undertaken.

What was unsurprising was that the health service and community care reforms should be linked to, and probably initiated by, concerns about costs and their containment. Governments influenced by radical right ideology would readily presume that cost containment will be especially problematic in the NHS since its finances continue to rely more significantly on general taxation than do those systems operating elsewhere in the European Community. The result is a system largely free at the point of use, and conventional economic analyses suggests that this a recipe for abuse and waste by consumers. However the evidence showed that the NHS provided 'a most efficient service ... a remarkably comprehensive service at a remarkably reasonable price' (Klein, 1995b, p. 309) leading to the seemingly paradoxical conclusion that a universal, open access, free service making little or no use of conventional market mechanisms is more successful at containing costs than more market-oriented systems. At least part of this success may be attributable to a modest degree of planning, the Service's traditional role as a monopsonist with regard to health care personnel and the absence of complex systems for charging and billing individuals or organizations – all of these features were now to be changed with the introduction of the 'internal market'.

To begin the 1980s with conventional administrative reform and to begin the 1990s with reforms based on 'internal markets' indicates a shift in government thinking from administrative to economic solutions to the perceived problems of a highly valued public service. Both modes were constructed to cope with what was perceived as the major problem confronting the NHS – escalating costs in the face of professionally defined need. This can be seen as a recipe for conflict with the professionals responsible for defining that medical care need; and with the public whose expectations are based upon a legitimate assumption of that need being met. Given a managerial and economic ideology that would attempt to control those who supply the need – doctors and managers – as well as those who demand the same – patients and their carers, it is not surprising that this particular ideology would come into conflict with an historically based experience of a public service meeting legitimate pubic health care needs.

In the event any long term contradictions or conflicts associated with the health and community care reforms would not be the responsibility of governments led by Mrs.Thatcher. By the time the reforms were being enacted another Conservative adminis-tration with Mr.Major as Prime Minister would face up to the consequences – good or bad – of these market-led reforms.

8
Rationing and rights

In this country when you are ill they take your temperature,
in other countries they take your credit card; while I'm in
Downing Street that will never happen here. (John Major in
a speech to the Conservative Party Annual Conference, 11
October 1996, reported in *The Independent*, 12 October,
1996)

Introduction

The previous chapter charted the progress of the Conservative
governments of the 1980s towards the idea of introducing an
internal market into the British health care system. This was not
the preferred alternative of the 'radical right' who would certainly
have abandoned the NHS and taken as much health care as
possible into the marketplace if it had been politically feasible.
Given the continuing popularity of the NHS the alternative was to
bring the market into the NHS through compulsory competitive
tendering, private sector management approaches and most radically the introduction of an internal market and the purchaser /
provider split.

Markets, quasi-markets and health care

This introduction of the internal market might be seen as something of a victory for one side in the long-running intellectual and
policy debate between Keynes and Friedman – demand management versus monetarism. The outcome of this debate affects the
Health Service because it structures public spending decisions.
Believe one theory and you believe in public expenditure and the
benefits of state intervention; believe another and you believe in

private expenditure and the power of the market. The two simple conceptual models used are opposite ends of a spectrum, at one end a command system (Appleby, 1994), at the other end the free market. The command system being tax supported, is based on the public sector and has something approaching a monopoly. This system tended to characterize post-Second World War European public health care systems whose main objective was to extend coverage to all based on ideas of social justice and moral obligations. The economic idea was to invest in human capital stock. The case for this has always been that a command system covers all members of the population, so that all are eligible. A basic minimum is provided, costs are controlled, and distribution is equalized.

The case against such systems has always been that they tend to generate large administrations. They become rigid, they cannot respond to changes in technical and social environments quickly. They become unresponsive to client concerns. The preference of the provider or professional takes precedence over the consumer or patient. Administrative regulations with fixed budgets and salaries means that there are no serious incentives to improve efficiency and productivity. They may even lead to perverse incentives; you punish efficiency by closing down successful services. Such services are in danger of becoming unaccountable and are professionally led. There is no price mechanism, so demand and supply relationships become distorted. Political or professional rationing is needed and is done arbitrarily by queuing. As a result of this, public health systems have, it is claimed, been faced by growing public demands, fiscal constraint and bureaucratic rigidity.

The second model, the free market, is one which under certain ideal conditions allows the market to deliver maximum social and economic benefit. The theory is that an efficient outcome is achieved by individuals pursuing their own self interest. Consumers seek to maximize utility and producers to maximize profit. But three conditions are necessary for a perfect market. Firstly, perfect competition; one requires a large number of buyers and producers in the market, none of which can influence price, with no entry or exit barriers. Secondly, there are no externalities; no spill overs from other people's production or consumption which are not accounted for in market transactions. Thirdly, perfect information is required, disseminated freely, understood, and capable of being used.

These three conditions are problematic for health care. With regard to the first condition, perfect competition, there is a tendency towards monopolistic provision, especially in secondary care. For the second condition, health care is especially prone to externalities, especially communicable diseases. Individuals gain from vaccination as does the rest of society. As for the third condition, perfect information, there are a range of uncertainties associated with consuming medical care (see Chapter 11 for a more extensive discussion of this point). In particular the latter produces two main problems. First 'adverse selection', which leads to gaps in the insurance of the population, especially those with high risks of certain conditions. Secondly, what has been called moral hazard; you are insured so there is an incentive to overuse the health care system, leading to excess and clinically inappropriate demands. Consumers and providers change their behaviour towards the provision and consumption of health care, resulting from the fact that the insured are insured against the full cost of health care. So unnecessary procedures and unnecessary diagnostic tests are insisted upon. Therefore free markets in health care can be both inefficient and inequitable, ability to pay being not necessarily related to need. The result is that you cannot assume that a real market in health care will replicate the theoretical market efficiencies promised by its advocates. This may be one reason why government intervention in health care is virtually universal throughout the industrial world.

Set against the claim that 'there is nothing like a competitive market to motivate quality and economy of service' (Enthoven, 1985, p. 43) is a questioning of the evidence that competitive markets in health care automatically have these outcomes (see, for example, Mooney, 1992). Would it be possible to capture the advantages of the free market, efficiency, and still safeguard equity in an 'internal market'? The reforms begun with the passing of the NHS and Community Care Act, 1990 were soon followed by the announcement of major job losses in two prominent NHS Trusts (Harrison and Wistow, 1992, p. 123; Klein, 1995a, p. 205). The Government ordered a 'steady state', indicating it was not prepared to countenance the political consequences of dramatic switches of contract by purchasers. The internal market was to be a managed or quasi market (Klein, 1995a, p. 204 and 1995b, p. 302).

So how much of a 'market' is this 'managed internal market' in the NHS? There is competition on the provider side, in so far as a simple state monopoly is replaced, but it is predominantly not-for-profit organizations that are competing for public contracts. On the demand side, consumers are represented by agents who manage the budget and carry out purchasing decisions. Competition may be limited also by the significance of emergency treatments (Harrison and Wistow, 1992, p. 127). This is the 'internal quasi-market' and its perceived failings and successes are a major theme in the current health care policy agenda. Is the quasi market improving efficiency, choice, responsiveness and safeguarding equity in the NHS?

Managing the internal market

The goals of the internal market model are hardly new. They include better care that produces better outcomes for patients; better access and greater patient satisfaction; less costly care and hence more care; and more responsive care with inevitably limited resources. It is not always apparent that health care purchasers are able to use market structures to achieve these ends. Purchaser choices are often limited; sometimes there are monopolistic providers locally and hence restricted leverage for improved provider performance. Entry barriers are there for new suppliers, there are heavy capital costs and private competitors are deterred. The existing pattern of referrals may be retained, as the willingness of patients to travel limits the use of distant providers; a high value being placed on local convenience. On the purchasing side, DHAs are monopolistic but general practice fund holders introduce an element of competition but raise inevitable concerns about the fragmentation of health care planning. What is the model of purchasing that best reflects individual needs and demands? Is the system concerned with consumer choice or the needs of the population and public health?

There are information deficits, a major area of difficulty being that purchasers are especially dependent on providers for information. These deficits may have the serious consequences of opportunistic behaviour by providers, inadequate contracts, poor strategic decisions by purchasers, and long term impacts on provider markets. There are also serious equity concerns. Of course the information problem is hardly new; there were pressures on hospitals to massage the statistics when they were competing for funds in the nineteenth century (see Woodward, 1974, pp. 139–42).

Concerns have also been expressed about the numbers and associated costs of the managers of the new internal market. There is a paradox here since critics of traditional bureaucratic modes of operation are often the strongest advocates of a market approach – and part of that advocacy will relate to presumed administrative costs and inefficiencies associated with bureaucracies. But the internal market has increased managerial costs. The numbers of managers were bound to rise and they have risen by about 20 per cent between 1991 and 1996. There are also transaction costs involved in negotiating, managing, and monitoring contracts. This process is time consuming and there are additional information costs, accounting costs, and management costs associated with long term relationships between buyers and sellers. There are also transitional and start up costs already estimated at £2 billion between 1991 and 1995. A huge management agenda has been imposed on purchasers and providers. If you switch from a non-market administered system to a managed market system with a million employees and a £40 billion budget, increased management costs are both a natural corollary and a necessity (Klein, 1995a, p. 205 and 1995b, p. 320). From 1990 £70 million per annum extra was allocated to the NHS in England and Wales to bolster finance, personnel and information services (see Audit Commission, 1995, p. 2).

So, have quasi markets in health care succeeded? Of the two national surveys done of district general managers, the advantage of the reforms appear to be that the purchaser provider split has clarified the roles of each. There has been a focus on health needs, and care has been more patient centred. Secondly, quality issues have been emphasised more. Thirdly, there is now better information available. Fourthly, provider accountability has been increased. In particular, market pressure may have opened up and made visible long standing problems (see also Chapter 9). But the restructuring, by changing provider patterns and closing hospitals, has involved significant social and political costs. The conditions for operating a successful internal market are not nationally met in terms of market structure, accurate information, and transaction costs, with particular problems in general practice over concerns about a 'two-tier arrangement' in which unacceptable advantages might accrue to the patients of fund-holding practices especially over faster access to hospital services, one example of an equity issue being exacerbated by a market condition.

The model of GP fundholding aimed to introduce competition on both the purchasing and providing sides of the internal market. In this case patients would be able to choose 'between those who would purchase services on their behalf' (Glennerster, Matsaganis, Owens, Hancock, 1994, p. 166). Since 1991 GPs have actually become involved in the purchasing process in a variety of ways, quite apart from fundholding (see for example, Glennerster, Cohen and Bovell, 1996). Studies of fundholding itself have found efficiency gains to be set against possible, although not inevitable equity losses; and that consumers lack the knowledge and interest in choosing between practices (see Glennerster, Matsaganis, Owens, Hancock, 1994, p. 175, p. 179 and Klein, 1995a, p. 239). For the moment it seems 'we know too little for sure about the relative effectiveness ... (of) ... fundholding or locality purchasing' (Glennerster, Cohen and Bovell, 1996, p. 55) and this is indicative of a justifiable uncertainty surrounding the impact of the 'internal market reforms'.

More generally, inpatient numbers, day cases and outpatient attendances have all risen; but we would have expected these trends with or without the quasi-market since they were well-established before its introduction and are evident throughout the history of the NHS (see for example, Chapter 5). Furthermore, in 1990/91 NHS spending in real terms increased by 2.8 per cent and in 1991/92 by 4.1 per cent. This coincided with the introduction of the quasi-market and the run up to the general election of 1992. Given that the alternative explanation of the pre-*Working for Patients* crisis was inadequacies in resources rather than structure, proponents of that view would argue that the NHS would show signs of improvement, or at least a 'steady state', given appropriate resourcing. Finally, the underlying trends of changes in medical science and medical practice continue. These changes, given appropriate funding which takes account of their resource implications, have the potential to lead to improvements for the health service-users. If the funding of the NHS also takes account of both 'medical inflation' (inflationary pressures adjusted for the distinctive costs of health care) and demographic change, we would anticipate these improvements to be sustainable and not 'counterbalanced' by a loss of service-quality elsewhere 'in the system'. However, given that firstly, this 'rational' approach to resourcing the NHS has not been a consistent feature of government funding of health care – especially in the period leading up to the setting up of the review that led to *Working for Patients* (1989a); and given secondly, the ongoing influence of other long-term factors (eg: changes in medical science); then arriving at anything resembling a definitive judgement on the recent reforms is inherently problematic. Perhaps the only clear conclusion that can be reached is that it will be very difficult to assemble the evidence that the general managed quasi-market NHS is 'better' than either the consensus team managed post-1974 NHS or the historic cost budgeted tripartite pre-1974 NHS (see also Klein, 1995a, pp. 224, 230–1, 236–40; Klein, 1995b, pp. 309–10; and Robinson and LeGrand, 1994, p. 243). Another 'NHS cash crisis' linked to concerns over whether there had been (for the 1996/97 financial year) a 'real increase' (of 0.1 per cent) or a 'real cut' (of 0.3 per cent) in spending on health and personal social services (see *The Independent*, 5/11/96, p. 2), illustrated again the significance of the overall level of resources going to the NHS. It may also lend support to the concern that 'the Tory reforms of the health service are now blamed for everything that goes wrong' (Abel-Smith and Glennerster, 1995, p. 1)

Of course some things will be 'going right', and these things also present difficulties of interpretation. The NHS of 1996 will on a number of counts be 'better' than that of 1986 and 1976; but that may have happened anyway without any of the changes introduced and then dismantled (eg: consensus team management) by various, mostly Conservative, governments. The picture is further confused by the possibility that some improvements might be attributable to 'old-fashioned Stalinism' (ie: direct political intervention) rather than 'free market liberalism' (Ham, 1994). In the rather unlikely event that we might be able to state with some degree of certainty and precision the benefits that have flowed from the 'internal market', we then have to set those benefits against the costs involved in operating such a market. Some of the latter may only just be emerging with regular press reports of shortages of specialist staff. If, in pursuance of quasi-market ideals, health care providers start competing more vigorously for such staff we might find that the cost-containment virtues of the quasi-market are overwhelmed by the well-documented cost-enhancement qualities of market orientated health care systems.

Rationing

The internal market has made more explicit this most sensitive issue. If rationing is used, then how, and by what criteria? Rationing has always taken place by delay through waiting lists, by deterrents through an unpleasant environment, by deflection onto other agencies, by dilution – reducing the number of treatments and the length of stay – and by charges (see Parker, R., 1975, 1976). If rationing is to become more explicit should the NHS adopt the model developed in Oregon and exclude certain services (see Dixon and Welch, 1991) thus falling below the comprehensive standard supported by the wartime 'near-consensus' (see Chapters 3 and 4). Recently, Berkshire Health Authority announced an Oregon approach, excluding, for example, tattoo removal, buttock lifts, GIFT, rhinoplasty and liposuction. Oregon has been described as a 'rational and democratic' model (Klein, 1994, p. 109). 'Rational' because it uses cost utility analysis weighing relative benefits of different procedures, and 'democratic' because community values are polled and the citizens participate.

But the Oregon model has been criticized. With regard to community values, it is suggested that health professionals dominated the citizens meetings. The cost utility approach depends heavily on using data like the British quality adjusted life year, the so called 'Qualy'. Key problems with this approach are informational outcomes and costs – that is the quality of data. How homogeneous are patients? When is a cosmetic procedure to be done for psychological reasons? If the information is reliable and valid do you give 5 units to 20 people or 20 units to 5 people? – the classic utilitarian problem. This approach may be relatively unproblematic for the macro decisions of public health, based on utilitarian philosophy. The micro, or clinical decisions where individuals are concerned produce other problems. The problem of who should be treated remains.

Because patient populations are heterogeneous, many medical interventions involve uncertainty, and the clinical decision-making process is iterative (using information obtained from the relationship between professional and patient), an effective health care rationing system must take into account the need for flexible physician response to numerous unprovided-for circumstances. Implicit rationing allows for needed sensitivity to variance by relying on clinical discretion. (Mechanic, 1992; quoted in Klein, 1994, p. 111).

Mechanic's view may be seen as conservative but relevant; that implicit rationing by clinicians may be more rational than explicit rationing by exclusion (Klein, 1995b, p. 325).

There is no doubt that clinical autonomy remains an important dimension of the NHS. In September 1995 the Minister of Health suggested that clinical need was the basis of broad political support for the NHS (BBC Radio 4, *Today*. 19/9/95). Indeed given the enduring popularity of a Service that has placed considerable emphasis on that autonomy, it may be that it still represents an appropriate basis for decisions if suitably informed by research, guided by ethical considerations and moderated more by concerns about economic costs to the community than the economic benefits to the individual professional (or health care provider). It may be that economic theory is best left in the text books where it works, and used rather sparingly in the real world of health care – given the propensity of health care markets to depart significantly from the text book.

Rights
What is the real world of the NHS like? The British system, despite the reforms, remains highly regulated, not just by the Treasury but by statute and Common Law. In public law and private law cases, the introduction of a quasi-market does not alter the obligations imposed under the legislation. Section 10 of the National Health Service and Community Care Act 1990 leaves unchanged the obligations imposed by the National Health Service Act 1977 sections 1 and 3. The latter when tested did not impose an absolute duty to provide services without considering economic decisions taken at national level about the amount of resources

going into the service, as well as the importance of local decisions (see Newdick, 1995, Chs.2, 4 and 6). The question becomes – are they reasonable decisions?

In R v Secretary of State, West Midlands RHA and Birmingham AHA (Teaching) exparte Hincks and others, the allegation was that the West Midlands RHA and Birmingham Health Authority had failed to fund the building of an orthopaedic unit. The Minister of Health had agreed the need to build such a unit. Lord Denning said in the Court of Appeal that:

> the Secretary of State says he is doing the best he can with the financial resources available to him: and I do not think that he can be faulted in the matter. (1992, 1 BMLR 93, p. 96)

Lord Bridge agreed with Denning stating:

> the situations revealed here are not unique. As the evidence shows and as we all know as a matter of common knowledge, the Health Service currently falls far short of what everyone would regard as the optimum desirable standard. (1992, 1 BMLR 93, p. 96)

In a case concerning a premature baby requiring a 'hole in the heart' operation, Sir John (later Lord) Donaldson, Master of the Rolls, rejecting the case for baby Walker and refusing to quash the decision of Central Birmingham Health Authority not to carry out the operation, although all concerned agreed the baby needed the surgery, went on to say that:

> it is not for this court, or indeed any court, to substitute its own judgement for the judgement of those who are responsible for the allocation of resources. This court could only intervene where it was satisfied that there was a prima facie case, not only of failing to allocate resources in the way in which others would think that resources should be allocated, but of a failure to allocate resources to an extent which was ... unreasonable. (1992), BMLR 32 [decided 1987] 1992, 3)

The argument was that unless the behaviour was unreasonable the court would not intervene to divert facilities from one patient to another.

In R v Central Birmingham Health Authority, exparte Collier, 1988, Judge Stephen Brown said, 'the courts of this country cannot arrange the lists in the hospital' (Kennedy and Grubb, 1994, p. 429). This was a child requiring urgent cardiac surgery. Again in re-J (a minor) (wardship: medical treatment)[1992] 4 AER.614 CA, Balcombe.L.J. said:

> I would also stress the absolute undesirability of the court making an order which may have the effect of compelling a doctor or health authority to make available scarce resources (both human and material) to a particular child, without knowing whether or not there are other patients to whom those resources might more advantageously be devoted. (Kennedy and Grubb, 1994, p. 275)

So although clinical need is proved neither the Secretary of State nor the DHA nor the purchasing authority can be ordered to fund or carry out procedures.

In the recent case of Child B (R v Cambridge Health Authority, Ex.p B) there was dispute over the prognosis of myeloid leukaemia, and whether the treatment was experimental. Discussions took place between Dr Zimmern of the Cambridge Health Authority and doctors at the Hammersmith, Marsden and Addenbrooke hospitals on the likely outcome of the treatment. Dr.Zimmern was criticized in the court of first instance, on three counts; one, for failing to regard the wishes of the patient; secondly, for describing as experimental, a treatment with a 10 to 20 per cent chance of success; and thirdly, because of his alternative use of resources. The Court of Appeal however, upheld the decision of the health authority to deny the resources to Child B in the following way:

> Difficult and agonizing judgements have to be made as to how a limited budget could best be allocated to the maximum advantage of the maximum number of patients. That is not a judgement which the court can make. (*The Weekly Law Reports*, 16 June 1995, p. 906)

What all these cases demonstrate is that a combination of clinical judgement, estimates of financial resources and likely opportunity costs, do structure health care decision making. So if 'the law' protects health authorities, can the Treasury help by releasing more cash into the system? There are two linked questions here. The first is, can society afford a NHS? And if the answer is 'yes' to that first question, how should we pay for the Service?

Resources

Over time expenditure on the NHS in cash terms has escalated rapidly. But in comparison with other countries, the UK spends a relatively modest amount of GDP on health care (see Figure 38, Hills, 1993, p. 56). Furthermore the increases over time are less dramatic when some account is taken of inflation (the general increase in prices represented by the Retail Price Index). When a more sophisticated inflationary adjustment is included – the volume which health care resource spending could pay for (eg: doctors and nurses) adjusting for NHS prices, the increases in 'real expenditure' become quite modest (eg: only 1.8 per cent between 1979 and 1992). When the crucial dimension of demographic trends is also accounted for, on an index of resources available in relation to need, needs have actually been growing faster than resources at certain points in time (eg: 1979–1992). If you add in new technologies and the impact of RAWP, then relative to needs one can see why, despite growth, services available to meet those needs were seen and felt, both by the professionals and the public, to have declined. Whether an organizational reform was necessary or not, it seems clear that the 'NHS crisis' that precipitated *Working for Patients* and the introduction of the internal market was a product of insufficient resources rather than any 'new problems' in the system for allocating such resources.

Can we afford the NHS? This is ultimately a matter of choice based on a combination of empirical evidence and value judgements. Looking at consumer expenditure patterns, it might be presumed that if we can spend £24 billion per annum on alcohol and £11 billion per annum on tobacco, that we could afford £40 billion per annum on a national health service. And if we cannot afford the NHS, can we afford what would replace it? International comparisons indicate that most other health care systems require more resources.

The UK is not an over-taxed nation, at least on some of the more obvious measures. Comparisons of taxes and social security contributions as percentage of GDP and GNP place the UK roughly halfway down the relevant OECD league tables (see CSO, 1995, pp. 37 and 38) a little higher than Portugal and Spain, but lower than Austria, Belgium, Canada, Denmark, Finland, France, Germany, Iceland, Irish Republic, Italy, Netherlands, Norway and Sweden (see CSO, 1995, pp. 37 and 38). Furthermore, it would seem that the NHS makes a valuable contribution to this lower level of taxes and social security contributions by significantly moderating the UK's expenditure on health care. The latter, as a percentage of GDP, has been consistently well below the OECD average for at least a quarter of a century. From 1970 to 1990 only Greece and Turkey (amongst OECD countries) consistently recorded lower health care expenditures than the UK (relative to GDP). On these measures the most market orientated system (the USA) emerges as the most expensive, and a marked divergence between Canada and the USA can be seen when the former moves away from a USA-type model of health care (see Ensor, 1993, pp. 41–2, 66).

The comparative figures on taxes, social security contributions and health care expenditure suggest that the NHS is only a 'public burden' in relation to some theoretical world where health care demands and needs are much less than they are at present. On international evidence a different mix of public and private health care provision would increase the 'burden' of health care costs on the economy as a whole and on many individual households. Since the USA spends a similar proportion of its GDP on a residual model of state health care for older and poorer people only, the savings in tax expenditure on health care by abandoning the NHS would seem to be relatively modest.

How should we pay for the NHS? One solution has been to suggest hypothecating taxation or raising National Insurance. Hypothecating taxation means earmarking taxation specifically for health services. This keeps the universal principle but has always been resisted by the Treasury – if for health, then why not for education or housing? Is it worth pursuing some sort of 'middle way' in which the basic format of the NHS is retained, but a much more significant source of its revenue is user-charges? There are usually five main purposes to charging, all of which are mixed up and often never made explicit. Either to raise revenue, or to reduce demand or to shift priorities or to check abuse, or the symbolic purpose of emphasising to people their responsibilities (Parker, 1976; see, also, Ensor, 1993, pp. 25–30). This multi-purpose remedy of charges fits in with a philosophy of independence based on the individualist notion of 'paying one's own way in life', but it is only useful where it is easy to calculate and collect and where there are marginal users, that is people who are 'not really sick'. Charging is clearly problematic where it is not appropriate that consumption be discouraged, for example vaccination; and where notions of social justice are affronted, that is charging the war injured, the chronically sick and the disabled. The problems of taking an equitable approach to user-charges, and remission of charges, was summed up many years ago by Titmuss. The statistics and some of the terminology, may have changed but the essential elements in the argument remain. He began by asking

should all ... victims of industrial accidents and their families ... be charged ... with part of ... (their health care) ... costs, and be means-tested to decide whether the charge should be remitted ... (and) ... if industrial accidents and diseases are to be excluded ... (from charges) ... though there is an appallingly difficult medical problem of diagnosis, attribution and checking in distinguishing these medical needs from other medical needs ... what about road accidents, medical error, cross-infection in hospitals, and many other categories of accidents and disease? How would one justify and administer charges and means-tests for a variety of services for some groups (eg: on criteria of occupational causation) and not for others? ... What about the war disabled, war widows and industrial widows, the blind, the mentally retarded, the mentally ill ... the large number of over-70s in hospital, those who die in hospital, those with infectious diseases, the tubercular, the chronic bronchitic victims of the coal mines and other industries, the unemployed and their families, unmarried mothers, deprived children, fatherless families, and so on and so on ... where in the end does one draw the line among over 5 million inpatient cases and over 35 million outpatient attendances annually and how often ... if equity is to be served ... then the content, scope, characteristics and frequency of means-tests and charges must differ according to the type of service provided. Different rules must apply to different groups in different circumstances for different types of services. There is no standardised answer. (Titmuss, 1968, pp. 117–18).

In the end there are few clear-cut cases for user-charges, many cases for exemptions and with the latter substantial administrative costs in operating such exemption systems (see Chapter 11 for a further discussion of this).

User-charges usually form part of another answer to 'the problem' that is canvassed; this is 'topping up' (see *Health Care 2000)*. Taxation remains the principal source of funding but some have suggested that it is unrealistic to close the gap between current provision and future aspirations by tax funding alone, arguing that instead there should be increased private expenditure. Taxation would fund a core set of services, with individuals allowed to buy additional services if necessary, with a range of user charges and patient co-payments as part of the system. The result would seem to be discretionary expenditure on the NHS, but the problem with discretion is that it can lead to inequity. *The Times* commenting on the proposals in *Health Care 2000* said:

This would represent a dilution of the principles of the NHS. The core would undoubtedly be whittled down. To pay to jump the queue means people languishing on waiting lists. (Leading Article, *The Times*, 19/9/95)

For the moment at least the NHS remains a very popular public institution and one for which most people seem prepared to pay. The *British Social Attitude Survey* has found that

despite all the political exhortations in recent years, which stress the desirability of cutting State spending, the public still wants Government expenditure on the NHS to be increased ... there remains persistent – and indeed increasing – support for the idea of a universal service. (Bosanquet, 1989, p. 102; see, also Klein, 1995a, p. 157)

Other things may have changed, some rather significantly, but the wartime 'near consensus' has held. The Beveridge Report was principally about social security and even there the 'Back to Beveridge' model has its place in contemporary debates. But when that Report ventured into health care and proposed a genuinely universalist and comprehensive service it identified a concept that has continued to have a particular resonance for successive generations of patients, voters and indeed politicians.

But this support for the principles of the NHS may be combined with dissatisfaction with the service actually provided. This high satisfaction for the performance of health workers, but concerns about staffing, organisation and the ability to deliver treatment at an acceptable speed, is apparent. A common concern is that in the 'generally managed' internal market of the current NHS, one's attitude to the Service may 'depend more on where you live than on what you believe in principle'; that 'NHS funding will come to be seen as a series of local problems' (Bosanquet, 1993, pp. 219, 218).

Conclusions

Histories of the more competitive (pre-NHS) environment in British health care tended towards conclusions that it 'did not bring economy' but rather led to 'uselessly expensive adminis- tration', to 'waste' and to 'behaviour which had no discernible relevance to medical needs' (see Eckstein, 1958, p. 68 and Gilbert, 1970, p. 300). There is no doubt that the recent revival of compet- itive elements in British health care has generated a rather similar set of concerns, especially since the deficiencies of markets in health care are widely recognised and the state supported NHS has become a dominant guarantor of such care in the UK.

The state as guarantor has moved from being the sole source of finance and provision of care (with a small private sector, with up to 10 per cent of the population covered by company schemes) to being a source of finance but allowing an internal quasi- or managed-market to deliver health care. Such a compromise between a full-blooded state monopoly and an equivalent free market has been arrived at in the last few years following the 1991 reorganization of the NHS (see Chapter 7). Whereas at first sight this appeared to be an attempt to replace state dominance with private market principles it has, within the first few years, settled down to a halfway house of state finance through general taxation and quasi-market relations in purchasing, administration and local assessment of need. Even the most radical of Conservative Prime Ministers (Mrs.Thatcher) was obviously unable to convince her government, her party and the general public that an attack on the presumed drawbacks of state provision (monopoly, inflexibility, bureaucracy, providers concerns more dominant than consumer interests) was so serious that a wholesale switch to a free market arrangement was preferable. In the end, the introduction of the 'internal market' may be most appropriately viewed as the latest, and most radical, attempt to reorganise the internal workings of the NHS (see Chapters 5 and 14). Indeed what the NHS Executive described as 'the final stage of the NHS reforms introduced in 1991' involved a conventional organizational restructuring in which the Regional Health Authorities disappeared (to be replaced by eight regional offices of the NHS Executive) and District Health Authorities and Family Health Service Authorities were to be merged to form new health authorities (NHS Executive, 1993, p. 2). Some might see this as the long-delayed implementation of key elements of the First Green Paper (Ministry of Health, 1968). This NHS reform takes place in parallel with the introduction of unitary local authorities across much of the country – one of the recommendations of the Royal Commission on Local Government in England (1969).

For the moment the rights of NHS users and the responsibilities of the state remain broadly unchanged – the key issue remaining the volume of resources the state is willing to commit to the NHS in recognition of these rights and responsibilities.

So, we remain with a universal service, tax funded but with resources rationed, and audited as to their effective use, openly and explicitly. There is public knowledge not only of rationing in the form of queues, waiting lists and waiting times, but also of the denial of certain services to elderly people, intensive care for example; the rationing of renal dialysis; smokers being refused coronary bypass artery grafts; and alcoholics being refused liver transplants. Is the comprehensive service under siege in the face of acknowledged scarcity?

We can begin a process of assessing what is effective and appropriate while keeping the state's commitment to a universal service (see Chapter 10). We can maintain the Beveridge and Bevan principles and the commitment to the collectivist approach. With regard to what is effective and appropriate, the key questions that are still asked by professionals are 'will the treatment benefit the patient?' This is clearly a question of clinical audit. If the treatment is paid for, who else is denied – this is the economic question of opportunity costs. How have resources been distributed to the community as a whole? This is not just an economic question but also an ethical one. Is the case approving experimental treatment one to be defended, in case it works – a question of science and high quality protocols (and there has been much activity on the latter since 1991, see, Klein, 1995b, p. 323).

Subsequent to the publication of *Health Care 2000* the case has been made that a commitment to universalist, comprehensive and evidence-based health care is eminently affordable. We can afford the NHS; we are frugal spenders compared with other industrial countries (see for example, Ensor, 1993). Efficient, effective and equitable spending decisions are needed and that will need a combination of economic and ethical thinking. There is the recurrent fear of elderly people as a 'burden', but this is much exaggerated. Only 3.5 per cent of the population will be over 85 years of age by the year 2031; this is something that can be planned for over a 35-year period. The law at the present will not support forcing Health Authorities to spend in specific ways unless their decisions are obviously unreasonable. Our own consumer spending decisions might be subject to deterrent taxation on health damaging products, and finally, technology has to be evaluated by audit and the results published and openly debated. And if a universalist, comprehensive and evidence-based NHS is affordable we might reasonably oppose attempts to rewrite the Beveridge commitments in the following way.

A comprehensive National Health Service might, if resources are available, be offered to those who can prove they are citizens of the U.K. in the form judged most appropriate by the medical profession after considering all other calls upon scarce resources. Responsibility for organising the service, funding the service and employing Health Service staff shall be the legal duty of the Treasury whilst the Chancellor of the Exchequer can if he deems it necessary veto any policy of the Minister of Health. Although the National Health Service shall be funded out of general taxation, charges for non-life threatening episodes requiring medical advice and treatment, shall be levied, at the discretion of the DHA, Trust Hospital or General Practice Fund Holder, and be enforceable at law. Self-induced ill-health or injury through health-threatening activities, for example, smoking, excessive drinking, unsafe sex or dangerous sports shall be paid for by an additional levy on the National Insurance Contributions by the individual concerned. The local Director of Health shall have the responsibility to assess on behalf of the DHA and the Trust and the General Practice Fund Holder which individuals shall be so charged. Individuals will be allowed to top up the health care they are entitled to receive by additional contributions. Such topping up once agreed, will be reflected in different waiting times for top-up and non-top-up patients.

(Given the change of government in May 1997 it seems that the above policy agenda for the NHS has been ruled out for the foreseeable future (see, our discussion of New Labour in the Postscript to this book). Of course this does not exclude the possibility of these ideas being revived at some future stage.)

9
London

Medical facilities were completely unorganised and virtually uncontrolled, except in the immediate vicinity of London. (Woodward, 1974, p. 2, with regard to the late seventeenth century)

The conditions in London hospitals appear to have been worse than those in provincial hospitals. (Woodward, 1974, p. 101, with regard to the late eighteenth century)

Urban poverty, especially in London, attracted more attention and alarm than that in the countryside, and poorer rural areas were last to receive adequate schooling, housing, sanitation or other services – not to mention adequate wages. (Thane, 1982, p. 8, with regard to the late nineteenth century)

During much of the twentieth century, the capital's hospital services, medical education and clinical research have been fixed in a gridlock imposed by history, buildings, institutions and the fierce loyalties each has engendered. (Kings Fund, 1992a, p. 66)

We conclude the first part of the book with a case-study – an examination of the health care problems of London. London health services serve as a useful example of some of the key themes that have emerged so far. They also pose some interesting problems of interpretation, represented by our opening (historical) quotations, in which a greater attention and concern for the health care needs of the capital city sits alongside service quality which is in some respects superior and in other respects inferior to provincial provision.

As with the rest of Part One, we have taken an historical perspective to London's health care provision and problems. This will indicate the enduring qualities of the debates concerning health services in London. These include, firstly, the apparent disparity between the resources in London and the rest of the country, but also the disparities within London itself most graphically illustrated by the concentration of high quality acute hospital resources in a relatively small area in central London – a spatial and service inequality.

Secondly, the role of the medical profession in influencing health service organization will emerge as a potentially important theme in understanding changes (and the absence of changes) in London's health services. As the location, throughout the period under review, of the majority of the country's teaching hospitals, London has also been home to the major organizations of the medical profession (BMA, GMC and the Royal Colleges) and has been seen as the location of the medical establishment. As such, the doctors based in the London teaching hospitals have been seen as the most influential section of what has been regarded as the most influential of the health professions (and indeed one of the most influential of professional groups). We have noted their influence on successive organizational arrangements for the NHS (see especially Chapters 4 and 6). In this chapter we can concentrate more specifically on how well the health care needs of Londoners have been served by the organizational structures which owed a good deal to the views of at least some London-based doctors.

Thirdly, London's health services provide good examples of the conflicts that have been an integral part of the development of health care in the UK; between the aspirations of professionals, politicians and the public and the limitations of essentially voluntary institutions; between the ideals of 'rational planning' and 'professional autonomy'; between the concept of a National Health Service and the demands of private practice; between hospital and community-based health services; between territorial justice and centres of excellence.

Social assistance and voluntarism

London was the world's largest city and the capital of its greatest empire during the period 1850 to 1930, when the emergence of bio-medical science prompted the construction of hospitals throughout the industrialised world. (Kings Fund, 1992a, p. 22)

As we have seen, paupers had access to medical treatment by virtue of the Elizabethan Poor Law of 1601 (Chapter 1) and in the first half of the eighteenth century, 50 of the 155 workhouses in Great Britain were in London (Woodward, 1974, p. 4). By the 1780s there were seven general hospitals in London contributing to a situation where there were as many hospital beds in London as the whole of the rest of England and Wales (Abel-Smith, 1964, pp. 4–5, see also, Woodward, 1974, p. 36). In 1861 there were three times as many beds per thousand population in London as there were in the provinces (Pinker, 1966, p. 84). As well as having a significant proportion of the beds in voluntary hospitals (35 per cent in 1861, see Pinker, 1966, p. 81), London had a higher proportion of beds in public hospitals per thousand population (0.76 compared to 0.34 in 1891, see Pinker, 1966, p. 90). It was also in London that 'the greatest improvements in furnishing hospital service to the poor' took place and by 1877 'only six London parishes housed their sick poor in mixed workhouses' (Brand, 1965, p. 95; see also, Abel-Smith, 1964, p. 127). Finally it was in London in the 1880s, that the first demands for some system of hospital planning were voiced – this being partly attributable to the sheer volume of hospital resources in the capital (Abel-Smith, 1964, p. 161).

Part of this considerable volume of hospital resources was a significant preponderance of teaching hospitals. By 1858, there were twelve London hospitals with medical schools and 80 per cent of the general hospital beds in London were in teaching hospitals (Abel-Smith, 1964, pp. 17–18). Furthermore this considerable quantity of distinctive hospital resources was also associated with profound spatial inequalities within London itself. Thus:

a voluntary hospital, it was thought, had to be within easy coaching distance from the centres of private consulting practice. Thus, where there were fewest poor was the greatest provision for them. Within a radius of a mile from the Middlesex Hospital there were eight general and twenty-six special hospitals. (Abel-Smith, 1964, p. 161).

Those factors that led to a concentration of voluntary hospital resources in London and other major areas of population (Chapter 1), led also to a further concentration of those resources within London itself. In marked contrast to this concentration in inner London, continuing care developed on the outskirts of London leading to 'the great concentrations of psychiatric and mental handicap hospitals in Hertfordshire and places like Epsom' (Kings Fund, 1992, pp. 22–3). All this posed particular problems for any notion of 'rational planning' of health care for London.

One such attempt to rationalise the provision of health care in London – at least for the poor – came in the form of the Metropolitan Poor Act of 1867. This provided for the establishment of district infirmaries, formed by combined parish action, for the sick, infirm or insane. A Metropolitan Asylums Board was set up to 'superintend the new facilities' (Brand, 1965, p. 87). Another historic precursor of more recent publications was the petition presented to the House of Lords on 29 July 1889 calling for an inquiry into 'the financial and general management and the common organization of medical institutions ... (and) ... Poor law institutions for the aid of the sick in the Metropolis' (Hansard (H of L), Vol. CCCXXXVIII, 29 July 1889, col.1548, see also Abel-Smith, 1964, pp. 163–5). A House of Lords Committee was subsequently set up, accumulating a substantial body of evidence before reporting in 1892 – the first of seventeen enquiries into London's health care over a one hundred year period (see Kings Fund, 1992, pp. 27–9).

Some of the evidence taken by the Committee identified the need for co-ordination and planned development and the Committee recommended that a central board be set up, although with 'no statutory powers as regards the formal licensing of any hospital built, or about to be built'. However the board would receive audited copies of accounts and statistics, report on proposals for new hospitals and hopefully 'have a powerful influence on preventing the building of useless hospitals' (House of Lords Select Committee on Metropolitan Hospitals, 1890–93, Third Report, p.cv and p.cvii; quoted in Abel-Smith, 1964).

The report had no immediate effect; 'it was one thing to show that some central board was needed but quite another to get one set up, in view of the rivalry and jealousy of the different hospital authorities' (Abel-Smith, 1964, p. 173). However within five years of its publication, the recommendation for a central board was effectively implemented by the establishment of The Prince of Wales's Hospital Fund for London to commemorate the Sixtieth Year of the Queen's Reign (later The King Edward's Hospital Fund for London). 'What was impossible by any other means was achieved through the almost mystical influence of the monarchy' (Abel-Smith, 1964, p. 182). Tasks undertaken by the Fund included the amalgamation of small hospitals 'by persuasion backed up by the promise of substantial grants'. By these means the three orthopaedic hospitals were amalgamated between 1903 and 1906, but it was only possible to get two of the five ear, nose and throat hospitals to amalgamate. In addition, money was given to enable two hospitals to move south of the River Thames. However when, in 1906, the Treasurer of St.George's Hospital wanted to move the hospital from Hyde Park Corner, he could not gain the support of the governors. Whilst the Fund could perhaps prevent the situation getting worse, it could, for example, 'do nothing to plan a rational division of responsibilities between the voluntary hospitals and public infirmaries' (see Abel-Smith, 1964, pp. 183–5).

In 1902 a plan was announced involving the establishment of a central medical institute in South Kensington to take over the teaching of the basic sciences to medical students from the medical schools. After a substantial sum of money had been collected the scheme was rejected by the Medical Faculty of the University due 'partly to jealousy of University and King's College' (Young, 1968, p. 298).

Social insurance and local government

At the time the major social insurance measure of the New Liberalism was being enacted the characteristic London hospital was still a teaching or special establishment. By contrast 'in the provinces general hospitals were the more usual form of accommodation' (Pinker, 1966, p. 82). Indeed general hospital provision remained relatively limited 'and it was not until 1938 that general provision exceeded teaching provision in the metropolis' (Pinker, 1966, p. 83). In terms of overall provision the general disparity between London and the provinces (as measured by beds per 1000 population) diminished in this period. By 1921 the amount of voluntary hospital accommodation was nearly 50 per cent higher than in 1891, but over the same time period the number of provincial beds had more than doubled. The gap continued to be narrowed during the 1920s and 1930s (see Pinker, 1966, pp. 83–6).

When the offices and institutions of the Poor Law were transferred to local government by 1 April 1930 (following the Local Government Act, 1929) the London County Council (LCC) was in a position to take a systematic approach to its extensive range of hospital facilities – a total of 77,000 beds compared to the 14,000 in the voluntary hospitals within the LCC boundaries (see Abel-Smith, 1964, pp. 368–73). 'It was the largest municipal hospital system in the world' (Kings Fund, 1992a, p. 24).

The London teaching hospitals figured in another planning initiative when they ran into financial difficulties in 1938 due to the rising costs of medical education and the growing demands for pay from hospital doctors (see Chapter 2; see also Honigsbaum, 1989, p. 16). It became apparent that the Ministry of Health wanted the LCC to resolve the problem and by so doing facilitate co-operation between municipal and voluntary hospitals; 'perhaps even force the closure of inefficient units'. In addition the Ministry did not want to single out the London teaching hospitals 'since it was felt that London had too many medical schools' (Honigsbaum, 1989, p. 16). In the event no action was taken and the immediate financial difficulties of the hospitals were resolved by the introduction of the Emergency Medical Service (see Chapter 3). One indicator of the continuing dominance of London in certain areas of health care – and of the wider problem of territorial injustices in the distribution of health services – was the location of specialist doctors, more than one third of whom were still based in the capital in 1939 (Stevens, 1966, p. 3)

War and welfare

The administrative arrangements for the EMS in London paid particular attention to the interests of the voluntary hospitals. London was divided into ten sectors radiating from Charing Cross, each including a teaching hospital. This scheme 'enabled the teaching hospitals to preserve their natural catchment areas ... but did nothing to promote co-operation among themselves or with LCC hospitals' (Honigsbaum, 1989, p. 17, see also p. 171). When the Goodenough Committee were reviewing postgraduate medical education in London in 1944 they talked in terms of '*the* hospital authority for London' (see Royal Commission on Medical Education, 1968, p. 183, our emphasis) – indicating the more 'rational' approach to health care organization that might be anticipated when the National Health Service was set up. Any such expectation was not realised by events.

Political parties and pressure groups
The distinctive approach taken by the EMS in London was retained in the arrangements designed for London's hospital services when the NHS was established. The non-teaching hospitals would be administered by four separate Regional Hospital Boards (Honigsbaum, 1989, p. 144). With London's twelve undergraduate teaching hospitals under separately-administered boards of governors, the scene was set for an administrative arrangement that could have been designed explicitly to prevent any significant amelioration of the problems that had been inherited by the new Service with regard to both resource allocation in London, and between London and the provinces. There seems little doubt that this administrative system was designed to accommodate the concerns of those who staffed the London teaching hospitals (see Honigsbaum, 1989, p. 171). Not only was London carved into four hospital regions but

> the bulk of the inner city acute services were provided by 12 undergraduate teaching hospitals and 14 postgraduate teaching hospitals, each of which had their own Board of Governors. In the regions which had their own teaching hospital, the problems of concerted planning did not pose major problems. But in London they were formidable. (Abel-Smith, 1978, p. 36)

Given the distinctive history of health care in the capital, it was paradoxical that the commitment to 'rational planning' represented by the NHS should do nothing to facilitate the sort of London-wide health service planning that was long overdue.

Efficiency and equity

> The varied and accidental factors that led to the foundation of the twelve main London undergraduate teaching hospitals and their associated medical schools could not be expected to have produced a pattern of distribution of hospitals that would be the most appropriate for the purposes of modern medical education. (Royal Commission on Medical Education, 1968, pp. 196–7)

We have already noted the significance of historic cost budgeting (Chapter 5) which led to NHS funding being significantly determined by the historical pattern of health service provision. The outcome was that traditionally well-endowed areas like central London maintained that position within the NHS (Benzeval, Judge and New, 1991, p. 26). The 1962 Hospital Plan did little to redress the imbalance of resources between central London, the Home Counties and the rest of the country. The rebuilding of teaching hospitals was given priority in the plan – because of the need to expand medical education – and within that priority the emphasis was on the cheaper option of expanding existing institutions. The result was that:

> nearly all the twelve London undergraduate teaching hospitals were rebuilt on their existing sites or only a few miles further out from the centre. While the population of central London declined and there was a rapid growth of population beyond the green belt, London's teaching hospitals were expanded all within easy reach of Harley Street. (Abel-Smith, 1990, p. 13)

This continuing concentration of a particular set of health care resources in London was not matched by complementary community health services. London gained proportionately less than other parts of the country from the 'health centre boom' of the late 1960s and early 1970s (Chapter 5). The Royal Commission on the NHS would subsequently note that the increase in health centres had been less rapid in conurbations generally, and that within that category Greater London appeared to be faring worse than other conurbations (eg: Greater Manchester) (see Royal Commission on NHS, 1979, pp. 86–7)

In 1968 the Royal Commission on Medical Education identified the continuing pre-eminence of the London medical schools, which at the time were teaching nearly one-half of those graduating in medicine at British universities (Royal Commission on Medical Education, 1968, p. 171). With so many medical schools in London in competition for funds, the Commission expressed themselves unsurprised that despite much goodwill, each of the medical schools in London has found great difficulty during the past thirty years or so in attracting financial support comparable with that made available to other medical schools in other British centres (Royal Commission on Medical Education, 1968, p. 174). This, the Commission concluded, should not be allowed to continue. The general pattern of the London medical schools was 'no longer satisfactory' and the 'present number of separate medical schools in London is ... no longer desirable or ... possible'; the Commission identified the need for a 'comprehensive and rational plan for future development in London' without which 'rebuilding could involve waste of scarce national resources, not only of money but of human skill and effort' (Royal Commission on Medical Education, 1968, pp. 172, 175, 177).

The Commissions 'radical reorganization' involved reducing the number of undergraduate medical schools in London by six involving a series of amalgamations (eg: St.Bartholomew's Hospital Medical College with the London Hospital Medical College). Each of the new medical schools formed by these mergers would become a faculty of medicine of a multi-faculty university institution (see Royal Commission on Medical Education, 1978, pp. 175, 177–8). When the Commission turned its attention to the organization of postgraduate medical education it found a similar situation. Major problems persisted, despite the lengthy consideration that had been given to the issues (now approaching a quarter of a century). The Commission's conclusion was that 'only a small minority of the postgraduate institutions and their associated hospitals are housed in reasonably modern and adequate buildings'; this was another set of circumstances which 'clearly cannot be allowed to continue indefinitely' (Royal Commission on Medical Education, 1978, p. 185). It was the Commission's view that the postgraduate institutes should for all academic, financial and administrative purposes become an integral part of the reorganised medical schools.

The commitment to more equitable funding of the NHS represented by the RAWP process (Chapter 5) involved an attempt to 'redress the imbalance created by historical patterns of funding by shifting resources away from London to the North and North-West' (Benzeval, Judge and New, 1991, p. 26). In fact the implications of the RAWP approach were more complex than this since the same analysis that showed the Thames Regional Health Authorities had more resources relative to the populations they serve than the rest of the country, also confirmed that much of this apparent over-provision was

> focused geographically upon Inner London, and functionally upon the group of services known as Local Acute Hospital Services and, in some districts, upon other services as well, such as those for the mentally ill and handicapped. (Kings Fund, 1987, p. 3)

The result was resource allocation policies designed to re-allocate resources both *away from* the Thames regions *and within* the Thames regions – from central London to outer London and the home counties. The resulting 'squeeze on health services in London . . . contributed to the closure of a number of smaller local hospitals' with sixty-two smaller hospitals being closed in the London area between 1979 and 1987 (see Kings Fund, 1992a, pp. 30, 32–3).

The Royal Commission on the NHS reviewed and restated the particular problems of health care in London. These included the high proportion of single-handed GPs (almost twice the national average), shortages of nursing staff, and the use of GP deputising services. It concluded that in parts of London the NHS 'is failing dismally to provide an adequate primary care service to its patients' (Royal Commission on the NHS, 1979, p. 89). Ameliorative policies and practices identified included financial inducements to attract GPs and other health personnel to work in inner London, health authorities giving priority to building health centres in 'health-deprived' localities, and experimenting with salaried appointments with reduced list sizes to attract groups of doctors to work in them. The Commission suggested that teaching hospitals have not always taken appropriate responsibility for fostering and improving the quality of primary care services in their surrounding areas. The Commission recognised that the expenditure of health authorities in London was being adversely affected by the application of the RAWP formula, but urged the London RHAs to make additional provision for distributing funds for primary care services to inner city AHAs (see Royal Commission on the NHS, 1979, pp. 89–90).

They also noted a longer term major failure of previous planning, that despite the recommendations of the Royal Commission on Medical Education (1968), little progress had been made in reducing the number of medical schools in London. They concluded that 'there is still an excessive concentration of teaching and research facilities in London and more hospitals than its population need' (Royal Commission on NHS, 1979, p. 274). The recommendation of the Royal Commission was that an independent enquiry should be set up to consider the special health service problems of London. The latter were identified as including the following:

the administration of the postgraduate teaching hospitals;
whether London needs four RHAs;
whether some special adjustment to the RAWP formula is required to take account of the high concentration of teaching hospitals in London; and
what additional measures can be devised to deal with the special difficulties of providing primary care services and joint planning in London. (see Royal Commission on the NHS, 1979, p. 282)

Reorganizations

It was not until 1974 ... that most of London's teaching hospitals accepted responsibility for providing a full range of hospital services to their local populations. (Kings Fund, 1992a, p. 25)

As with the Service as a whole, the themes identified in Chapters 5 and 6 have a particular significance for what has happened to the health services in London. Alongside the *over-provision* of acute hospital services in inner London there was the *under-provision* of community health services – a particularly graphic example of the failure to plan effectively for a more efficient and equitable health service. The particular organizational structure bequeathed to London by the political compromises of 1945–1948 was a potentially major obstacle to such planning.

To the universal problems posed by 'tripartism' (see Chapter 6), were added the division of London between four regional hospital boards and the presence within those regions, and particularly within London, of a larger number of relatively autonomous units associated with the teaching hospitals. Whether the RHBs would be able to carry out their functions of planning hospital and specialist medical services in these circumstances was questionable.

A new pattern of local government was established for London in 1966 following a Royal Commission. But although the Commission had to take account of issues relating to local authority health services, they did not have to consider the rest of the 'tripartite' NHS (see Royal Commission on Local Government in Greater London, 1960). A subsequent Royal Commission – this time on medical education – criticised the arrangement where there were thirty separate hospital authorities in the territory of the four Metropolitan regions each with its own finance and direct access to the Minister of Health. It did not, in the Commission's view, lead to either 'efficiency or to economy in the provision of clinical facilities for medical education'; nor did this arrangement serve the needs of other areas of hospital and health care planning (Royal Commission on Medical Education, 1968, pp. 195, 197).

The Commission's key recommendation on this matter was that 'the teaching hospitals in England and Wales should be brought within the framework of administration of the regional hospital service' to be accommodated in London by having five rather than four metropolitan regional hospital boards, if possible with boundaries coterminous with local authorities; and in an historical parallel with the central board proposed in 1892/93, the Commission proposed the establishment of a Committee for Medical Education in London which would take general responsibility for the implementation of all aspects of the complete plan for London (see Royal Commission on Medical Education, 1968, p. 198, para.479 and p. 201). Despite the 1974 reorganization the Royal Commission on the NHS made further critical comment on the arrangements in London noting that 'problems arise through the lack of coterminosity which affects 12 out of 16 London AHAs' (Royal Commission on the NHS, 1979, p. 325).

Benzeval and others effectively summarised the views of commentators, committees and commissions with their observation that:

> the fragmentation of responsibility between a multiplicity of regional, district, family health services and special health authorities means that the development of a coherent plan for health services in the capital has proved extremely difficult. (Benzeval, Judge and New, 1991, p. 31)

For many of those commentators, committee and commission members it was far from clear that an internal market of the sort proposed in Working for Patients would be any more successful in developing a coherent set of services for the capital.

Managers and markets

> There is no shared, positive vision of what London's health services ought to be like. (Maxwell, 1990)

> In relative terms, London is over-endowed with acute hospitals, poorly provided with community health services and lacks the organizational capacity to deal with the complex issues it faces at a strategic level high enough to make the impact which is required. (Benzeval, Judge and New, 1991, p. 25)

In 1980 the London Health Planning Consortium (LHPC) drew attention yet again to the concentration and fragmentation of acute speciality medicine and surgery in London – and the continuing inadequacy of primary care in London (LHPC, 1980). Meanwhile the Flowers Report recommended the formation of six schools of medicine and dentistry out of the existing thirty-four schools; and the integration of postgraduate institutes with general medical schools (Flowers Report, 1980). Also in the same year a

Fabian Tract emphasised again the problems posed by the administrative arrangements for NHS health care in London (Carrier, 1980, pp. 31–4).

The following year the LHPC published its major review of primary health care services in inner London chaired by Sir Donald Acheson (LHPC, 1981). The report confirmed much of the analysis of the Royal Commission including the large numbers of single-handed GPs; large number of GPs with small list sizes; unsuitable premises; a lack of support staff; problems of accessibility and availability of GPs and a lack of co-ordination with hospital services; and poor medical education in general practice. One conclusion was that

> in areas with major social problems the primary care services are less well organised to cope with the extra burdens involved in caring for patients in the community and many more people end up being treated in hospital (LHPC, 1981, p. 19; see also, Jarman, 1981, pp. 2–4).

Also published in 1981 were the reports of the London Advisory Group chaired by Sir John Habakkuk. Recommendations included reductions in acute beds to free resources for mental health services and services for elderly people – including more community-based provision (see London Advisory Group, 1981).

Between 1982 and 1989 the continuing effects of the RAWP policies were demonstrable in London with a reduction of 3,700 acute services beds in inner London – a faster rate of decline than that experienced nationally. However despite this decline in bed numbers, specialist provision and medical staffing levels in teaching hospitals remained much as before – the reductions affected general medical and surgical beds, leaving specialist provision relatively unaffected (see Kings Fund, 1992a, pp. 30–1, 52).

In 1987, the Kings Fund published a report commissioned by the Chairmen of the ten DHAs covering inner London. It covered the planning period 1983/84 to 1993/94 and its Foreword included the interesting observation that there was an absence of a systematic factual basis against which to judge the current concerns about London's health services being expressed by Health Authority members, NHS staff and the general public (Kings Fund, 1987,

p. iii). Given that observation, one of the Report's central con-clusions was perhaps less startling than it might otherwise have been; this was that

> it is not in fact possible to draw a coherent and comprehensive picture of inner London's future health services from the published plans of the four Regions, nor indeed from the unpublished documents to which we have had access. (Kings Fund, 1987, pp. iii, 1)

As well as providing a further reminder that 'the populations of districts in Inner London are relatively deprived compared with many other parts of the country', the Report also confirmed the long-expressed concern that the regional authorities (now the RHAs) had not been able to co-ordinate their approach to planning on a London-wide basis (Kings Fund, 1987, p. 9 and p. iii). The Report's detailed analysis of then current plans and trends was particularly disturbing. Substantial bed reductions had occurred in inner London's local acute services prior to the planning period under review; and the then current RHA plans involved further reductions. These planned reductions were based on a projected decline in hospital admissions in inner London. However not only were the planned service reductions proceeding at an alarming rate – 74 per cent of planned 10-year bed reductions occurring within the first two years of the plan – but were also yielding substantially less spending reductions than had been anticipated – only 34.5 per cent of the planned reduction in spending had been achieved by undertaking 74 per cent of the planned reduction in beds. Furthermore this reduction in beds was taking place against a background of an *actual increase* rather than the *anticipated decrease* in hospital admissions – perhaps an indication of the continuing limitations of London's community health services and the social and economic circumstances of at least some inner-city areas. One conclusion was that

> either more than the planned reduction in local acute services will be required to release the required resources, or revenue reductions may have to be extended to priority services (see Kings Fund, 1987, pp. iii–iv, 12).

Given that effective investment in priority services was one policy which might facilitate the anticipated, but not yet realised, reduction in hospital admissions, there appeared to be considerable potential for an emerging 'crisis' in London's health services – combining both 'over-spending' and 'insufficient services'.

In December 1990 the Kings Fund appointed a Commission 'to examine the future of acute health services in London' in response to growing concern about the future of health services in the capital. Its terms of reference required it to 'develop a broad vision of the pattern of acute services that would make sense for London in the coming decade and the early years of the next century' (Kings Fund, 1992a, p. 15, 104). The Commission's report on health services, medical education and research in London was published in June 1992. Its conclusions about policies during the 1980s were particularly scathing:

> What has happened to the capital's hospitals since 1980 has been almost the worst of all possible worlds; acute specialities have retained their grip on the capital's hospitals; there has been virtually no redistribution of medical manpower away from central London despite the decline in bed numbers; and little progress has been made in concentrating specialist resources into fewer, stronger centres. (Kings Fund, 1992a, p. 58)

The key issues identified in the report were inevitably an updated re-statement of points identified in previous reports regarding the concentration of acute hospitals in central London; inadequate primary, community and continuing care; poor linkages between London's medical schools and the rest of London University; fragmented and inadequately supported specialist and clinical research units; ageing buildings and equipment; and inadequate management and planning structures for London. (see Kings Fund, 1992a, pp. 22,26,34).

Despite the operation of the RAWP criteria, and the very limited role played by London as a national referral centre, it was noted that around 20 per cent of all English hospital and community health services expenditure was devoted to London which contained 15 per cent of the relevant population. This calculation excluded the expenditure on London's Special Health Authorities, which also had a largely London-based caseload. Health care in inner London was costing 45 per cent more than the national average – contributory factors to the latter would include a longer average length of stay in hospital and a much more marked difference between teaching and non-teaching hospital costs in London than elsewhere (see Kings Fund, 1992a, pp. 9, 30, 45, 46, 48, 51, 52).

Concerns about the effectiveness of this higher spending were related to a number of issues. Firstly, competition between, and the duplication and fragmentation of, specialist expertise and equipment – for example four cardiothoracic surgery services, three renal units, three plastic surgery centres and three sites for radiotherapy services were operating within three miles of one another in south-east London (see for example, Kings Fund, 1992a, p. 63). Secondly, the dissatisfaction with their health services expressed by Londoners (Kings Fund, 1992a, pp. 9, 42). Thirdly, there was also evidence of problems of access to standard hospital services for inner London residents and to specialist hospital services for outer London residents (Kings Fund, 1992a, pp. 53,69). Finally, the overall higher spending co-existed with relatively lower spending on, for example, family health services and drugs; and

> much less comprehensively developed primary and community health services than other parts of the country ... with frail elderly and homeless people, and those with mental health problems ... (receiving) ... a distinctly poor service (Kings Fund, 1992a, pp. 9,54,55,56,69).

The continuing major role of London based medical education – approximately one-third of all medical students in the UK were still being trained in London – was identified as problematic in terms of fragmented research efforts, poorly developed formal postgraduate training opportunities and the quality of educational opportunities offered in an environment where bed numbers had declined significantly and further significant reductions were planned. All this was despite 'a succession of policy recommendations urging closer association between the medical schools and the multi-faculty colleges of London University' (Kings Fund, 1992a, pp. 10,60,61, 64–6).

If much of this was familiar, if somewhat depressing, to readers of the Royal Commission Reports of 1968 and 1979, the new report was able to add a significant new dimension in terms of the impact of the NHS reforms. The high cost of care in central London – exacerbated by the introduction of charges for land and equipment – might very reasonably be assumed to lead to possibly quite dramatic and significant changes in the traditional flows of patients into inner London. At the same time the new mode of funding health authorities as health purchasers (weighted capitation funding, see Chapters 6 and 7) would reduce the resources coming to inner London DHAs (Kings Fund, 1992a, pp. 9,35). The implication was clear; the workings of the internal market would significantly extend the range and intensity of the potential problems for inner London health services that had been identified in the previous Kings Fund report on plans and trends (Kings Fund, 1987).

Before putting forward their proposals for reform, the Kings Fund Commission identified changes in the social and economic context within which health care is delivered and which needed to inform plans for the future shape of health services in London and indeed throughout the UK. These included requests for improved information about health and involvement in choices about health care, a closer scrutiny of the quality of health care – including waiting times for operations and expert opinions. In addition there was evidence that well-established trends would continue as further developments in pharmaceutical and less invasive methods of diagnosis and treatment afford the opportunity both to shorten even further the lengths of hospital stays (eg: day surgery) and to relocate activities which currently take place in outpatient and other acute hospital settings to primary and community health care (see Chapter 13). In addition, as the primary causes of disease and death have changed and continue to change (from acute infectious diseases to chronic degenerative diseases and cancer) so the management of disability becomes as relevant as treatment to the needs of patients and the aims of the health services (see Kings Fund, 1992a, pp. 10, 71–4). Some of these trends pose particular challenges for London's health care given the 'intense concentration of specialist units in inner London' (Kings Fund, 1992a, p. 52) and the long-standing and widely acknowledged limitations of primary health care in London.

The interpretations of demographic, technological and social changes contained in the report led the authors to recommend what they termed a 'radical programme of investment and restructuring' to reshape London's health services (Kings Fund, 1992a, p. 9). The resulting strategy was an interesting combination of familiar and less familiar suggestions. The key point had been made before; that there needed to be

> a major shift of services and resources from hospital-based to primary care. The aim must be to locate many diagnostic and investigative procedures, and much treatment and care, in primary and community health settings close to where Londoners live, where this can be reconciled with quality and cost criteria. (Kings Fund, 1992b, p. 3, para.7.3).

Some of the supporting points reflected developments that had taken place since the Royal Commissions of 1968 and 1979 including the handling of a high proportion of planned acute interventions through dedicated day care facilities, hospital-at-home schemes, and a wide-ranging role for primary health care practitioners – including convalescent and respite care, rehabilitation, care for people who are dying, and for people experiencing mental health problems (see Kings Fund, 1992a, p. 77)

If the vision of health care in London in 2010 was radical but well-founded in terms of evidence and judgements, the Report's attempt at 'costing the vision' was more problematic. Most significantly for its acceptability to the Government, the Report concluded that 'there is sufficient scope within the capital's existing resources to achieve a significant transfer from acute to primary care without requiring additional funding for the NHS over the whole period' (Kings Fund, 1992a, p. 87). As with other major shifts of resources towards primary and community health care (see Chapters 5 and 13) key assumptions concerned the potential reduction in core speciality hospital beds (25 per cent) over a specified time period (18 years) and the volume of resources released by this planned reduction (see Kings Fund, 1992a, pp. 84–5 and Appendix 4). Given existing experience in relation to both previous national and London-based plans, such assumptions might be regarded as unduly optimistic.

To carry forward the vision, the Report recommended the establishment of a Task Force to undertake the reshaping of services in London including a £250 million primary and community care development programme to address the current deficit in these services, encourage primary health care practitioners to undertake aspects of treatment currently taking place in acute hospital settings, and to involve Londoners in designing services to meet needs which they have helped to identify. Other tasks identified for the Task Force included planning the more rational disposition of specialist services; and the consolidation and reorganization of undergraduate and postgraduate medical teaching, involving an overall reduction in the number of medical students trained in London (see Kings Fund, 1992a, pp. 10, 89–91, 95–6).

Rationing and Rights

The 'unchecked internal market' posed particular problems for London's health services. For example, the new NHS Trust hospitals were given three statutory financial targets to meet, their External Financing Limit (EFL), their 'break-even' on income and expenditure, and a 6 per cent return on capital. But the meeting of these targets would be difficult with evidence that 'the more costly London hospitals have begun to lose contracts for patient care to the cheaper provider units in the home counties' (Bartlett and Harrison, 1993, p. 88). It was in this context that the government commissioned (October 1991) and published (October 1992) the Tomlinson Report to 'advise on the organization of, and inter-relationships between, the NHS and medical education and research in London . . . focusing on the management action needed to resolve immediate and foreseeable problems in London' (Tomlinson Report, 1992, p. 1). The essential questions to be answered were those posed many times in the past. Should London have so many acute hospitals? (see Tomlinson Report, 1992, pp. 8–19); and why is primary care in London of such poor quality? (see Tomlinson Report, 1992, pp. 20–30).

Tomlinson identified and reviewed the same issues as the Kings Fund Report recommending a managed rationalisation of hospital services in London in recognition that acute health services in

London could be delivered equally well and cost effectively from fewer sites and with less beds – especially when considering likely contracted activity levels. The latter was likely to involve a 'withdrawal of patient flows from outside inner London as purchasers secure high quality, but cheaper, services locally (Tomlinson Report, 1992, p. 4). The answer was to close and merge several teaching hospitals including University College and Middlesex; St.Bartholomew's and Royal London; St.Thomas's and Guys; Charing Cross, Royal Brompton and Royal Marsden (see Tomlinson Report, 1992, pp. 32–8). Like the Kings Fund, Tomlinson also recognised the need to invest in London's 'comparatively undeveloped . . . primary and community health care services' (Tomlinson Report, 1992, p. 4). The Report recommended 'a gradual and systematic transfer of resources from the acute sector to community health . . . and family health service budgets' (Tomlinson Report, 1992, p. 9). The associated transitional costs were dealt with very briefly commanding only one, three sentence paragraph (Tomlinson Report, 1992, p. 59). The Report noted the need to manage the reduction in demand for London's acute service in order to prevent chaos.

> If this change is not managed firmly and in certain cases urgently the result will be serious and haphazard deterioration in health services in London. (Tomlinson Report, 1992, p. 3).

Faced with its first major and most predictable problem, it was being recommended that the managed quasi-market would need to be complemented by a substantial degree of directive 'command planning' of the sort the NHS has been set up to facilitate (see for example, Tomlinson Report, 1992, para.42, p. 12; para.53, p. 15; para.58, p. 16; and para.65, pp. 18–19; see, also Donaldson, 1993, pp. 22–34). The Report also revived an organizational device with a lengthy history – 'that NHS commissioning authorities . . . should be coterminous . . . (and) . . . that health purchaser and local authority boundaries should be coterminous' (Tomlinson Report, 1992, p. 45 and p. 19).

The Secretary of State promised to consult widely over the Tomlinson proposals before reaching firm decisions in early 1993 (Smith, 1993, p. x). The Tomlinson Report, like that of the Kings Fund, generated considerable opposition from a disparate range of groups including the medical and nursing professions; manual and non-manual trade unions; community health councils; and voluntary organizations like Age Concern. The essence of the opposition was that both reports were wrong – they were rushed and were about 'rationalisation' rather than health care needs. Existing waiting lists were used as evidence that Londoners needed not only all their current services, but more services rather than enforced closures and mergers. Particular issues identified included the impact on the development of community care (Jowell, 1993, pp. 46–53); the future of clinical research (Green, 1993, pp. 63–76); and the ongoing post-RAWP debate about the measurement of variations in health care needs. For London, issues of continuing concern included the significance of transient populations and the health care needs of people from minority ethnic groups. In addition there were reservations about the 'assumption that hospitals serving deprived populations can increase efficiency to the level of the top quartile of health providers' (Jacobson, 1993, pp. 43–4). Then there was the national picture. If the NHS needed more resources, then London should not be penalised because the government was not providing sufficient resources for the country as a whole.

In early 1993 the Government published its own proposals *Making London Better* (DoH, 1993a) which concluded that 'no change in London is no option' (DoH, 1993a, p. 20). A House of Commons statement by the Secretary of State (16/2/93) indicated that the Government proposals took account of the Tomlinson recommendations; of evidence submitted since that Report was published; and also the informal consultations with the institutions affected by the proposals. *Making London Better* set out a strategic framework for London's health services with four main elements:

> developing higher quality, more accessible local community and primary health care services;
> providing a better balanced hospital service, on fewer sites, to meet the needs of London's resident working and visiting populations;
> rationalising and developing specialist hospital services to safeguard standards in patient care and medical education and research whilst securing value for money; and

merging free standing undergraduate medical colleges with multi-faculty colleges of the University of London for the benefit of medical teaching. (DoH, 1993a, p. 3)

Making London Better confirmed the establishment of the London Implementation Group (LIG) as part of the NHS Management Executive. The LIG would be responsible for overseeing and implementing the major programme of work following from the Tomlinson Report, by working with existing health agencies in the capital (see DoH, 1993a, p. 37). *Making London Better* confirmed that the criticisms of London's primary health care were accepted and proposed the creation of a London Initiative Zone (LIZ) as a focus for new investment and new approaches to improve primary health care and community based services in those areas of inner-London with high population needs (DoH, 1993a, pp. 4–8). An additional £43.5 million was allocated in 1993–94 to support primary care development plans in the LIZ with £170 million made available over six years for community and primary health care capital projects, £7.5 million over three years for voluntary sector schemes to reduce the need for hospitalisation or to enable early discharge, and £10 million allocated to help tackle waiting times in London (DoH, 1993a, p. 35)

The overprovision of acute hospital beds and duplication of specialist services was also accepted (DoH, 1993a, pp. 8, 9). For the latter a series of parallel but separate Speciality Reviews were ordered to be carried out to determine how the six specialist services (cancer, cardiac, neurosciences, plastic surgery and burns, renal and children's services) should be organised. Each review was to be led by an eminent clinician from outside London and a senior NHS manager from a health purchasing authority. The key aim was to reduce unnecessary duplication of specialist services and suggest a more rational disposition to provide a stronger service and academic base. LIG would be responsible for providing medical project management, information, and drafting support to the teams.

Making London Better also identified some specific proposals; these included ending Accident and Emergency Services at some hospitals (eg: Charing Cross), continuing proposed rationalisation (eg: UCH and Middlesex), and indicating the uncertain future of St.Bartholomew's (see DoH, 1993a, pp. 10–15). Unsurprisingly, given that it would confirm the views of critics of the post-1979 Conservative administrations, it was concluded that the 'root cause of London's problems is not a lack of resources' (DoH, 1993a, p. 18).

The Speciality reports were published on 23 June 1993 following an 'extremely – some would say dangerously – tight timetable' (Maxwell, 1994, p. 5). The reports were separate entities with recommendations in one speciality being made without reference to the position in other specialities. Therefore no overall conclusion was published (or was possible). However except for the report on plastic surgery, all the reviews proposed to consolidate services on fewer centres, with thirteen London hospitals to lose specialities and services being concentrated in high quality centres to be two to three times their current size for research and patient cover. Overall half of London's tertiary services would disappear as separate entities. In a letter to all interested parties, the Chairman of LIG stated that the speciality reviews were 'only one element in a complex jigsaw ... they are independent advice to the Minister ... not policy ... and not for formal consultation' (see LIG, 1993 and Dillner, 1993). The proposals were condemned by the Royal College of Nursing and the Association of London Authorities; amid Opposition protests in the House of Commons, the Secretary of State for Health would not commit the Government to implementing specific recommendations contained in the Reviews (see *The Independent*, 24.6.93, p. 2). Subsequently some of the assumptions and conclusions of the Reviews were criticised (see for example, Farrell, 1993).

In October 1993, the Secretary of State announced that the existing 14 RHAs would be replaced by 8 regional offices of the NHS Management Executive. North and south London would be covered by the North and South Thames offices. On December 15, 1993, the Secretary of State incurred further unpopularity with Labour Party MPs when a series of decisions were communicated to the House of Commons through written answers. Among the decisions announced was the end of most services on the St. Bart's site and confirmation that Camden and Islington health authority would not be allowed to switch contracts from UCH and Middlesex Hospital (see *The Guardian*, 16/12/93, p. 11). Less than two months later came the announcement that Guy's Hospital would effectively become the junior partner in a merger with St.Thomas's

– a strange outcome for an institution identified as one of the flagship NHS Trusts in the new 'internal market' (see *The Guardian*, 11/2/94, p. 2).

In March 1994 the government reported that 'good progress was being made' in relation to London (see DoH/OPCS, 1994). But the following month there were press reports that a NHSME review of allocation criteria would conclude that rather than being overprovided by £70 million, London was underprovided by £200 million (see *The Independent*, 29/4/94). The implication was that current plans to reduce beds should be halted; and four months later (August 1994) a well-known health policy analyst argued that there should be no more overall acute bed reductions (Maxwell, 1994, p. v). Maxwell's report suggested that whilst the overall case for change remained valid (along the lines of the Kings Fund and Tomlinson recommendations), current concerns and experiences underlined 'the difficulties of making changes on the scale proposed' (Maxwell, 1994, p. 1), Whilst progress on London's primary health care (notably in the LIZ) had been 'slow' but 'uncontroversial', the proposals for acute hospitals services had proved to be very controversial with deleterious effects on nursing and medical morale, and public confidence (Maxwell, 1994, pp. 8–9). Against this background were the unexplained rises in emergency admissions being experienced in London and elsewhere; and the arguments that London is not 'overbedded' (see Jarman, 1993 and Jarman, 1994). Maxwell expressed particular concern about the scale of bed closures (2,500 before any major hospital closure occurs) and their piecemeal, unplanned nature (by implication internal-market led) (see Maxwell, 1994, pp. 11–13). A month after Maxwell's report was published, the Kings Fund published another report indicating that patients needing emergency treatment in London face long waits before and after they reached hospital; and that there was no evidence to support claims that attendances at casualty departments are higher in London because of inappropriate referrals by GPs (see *The Times*, 2/9/94).

In February 1995, the theme of a moratorium on hospital bed closures in London was pursued not only through an Opposition motion in the House of Commons but also in a report from the Kings Fund (Kings Fund, 1995a; see also *The Independent*, 23/2/95, p. 7). The same month also saw the publication of report commissioned by the Inner London Health Authorities,. Its brief included 'examining what is happening to London's hospitals at the present time' and its overall conclusion was that 'London's acute hospitals are operating under very considerable pressure' (Inner London Health Authority Chief Executive, 1995, pp. 1, 3). The following month members of the London Health Economics Consortium were reported as concluding that 'there is no evidence to support ambitious targets for a reduction in hospitalisation' (see *The Independent*, 6/3/95, p. 2)

Meanwhile the Government reported continuing 'good progress' with medical school mergers in London and indicated that there would soon be an announcement relating to proposals for 'the reconfiguration of the acute hospital service in London' (DoH / OPCS, 1995, p. 37). In April 1995, Virginia Bottomley, the Secretary of State for Health, came under unprecedented attack in the House of Commons from senior Tories (especially from Sir Peter Brooke, MP for City of London and Westminster and former Secretary of State for Northern Ireland) as she avoided making a Commons statement on this 'reconfiguration' which involved a string of London hospital closures that finally signed the death warrant for St. Bartholomew's in the City (House of Commons, 1995a, Cols.1651–52) The same announcement, made in a Commons written answer, consigned Guy's to becoming a peripheral part of St. Thomas's, its £140m state-of-the-art Sir Philip Harris House (south of the Thames) turned into a white elephant. Mrs. Bottomley's decisions affected nine London hospitals, and involved the closure of the Brook and Greenwich District general hospitals, an end to kidney transplants at Dulwich, the closure of Accident and Emergency and in-patient services at Edgware General, confirmation that most of Barts' services would go to the London, and that Guy's would be restricted to minor injuries, day and outpatients, mental health and academic units. The Queen Elizabeth military hospital at Greenwich would be developed as the NHS hospital for Greenwich. The changes involved capital investment of £400m and a £210m investment in primary care. In May 1995 the Opposition again asked the Government 'to halt the withdrawal of hospital services and moderate the pace of change' (House of Commons, 1995b, Col.765). In the subsequent debate there was further critical comment from London-based Conservative MPs (see House of Commons, 1995b, Cols.789–792; 804–806; 813–815; 837–838)

Conflicts

The London case study just described exemplifies the constant presence of conflict when attempts to change existing patterns and distributions of care are attempted. Whilst the Government seems prepared for a programme of investment in primary and community health based health services, there are a number of endemic problems. It is difficult to achieve a planned and integrated service that meets the needs of a diverse and often disadvantaged population. Within the primary sector there are co-ordination problems between the agencies and professional workers who provide different elements of primary care. There may be different planning and budgetary cycles; different and incompatible forms of accountability; and differences in ideologies and values. There is professional self-interest; concern for threats to autonomy and job security; and conflicting views about consumers interests are also uncovered when change is mooted.

Specialist services require cross-boundary regional planning which seems to be diminishing. There is considerable potential for conflict over the development of health services in London given the historic domination of the teaching hospitals in inner London. There is an over-resourced system – by national/RAWP type standards – and especially with regard to the duplication of expensive equipment – allied to inadequate provision for certain groups (and of certain services). New technologies and techniques afford opportunities for more effective use of expensive hospital resources (eg: day surgery) and there has been a long-running and ongoing plan to reduce acute beds in inner London. But with a continuing tradition of teaching hospital autonomy – enhanced by NHS trust status – there are questions regarding the move towards a more effective set of health services for London.

The Tomlinson Report, based upon 'principles of administrative rationality' had recommended the reorganization of London's health care services (hospitals and primary care), similar to those of the Kings Fund, but with the political backing of the government of the day. Conflict was perhaps inevitable, with opposition from London health professionals, London Members of Parliament, sections of London's population, and prominent sections of the London media – especially the *Evening Standard*. For a change of such magnitude for the capital's health care services to be promoted without expecting conflict would have been naive, if not wholly lacking in any feel for the history of London's health care and the allegiances, loyalties and jealousies with which the institutions and services would be defended.

Is there a conflict between the commitment to a managed 'internal market' and the London problem? Was there a problem with 'the planning process chasing the tail of the market'? For the moment the 'familiar pattern ... (remained) ... of underdeveloped primary services and relatively high expenditure in the hospital and community services sector' (see Kings Fund, 1994, pp. 18, 26).

Conclusions

Well before the foundation of the NHS, the deep-seated nature of the problems facing London's hospitals was recognised by policy-makers and health care professionals ... key elements of the (London) problem have remained entrenched for many years: a tribute to the power of the many interests involved. (Kings Fund, 1992a, pp. 25, 35)

There are circumstances in which a managed health market requires intervention – that's always been the case (Virginia Bottomley, Secretary of State for Health, referring to changes in London, quoted in *The Independent*, 16/12/93, p. 11)

Far from being left to the market, the re-structuring of London's health services was to become one of the most ambitious planning exercises in the history of the NHS. (Klein, 1995a, p. 207)

Health needs in London are unique in that its resident population (1989) is 6.7 million, but every day there are an additional 1.3m commuters plus an annual 8.4 m tourists. It has a unique (in the UK) density of population and range and diversity of individuals. Extremes of poverty and wealth exist, as well as a high proportion of people from other cultures for whom English is not a first language, including 120,000 refugees. There are also an estimated 26,000 homeless people. London also has a high proportion of people with psychiatric problems due to mental illness, drug addiction, and other social problems.

The publication of the report of the Kings Fund Commission in 1992 produced a rather attractive historical symmetry with the first report of the House of Lords Committee in 1892. Less attractive is the consistency of analysis and the persistence of problems identified in the series of reports generated between 1892 and 1992; this seems to indicate a certain intractable quality about the problems despite their serious consequences for the quality of health care provided in London.

On the other hand, an analysis of the means available to resolve the problems may put the latter in a different perspective. Until the establishment of the NHS, the lack of any coherent organizational framework for health care in Britain was such that it was perhaps inevitable that nothing was done (see Chapters 1 and 2). Unfortunately the political compromises associated with the establishment of the NHS and its organizational structure (Chapters 4 and 6) and the politics of planning and cost containment (Chapter 5) severely limited the ability and willingness of successive governments to address the issues. It might be fairly concluded that it is only since the mid-1970s that we have earnestly sought to realise the potential of a NHS to deliver a 'rationally planned service' informed by considerations of 'equity'; and from this perspective the problems of London's health services may be seen as palpably persistent but not inevitably intractable.

Apart from providing further illustrations of all the conflicts we have identified with state provided health care throughout Part One of this book, the case of London illustrates a long-standing conflict in its newest guise – at least in Britain. Should London's problems be resolved by traditional modes of public service planning and professionalism or by a new managerialism operating in quasi-markets? Advocates of the latter might well claim that it is the new internal market that has so 'sharpened up' our appreciation of London's problems that we are at last going to do something about them. Advocates of the former might well claim that it was the operation of the older quasi-market of pre-NHS health care that created London's problems in the first place and it was the first effective operation of public service planning and professionalism (via RAWP) that really 'sharpened things up'.

Certainly the Kings Fund did not recommend leaving London to the workings of the 'internal market'; rather the proposed Task Force should be given the *powers to* ... *direct* NHS commissioning consortia, health authorities, health service providers, local authorities and other agencies to reshape the pattern of health services in the capital. (Kings Fund, 1992a, p. 90, our emphasis)

Indeed the argument that some stays in London hospital beds are prolonged as a result of insufficient sheltered housing, nursing home and domiciliary care (see Murphy, 1992) might serve as an eloquent testimony to the failure of successive governments to provide an organizational infrastructure to sustain the effective planning of health and social care in London. Certainly the argument that evaluative research will continue to endorse the case for the centralisation of certain kinds of treatment in specialist centres (see Kings Fund, 1992a, p. 73) raises questions about how, and indeed whether, this research-based outcome can be achieved through the 'internal quasi-market'.

The principles identified by the Kings Fund as the basis for change in London would not be problematic for those who argued for a National Health Service half a century ago;

London's health services must be *planned* and managed to serve the population rather than to perpetuate institutions ... (and) ... Londoners should be much more actively involved in their own health and health care. (Kings Fund, 1992a, p. 75, our emphasis)

Indeed one of the Commission's conclusions contains elements of some of the key arguments in favour of a National Health Service

We are also convinced that changes of ... (this) ... scale and depth ... will require *strategic guidance* and *co-ordinated development* at national, regional and local level. Success will depend on coherent, system-wide implementation. (Kings Fund, 1992a, p. 75, our emphasis)

Part One Conclusions

At the Middlesex Hospital in 1821 the apothecary had been equally lavish and had issued leeches at the rate of a hundred a day. The Board ordered that in future after the leeches had been used they should be properly preserved for future application. (Abel-Smith, 1964, p. 35)

The new buildings were opened by Queen Victoria who planted a tree with a diamond-studded trowel. But almost immediately the hospital ... (St.Thomas's) ... was beset with chronic financial shortage. For several years, 13 of the wards were kept closed for lack funds. (Harris, 1979, p. 288)

A number of inner London hospitals are ... in financial difficulty. (Tomlinson Report, 1992, p. 4)

Hospital trusts go broke as NHS is bled dry. (Headline in *The Independent*, 4/11/96, p. 1)

We have sought to base our historical audit of the National Health Service on a range of existing accounts of health care developments in the UK. In so doing the aim has been to search out consensus between scholars. Therefore the resulting audit is perhaps most distinctive in the chronological time span covered embracing almost a century and half before the NHS was established, as well as the half-century since the NHS Act of 1946 was passed. An historical perspective on the state provision of health care in Britain illustrates both a changing role for the state (from a 'minimal state' of the pre-Public Health poor law to a 'welfare state' of the NHS) and some of the arguments generated by this changing role. Once political commitment became attached to the provision of health care for the population in the late nineteenth and early twentieth century, long and acrimonious debates took place upon exactly what it was the population required to meet their current health needs, how could this best be organised, its cost, and likely outcomes in terms of improvement in health status. In terms of understanding the significance of contemporary conflicts our historical audit is instructive in relation to three pre-NHS themes.

Firstly, and perhaps most significantly, that the provision of health care has been a source of conflict before there was any substantial state intervention in the provision of such care. These included conflicts relating to costs, to lay / professional relations, to professional / bureaucratic relations and to inter- and intra-professional relations. Whilst these conflicts may have assumed particular and distinctive forms as state intervention in health care has been extended, their origins seem to lie more in the emergence of something we would recognise as modern health care and modern professional groups. *There has never been a golden age of conflict-free health care to which we might return if we abandoned our commitment to a national health service.*

Secondly, some degree of state involvement in health care has a very long history which can be traced back even before the New Poor Law. More extensive state intervention was the subject of Rumsey's *Essays on State Medicine* in 1856. Indeed social and economic circumstances appear to have drawn the state into significant intervention in aspects of health care (eg: public health, Poor Law medical services, and the asylums) long before the more overt reformism of New Liberalism and the Labour Party formulated 'national health' legislation in 1911 and 1946. *There has never been a golden-age of state-free health care to which we might return if we abandoned our commitment to a national health service.*

Thirdly, as soon as the state was drawn into something more than a minimal state model of 'less eligibility', institution-based health care, then successive governments became embroiled in some of the fundamental conflicts of modern health care (how much is it costing; and can we afford it?) and of modern state welfare (who should benefit; and who should pay?). Over virtually one hundred years – from nineteenth century Poor Law and Public Health reforms to the Medical Planning Commission of the 1930s

– conflict was endemic between participants and government. *There has never been a golden age of more limited state intervention in health care which was conflict-free.*

What can we say of the half-century since the NHS Act was passed? With the establishment of the NHS, Britain became the first country in the world to offer free medical care to the whole population. The principle of universality – of providing the same rights to services to all residents – has since been emulated by many other countries, for example, Canada, the Scandinavian countries, Portugal, and Italy and was being planned for in Greece and Spain by the 1990s (see Abel-Smith, 1990, p. 11). It is commonplace for judgements about the NHS to suggest that the period up until 1979 was characterised by a high degree of consensus on the need for, the reasons underlying, and method of guaranteeing, health care for the population of the UK. This judgement is based upon the successful implementation of the NHS following the early days of professional opposition. But the Service came into existence in an atmosphere of conflict generated by the strong ideological commitment of the post Second World War Labour Government, and the opposition of the Conservative Party, and some sections of the medical profession to what was perceived as the most symbolic of socialist aspirations; a universally available, comprehensive, centrally-planned and free at the time of need, medical care service.

Even though the political battle was won to establish the Service, conflicts and arguments have dominated the Service since its inception to the present-day. Indeed, given agreement on the revolutionary nature of the NHS (universal provision and access, comprehensive coverage, absence of a cash nexus, retention by professionals of independence within a state system) and a context of scarcity with the necessity to reconstruct a war-battered society it seems remarkable that within a decade the NHS had become an accepted and well-regarded social institution, resting upon public and collective rather than private and individual values.

The state's acceptance of financial responsibility for health care could be sustained by a range of arguments based on efficiency, equity, the welfare of the community, the support of the community and the limitations of the alternative institutions (eg: private charity and endowment) (see Chapters 11 and 12 for a further discussion of these issues). These arguments did not allay the concerns of politicians regarding the costs of a national health service especially when it seemed as though the costs of the new service had been seriously underestimated. The outcomes were predictable; only twenty-one months elapsed before the first cash limits were introduced in the NHS (Abel-Smith, 1990, p. 12) and the first major committee of enquiry into the new service was concerned with its cost (Guillebaud Report, 1956). The latter was the most obvious indication that the initial Conservative opposition to the passage of the Bill would not disappear. But the main conclusions of the Guillebaud Report were that far from the NHS being over-resourced and wasteful, it was on the contrary under-resourced and efficient given its objectives and the unsympathetic economic environment in which it was established. The publication of Guillebaud became the launching pad for another area of potential conflict – that between old-fashioned public administration of the NHS and the novel concern with managing such a Service. Between the twin concerns of money and management, other more 'technical' changes were affecting the Service, all of which raised sharply the economic and management questions for professionals, politicians, planners and eventually the public.

Our audit must judge the infant NHS a success in not succumbing to a morbid or fatal condition in its early years; furthermore this might be interpreted as a testimony to its likely longevity. Just to survive in that context was a remarkable achievement. Between 1948 and the first major reorganization of 1974 there were concerns about general practice conditions of service, constant Supplementary Estimates from the Exchequer to meet rising demands and costs, and a continuing concern that the 1948 structure was a compromise that could never meet the goal of an integrated service. At the same time there was an increase in the knowledge base of the general population about health and medical matters. In a context such as this, conflict rather than consensus was bound to be more common, because the risk of change, however necessary such change, could always be interpreted as potentially jeopardising those values underpinning the Service which had been achieved. Hence the continuing debate about management, issues about the distribution of health care resources to the most 'health care needy' of the population; and the long-running saga of a powerful medical profession which always wished for an arms-length relationship with government and the state over their clinical autonomy, yet at the same time took it as axiomatic that the concerns of the medical profession should give them automatic access to the corridors of power.

If conflict in the Service seemed to increase with the introduction of indicative planning, managerialism, and the use of specifically economic criteria to measure health service performance and outcomes then the start date for this might be 1974 rather than 1979. This was in part a conjunction of a clearer commitment to 'real NHS principles' (eg: equity in resource allocation) and less than propitious economic circumstances. Subsequent structural change produced new administrative cadres (general managers); efficiency criteria have been used to measure the performance of the service, accompanied by much criticism of the validity of the measures used; and public expectations have risen inexorably along with the mass production and distribution of medical knowledge about what is now feasible (DNA, genetic engineering, technological applications in medicine). At the same time, the elderly population are now being defined as a 'burden' upon the resources of the service, as mortality is delayed, and 'medicated survival' becomes a costly process.

No-one could predict the current system as recently as 8 years ago. No hint of it was in the Conservative Manifesto of 1987. Following the election a steady state in purchasing power to the National Health Service took place throughout the 1980s but with hospital price inflation always ahead of the Retail Price Index. The '2 per cent argument' began to be heard – if only we could increase the size of the National Health Service Budget by a further 2 per cent all would be well. This it was said would cover population changes, really the growth of the elderly population; it would keep the National Health Service in line with innovation and new technology; and it would meet the legitimate expectations of the population for an 'end of the 20th Century quality' health service to match the expectations generated in the market place by high quality stores.

However it was far from clear that governments in the 1980s were taking account of 'health care inflation'; in addition there were problems associated with major uncertainties over the scale of funding from one year to the next. The sort of reductions imposed at relatively short notice by the Chancellor of the Exchequer (Lawson) in 1987 generated a 'crisis' that precipitated the review that led to *Working for Patients* (Carrier and Kendall, 1990a, pp. 90–1). The successes and failure of the resulting 'internal market' seem to remain inextricably associated with the overall budgetary situation. Running 'smoothly' if resources keep pace with 'health care inflation', generating 'crises' when they did not. The resulting dilemmas were most acute for the government in London. Should you let the market clear at prices purchasers were willing to pay or 'downsize' through old-fashioned 'rational planning'. The establishment of the Tomlinson Review and the acceptance of its recommendations was perhaps indicative of at least the political limitations of 'internal markets' in a context where the government retains ultimate responsibilities for rights to, resources for, and the regulation of 'a comprehensive health service'.

An audit of the NHS can be an artificial exercise in which an order is imposed upon a series of unco-ordinated and complex events which together determine the quality of health care delivered to those with defined medical/health needs. Nevertheless, after half a century of statutorily recognised health care in the UK, it is possible to review the past decades both in the light of experience, critical comments and future judgements. This long period can be interpreted as one in which the National Health Service has moved from a professionally-led service, in which professionals are responsible for defining clinical need to a service in which needs are judged against resource, financial, and manpower considerations as well as legal restraints. The system has always been cost contained and rationing has been implicit in this. In theory, the new system sets priorities through purchasing decision making, and rationing is made explicit. However, a managed market retains features of the pre 1989 system, particularly the principles of a national system, tax financed, comprehensive coverage and no explicit limits on health care.

The audit report for the most enthusiastic advocates of the health care reforms introduced by Mrs.Thatcher's governments is that a combination of cash-limited devolved budgets, general managers and internal markets has not, and we would suggest will not, usher in a golden age of conflict-free state health care. The audit report for the sternest critics of those same governments must include a reminder that there was conflict in the NHS before the election of a Conservative Government under Mrs.Thatcher in 1979. *There was no golden age of a conflict-free NHS between 1948 and 1979.*

Finally, two further points can be derived from our historical audit. Firstly, although the NHS has brought along the luggage of conflict from the nineteenth and first half of twentieth century, it should not be assumed that there is not consensus about aims. That alongside the endemic and at times continuous areas of conflict there have been elements of continuity and long and unchallenged periods of consensus about key elements of health care. In particular the growing recognition that the NHS was one of the cheapest health care systems in the developed world has in the end united a broad spectrum of 'political opinion' and 'public opinion' in support of its fundamental principles. Secondly, given the scarcity of 'conflict-free golden ages' we should perhaps be more accepting of the conflicts engendered by the attempt to contain within the institutional arrangements of the NHS a number of dissident and potentially conflicting elements. Part Two of our audit focuses on some of these elements. As a final concluding point to our historical audit we can identify the potential of conflict to act at times at least as catalysts for needed changes. Perhaps one of the challenges and achievements of the NHS has been the management of conflicts and changes within the broad parameters of a near-consensus about the concept of a national health service which Beveridge captured in his Report. On that occasion at least (February 1942) queues outside a shop (Her Majesty's Stationery Office) and public opinion surveys (Gallup) were identified with something more than the transitory.

Part Two:
A Contemporary Audit

Introduction

One of the themes that emerged from our Historical Audit was not only a long-standing history of conflicts but a history of long-standing conflicts. The implication is that some of these conflicts centre around enduring themes. The aim in our more Contemporary Audit is to explore some of the more obvious sources of long-standing conflict.

Our history has looked at differing models of health and health care with initial state intervention focusing on public health programmes for which the prevention of ill-health might be deemed the most appropriate criteria of success or failure. Subsequent extensions of state intervention into the direct provision of personal health services involves curing and caring and draws us into a long-running debate about the relative merits of particular curative and preventive approaches. This has been most obviously represented in the assertion that modern health care systems, like the NHS, have a distinctive bias in the direction of curative, hospital-based health care, deflecting attention and resources away from health service and other social services programmes and policies that could diminish ill-health through proven preventive measures. The post-NHS development of 'high technology' medicine was greeted with a mixture of reverence and awe as well as suspicion and criticism. On the one hand innovations saved and prolonged life for the few, but was thought to compete with the basic and more utilitarian functions of the health care system. The disillusion with high technology during this period raised questions of non-health care interventions having an impact upon life expectancy and lower morbidity. In particular, the emphasis on nutrition, improved housing, ante and post-natal care and education was used to counteract an uncritical commitment to medical technology reminding the population of prevention and the importance of non-medical factors influencing health status. Such 'environmental' factors were used to remind all that a NHS did not necessarily contribute to the increased life expectancy and improved quality of life over and above that which could be derived from old-fashioned public health policies. Nevertheless it was also becoming well-documented that the medicated survival of old people living well beyond the statutory pensionable age required more health care resources than younger age groups and thus again the 'can we afford?' question was present throughout the first 40 years of the NHS. Chapter 10 explores these issues around the concepts of health and health care and the relationship between them. What does modern health care contribute to the health status of the community at large?

Chapters 11 and 12 address the issues associated with any moves beyond the residual model of state welfare represented by the New Poor Law. Chapters 1 to 4 traced the changing roles of voluntary and state health care institutions and the emergence of a commitment to a universal, comprehensive health service. Chapters 10 and 11 seek to identify the key arguments deployed for and against state intervention in health care and the universalist approach that has formed the basis of the NHS.

The New Poor Law was intended as an 'institution-based' system although it proved impossible to eliminate 'outdoor relief'. The apparent choice (or conflict) between institutional and community care has therefore never been a simple one. Community-based traditions of health and social care (eg: district nursing) developed in an era when there was considerable investment in an institution-based approach; and the problems of the latter were recognised alongside their construction (eg: Dr. Barnardo's concern about the 'problems of institutionalism'). Chapter 13 seeks to identify the main arguments that have been deployed in relation to both institutional and community care.

In Part One we identified the power and influence of the medical profession in being able, and allowed, to set the health care agenda both pre- and post-1948. This interpretation draws upon radical and critical reviews of the profession (see for example, Illich, 1976; Stacey, 1988; and Ham, 1992) and assesses the influence of professional authority in general, not just the NHS (see for example, Friedson, 1986; Mechanic, 1976; Berlant, 1975; Starr, 1982; and Wilding, 1982) upon policy initiatives and policy inertia in the field. This view is supported in the USA by Alford (1975), Marmor (1983) and others. There also exists a decision-making literature which accounts for current health service debates in terms of unequal power between participants in the system (see for example, Ham, 1992; Stacey, 1988; Jeffreys and Sachs, 1983; Lee and Mills, 1982; Allsop, 1995; and Seedhouse, 1993). Chapter 14 explores some of the issues relating to the organizational formats utilised for health care both pre- and post-NHS. How health care professionals are accommodated in these formats is a key theme, but in the end is identified as only one of a range of organizational dilemmas posed by the commitment to provide a national health service. In particular, the advent of Griffiths has brought the NHS into the age of managerialism in a major public service, and this is to be welcomed for the stress this has placed upon authority, accountability, review and planning. The administrative structure may be judged by its responsiveness to requests for 'reasonable' change, especially in the area of patient's complaints; how it meets requests for information; how it treats 'reasonable' expectations; and whether it treats individuals as autonomous beings, with integrity, able to make conscious choices, even though their status as 'patient' is that of dependency.

Finally we come to what might be considered the central question of any audit of the NHS – has it been a success or failure? Predictably there is no one definitive answer to this central question. However in Chapter 15 we have tried to indicate how that final judgement is influenced by the criteria deployed and suggest which criteria are most appropriate. We concur with a number of other commentators in concluding that in a number of crucial respects the NHS has been a success.

10
Health or health care?

(The death rate) . . . instead of being the measure of a single influence on the health of hospitals, is in truth the sum of the influences of an almost infinite number of causes, all of which require to be duly considered and allowed for before any useful comparison can be made. (Bristowe and Holmes, 1863, p. 513)

We can buy human life. Each country, within certain limits, decides its own death rate. (Sand, 1935; quoted in Titmuss, 1950, p. 535)

Health and health services: a plausible relationship

The growth of modern biomedicine has closely paralleled a significant improvement in the health status of populations in relatively affluent, industrial societies. There have been dramatic decreases in the death rates for common infectious diseases and other conditions in the twentieth century (see Table 1). These decreases have taken place over the same time period in which there have been dramatic changes in health care. In place of hospital care of dubious value (see for example, Eckstein, 1958, p. 15) and deficient medical education (see for example, Stevens, 1966, p. 23) we have experienced a range of improvements in relation to diagnostic techniques, chemotherapy, radiotherapy, organ transplantation and other forms of surgical intervention.

One obvious outcome of these improvements in health care has been the increasing costs of health care (see for example, Chapters 2 and 5), but another plausible outcome has been improvements in health status. Indeed part of the rationale for the National Health Service was derived from the 'inverse care law' by which

Table 1 Standardised death rates (per million) from certain diseases: England and Wales

	1848–54	1971
Bronchitis, influenza and pneumonia	2239	603
Tuberculosis (respiratory)	2901	13
Scarlet fever and diphtheria	1016	0
Whooping cough	423	1
Measles	342	0
Smallpox	263	0
Infections of ear, pharynx, larynx	75	2
Cholera, diarrhoea, dysentery	1819	33
Typhoid, typhus	990	0
Convulsions, teething	1322	0
Syphilis	50	0
Appendicitis, peritonitis	75	7
Puerperal fever	62	1

Source: McKeown, 1976, pp. 33–7.

communities with poor health care facilities had poor health status – a relationship which provided further evidence of this link between health and health care (see Chapter 2). The 1944 White Paper implied a 'causal relationship between the provision of medical services targeted against illness and the reduction of ill-health' (Seedhouse 1987, p. 146; see also Chapter 3). This implication served as the basis for certain assumptions about the cost of running a comprehensive, national health service.

The resulting expectations were three-fold. Firstly, that a more efficient health service would have a marked impact on the health status of the population as a whole. Secondly, that a fairer health service would have a marked impact on inequalities in health status. Thirdly, that stable, or perhaps even declining real costs, would result from the impact of this fairer and more efficient health service.

Health of the nation and an efficient health service

The view that a more efficient health service would have a marked impact on the health status of the population as a whole, has been significantly challenged since the publication of the Beveridge Report, most notably by McKeown (1976) who demonstrated that

Table 2 Death rates and the introduction of specific measures

Cause of death	(A) Fall in Standardised Death Rate (SDR) between 1848/51 and 1971	(B) Year when specific measure became available	(C) Fall in SDR by 1971 after introduction of specific measures	(D) C as a % of A
TB (respiratory)	2,888	1947 (streptomycin)	409	14.16%
Measles	342	1935 (sulphonamide)	50	14.6%
Bronchitis, pneumonia and influenza	1,636	1938 (sulphonamide)	531	32.4%
Smallpox	263	Before 1848 (immunisation)	263	100%

Source: McKeown, 1976, p. 52

for many causes of death (with the notable exception of smallpox) the proportionate fall in the standardised mortality rate which could be attributed to specific personal health care innovations was relatively modest, the largest fall coming before such innovations (see Table 2). This appraisal of important medical advances 'leaves little doubt that their impact was much smaller than is generally supposed' (McKeown, 1976, p. 92). Indeed given that the factors reducing death rates might be presumed to remain active after the introduction of the specific measures (eg: streptomycin in relation to TB), then the reduction of the death rate attributable to immunisation and therapy was less even than these figures suggested. Mortality from all diseases was declining before, and in most cases long before, effective procedures became available (McKeown, 1976, p. 53).

To what then might we attribute our improving health status in industrialised societies? McKeown's appraisal of influences on health in the past led him to conclude that:

we owe the improvement not to what happens when we are ill, but to the fact that we do not so often become ill; and we remain well, not because of specific measures such as vaccination and immunisation, but because we enjoy a higher standard of nutrition and live in a healthier environment. (McKeown, 1976, p. 94)

Part of this healthier environment can be attributed to the epidemiological tradition from Snow and Semmelweis through Pasteur, Koch, Erlich and up to Salk. This has certainly had an impact in terms of preventing and alleviating human misery, disability, disease and death. But other factors start to take us beyond the 'medical tradition' when for example more detailed analyses focus on improvements in the quantity and the quality of milk supplies in urban areas (see Beaver, 1973) in which improvements in the transport system (and therefore the knowledge of civil engineers rather than doctors) play an important role (see also Szreter, 1988).

This general link between quality and quantity of food intake on the one hand, and general levels of health on the other, was accepted by the World Health Organization -

for the time being an adequate diet is the most effective 'vaccine' against most of the diarrhoeal, respiratory and other common infections. (WHO, 1973)

This applies particularly to developing societies but is also applicable to the analysis of the contemporary pattern of disease in the more affluent societies. For example, Burkitt identified twelve 'common and serious diseases of the western world' including coronary heart disease, cancer of the large intestine, appendicitis, and diverticular disease of the large bowel. He labelled these 'diseases of modern economic development' because they are 'rare or unknown in communities little touched by Western civilisation, and Western dietary customs in particular' (Burkitt, 1973, p. 141). Given other conclusions that, for example, 'most cancers are due to environmental factors' (Doll and Kinlen, 1972), the contribution of health care to health status was being seriously questioned in relation to both historical and contemporary evidence.

Although McKeown's conclusions have been subject to further critical appraisal (see for example, Szreter, 1988), the general argument that the environment has a major impact on health status is now broadly accepted in policy and clinical initiatives. In the UK the Chief Medical Officer of Health identified an epidemic of stress-related illness resulting from the demise of 'jobs for life' (see Chief Medical Officer, 1995). Meanwhile the WHO identified migration, world travel and rapid population growth with increases in infectious diseases such as tuberculosis and malaria.

Debates still continue around the relative contribution of different elements in the environment (eg: nutrition, pollution) and more specifically about the benefits and dangers to health of individual items within these elements (eg: different foodstuffs). However these debates do not substantially challenge the fundamentals of an argument that consign personal health services to a more modest role in improving the health status of the population. More controversial are differing assumptions about the individual's ability to manipulate these environmental factors.

(In) the past century the improvement in expectation of life of mature males from all causes has been reduced by at least half by smoking alone ... (this) ... indicates that in technologically advanced countries behaviourial influences are now more important than all others. (McKeown, 1976, p. 99)

This conclusion inevitably raises questions of individual responsibility for health status and has led both to advocacy of, and accusations of, discrimination against smokers when presenting for treatment within the NHS. The estimate that smokers are costing the NHS more than £1.67m per day in medical treatments and consultations indicates the significance of the problem in resource terms (HEA, 1993; see also Underwood and Bailey, 1993, Shiu, 1993; and Higgs, 1993).

The status of health care in relation to health status has been diminished by other evidence. This includes the so-called 'submerged iceberg of sickness in society' (Last, 1963) the label attached to the substantial volume of treatable illness in the community identified by researchers but not recorded in the routine record keeping of health service professionals. This indicated, amongst other things, the imperfect relationship between individuals with treatable conditions and health care systems – even ones like the NHS where some of the more obvious barriers to access and utilisation (eg: charges and stigma) – had been much reduced in significance. From a simple equation attributing improvements and variations in morbidity, to improvements and variations in health care, a more complex picture has been emerging since the establishment of the NHS. Differences in morbidity between different parts of the country might be

> the result of age/sex differences, socio-economic differences, physical aspects of the environment, or merely an artefact of differences in the availability of GPs and the preparedness of patients to consult them about the iceberg of untreated illness. (Buxton, 1976, p. 25).

This perspective leaves the status of the NHS as a major preventer and alleviator of disease and illness as problematic. One conclusion might be that we can safely reduce the resources going to the NHS without having a detrimental effect on the health of the population as a whole. The policy implications of this are obviously quite profound, although probably politically unacceptable whilst the NHS retains a substantial degree of public support and is perceived as being under-funded rather than over-funded (see Buxton and Klein, 1978, p. 4 on 'standards' or 'rations').

The situation is further complicated by the problematic nature of a range of widely used terms including 'health', 'health care' and 'health policies'. Firstly, the very concept of 'health' is problematic. For example at the most general level there is the early and widely quoted World Health Organization's (WHO) definition that

> health is a state of complete physical, mental and social well-being and not merely the absence of disease and infirmity. (WHO, 1948)

What would be the appropriate services required to deliver such a theoretical and abstract aspiration. Given the problems involved in measuring 'mental', let alone 'social' well-being, this admirable goal is probably indefinable as well as unattainable. More recently the current WHO's ambition of 'Health for All by the Year 2000' (WHO, 1977) seems somewhat remote when health surveys in the more affluent sections of the world 'have noted that as much as 90 per cent of their apparently healthy subjects had some physical aberration or clinical disorder well worthy of treatment' (Robinson, 1973, p. 34). The goal of health for all is linked to a 'right to health' (see WHO, 1981). Like the 1946 definition, this sounds not merely improbable but impossible; even if one of the WHO's primary goals were to be achieved – that is the cessation of war.

Moving from the global and general to the more specific, the evidence for the 'submerged iceberg' provided some striking illustrations of the problematic concept of health. For example, it was realised that not only did there appear to be many unrecognised and recognised sufferers from diabetes mellitus (Last, 1963) but that various studies indicated that

> blood sugar levels in the population show a continuous distribution (a skewed normal distribution) and that there are not two distinct groups. This means that diabetes ... has to be arbitrarily defined somewhere along the scale of this continuous variable. Thus the only boundaries between normality and abnormality are those created artificially by definition. At what point does one divide the population into diabetics and non-diabetics? (Israel and Teeling-Smith, 1967, p. 47)

What some social scientists (especially sociologists) refer to as 'health status' and others (especially economists) as a form of 'human capital' is hardly capable of precise measurement in these circumstances. If the concept of 'human capital' rests upon the assumption that there is a 'stock of health' (the result of genetic and other more difficult to measure factors) which will be expended over the lifetime of the individual, the more wary 'health accountants' might well decline to be responsible for defining levels of depreciation!

Secondly, there can be confusion over the terms 'health care' and 'medical care'. The two might be distinguished in so far as the latter can be taken to refer to individual assessment, diagnosis, prognosis, and treatment delivered by professionally trained individuals in the clinical nursing and medical sciences to those who 'present' themselves for such attention with a bio-social condition defined as pathological, abnormal, morbid or below an optimum or normative level. Such intervention presumes to improve and maintain health status wherever this is feasible. On this reading, 'health care' might apply to a broader category of intervention including the application of the scientific principles of preventive medicine in attempting to promote good health, and the more caring role that has been such a crucial, although often relatively neglected (see Chapter 5) dimension of the NHS.

These categorisations should not discount other aids to health (social services, housing policy, nutritional policy, social security, and industrial safety); they simply focus on the role of health professionals in maintaining and improving the health status of individuals. 'Health policies' may not require any specific medical or health care interventions but will include important services having an impact on health such as housing, social security, education and food (for school children). Although they have not been counted as part of the NHS, their significance for health status was recognised in the Beveridge Report and earlier.

All the above is subject to fierce scientific and lay disputes. There are medico-legal disputes about the meaning of death – when to 'switch off the machine' – especially in situations of 'persistent vegetative states' (see for example, Airedale NHS Trust v Bland [1993] 1 All E.R. 821). There is also the long-running debate often expressed as the medical versus the social model of health. This leads us to the socially and scientifically defined distinctions between disease, illness and disability.

None of the above categories are capable of simple definition. What is clear is that there is a division of labour; different sectors of the health service are more appropriate to the maintenance of health, the cure of disease and illness; whereas other sectors (eg: occupational therapy) are more suitable to the alleviation of disability. Because the causes of each condition differ, so must the appropriate service responses. Decisions which are reached about the balance between the resources necessary for these sectors to flourish is the outcome of the relationship between 'approved' knowledge and social/political values and choices (see Chapter 5). Such choices we have shown, are rooted in the background of the NHS, with the long haul from public health concerns of the latter half of the nineteenth century (for example, Chadwick, Simon, Snow) to the concerns with individual health status in the first half of the twentieth century (the Webb's, Dawson, the British Medical Association, Political and Economic Planning, the Socialist Medical Association and Beveridge). The trend is exemplified by the move from the classic nineteenth century epidemiological concerns (sanitation, clean water and prevention of cholera and typhoid) to the highly sophisticated methods applied to the treatment and cure of the conditions of individual patients. The ideals underpinning these developments are a mixture of political and professional concerns with equity, for which a universal and comprehensive medical care service was justified (see Chapters 3 and 4).

The relationship between health services and the health of the nation is a complex one. In part this reflects potential conflicts around how we might define and measure the health of the nation and what we include within the category of health services. Nonetheless two conclusions might reasonably be said to have a broad measure of agreement. Firstly, that the health of more affluent nations like the UK has improved over a period of 150 years and a set of factors operating largely outside the boundaries of the health services (broadly defined) has played a crucial role in this improvement. Secondly that within our broadly defined health services it is the public health rather than the personal health dimension that has contributed most significantly to improving the health of the nation.

These conclusions might be seen to exacerbate rather than ameliorate some of the conflicts we have identified in Part One. Indeed the government's concern with cost-containment might be seen as more legitimate when additional expenditure on the NHS is not going to improve health in some obviously self-evident manner. Certainly, the balance of priorities within the NHS will remain a source of conflict given the continuing case that can be made for those activities which might be seen as less popular with the professionals and the public (see Chapter 5); for in an individualistic more privatised society it is the contribution of medical care to personal health status that has taken centre stage.

Health inequalities and a fairer health service
One understandably disappointing feature of post-war Britain has been the failure to eliminate the health inequalities that so disfigured pre-war society and which form part of the powerful case for health care reform (see Chapter 2). By the 1960s, studies were indicating the persistence of social class and spatial inequalities (see for example, Titmuss, 1968; Tudor-Hart, 1971). This and

subsequent evidence was collated and summarised by the *Black Report* (1980). The Report confirmed the persistence of significant inequalities in health. It concluded that relative material deprivation was the most important factor in explaining the links between social class and health, thus confirming the perspective on the relationship between health and social and economic circumstances which emerged from the historical analyses of McKeown (1976) and Burkitt (1973) and more contemporary comparative analyses (see Abel-Smith, 1994, Chapter 2 for a review of the latter; see also, Phillimore, Beattie and Townsend, 1994; Power, 1994; and HSE, 1996).

The recommendations of the *Black Report* identified not only more information, research and more effective planning of health and social care as being necessary, but also increases in social security benefits to improve the economic circumstances of the most disadvantaged sections of the population. In 1987 the evidence was updated with the publication of *The Health Divide* (Health Education Council, 1987) which concluded that little progress had been made since the publication of the *Black Report* and that higher levels of unemployment were now contributing more significantly to social deprivation. Since the conclusions and recommendations of the *Black Report* had not been welcomed by the government (see Chapter 7) it is perhaps unsurprising that *The Health Divide* should record a rather similar picture.

Whilst the government's reaction to the *Black Report* and *The Health Divide* might be characterised as essentially ideological – an unwillingness to accept explanations that called for more government expenditure and more government intervention – there were other critiques of the Report. In particular it was suggested that the apparent persistence, or even widening of health inequalities, might be a function of the limitations of the data, especially with regard to the inconsistent classification of social class over time (Illsley, 1986). Furthermore it was suggested that lower class status might for some people be a function of poor health and disability, rather than the other way round (Stern, 1983; Wilkinson, 1992; Judge, 1995; and Wilkinson, 1995).

The themes of the *Black Report* and *The Health Divide* were to be replayed again with the publication of *Tackling Health Inequalities: An Agenda for Action* (Kings Fund, 1995b). This showed death rates amongst the poorest groups to be rising for the first time in at least fifty years with the widening of social inequalities and social divisions in the 1980s as a likely cause. The resulting policy agenda focused, like the *Black Report*, on incomes and housing plus action to diminish the incidence of smoking (advertising restrictions and tobacco taxes). Meanwhile the Government's own *Health of the Nation* strategy (DoH, 1992) largely ignored the relationship between poverty, inequalities and health in contrast to initiatives taken by governments elsewhere (see for example, Bayley, 1995, p. 7).

The relationship between the NHS and health inequalities can be understood in part as one dimension of the broader relationship between health and health care. If factors other than health services have a profound impact on health status – including health inequalities – then the NHS, however fair its policies and procedures on access and utilisation, will have a modest impact on health inequalities. This point is made in effect by the *Black Report* and the subsequent reports, where emphasis is laid as much on social security and housing policies as on health service policies. Our conclusion might be again to provide support for governmental concerns with cost-containment when additional expenditure on the NHS is not going to ameliorate health inequalities in some obviously self-evident manner.

Health care and health costs

Reductions in the costs associated with providing both health and social security systems was one anticipated consequence of establishing a more efficient and fairer health service. That the National Health Service was not delivering stable or declining health care costs was recognised widely and early in the history of the service (see Chapter 5). Despite being readily attributable to trends apparent before the NHS was established (see Chapter 2) and in other countries, successive (especially Conservative) governments have never been able to free themselves entirely from the notion that there might be some reorganised NHS that is demonstrably more efficient and that the associated efficiency gains would generate really significant savings in the delivery of the service (see Chapters 6 and 7).

The perspective on health and health care identified above provides not only a rationale for a policy of cost-containment, but also an indication of its inherent limitations as a policy goal. For if the nation's health status is significantly influenced by the social and economic circumstances of the nation, then the demands for health care and the costs of the nation's health services may be only marginally influenced by the way these services are organised. The exceptions to this stricture might lie only in the form of three radical policy options which involve the significant re-ordering of the role of medical and health care; a re-ordering of the role of health policies; and a recasting of the role of the state.

The role of medical and health care

At the centre of this policy option are a series of policies known interchangeably as preventive health, health promotion, disease prevention and preventive medicine. The major thrust of such policies is to concentrate upon 'non-medical' health services which will prevent disease, illness and disability from occurring thus obviating the need for, and hence expenditure on, medical care. This is essentially a recognition of the equation of much nineteenth century social policy with the prevention of ill health, disease and disability avoidable through knowledge of risks present in an economically and oppressive environment (see Chapter 1). However there are a number of problems associated with making this the basis of a radical policy agenda.

Whilst the essentials of the preventive approach might be broadly accepted – that there is a range of environmental factors impacting on the health status of individuals and the wider community – these essentials cannot always be translated into clearly defined and/or widely accepted detailed policy prescriptions. Policy-makers in the preventative care field face a number of uncertainties, especially about knowledge and 'whether or not to act on the basis of inadequate information' (DHSS, 1976d, pp. 66–8). Other uncertainties include measuring the outcome of preventive services (do they make a difference?) and those surrounding the alternative use of scarce resources, especially where these are known to make a difference in the short-run against the hoped for long-term effects of preventive services.

These uncertainties are reflected in the language of prevention including the 'shadowy concept' of 'positive health' (Illsley, 1980); the contradictory sounding concept of 'preventive health care'; the defensive sounding 'disease prevention'; and the almost evangelical sounding 'health promotion' (Expenditure Committee, 1977). Indeed the linguistic styles in legislation and education employed by those concerned with the preventive approach have been identified as obstacles to understanding and comprehension in the community at large. Other obstacles to behavioural changes include the psychological defence against anxiety, the empirical folklore ('my grandad smoked until he was ninety') and the financial (the return from investment in prevention takes years to materialise and even then it is difficult to attribute cause and effect) (Muir-Gray, 1979).

The evidence on factors influencing health is such that it is impossible for the preventive approach to ignore the issue of behavioural changes (see especially the evidence on smoking referred to earlier in this chapter). But does 'behaviour change' involve 'blaming the victim' (Ryan, 1976)? Does the focus on behavioural change lead to a neglect of the impact of environment, the socio-economic context in which groups and individuals are located, and differing responses towards health education and behaviour changing messages? Studies continue to confirm the long-standing finding that health messages are failing to influence the groups who most need advice (see OHE, 1994). Thus preventive policies may be preaching to the converted. This is a dilemma for any policy maker; devise a preventive programme for changing individual life styles and the disparity in health status between rich and poor is as likely to increase as decrease.

Finally, there is the political dimension of medical care. Since the emergence of 'modern medicine' and 'modern health services' professional and public attention has focused on the 'interesting cases' represented in the acute hospital sector of the NHS (see especially Chapters 1 and 5). What are now well-established trends of burgeoning technology, raised expectations, and increased dependency through changing demographic factors, serve to maintain the focus on curing, and to a lesser extent caring; in these circumstances prevention might be seen to represent a less pressing concern. Indeed in one area where political pressure is exerted to develop preventive measures (screening) it is not clear that the outcome best serves 'a rational approach' to prevention. For example, doubts continued to be expressed about the cost-effectiveness of screening programmes for both cervical and breast cancer.

The dilemmas in the preventive approach have meant that the search for conceptual clarity has led to policy uncertainty. The appropriate resources cannot be easily identified and shifted from acute to preventive work. While a holistic approach is conceptually attractive it presents problems for monitoring of policy. The organizational context, until the 1991 reforms, was not really suitable for giving the preventive approach high visibility (see Chapter 5). Since 1991, with Directors of Public Health replacing Community Physicians and providing advice to health purchasing authorities, the situation may be changing (see Chapter 7).

There is also a danger of deprofessionalisation in which everything in the environment, especially the socio-economic, is said to determine health status, and the result is a 'buckshot' theory of policy in which all explanations of health have equal value and consequently devalue the professional input. Some of the advocates of the preventive approach are at the same time 'deprofessionalisers'. This presents us with another uncertainty; the constant criticisms of the practitioners of a craft can lead to a professional retreat and a withdrawal from the sort of interdisciplinary co-operation which is an essential element of all preventive programmes.

The potential significance of illness and disease prevention and health promotion are substantial; but there are associated dilemmas. The costs of acute medical care might be diminished, but other parts of the NHS budget may have to rise; furthermore the former is in the long-run and somewhat uncertain, whilst the latter is in the short-run and is less uncertain. The power and status of the medical profession might be moderated in the long term; but in the short-term, preventive policies may need the prestige of a health care profession to get their message across.

Finally, if the preventive approach derives part of its rationale from our awareness of the social production of health, disease and disability, its development must inevitably be constrained by the social production of health care. Communal support for the NHS may rest, in part at least, on our perception of the value of access to professional skills and knowledge as a means of avoiding, ameliorating or forestalling potentially life-threatening events which occur in the social context in which we currently live. Support may be less forthcoming for a health service that tells us to change this social context in order that we make less use of the health service. Indeed a community may exist in which smokers and drinkers willingly pay taxes on smoking and drinking to finance a health service where a substantial volume of resources are taken up with dealing with the consequences of smoking and drinking.

The case that there has been a relative neglect of the preventive approach in the NHS, and indeed other health care systems in other countries, can be well made. When resources are scarce an immediate response to the acute situation of pain or potential mortality takes priority over the longer-term investment in future health status. The case for a radical and short-term re-working of the NHS in the direction of preventive policies can be said to conflict with the uncertainties of the knowledge base, the problems of knowledge utilisation, the dangers of victim-blaming, the politics of prevention and the social construction of health and health care.

The role of health policies

The policy option here would be to place an increased emphasis on the intersectoral approach to health. Any health-challenging features of the 'normal environment' would be confronted by the full range of social and economic services. This would require a combined role for education, housing, nutritional advice and social security policies to be emphasised, not only as a counterweight to 'individual victim blaming' but also as a recognition of the importance of a multi-factorial explanation for disease and illness, which requires a multi-service response.

> (All) theories of health and all approaches designed to increase health are intended to advise against, to prevent the creation of, or to remove, obstacles to the achievement of human potential. These obstacles may be biological, environmental, societal, familial, or personal. (Seedhouse, 1986, p. 53)

This might justify a number of policies and services which have as their purpose the prevention of distress and disability, the alleviation of disease, the cure of illness and sickness, and the rehabilitation of the individual to social functioning. Such services go way beyond health care as conventionally labelled and include other social and public programmes that have an impact on the health status of the community at large and groups within that community (eg: social security, housing, education and environmental programmes). The administrative/inter-sectoral implications for government of taking this view seriously are quite profound:

> Quite apart from the DHSS, the policies of a whole range of government departments, including the Treasury (tobacco and alcohol excise duty), Department of Environment (atmospheric and other forms of pollution), Ministry of Agriculture, Fisheries and Food (food safety and agricultural policy), Home Office (narcotics), Department of Education and Science (health education in schools) to name only the most obvious, influence the health of the public. (Acheson Report, 1988, para. 4.2)

The significance of this 'necessary collaboration' between departments of state raises the spectre of an even more powerful and intrusive state; clearly anathema for those wedded to the concept of a minimal state (see below and Chapter 10). However in other respects the inter-sectoral approach might be characterised as both 'more radical' and 'less intrusive' than a more preventive approach within the NHS. A range of measures (eg: increasing the level of social security benefits, reducing environmental pollution and improved food labelling) can be justified on other grounds (eg: social justice, environmentalism and consumerism) and do not involve state or professional definitions of how individuals should behave (eg: how they spend the social security benefit or whether they read and make use of the information included in food labelling). However in making this point we are identifying what might be identified as one of the weaknesses of this approach – that its impact is more diffuse and even more uncertain than that attributable to more focused preventive policies. Accurate food labelling can be justified on a number of grounds including the promotion of 'healthy eating'. However the latter will not automatically flow from the former, even where the knowledge base underpinning the concept is soundly-based and widely-accepted. Once again the knowledge is likely to be interpreted and utilised differently by different groups. More generally these intersectoral policies acquire a legitimacy partly as an element in policies for health and partly through cost-benefit analyses which indicate the potential for savings in areas where conventional NHS expenditure might be expected but not necessarily efficient or effective. However once again it seems unlikely that these policies will readily secure support as an alternative use of money that would otherwise be spent on the NHS. It seems unlikely that radical changes would be supported on the grounds that they afforded an opportunity for dramatically reducing expenditure on 'conventional health services'.

The case that there has been a relative neglect of the intersectoral approach to health policies can be well made. However the case for a radical embrace of this approach, as a means of making significant inroads into health service budgets, seems problematic for a set of reasons similar to those identified for radically recasting the role of medical and health care. A final and quite telling point might be the difficulties encountered in getting an inter-sectoral approach *within* the NHS itself and *between* providers of health and social care (see especially Chapters 6 and 12).

The role of the state

Perhaps the only feasible alternative for a cost-conscious government is to change the role of the state as a provider of medical care and health care. In terms of the trends identified in Part One, the obvious alternative would be to return to the residual model of state intervention in health care described in Chapter 1. However more recent debates and developments might provide other means by which the state's role and state expenditure can be diminished. In particular critiques of contemporary health services relating to the medical model – its use and misuse.

These critiques vary in their roots and their radicalism. Perhaps the most radical is that of Illich in which the role of medical care is not simply much less dramatic and positive than sometimes imagined (the McKeown thesis) but is negative in its impact on those societies where it is the dominant approach – the result being what he terms 'iatrogenesis' (Illich, 1976). This critique does connect with that of others who decry the over-medicalisation of human activities ranging from 'maternity cases' to 'mental health problems' (see for example, Oakley, 1984 and Sedgwick, 1982).

The Illich critique is so radical that there are few, if any, signs that it has made it way on to the policy agenda – in this sense at least it is not realistically part of contemporary conflicts about health and health care. Other critiques of over-medicalisation seem to connect more with the experiences of at least certain service users and can be located in the long-running 'always potential' conflict between professionals and their clients (see Chapters 13 and 14). Other critiques might well be understood as part of equally long-running and ongoing conflicts between different professional groups (see Chapter 13) and there is no doubt that other professional groups – most obviously midwives, nurses and social workers – have seen themselves, and their approaches to needs and problems, as more appropriate than that offered by medical practitioners.

Whether they are intended to do so or not, it seems likely that these critiques of the medical model provide a rationale for restricting the scope of the NHS in relation to, for example, meeting the needs of people with mental health problems or providing long-term nursing care to frail elderly people. Whilst the theoretical implications of some critiques would be to switch resources away from provision based on a 'medical model' and towards provision based on a 'social model', the political reality would seem to be that the 'social model' lacks the popularity and legitimacy that has been attached to the 'medical model'. The respective 'economic' and 'political histories' of the NHS and the local authority Social Services Departments could be adduced as relevant evidence on this point. However the controversies surrounding particular cases (in relation to mental health services) and the general trend (in relation to long-term care for older people) indicate that the ensuing political conflicts may limit the ability of governments to reduce significantly the scope of an ostensibly comprehensive NHS.

The other critique that has been developed is one that might actually be characterised as 'taking the medical model seriously'. As developed by Cochrane (1972) it is partly rooted in the findings associated with the 'submerged iceberg' – that the diagnostic characteristics of 'ill' and 'healthy' people are not widely different. The problem then becomes one of discovering the point, or points, on the distribution at which therapy begins to do more harm than good. One solution to the problem is randomised controlled trials

(RCTs) to test the hypothesis that 'a certain treatment alters the natural history of a disease for the better' (Cochrane, 1972, p. 20). Cochrane's conclusion was that many procedures being applied were not soundly based on evidence drawn from RCTs. Furthermore there was available evidence to question, for example, variations in the length of hospital stays and treatments advocated or used in relation to ischaemic heart disease and mature diabetes. Some of his most devastating criticisms were directed at ENT departments where he concluded that

> we have two therapies which are probably effective in limited spheres; the first (tonsillectomy) is probably effective for only a small percentage of the cases operated on at present and has a definite mortality, but it is an urgent, dramatic therapy and is still rather fashionable. The other (audiological) is probably effective in improving the quality of life in some of a defined group of the population; it is dull, smacks of a local authority service, is not nearly as fashionable and serves the elderly. The first is applied inefficiently because it is too widely applied; the latter is applied inefficiently because it is under-applied. (Cochrane, 1972, p. 63)

He was even more critical of psychiatry, concluding that it uses a 'large number of therapies whose effectiveness has not been proven. It is basically inefficient' (Cochrane, 1972, p. 60).

Cochrane's themes continue to be pursued and supported by relevant evidence with variations in practice being identified by Yates (1987), the National Audit Office (1987) and in Frankel and West (eds., 1993). More recently it has been suggested that of those procedures used by doctors in pregnancy and childbirth which have been subjected to RCTs, 60 per cent are of doubtful value or positively harmful (see Bayley, 1995, p. 11). These figures do suggest that there remains considerable scope for focusing NHS activities more explicitly on evidence-based medicine grounded in sound medical research and communication of research results to all NHS doctors (see Fries et al, 1993 for a presentation of this argument).

Does this approach provide an opportunity to significantly diminish public expenditure on health care by focusing much more precisely on those activities with proven efficacy? The answer is probably 'no', given that the evidence can also support increased activity and expenditure (for example, in relation to audiological services for elderly people and reducing social class inequalities in the use of health services, see, Cochrane, 1972, pp. 61–3, 75). Furthermore since 'wasteful use of diagnostic tests and the excessive use of X-rays, and unnecessary intervention (including unnecessary surgery)' seem to be features of more market-driven health care systems – especially the private insurance and private market system in the USA (see Abel-Smith, 1976, p. 62), it may well be that a universal, comprehensive health service has the greatest potential to make progress towards the model of evidence-based medicine. In the end, given the limitations (political and others) on the scope for a radical recasting of the roles of medical care, health care and health policies, the radical reduction in government expenditure on health care will probably only come from recasting the role of the state in the manner referred to at the beginning of this section – retreating back from the universalist model embodied in the NHS. We will examine the arguments relating to this radical alternative in the next chapter.

Conflicts

The only purpose for which power can be rightfully exercised over any member of a civilised community, against his will, is to prevent harm to others. His own good, either physical or moral, is not a sufficient warrant. (Mill, 1859, p. 73)

No man is island entire of it self; every man is a piece of the Continent, a part of the main. (Donne, 1624, pp. 1108–9)

In terms of the long-running conflict about the role of the state the debates about health and health care afford relatively little comfort to the libertarian standard, used for the last hundred years by those philosophically against the role of the state in social and economic life. While clearly a philosophical value, it nevertheless raises a number of important practical questions. For example, what sort of response, if any, would be forthcoming from a contemporary supporter of a minimalist state in the face of a professional judgement about what is regarded as the minimum necessary to enable an improved health status of the population to be achieved?

The implications of accepting an inter-sectoral approach are germane to discussions about the scale and scope of state intervention in society. Advocates of a minimalist state position run the danger of equating health policies with medical care, thus confusing health as an objective with medical care as one possible means to that goal, and relegating, ignoring, or being unconscious of, the relationship between societal sources of ill-health and the societal institutional responses to that condition.

The conflict surrounding the relative roles of health interventions relates to Dubos's conceptualisation of the differences between the myths of Hygieia and Asclepius symbolised as 'the never-ending oscillation between two different points of view' in medicine, between those who believe in 'the discovery and teaching of the natural laws which will ensure a man a healthy mind in a healthy body', and those who believe 'that the chief role of the physician is to treat disease, to restore health by correcting any imperfection caused by the accidents of birth or life' (Dubos, 1959, pp. 109–11).

This conceptual dichotomy is dangerous for the advancement of both the preventive and alleviative roles of medicine. Whichever wins the philosophical battle, it will be at the expense of the other and will further the erosion of the resources going to the already embattled public sector. Is there an inevitable conflict between conventional medical practice and preventive medicine? Not necessarily; one ideal goal promulgated by critics of the western scientific model, in the face of the subordinate position of preventive medicine and health promotion, is that of a partnership between scientific knowledge and humane ethics so that the NHS can as far as possible strive to guarantee an equal diffusion of knowledge-based services in a sensitive manner. A summary of the critics arguments is that the health care system (NHS) should have two key objectives. Firstly, to keep the individual out of the health care system if at all possible by emphasising the impact on health status of socially produced conditions, thus re-instating the importance of prevention. Secondly, once the individual enters the health care system, they should as far as is feasible be enabled to return to their 'normal environment' as soon as possible. If unable to return to 'normality', then the most sensitive and 'caring' setting for their future should be planned with and by the individual.

Conclusions

There is not a conflict between health and health care; nor do we have to choose one or the other. Health and health care are related, but the relationship is a complex one mediated through the impact of social divisions, lay/professional relationships, and attitudes towards health and sickness. In particular the evidence seems clear for the impact of factors *other than* quality and quantity of health care on the health status of populations. *Policies for health* must therefore involve substantially more than *policies for health care*; and the persistence of many 'health problems', including many health inequalities are to a significant degree beyond the powers of the NHS to ameliorate to any significant degree.

In these circumstances it is unsurprising that the health policy priorities of the *Black Report* (1980), *The Health Divide* (Health Education Council, 1987) and *Tackling Health Inequalities* (Kings Fund, 1995b) focused on social security and housing policies rather than health care policies. In many respects this orientation is not particularly new. It reasserts the significance of environmental factors for health status first developed in the public health movement in the nineteenth century (see Chapter 1). It accords with the conclusion that the country was far healthier in 1948 than it had been ten years earlier (Briggs, 1978, p. 448) – testimony to the impact of a range of social policies deployed in the Second World War and especially targeted at children (see Titmuss, 1950). It also emphasises the intersectoral approach to social policy that was a feature of the Beveridge Report for whom the National Health Service was but one part of a broader programme of social policy reform (see Chapter 3). One implication of this more limited role for the National Health Service in the nation's health might be to clarify the role of the Service and free it from the burdens of unjustified criticism – especially in relation to health inequalities. On the other hand if there is less faith in the ability of a National Health Service to diminish disease and disability will this lead inevitably to a questioning of what the National Health Service is for?

We have already referred to the problematic nature of the concept of health as one not capable of simple definition. The assertion that good health is desirable is not sufficient warrant for ignoring this uncertainty. It would be strange if the political and economic case for directing resources to a National Health Service could not be supported because of the absence of a core definition of the target of such resources. Although there are some conflicts and dilemmas involved in this task (see for example, Seedhouse, 1987), these should not be seen as forever irresolvable or insurmountable – either politically, economically, intellectually or morally.

Although not entirely satisfactory the Royal Commission did go some way towards clarifying the objectives of the NHS. It is particularly relevant to note that the Commission's recommended objectives avoided any ambitious commitments to making an impact on the health status of the nation. The Royal Commission defined the objectives as being to:

(a) encourage and assist individuals to remain healthy;
(b) provide equality of entitlement to health services;
(c) provide a broad range of services to a high standard;
(d) provide equality of access to these services;
(e) provide a service free at the time of use;
(f) satisfy the reasonable expectations of its users; and
(g) remain a national service responsive to local needs
(See, Royal Commission on the NHS, 1979, p. 9)

These aims do accord, in part at least, with the well-known paragraphs in the Beveridge Report as well as the duty of the Minister as laid down in the National Health Service Act, 1946 and subsequent legislation. The current statutory definition (in the 1977 NHS Act) states that the Secretary of State has a *duty* to provide a comprehensive health service to secure improvements in health, and in the prevention, diagnosis and treatment of illness.

What this suggests is that there are a set of substantial purposes for the NHS, separate from the more ambitious goals of enhancing the health status of society as a whole or of particular groups within society. Furthermore, if all members of society are to receive at least some assistance in remaining healthy (goal a, above) then some state intervention in society is inevitable. Goal (c) may require substantial state intervention in health care of the sort represented by the National Health Service and goals (b), (d) and (e) seem inseparable from a national health service. We will pursue these arguments in the next two chapters.

11
State or non-state?

The right to health care and the role of the state

> Special care is first taken of the sick who are looked after in public hospitals . . . these hospitals are very well furnished and equipped with everything conducive to health. (St. Thomas More, 1516, see Surtz and Hexter (eds) (1965), pp. 139–41)

> There has been a growing acceptance that access to medical services is one of the modern social rights. (Stevens, 1966, p. 6)

> Health care thus became an inalienable right rather than being a benefit dependent on the vagaries of the market. (Webster, 1990, p. 149)

The idea of the public provision of good quality health care is not new; but it has been a source of ideological and political conflict in Britain for at least one hundred and fifty years, as Part One of this book has documented. The previous chapter noted the conceptual difficulties associated with the concepts of 'health', 'health care' and 'medical care'. Despite these difficulties there have been advocates of a 'right to health' (see WHO, 1977); however the focus of this chapter is on the much narrower concept of a 'right to health care'. For the purposes of the arguments that follow we take health care to refer to the range of health services we associate with the National Health Service. That is essentially access to the professional skills and expertise of the medical and nursing professions and the range of professions allied to medicine. We might represent the right to health care operationally as 'minimising the gap between new biomedical knowledge and its application and availability to the community as a whole' (Carrier and Kendall, 1990c, p. 10).

The case *against* a national health service

There is no doubt that the preferred alternative of the radical right is that health care should be provided with the minimal involvement of the state on the assumption that there are more appropriate institutions for meeting an individual's health care needs – for example, the private market and the family. This radical right critique is not necessarily an attack on all state intervention in health care. It focuses on a particular model of state welfare and particular forms of state welfare. Essentially the focus is on the institutional model of state social welfare programmes – that is the state having a major role as a guarantor of social rights through comprehensive service provision (eg: health care, pensions, education) on something approaching a genuinely 'universal' basis. This inevitably involves a substantial proportion of GNP being devoted to government expenditure and a substantial proportion of that government expenditure being devoted to welfare expenditure. The British National Health Service constitutes something approaching a perfect exemplar of the institutional model of state welfare given its explicit aims to provide a comprehensive, optimum standard service – comprehensive 'in two senses – first, that it is available to all people, and second, that it covers all necessary forms of health care' (Ministry of Health, 1944, p. 9) with access based on citizenship (universal) and with limited user charges.

By contrast with the NHS, the radical right's preferred alternative is the residual model of state social welfare in which the provision of services is limited to a narrowly defined proportion of the population. The Poor Law medical service would represent an exemplar of this residual model of state welfare. Returning to the historical perspective of Part One, the radical right critique of state welfare, applied to health care, implies a reversal of the trends identified in Chapters 1 to 4. The basis for this significant re-ordering of the role of the state in health care can be said to be based on four sets of arguments:

(1) the perceived failings of 'welfare states';
(2) the nature of industrial societies;

(3) attitudes towards 'welfare states'; and
(4) alternatives to 'state welfare'.

1. The failings of 'welfare states' – by which is meant the failings of the institutional model of state welfare – can be broken down into six sub-headings as follows:

(a) micro-economic;
(b) macro-economic;
(c) political;
(d) social needs;
(e) freedom; and
(f) social costs.

The *micro-economic* argument centres on the virtues of competitive private markets as a means of allocating resources. Competition affords choice to the consumer – 'the market is generally superior to the ballot box as means of registering consumer preference' (Lees, 1961, p. 76) – and ensures the efficient use of resources (the inefficient competitor goes out of business). This is contrasted with the inefficiencies and non-existent consumer sovereignty associated with monopolistic state welfare bureaucracies of which the NHS would be a prime example.

> The NHS has a virtual monopoly of medical care and the absence of substitutes means that there are no strong external forces making for improvements in quality and efficiency ... the insistence on a single standard of service for all eliminates the internal forces making for improvements that would be generated by emulation between diverse standards. (Lees, 1961, p. 77)

This leads to the conclusion that not only are private markets more efficient and offer more choice, but that 'so-called welfare goods' like health care are no different to any other consumer goods that might be distributed through the market (see for example, Lees, 1976, pp. 6–7 on cars, TV sets and health care).

The *macro-economic* argument is represented by the long-standing concept of the 'public burden model of welfare' which 'sees public welfare expenditure – and particularly expenditure which is redistributive in intent – as a burden; an impediment to growth and economic development' (Titmuss, 1968, pp. 124–5). The implications are that an egalitarian welfare state erodes differentials, an expansive welfare state establishes major tax burdens on employers and employees alike resulting in disincentives to invest and to earn and a general redirection of resources from productive to non-productive sectors of the economy (the latter being one particularly widely quoted 'crowding-out' argument developed by Bacon and Eltis, 1976).

The *political* argument is that inevitably the government becomes overloaded with tasks beyond its competence and knowledge. This leads to a concern with accounting for public expenditure which dominates over the quality of the service which should be delivered. Government therefore becomes obsessed with administrative means of delivery and control (the process) rather than with the inputs necessary to deliver high-quality outputs (for which read health care according to professionally defined need). This bureaucratic control denies the existence of public choice and makes systematic what should be a form of professional flexibility based on individual need. The end result is the public burden model of state health and welfare, reluctantly assumed by government and suspiciously used by the public (see for example, Dunleavy, 1991; Hayek, 1976; and Murray, 1990).

The *social needs* argument points to the failure of welfare state programmes to achieve their stated goals. The giants identified by Beveridge – idleness, poverty, squalor, ignorance and disease – still stalk through British and other societies. The Beveridge-inspired social welfare programmes have singularly failed to achieve their basic goals and seem to be impotent in the face of apparently intractable problems of poverty, homelessness, child abuse and newly emergent problems such as AIDS. For the NHS the persistence of inequalities in health and health care (Chapter 10) and the continuing problems of waiting lists (Chapter 8) can be construed as damning evidence of the failure of this particular welfare state programme.

The *freedom* argument derives from the established liberal tradition which identifies the state as the major threat to individual freedom. The extensive state activity associated with the institutional model is inevitably associated with a diminution in freedom as the state takes away individual resources in the form of taxation and then spends them on health and other services designed and delivered by politicians, state welfare bureaucrats and professionals. 'Political decisions replace personal choice' (Lees, 1961, p. 76).

The *social costs* argument focuses on the socially and morally debilitating effects of the welfare state on the wider society.

> Not only is the present welfare state inefficient and destructive of personal liberty, individual responsibility and moral growth but it saps the collective moral fibre of our people as a nation. (Boyson, 1971, p. 7)

So it is not just freedom – the ability to act – that is eroded by the welfare state, but also the willingness to act, as society (or at least sections of society) gets drawn into a dependency culture.

2. The nature of industrial societies The arguments relating to this section can be broken down into three sub-headings as follows:

(a) egalitarian trends;
(b) greater affluence; and
(c) limited social costs.

The *egalitarian trends* argument and the *greater affluence* arguments use different empirical evidence to the same end. As societies like the UK become more egalitarian and affluent the 'increasing equality of income makes it wasteful to redistribute through taxes, grants and free services' (Seldon, 1966) and the increasing affluence associated with 'full employment and economic development' (Lees, 1961, p. 75) enables more and more individuals to purchase their own health care rather than rely on a tax-financed state health care system. Basically changes in income levels and 'the more equal distribution of income' (Lees, 1961, p. 75) in industrial societies leaves only a 'dwindling minority unable to pay' (Lees, 1961, p. 77) for themselves through a competitive private market in health care. We can all afford to be health care consumers in the private market even if it involves some modest sacrifices. The *social costs* argument relates to an assumption – sometimes unstated – that there are no significant social costs and diswelfares associated with the economic growth that is creating greater affluence. Certainly such social costs are sufficiently limited to provide no justification for extensive state social welfare programmes such as the NHS.

3. *Attitudes towards 'welfare states'* focuses on the growing unpopularity of extensive state social welfare programmes like the NHS and evidenced by surveys of popular opinion (Harris and Seldon, 1979) and actual voting behaviour. If valid this evidence seems to call into question the legitimacy of the modern 'welfare state'.

4. *Alternatives to 'welfare states'* are a key element in the radical right perspective since the residual model of state welfare presumes a diminished role for the state being compensated for by a much more extensive role of non-state providers of health care – primarily the market, but also possibly voluntary associations, communities and families. It is presumed that the resulting pattern of provision is relatively unproblematic and indeed that for most service-users the outcome will be improvements in relation to issues such as choice and service quality.

The right to minimal health care
The principles of the National Health Service appear to rest on something more elaborate than the right to minimal health care. However establishing the basis of this 'more modest right' is a useful (and logical) precursor to establishing the basis of an argument for the sort of state commitment embodied in the NHS.

The position of radical right writers that 'medical care is a personal consumption good, not markedly different from the generality of goods bought by consumers' (Lees, 1961, p. 76) and that 'we should all be consumers paying for all our purchases' (Seldon, 1966) seems at odds even with the concept of a minimal right to health care. Seldon goes on to suggest that

if some paid higher school fees, health insurance premiums, rents, mortgage repayments or saved more through pension schemes than others they would be no more regarded as morally different than people who spend more on shoes, sherries and shampoo. (Seldon, 1966)

This apparent equation of health care with shoes, sherry and shampoo appears to rule out any common ground on rights since there have been few notable advocates of rights to minimal sherry supplies – either in terms of quality or quantity

The perspective of Lees and Seldon appears to totally by-pass Arrow's concern about uncertainty in providing medical care (Arrow, 1963). The most notable critic of this equation (shoes, sherry and medical care) was Richard Titmuss who produced a non-exhaustive list of the characteristics of medical care that distinguished it from other goods and services which included the following suggestions:

1. Most consumers of medical care enter the doctor-patient relationship on an unequal basis; they believe that the doctor or surgeon knows best. Unlike market relationships in the case of consumer durables, they know that this special inequality in knowledge and techniques cannot for all practical purposes be reversed. It is thus no accident that Titmuss highly recommends Arrow on the uncertainties surrounding the medical care market and the obverse need for certainty guaranteed by the state through professional trust.
2. Many consumers do not desire medical care
3. Many consumers do not know they need medical care
4. Consumers who want medical care do not know in advance how much medical care they need and what it will cost
5. Medical care can seldom be returned to the seller, exchanged for durable goods or discarded. For many people the consequences of consuming medical care are irreversible.
6. Consumers of medical care experience greater difficulties in changing their minds in the course of consuming care than the consumers of durable goods. (See Titmuss, 1968, pp. 146–7 which also includes further examples)

These dilemmas for the so-called consumer and the distinctive qualities of medical care were also neatly summed up by Abel-Smith when he observed that:

It is somewhat unreal to envisage a motor accident victim with multiple fractures weighing up at the hospital door his preferences for medical treatment compared with food, clothing, or a new car. In such situations, money is no object. (Abel-Smith, 1976, p. 36)

Paradoxically the strength of these arguments has been recognised by advocates of private market provision. Lees has argued that there should be a means-test for those unable to pay hospital costs directly, or indirectly through insurance, and that the state 'would retain a special responsibility for the mentally ill and the chronic sick' (Lees, 1961, p. 77). But why should this be, if medical care is a personal consumption good not markedly different from the generality of goods bought by consumers? In a similar vein, Seldon has argued that

there could be minimum requirements by law of spending on education and health so that if 'parents won't pay for the desirable minimum of education', logic points in the first place to methods of impelling them to do so by state requirements ensured by inspection. (Seldon, 1966)

One is led to wonder whether there is a similar desirable minimum for spending on shoes? And finally there are the long-standing arguments for voucher schemes (especially education vouchers, but also health vouchers) ensuring that the poor are not prevented from becoming 'education consumers' or 'health consumers'. We still await a 'radical right text' advocating similar vouchers for sherry or shampoo! (See also Sugden, 1982 on this inconsistency in the radical right approach to minimal state welfare).

It seems that health and education might be, after all, 'markedly different' from the generality of goods bought by consumers. Even whilst they defend a private market model, the radical right writers concede the case for a residual model of state welfare – that is people should have some sort of right to at least a minimal level of health care and their children to some sort of education. We will return to the basis of this apparent wide-ranging consensus below.

Alternatives to state health care

The concept of a right to minimal health care does not lead immediately to some sort of state intervention. Do we need state-provided and/or funded health care as against health care made available by alternative providers and alternative forms of funding? The radical right have always argued the virtues of alternatives to state welfare for reasons we have noted above. The major alternative mechanisms being:

(a) profit and competition – health care through the market and employers
(b) altruism and mutual aid – health care through voluntary associations
(c) informal caring networks – health care through families and communities.

Profit and competition

In reality the major mechanism is private insurance, since few individuals can afford to pay on demand when medical need arises. The potential for such private insurance in the area of health care is considerable (as the example of the USA indicates). The operation of such a market / private insurance based system of health care has traditionally raised a number of concerns relating to both inequalities and inefficiencies. However in the terms of our initial argument these concerns are not central, although they will enter the argument at a later stage. The key issue is well represented by Abel-Smith's comments on the operation of private health insurance in industrial societies:

> no private insurance company is prepared to provide in full the health insurance cover which people want . . . (and those) . . . who most 'need' insurance cover are least likely to be able to purchase it. (Abel-Smith, 1976, pp. 37, 39)

Whilst we may have justifiable concerns about the extent to which markets in health care do match up to the benefits (choice and efficiency) of the theoretical model, a more fundamental issue concerns groups whom the insurance industry will effectively label as the 'bad risks of an industrial economy'. For these 'bad risks' the limitations of health care markets will be of less concern than their inability to enter the health care market in the first place. The classic 'bad risks' for health care insurance may include elderly people, people with physical disabilities and/or chronic health problems, those with AIDS, people with mental health problems, and people with disabilities. For these groups the difficulties of exercising genuine consumer choice in a 'market for medical care' are of theoretical interest, because their needs and income are such that they cannot afford to be consumers in the market in the first place!

Whilst employer-based welfare schemes may include health care, and extend the market beyond those who can afford conventional health insurance provision, the evidence on *deregulated* occupational welfare suggests a pattern of inequalities and exclusions that replicates that of market and insurance-based provision. Most obviously serious health problems can lead to a marginal position in, or exclusion from, the labour market and the latter is inevitably associated with limited or no access to occupational welfare.

Altruism and mutual aid

Philanthropic and mutual aid voluntary associations have played a key role in the development of health care in most industrial societies (Chapter 1). In Europe, contemporary health care systems are invariably based upon the foundations of charitable hospitals and medical benefits provided by mutual-aid organizations (trade unions, friendly societies) (see Abel-Smith, 1972). However this historical role also provides ample evidence of the potential limitations of a reliance on altruism and mutual aid as the means of providing a right to minimal health care.

Despite their considerable merits as providers of good-quality hospital care to those who would be unable to purchase such care in a private market, Britain's voluntary hospitals were limited in their coverage both to certain areas of the country and to certain areas of health care. The mutual-aid institutions of nineteenth century Britain – the Friendly Societies – were also limited in their coverage of the population (Chapter 1).

Supporters of a scenario in which voluntary institutions reclaim something of their presumed earlier predominance in welfare provision, including health care, have to contend with historical evidence of their limitations in an era untrammelled by vast state welfare bureaucracies and the observation that the existence of the latter in industrial societies

> suggests not so much these societies are uniquely compassionate, but is a recognition of the fact that the spontaneous dictates of compassion consistently fail to meet the volume of unmet human needs. (Pinker, 1971, p. 170)

To this point we might add the seemingly paradoxical point (at least for some political perspectives) that a state-run health care system may have done more to sustain a sense of altruism than those systems dominated by not-for-profit voluntary institutions. Titmuss's international survey of different modes of obtaining blood for transfusions is an interesting illustration of this point (see Titmuss, 1970, especially Chapters 13 and 14).

Whether a modern day version of mutual-aid would be more successful is equally questionable. Partly because there would have to be questions about the ability and/or willingness of the contemporary equivalent of the 'grey, faceless lower third of the working-class' (Gilbert, 1966, p. 166) to participate in such institutions. More especially contemporary health care examples indicate that non-profit voluntary health insurance institutions, like Blue Cross in the USA, have to adjust their premiums to risks or they

> will be left with the bad risks, as the good risks are offered cheaper policies elsewhere ... (with the result that) ... while voluntary health insurance can meet the requirements of the healthy, it cannot provide for those who require most medical care. (Abel-Smith, 1976, p. 39)

Families and communities
For the radical right, families and communities constitute another set of alternative welfare institutions who might reasonably reclaim their historical role as pre-eminent welfare institutions and thus aid the replacement of extensive state welfare activity. This perspective seems to be at least in part based on assumptions that the family and state are competing welfare institutions, and that the diminished contemporary welfare role for families is attributable to an extending and intrusive role for the state.

Diminish the role of its competitor by 'rolling back the frontiers of the welfare state' and the frontiers of the 'welfare family' are presumed to begin expanding. This perspective reverses a traditional sociological perspective in which the causal relationship runs the other way, and the increasing role for the state is partly caused by a declining role for families which in turn is caused by fundamental changes in structure and function brought about by industrialisation and urbanisation. Whilst this conventional sociological wisdom has been called into question – at least with regard to the British experience – the alternative scenario offers no more sustenance to the radical right perspective. This contends that the dramatic decline in the welfare role of families and communities has been equally dramatically overstated. At one end of the time continuum, historians like Anderson (1980) and Laslett (1965) have questioned the historical veracity of extended families as effective welfare institutions and at the other end, social policy researchers have undertaken a more precise delineation of a formidable army of contemporary informal carers.

On this evidence the welfare role of families might be expanding rather than declining, and be complementary to, rather than competing with, the welfare institutions of the state (such as the NHS). Contemporary families and communities might also be somewhere near the limits of their capacity in terms both of the 'burden of caring' borne by many 'informal carers' and of past demographic and current employment trends which may be about to cut a swathe through some of the traditional sources of this army of informal carers. Even without these trends there are questions about the ability and desirability of substituting familial care for the sort of specialised nursing and other forms of care and support that could be delivered through a state health care system like the NHS. Reliance on families inevitably raises concerns about inequalities in familial resources – compare a large, rich family with an impoverished single-parent family with few relations. Advocates of greater economic inequality in society may not be much impressed by this comparison but it does lead to a more basic point – some people have little or no kin.

Around the three major alternatives to state-provided health care; firstly, of profit and competition; secondly, of altruism and mutual aid; and finally, of families and communities, there are clearly concerns of equity, fairness, and efficiency all of which may claim a part in a later stage of the argument. But at this stage we encounter even more fundamental points. We can identify firstly, a degree of consensus around the concept of a right to minimal health care, and secondly, a substantial body of historical and contemporary evidence that the major alternatives to state provided health care will not guarantee this right to at least a substantial minority of the population – particularly those with limited income and/or limited kin networks afflicted with particular physical and mental health problems. This is perhaps most eloquently summed up in the concept of the 'bad risks of an urban/industrial society'. The historical and contemporary evidence suggests that a significant minority of the population would be denied access to even minimal health care without some form of government intervention. The result is a wide-ranging consensus around the concept of minimal state welfare.

Rights and responsibilities

Before we move on to examine the case for going beyond a right to minimal health care (beyond the residual model of state health care) we can look briefly at two other strands of the radical right argument against state provision of health care (and other dimensions of state welfare). We have labelled these the 'personal capabilities argument' and the 'personal morality argument'.

The personal capabilities argument recognises that personal capabilities vary and poses the question of why the more capable members of society should be forced to compensate the less capable for their poverty and disadvantage. This is associated with 'Social Darwinism' and is linked in social policy literature to the late nineteenth/early twentieth century proposals of the Eugenics Society in relation to people with learning difficulties and to the work of Spencer (see for example, Pinker, 1971, pp. 24–31). It is however an argument that can have a continuing resonance as advances in medical care increase the life expectancy of individuals with a range of life-threatening and disabling conditions – particularly those which are genetic in origin.

One 'social science' response to this argument has been an 'empiricist' approach. This asserts that it is simply not true that 'the support of paupers and the mothers of illegitimate children would eventually lead to a deterioration in the biological and moral quality of the nation' (Pinker, 1971, p. 27 on Spencer). However this can be considered an inadequate response since it does not attempt to refute the underlying assumption that it would be quite proper to leave unmet the needs of certain individuals (eg: illegitimate children, people with learning difficulties) if by so doing, the rest of society derived some benefit.

The value arguments against this approach could include one from 'common needs' with its associated commitment to minimal/ subsistence rights (see below). One could also develop a 'fairness' argument employing the 'nature / nurture' debates about the extent to which individual capabilities are endowed / inherited or influenced by environmental factors. One does not have to 'take sides' in that particular debate since both lend support to this 'fairness' argument. For if it is conceded that personal capabilities are to any significant degree influenced by either genetic / biological or environmental factors, it can be argued that it is unfair that an individual's command-over-resources should be entirely decided by her / his personal capabilities. Expressed in that form the argument does not seem 'strong' enough to justify extensive state welfare activities, but does provide an additional argument for residual state welfare and the right to minimal health care.

The personal morality argument refers to the long-established 'personal pathology' argument that people are poor or disadvantaged through their own moral failings. This might include an unwillingness to work hard, to spend money wisely, and in the case of health care, an unwillingness to cease health-threatening behaviour (smoking, over-eating). It is an argument that has been linked to the 'personal capabilities argument' and it has also been refuted in the same 'empiricist' manner; that it is simply not true (eg: the finding by Booth (1903) regarding the small proportion of poverty that could be attributed to questions of habit rather than circumstance of employment, see Simey and Simey, 1960, p. 182). However to counter the argument only on those terms could imply that one is accepting the idea that if an individual's poverty or ill-health could be reasonably attributed to some 'moral failing' then it would be acceptable to do nothing for them (people with AIDS are the contemporary group who seem most likely to be categorised in this way). This is clearly one of the limitations (for the purposes of normative theory) of the perspectives that conceptualise 'poverty' and/or 'ill-health' as predominantly 'structural problems' (Chapter 10). By themselves they do not invalidate the 'less-eligibility workhouse' for the 'undeserving poor'.

One argument to counter the 'personal morality' argument would once again be based on 'common needs' and the associated commitment to minimal/subsistence rights. One could also develop another 'fairness' argument. We know that the workings of a modern industrial society are not always fair. People do not always get their 'just deserts'; people can be poor and ill even if they work hard, spend their money wisely and follow the advice of health educators to the very best of their ability. Poverty and ill-health cannot therefore be necessarily linked to 'personal pathology'. This at the very least would seem to justify forms of residual state welfare for the 'deserving poor' and the 'deserving ill'. However given, if nothing else, the operational difficulties in identifying and 'separating out' the 'undeserving poor' and 'undeserving ill' from their more worthy counterparts, we are left with a compelling case for residual state welfare for the poor (for all practical purposes). We may of course note that this concept of the 'undeserving poor' may obviously have a profound impact on residual state welfare, providing the basis for 'anti-scrounger' controls and associated problems of stigma for, and under-utilisation by, the 'deserving' poor (see Chapter 12).

Minimal health care and the role of the state
If the state is drawn into an involvement in health care to guarantee the right to a minimal service, what form might this take. The implication seems to be some variant of the residual model of state welfare – a contemporary version of the New Poor Law (Chapter 1). However there are two other forms of minimal state welfare which can be explored and whose 'hands-off' approach would commend themselves to the radical right. These are judicial state welfare and fiscal state welfare.

Judicial welfare refers to the welfare role of the courts and the potential for 'redistribution by the courts' (see for example, Titmuss, 1974, Ch.6). Of interest for this argument is the extent to which the courts can effectively and equitably compensate groups and individuals for the social costs and disservices generated by a complex, changing society. This could clearly include those health problems which may be said to be attributable to the actions of others.

However there are the limitations on the problems that can be resolved in this way. This is another issue which Titmuss high-lighted with his observation that in a modern industrial society it is 'increasingly difficult to identify the causal agent or agencies, and thus to allocate the costs of disservices and charge those who are responsible'. This circumstance places obvious limitations on the potential welfare role of the courts for:

> if the identification of the agents of diswelfare were possible
> – if we could legally name and blame the culprits – then, in
> theory at least, redress could be obtained through the courts
> by the method of monetary compensation for damages. But
> multiple causality and the diffusion of disservices ... make
> this solution impossible. (Titmuss, 1968, p. 133)

Even where this solution is possible, there are also some well-documented problems with having recourse to the courts as a means of compensation for losses and injuries. These include problems of access, bias, delays, uncertainties and such conse-quences as the development of legally defensive medical practice (see for example the cases of Whitehouse v Jordan [1981] 1 WLR 246 and Sidaway v Board of the Bethlem Royal Hospital [1985] 1 AER 643; see, Carrier and Kendall, 1990b, pp. 25–31 for a review of these and other problems).

Fiscal welfare refers to the welfare role of the tax system. Will tax breaks enable more individuals to buy their own health care, more voluntary associations to provide health care and so on? The introduction of tax allowable health insurance for the over-60s in association with the *Working for Patients* reforms of the NHS is one indication that at least some members of Mrs.Thatcher's government held to this belief (Chapter 7). That this was a potentially significant and growing dimension of state welfare activity was first recognised in Titmuss's classic essay on the 'social division of welfare' (see Titmuss, 1958, Ch.4). Subsequent com-mentators were to note that we commit as many resources to state fiscal welfare (the 'tax allowance welfare state') as state social welfare (the 'traditional welfare state') (see Field, 1971). Another indication of the significance of state fiscal welfare programmes in the UK is the potential impact on the standard rate of income tax if all such tax allowances were abolished. Figures of between 10p and 12p in the £1 have been quoted. The concerns expressed in the social policy literature about this form of state welfare include its costs and complexity, and the problems of accountability and regulation. There are also concerns around the issue of inequalities including both the marked tendency for fiscal welfare benefits to be conferred on the better-off members of the community and perhaps more fundamentally their 'negative redistribution' effects. For example,

> the taxes avoided by the 11 million members of occupational pension schemes have to be paid for by the rest of the population. With the bias in pension fund membership towards higher paid groups, this burden has to be taken by the less well-off, including the low-paid, the retired, the unemployed and part-time workers. (James, 1984, pp. 10–11)

For the purposes of our argument the central point is that despite being potentially very costly, fiscal state welfare does not seem well-placed to guarantee minimal rights to health care and other forms of welfare. This point is illustrated by the tax-supported system of health insurance in the USA where 'over 30 million Americans have no financial protection against the expenses of medical care – they have no insurance cover ... millions more have only limited coverage that leaves them vulnerable to enormous financial risks' (Ham, Robinson and Benzeval, 1990, p. 60).

The dilemma for this form of state welfare is that if it 'pushes towards universality' (the right to minimal health care) it will become more complex, more costly, with more incentive and potential for abuse, and thus encountering more serious issues of regulation and accountability as an increasing proportion of public funds are dispensed to private individuals and institutions. At the same time its extension is likely to be of more benefit to the better-off whilst increasing the burden on the poor by making the tax-system more regressive. The result appears to be fiscal welfare for the better-off and fiscal diswelfare for the poorer members of the community, worsening the position of 'bad risks' and 'marginal bad risks' and making market-allocated health care even more selective .

Conclusions

We have identified a consensus around the concept of minimal state welfare – the right to minimal health care. The basis for this consensus is probably an argument from 'Common Needs' – that there are certain 'basic necessities' of life without which we cannot reasonably expect people to live and hence we all need access to health care when sick. But there is more to the argument than that since in that case food would qualify as well as health and education for 'desirable minimum' amounts of spending and for voucher schemes (and advocates of a National Health Service would presumably also advocate the establishment of a National Food Service).

It seems to us that the argument is based on linking together two elements. The goods and services that are a necessity for something resembling a 'normal life' in our sort of society (a 'common needs' argument); and the current free market conditions for the sale of these goods and services. The latter is an argument from 'market limitations' – that unregulated markets, employers, and voluntary associations will not meet this need. In relation to 'market limitations' we can contrast health care with food. For the latter, regulated private markets have been relatively successful in industrial societies, especially by contrast with command economies of state socialism. Of course the balance of this argument may change, and was generally agreed to have changed during wartime Britain when food allocation was more regulated (and with a 'welfare' orientation, see Harris, 1973).

The key elements of the 'market limitations' argument in relation to health care are as follows. Firstly, there are problems of costs and hence of consumer access to health care markets. Contrary to the expectations of Lees and Seldon, there has been no evidence of diminishing income inequalities in industrial societies; indeed recent trends in the UK indicate widening inequalities (Atkinson, 1996). Furthermore some of those elements underlying the health care 'cost containment' problem for societies (health care is skilled-labour intensive; changes in medical technology; rising expectations) mean that 'good quality health care' has not become relatively cheaper over time for the 'health care consumer'. The ideas that the 'problem of residual poverty is one of our time and not for all time to come' and that there is only 'a temporary problem of medical expenses in old age' (Lees, 1961, p. 75) appear to be absurdly optimistic; indeed at the time they were made they took no account of the existing and substantial body of evidence relating to an almost ninety year period of escalating health care costs and a stable income distribution.

Secondly, there remain the problems of consumer knowledge and uncertainty and the associated difficulties associated with exercising 'real consumer choices' in 'health care markets'. Thirdly, and finally, there are the consequences for consumers not only of not being able to make a choice (because they have insufficient money to enter the health care market) but also of making a 'wrong choice' – that is the dramatic, life-threatening implications of being denied access to modern biomedicine and the consequences of consuming low-quality health care.

The implication of a widespread consensus around the right to minimal health care implies minimal state welfare, given the overwhelming body of historical and contemporary evidence that the alternatives to state welfare cannot guarantee that right. Furthermore the limitations of judicial and fiscal welfare leads to a further consensus that there must, at the very least, be a commitment to the residual model of state welfare.

However in terms of the changes reviewed in Part One the residual model of state welfare would return state involvement in health care to a modern day equivalent of the Poor Law Medical Service. The case for a continuing commitment to the institutional model of state welfare, especially the universalist/citizenship model represented by the NHS, requires a more elaborate and substantial set of arguments than those reviewed in this chapter - although the arguments developed above do form part of this more elaborate argument. It is the case for the institutional model and universalism rather than the residual model and selectivity, which forms the basis of the next chapter.

12
Selectivity or universality?

Given a commitment to a right to minimal health care, there is a strong case for saying that this commitment can be realised only by the residual model of state welfare. This involves the provision of some sort of safety-net that guarantees at least the basic essentials of health care to the poorest members of the community and the 'bad risks' – that minority of the population whose access to health care is at risk if they have to rely on the mechanisms of profit and competition, mutual aid, philanthropy, familial and community support. The health services provided as part of the British Poor Law serves as a classic example of the residual model in the provision of health care.

The operation of such residual state welfare provision has attracted a number of criticisms. Such schemes are very costly to operate, although their overall public expenditure implications are normally less than a universal system. These administrative costs are perhaps an inevitable consequence of the complexity of schemes that seek to target a service (free or reduced cost health care) on a limited section of the population and to exclude the rest of the population. There are clearly issues of equity associated with this complexity, for example, a health voucher scheme would seem at the very least to convey a bonus to the healthy poor, whilst penalising those less healthy with modest incomes – the latter being a group identified as being disadvantaged by the income-limited National Health Insurance scheme that preceded the National Health Service in the UK (see Chapters 2 and 3). It is of course possible to devise schemes that would in theory compensate the poorest and least healthy in an equitable manner for the absence of a National Health Service. But such schemes are likely to be of daunting complexity and hideously expensive to administer. Such a scheme would be more complex than conventional means-testing since some mechanism would be necessary to meet the needs of better-off individuals faced with catastrophic medical bills. There is nothing in the history of conventional means-testing in the UK or elsewhere to lend any credence to the idea that such a scheme could be operated in a sensitive and equitable manner and indeed there is something of a paradox in the radical right's advocacy of targeting and means-testing given their critique of traditional forms of public administration. Conventional public administration has proved remarkably efficient at delivering straightforward, universal benefits (child benefit) and has attracted considerable justifiable criticism directed at its delivery of means-tested services and benefits!

Another consistently and widely reported problem of residualism is that of under-utilisation. Not all those members of the community towards whom the residual services are targeted come forward to claim them. This may reflect the way such services are administered and associated problems of stigma. Perhaps this could be resolved by better administration and attempts to minimise feelings of stigma (but, see below). However there may be a more intractable knowledge problem, or more accurately a knowledge/equity dilemma. The 'knowledge-problem' of potential service-users, and those who advise them, may be resolved by simplifying rules of entitlement to a residual state health care system. However it does seem likely that the simpler these rules, the less likely they are to serve the goal of equity and the more likely they are to offend widely-accepted notions of 'natural justice' (see for example, Titmuss, 1968, pp. 117–20).

This immediately raises the question of whether we have, in these issues of cost, equity and under-utilisation, the basis for saying we should move beyond residualism to some more elaborate and extensive form of state intervention in health care. The cost issue is certainly worthy of some consideration. The Americans spend more on their residualist Medicare scheme than the United Kingdom does on its universalist NHS; although this is less startling when one considers the volume of NHS resources directed at the British equivalent of Medicare-users – 'the health sector is largely a service for older people' (Phillipson, 1990, p. 59). Generally speaking it would take a particularly badly-administered and generous residual service and a very well-administered and austere universalist service for the former to be a greater 'burden' on public expenditure than the latter.

Issues of equity and under-utilisation are of more significance given the commitment to a right to minimal health care. The implication of these criticisms of residualism are that:

(a) the rules of entitlement exclude those who should properly be included and whose right to minimal health care is 'at risk' as a result; and

(b) the problems of underutilisation mean those whom the community has decided should be entitled to the service do not use the service and their right to minimal health care is also 'at risk'.

We should therefore move beyond 'residualism' on the basis of the 'minimal rights' of the minority who fail to make effective use of residual state welfare or who are excluded from making such use by inequitable rules of entitlement. However a number of arguments may be ranged against this proposition.

For the under-utilisers there would be an argument from freedom of choice. People can use a residual state health care system if they wish to. It is inappropriate to sanction massive extensions in state expenditure on health care because of the way certain individuals exercise their freedom of choice. There would also be an argument from need. People who do not use the services obviously do not really need them. There is some empirical evidence to back this up, since under-utilisation tends to be most marked where the benefit to be derived is least (ie: those entitled to small amounts of Family Credit and Income Support). It might also be argued that the problems of both under-utilisation and unfair entitlement rules may be resolved by better and fairer administration. Whilst the resolution of both these problems at the same time looks certain to encounter the knowledge/equity dilemma mentioned above, it has to be conceded that, for example, appropriate expenditure on modern information technology and better advertising might resolve these problems (although this may indicate a broader costs / knowledge / equity dilemma for residualism).

Given the implications for public expenditure (and state intervention in society) of the move from residualism to universalism, there does seem to be sufficient doubt and too much uncertainty surrounding the costs, equity and under-utilisation issues for them to provide a basis for saying we need universalism to deliver a right to minimal health care. We might also make a 'democratic realities'/'political expediency' observation that extensive state welfare with its associated features of more extensive public expenditure and higher taxation is unlikely to be sanctioned by the community as a whole, simply to make good the 'subsistence rights' of a small minority who do not make effective use of residual state welfare programmes. On the grounds of political expediency, if nothing else, there may be a case for formulating arguments for moving beyond the residual model of welfare on something more 'substantial' (in terms of political impact) than the observed tendency of residual state welfare to deny even 'subsistence rights' to a minority of poor people.

For the purposes of our argument the more central criticism directed at residualism is its association with poor quality services; that services for poor people will be poor services. This leads to a key question of whether residualism is almost inevitably associated with poor quality services and stigma. This is partly an empirical question. But it is also possible to locate these problems as inextricably bound up with the principles underpinning the residual approach.

We have already identified the problem of operating residualism in an equitable manner. The enduring problems are firstly, targeting the needy and deserving and secondly, excluding those who may seek to use the service but are not entitled to use it. The framers of the British Poor Law foresaw the problem and resolved it with the crude but effective device of the 'less eligibility' principle. A poor standard of service resolves a key administrative problem of equity. Any move away from this poor standard of service revives the problem. The improving medical services as part of the British Poor Law in the latter part of the nineteenth century encountered precisely this problem as it attracted usage beyond the conventional 'pauper classes' (see Abel-Smith, 1964, p. 217).

The market situation of residual state services may also contribute to their poor quality. As they seek to compete for resources, especially staff in the context of powerful private welfare markets ... they are able to recruit the worst rather than the best ... doctors, nurses, administrators and other categories of staff upon whom the quality of service so much depends. (Titmuss, 1968, p. 143)

There is also the political context within which residualism operates. If our health care system returns to residualism this implies a broad acceptance by the community of the 'public burden model of state welfare'. This approach makes a necessary virtue out of restraining and restricting all forms of state welfare expenditure. Whilst its advocates will see their major victory in the abandonment of universalism, this widely-accepted ideology (if the community endorses residualism) is likely to influence the scale and scope of expenditure on a residual health care system. Since the virtue of residualism is to confine state spending on health care to a minority, there are also likely to be significant democratic pressures to limit the quality of a service from which the majority are excluded. As Abel-Smith concludes:

if the same facilities were made available free to people who did not insure, even if they could have afforded to do this, this would discourage the growth of voluntary health insurance and be unfair to those of the same income who did pay the premium – in some cases at considerable sacrifices. For these and other reasons, the services provided for the poor are generally poor services and the processes of applying them for them is stigmatising. (Abel-Smith, 1976, p. 42).

That stigma should also be inextricably associated with residualism might be presumed to follow in part from what we have argued to be an almost inevitable association of residualism with poor quality services. The 'public burden ideology' could also contribute to stigma, for if the services themselves are appropriately categorised as a 'public burden' then this seems to convey the service-users to a similar, devalued and stigmatised category. It might also be argued that what is seen as a justifiable invasion of privacy – the scrutinising of individual eligibility to serve the goals of equity – is a potentially stigmatising experience in its own right. Given a personnel who may not always be the best people for the tasks in hand, an organizational / agency ideology that may stress the need to exclude the non-eligible and minimise abuse, and a government ideology of the 'public burden model' one cannot automatically exclude the possibility of operating a non-stigmatising residual model health care system – but the balance of probabilities, and much empirical evidence from different societies, seems to point to a rather different scenario as the likely outcome.

We should explore a final criticism of residualism that has a bearing on both the 'quality of service' argument developed above, and the argument developed for moving beyond 'residualism' below. This is the economic problem of disincentives associated with the extensive systems of means-testing associated with residualism. Even in the British context where the social security system retains major universalist cash benefits and operates in a context of universal health and education systems, researchers have consistently documented the extent to which a substantial body of low-wage earners may be subjected to the powerful disincentive effects of interlocking means-tested benefits. This problem is further compounded by the operation of a tax system that now makes more significant inroads into the income of low-wage earners (due in part at least to the growing burden of the fiscal welfare system, see Chapter 10). Fortunately for the operation of the economy, and contrary to the rhetoric of the radical right, the 'work-ethic' has not been eroded by guaranteeing ordinary people access to state health and education services and targeting is so ineffective (the under-utilisation problem) that the potential disincentive effects of means-testing are often less marked than might otherwise be the case.

The disincentive effect is also controllable through the quality of residual services. This brings us to a further dilemma of residualism – at least for those who claim that it affords the opportunity to target better benefits on the disadvantaged and so redistribute resources more effectively. Problems of disincentives, and indeed concerns about abuse, costs, equity and knowledge, may all be minimised or resolved by providing a simple, obviously poor-quality service which effectively uses the 'less-eligibility' principle as a guide to service-standards and an entitlement criteria (that is to re-invent the Poor Law Medical Service from the first half of the nineteenth century (see Figure 4).

Figure 4: Service quality and disincentives

Quality of service	Entitlement criteria	Disincentive problem
Very poor	'Less eligibility test'	None
Poor	Income (means) test	Of some, but limited, significance
Good	Income (means) test	Considerable

Other concerns – sometimes mistakenly presumed as new – about state welfare and a 'dependency culture' can also be answered by the 'less-eligibility' approach. It is when we seek to use residualism as a device for delivering good quality service to 'the bad risks' that the dilemmas and problems arise – the first evidence of which was apparent with the improvements in the Poor Law Medical Service in the latter part of the nineteenth century (see Chapter 1). For the critics of 'welfare state programmes', often much concerned with questions of 'economic efficiency' and 'dependency cultures', there is a real dilemma. There is no evidence that there is a substantial constituency of opinion prepared to sanction a return to 'less-eligibility' systems of public assistance as the basis of all existing state welfare programmes in education, social security and especially health care. Yet forms of residualism that move away from the 'less-eligibility' approach pose potentially significant problems for the operation of sizeable sections of the labour market and the creation of a 'dependency culture' in which many individuals, families and households are locked into economic circumstances where rises in income and/or savings disqualify them from access to good quality health care for themselves and good quality education for their children.

If we accept the argument for a right to minimal health care we are led to the minimal state (residual model) but not beyond. Beyond the minimal state requires a commitment to the right to optimal health care. This is something that, despite the theoretical claims advanced in its favour, residual welfare programmes seem to be incapable of delivering. There is a case for going beyond minimal state welfare programmes in health care. It could be based on the under-utilisation problems of residual state welfare, although given the cost and other implications of moving beyond residualism it might be argued that under-utilisation provides the case for a more dramatic and well-funded attempt to eliminate such under-utilisation. The quality of service argument is crucial. If our commitment to quality goes no further than the right to minimal health care, it may be conceded that the residual model may achieve this. If the commitment is to a reasonable or good standard of health care for all citizens then the evidence suggests this will not be delivered by a combination of residual state welfare and associated provision outside the state.

The right to optimal health care

In examining the case for a right to optimal health care a number of points become apparent. Firstly, the political division of opinion will become obvious and more marked and could lead to difficult questions of financing a greater than residual service (choice between social divisiveness of residualism and possible political divisiveness of universalism). Secondly, the right to optimal health care involves a significant extension in the activities of the state on behalf of the disadvantaged but with an uncertain political outcome and accusations of profligacy, support of non-contributors, and dependency creation. Thirdly, there will be an ongoing debate with professionals which challenges their definition of what is a deliverable component of service and over which they have control, but which is financed by general taxation – witness the disputes with doctors from 1911 onwards.

We do then need to address some of the key reservations that may be expressed about going beyond residualism associated with the potentially negative effects of extensive state welfare programmes on the operation of the economy (public burden model leading to a less affluent society which will lead to the relative impoverishment of 'good risks' and 'bad risks' alike) and on freedom, to say nothing of the Illich-type dependency creation argument about individuals surrendering their autonomy to professionals. On what grounds might we develop the argument for a right to optimal health care which given our equation of residualism with no more than minimal rights, would move us beyond residualism? We suggest the following might form the basis of such an argument:

fairness
freedom
social well-being
economic well-being

We are taking *fairness* arguments to be arguments based on ideas about how society should be organised. They could include an argument from democracy; that we should retain the present scale and scope of state intervention in health care in Britain for democratic reasons – it reflects the wishes of the vast majority of the population who appear to be willing to sustain existing levels of taxation in support of such a service (see for example, Bosanquet, 1989 and Bosanquet, 1993). However this might not provide a permanent rationale for moving beyond residualism since public sentiments about the NHS may change.

The same concern might be expressed about utilitarian arguments in favour of the right to optimal health care (and other welfare rights such as the right to optimal education). If increasing affluence were to do what it has so far failed to do, to enable a substantial majority of the population to purchase their own health care with few attendant financial problems, then the principle of the 'greatest happiness of the greatest number' might be as well served by a residual state health care system for the minority still unable to easily provide for themselves and their families.

One 'fairness' argument that might provide a more sustained defence of the move beyond residualism could be the concept of 'specific egalitarianism'. This is the belief that certain specific commodities should be distributed less unequally than the ability to obtain them through the means of profit and competition, mutual aid, philanthropy and familial support. Health care might be one such commodity (others might be education and legal services). The basis of such 'specific egalitarianism' might be derived from one or more of the following:

(a) a general commitment to equality;
(b) a general commitment to citizenship;
(c) a general commitment to fairness.

For (a) we could take the idea that 'no society showed concern and respect for its members unless it treated them as equals in certain fundamental respects' (Dworkin, 1978) and/or that such equal treatment expressed the idea of looking on persons as ends in themselves and not as mere means to further ends (such as 'economic' or 'social efficiency'). Seeking to minimise inequalities in access to health care might be one practical means of giving expression to a general commitment to equality by taking action in areas that are generally regarded as particularly important for people's welfare. In Rawlsian terms this more egalitarian alloca- tion of health care would be justified by the application of his 'difference' principle – that social and economic inequalities are only fair in so far as they work to the advantage of the least advantaged people in society (see Rawls, 1980, pp. 75–83).

For (b) we might develop an argument from some notion of citizenship that we should seek to avoid stigma-associated public services; once again this is something that it seems universal services may be capable of delivering and that residual services are unlikely to provide.

For (c) there may be some notion of the just or fair society that requires equality of opportunity in certain key respects. We could use Rawls' concept of 'primary goods' in this case (see Rawls, 1980, pp. 93, 62). Decent health care could be one such 'primary good' on the grounds that every rational person in our sort of society needs access to decent health care (and, for example, a decent education) as a basis upon which they can follow through their own individual life-plans (a link with concept of 'positive freedom', see below). The rationale for including health care in the category of 'primary goods' would clearly draw on the previous arguments from 'common needs' and 'market limitations' (see Chapter 10).

We need to be clear why the residual model of state welfare operating in these areas would not be sufficient to meet our social justice criteria. It is at this stage that the issue of inequalities referred to above (see Chapter 10) become crucial to the argu- ment. Residualism and non-state provision in health care are clearly compatible with 'extreme inequalities in access to health care with the uninsured dependent on often lower quality, public hospitals' (Ham, Robinson and Benzeval, 1990, p. 75 writing about the US health care system). There is also a concern that the provision of health care through profit and competition not only reinforces, but actually increases, inequalities through 'negative redistribution effects' (from the less well-off to the better-off) (see for example, Titmuss, 1968, pp. 181, 193–4 and Titmuss, 1974, pp. 90,97,99). These inequalities are not compatible with 'specific egalitarianism' whether derived from a commitment to equality (the Dworkin argument above) or from a commitment to fairness and equality of opportunity (the Rawlsian argument above). Residualism is also compatible with, indeed perhaps inevitably associated with, poor quality services and all these social justice arguments assume the provision of a good quality service. We might draw on Townsend's classic observations on defining poverty for this purpose.

> Society establishes the kind of diets people imbibe, the kind of accommodation in which they work,play and sleep, the clothing they wear and the kind of activities which they regard as natural ... the pattern may not be clearly laid down and in nearly all societies is changing rapidly. But this is the pattern to which people are expected broadly to conform and take for granted. It is a pattern that defines the needs of a population. Those with insufficient resources to satisfy this pattern can be regarded as being in poverty. (Townsend, 1970, pp. 1–2)

Townsend's attempts to operationalise this concept of poverty have been challenged on grounds of value-bias (see for example, Piachaud, 1981 and 1987). Nevertheless it provides a benchmark from which alternative values are assessed and with which alternative values have to engage. Such assessment and engagement is important – the former is the philosophical debate and the latter is the political struggle. For the purposes of our argument the 'operationalising problem' is not necessarily an issue. The inference of this 'relative concept of poverty', linked to the problematic concept of health (see Chapter 10), is that individuals need access to *more than a minimal* standard in the 'primary goods' (health care, education) if they are to participate effectively in society; and they are unlikely to get more than a minimal standard from a residual-model state health care service. To summarise, the arguments for moving beyond the residual model of state welfare could be based on some concept of specific egalitarianism linked to some notion of citizenship rights. They are based on the significance of access to certain key resources (eg: health care) of certain standards (ie: optimum standard), as a means to enable individuals to lead full lives in our sort of society, including the capacity to plan their own lives

Arguments from *freedom* have of course been deployed against any form of state welfare and certainly against moving beyond residualism. The modern 'liberal tradition' represented by writers like Dicey (1930) and Hayek (1944) has been summed up as follows:

> by these standards, the meddlesome interferences of the welfare state look like restrictions of people's freedom without any compensating gains in terms of freedom. (Goodin, 1982, p. 151)

There is an established response to these freedom arguments which we can review briefly using the following questions.

(a) what concept of freedom?
(b) whose freedom?
(c) what freedom?
(c) what state welfare activities?
(d) what other welfare activities?
(e) what happens?

'What concept of freedom?' involves the argument that freedom involves a power of choice between alternatives which is real, not merely nominal, between alternatives which exist in fact, not only on paper. This can of course be linked to the 'fairness arguments' – that social institutions should be organised in ways that ensure a fair distribution of key scarce resources (eg: education, health care) if liberty is to be maintained and enhanced for all citizens. This leads to the criticism of minimal state welfare arrangements. That such arrangements fail to provide the minimum conditions in which any significant degree of freedom can be exercised by individuals or groups who

> need medical help or education before they can understand, or make use of, an increase in their freedom. What is freedom

to those who cannot make use of it? Without adequate conditions for the use of freedom, what is the value of freedom? (Berlin, 1988, p. 124)

There are 'various conceptions of freedom ... and consequently varying evaluations of the welfare state will emerge depending on which conception we adopt' (Weale, 1982, p. 146). One need not reject the concerns of the 'liberal tradition' with the restrictions and interferences of governments and other people (see, for example, concerns expressed about essential freedoms in Tawney, 1966) in order to recognise the constraints on, restrictions on, and barriers to freedom associated with social and economic circumstances (eg: poverty, disability and ill-health).

The question of 'whose freedom' can be seen as linked to the issue of differing conceptions of freedom. To the young, healthy, affluent individual the presence of a universalist state health care system could be seen as restriction on freedom, requiring that person to spend more on health care through taxation than the market would require of them in commercial health insurance premiums. For the elderly person with physical disabilities and a limited income, a good quality state health system may hold out the hope of greater mobility, less physical discomfort and greater peace of mind than would be experienced if they were forced to rely on a combination of free market, charitable and residual state medical care. The latter's freedom may be enhanced in some quite tangible and dramatic ways whilst that of others – her young, affluent and able-bodied fellow citizen – are reduced.

The welfare state promotes certain kinds of freedom for certain people ... it restricts those or other freedoms for those or other people. (Goodin, 1982, p. 149)

Goodin's observation sums up 'whose freedom?' and introduces 'what freedom?'. Not all action nor all freedoms are compatible. What is possible for a single individual is not possible for all individuals – a walk in empty countryside for example (see Hirsch, 1977 on the 'positional economy'). In his answer to the very important health care-related problem of whether people should be free to sell their blood, Titmuss gave his answer as follows:

> In a positive sense we believe that policy and processes should enable men to be free to choose to give to unnamed strangers. They should not be coerced or constrained by the market. In the interests of the freedom of all men they should not, however, be free to sell their blood or decide on the possible destination of their gift. (Titmuss, 1970, p. 242)

This is an issue which is also of relevance to the social well-being arguments (see below).

More specifically, but not without relevance, we can also question an uncritical use of the term the 'welfare state' in these arguments. Under this heading one might for some purposes justifiably link together a range of social policy programmes. But their relative impact on freedom may be variable. State education is typically compulsory for certain age-groups; use of state health care is typically voluntary. Universalist services are typically less intrusive of individual privacy than means-tested residual services. This is not to deny there may be aspects of universalist, health care programmes that diminish certain people's freedom (see, for example, the arguments relating to preventive measures, see Chapter 9). However it is important that certain compulsory or particularly intrusive dimensions of state welfare are not used as examples to represent 'the whole'.

More significantly for this argument, if we are to disaggregate the 'welfare state', we should do the same for 'welfare activities'. Critics of the institutional model of state welfare not only concede, but also advocate, that diminished state welfare activity means enhanced non-state welfare activity. Are there no implications for freedom in the operation of private health insurance, employer-based (occupational) health care, and tax-allowable health expenditure?

> For the employee ... (occupational welfare benefits) ... are generally compulsory whether or not they are contributory and represent wages or salaries deferred on the theory of human depreciation. The employee cannot contract out. S/he cannot decide to spend his/her earnings in alternative ways. Moreover, even if participation is voluntary, s/he has no choice in respect of (a) the cover afforded or (b) the insurer. (Titmuss, 1974, p. 94)

Titmuss's comment on the lack of choice in occupational welfare benefits has only been remedied to some degree in the UK through state intervention. Similarly third-party intervention in health care, in the form of insurance companies (who intervene between consumer and producer) must inevitably distort the workings of the 'free market' and may certainly limit consumer choice in some important respects. It has been a paradox that those who hold that 'one vitally important principle is … that the patient pays the doctor directly' (Lees, 1976, p. 5) have failed to recognise the 'realities of the health care' market – that it is more likely to be dominated by large employers and insurance companies than individual consumers. Finally, tax allowances for expenditure on health insurance can also be construed as an interference in individual freedom – no tax allowances here for spending on shoes, sherry or shampoo!

Last, but by no means least, we can add the well-established feminist critique of policies for community care that rest on certain assumptions about the composition of the army of informal carers. It is far from clear that diminished state intervention in health care and more pressure on informal caring by female kin will enhance the freedom of the women drawn into such caring roles.

We might finally pose the question of what has happened to the 'welfare states' – all these societies that have set off down the 'road to serfdom' (Hayek, 1944). It is hardly likely that we will come up with a definitive answer to this question. However the league tables in Charles Humana's *World Human Rights Guide* (1992) are interesting. Social rights count for little in these tables, the health care achievements of Cuba and Kuwait do not prevent them languishing in the lower reaches of the table since the emphasis is on the traditional civil and political rights. Nonetheless it is the conventional welfare states of Europe – Denmark, Germany, Netherlands Norway and Finland – that achieve a higher freedom quotient than that 'reluctant welfare state' – the United States (see Humana, 1992, pp. xii–xiv, xvii–ix).

We must conclude at the very least, that contrary to the implications of the 'radical right' perspective, there is a debate about freedom and the state's role in health care, which does not simply resolve itself into an unproblematic and uncontentious assertion that more state health care means less freedom. We can add to this that there is within this 'freedom debate' a set of arguments in favour of the 'freedom-enhancing' implications of universalist state health care.

We have already indicated that a loss of *social well-being* forms part of the radical right critique of extensive state welfare. The latter is in effect a moral burden as well as an economic burden. There is inevitably a basic problem of evidence for the suggested changes. The sociological concept of 'moral panic' reminds us of the difficulty of judging changes in 'moral growth' and 'moral fibre' (see Boyson, 1971). Historians have also alerted us to the problematic concept of a 'lost' and 'better past' which we might seek to reclaim, for example the following:

> The idea of a tranquil, undisturbed evolutionary progress even for England, let alone the turbulent, fractured, schizo-phrenic history of the Celtic nations comes out here as little more than a myth, fit for the refuse heap of history, like romances of 'golden ages' over the centuries from Arthurian times onwards. (Morgan, 1984a, pp. vi–vii)

Comments and statistics on the role of the family may serve as one small example of an illusory 'golden age'. The following observation on the apparent unwillingness of children to care for aged parents was made in the report of the Royal Commission on the Poor Law in the 1830:

> The duty of supporting parents and children in old age and infirmity is so strongly enforced by our natural feelings that it is often well performed, even among savages, and almost always so in a nation deserving the name of civilised. We believe that England is the only European country in which this is neglected. (Checkland and Checkland (eds), 1974, p. 115)

One of the 'myths of the family' has been that the modern family was readier to place elderly relatives in institutions, although there was a higher proportion of people aged over 65 years of age in poor law institutions in 1906 than in residential and nursing homes seventy years later (Anderson 1983). These two linked social policy examples cast some doubt on the presumed decline in 'moral fibre' detected by Rhodes Boyson. As with 'the freedom debate' we can take the argument further.

One well-established theme of social policy writing concerns the socially divisive nature of the residual state welfare services. Townsend's comment was to the effect that selectivity and means-testing:

> fosters hierarchical relationships of superiority and inferiority in society, diminishes rather than enhances the status of the poor, and has the effect of widening rather than of reducing social inequalities. Far from sensitively discriminating different kinds of need it lumps the unemployed, sick, widowed, aged and others into one undifferentiated and inevitably stigmatising category. (Townsend, 1968, p. 6)

It is also argued that this treatment of the poorer sections of society may have unpleasant consequences for the non-poor (see for example, Rein, 1970, p. 46). Of course in conditions of scarcity some rationing devices are necessary. For state health care the question is how do you ration with equity and retain the support of the disappointed; preventing the disappointed becoming the disenchanted and ultimately the disaffected. The argument then becomes that the presence of state provision of health care allows the disappointed the opportunity to challenge with possible scope for redress. By contrast the presence of competing markets reinforces the dispossession of the disappointed. This viewpoint is quite well summed up in Titmuss's vision of a society which lets market relations dominate in the areas we have come to view as subject to state welfare activities.

> There is nothing permanent about the expression of reciprocity. If the bonds of community giving are broken the result is not a state of value neutralism. The vacuum is likely to be filled by hostility and social conflict ... the myth of maximising economic growth can supplant the growth of social relations. (Titmuss, 1970, pp. 198–9)

Bevan's view was that 'the field in which the claims of individual commercialism come into most immediate conflict with reputable notions of social values is that of health' (Bevan, 1978, p. 98). If there are 'moral burdens' associated with universalist state welfare, the alternatives of residualism and private markets may carry their own moral burdens. We have already raised the question of whether it is residualism rather than universalism that is most productive of a 'dependency culture'.

The pro-state welfare argument can have a further dimension beyond the lessening of social divisiveness; can universalist provision more positively promote social integration? This may be characterised as a citizenship effect in which there are social rights to complement civil and political rights (Marshall, 1963 and 1981); these rights give access to certain common services which may overcome class divisions and help create a bond of human feeling (Tawney, 1964). For Crosland greater equality would increase social contentment and diminish social resentment (Crosland, 1956) and forty years later there is an equivalent debate in a related field, suggesting that as social resentment rises consequent upon highly visible and deeply felt inequalities then criminal activity also increases.

This perspective is not readily susceptible to proof (there is an evidence problem here to!) and this whole dimension is viewed in a pejorative light in Marxist accounts (the 'social control' perspective). The key point is that this 'social well-being' terrain (like the 'freedom debate') is not the exclusive territory of the anti-state health care critics from the radical right, a point we can also make in connection with arguments relating to *'economic well-being'*.

Once again a starting point is a radical right critique of state welfare which holds that increased expenditures on programmes like the NHS diminishes economic welfare with deleterious effects for rich and poor alike – the 'public burden model of welfare' (Titmuss, 1968, pp. 124–5). The price of equality becomes both a loss of freedom and impoverishment. The social and economic crises of the state socialist societies of Eastern Europe which unfolded from at least the mid-1970s onwards is understandably cited as evidence of this apparent dilemma.

For Britain a least the historical evidence does not lend straightforward support to the concept of the public burden model of state welfare. The starting point for Britain's relative economic decline is often identified with the 1870s (see for example, Matthew, 1984, p. 510) well before the welfare reforms of New

Liberalism had any impact on the public finances, never mind the Beveridge Report and the NHS. That there were relatively significant increases in the proportion of the GDP spent on social services between 1924 and 1938 (see Hennessey, 1992, p. 127) is further evidence of the limitations of the rather simplistic equations of post-war 'New Jerusalems' and relative economic decline (see for example, Barnett, 1986 and 1995). Furthermore when post-war British state welfare expenditure is put in a comparative context, post-War British governments emerge as consistently low spenders (especially on health care) (see Chapter 8) and the

> generalised case for the existence of a parasitic welfare state, which since the 1940s has crippled the economy of Britain but not that of her economic rivals, therefore looks weak. (Harris, 1990, p. 181)

Of course it is possible that other aspects of public expenditure were problematic in this period. Barnett seems to be on stronger statistical ground when he notes that UK defence expenditure was 'up to double the proportion of GNP spent by European industrial competitors' (Barnett, 1986, p. 304) and there are related arguments to do with the impact of this expenditure on the pattern of research and development expenditure in post-war Britain. Similar arguments cannot be advanced in relation to Britain's frugal health care expenditure.

Finally when state welfare expenditures *and* economic growth is put in the broader comparative context of the OECD countries, the most striking point is the over-simplicity of this public burden model. It simply does not fit with what we know about relative economic performances of different societies. High spenders on state welfare and more specifically high spenders on state health care programmes have coped very well with the so-called 'public burden' and consistently outperformed lower spenders on health and welfare in terms of the conventional measures of economic growth (see for example, Wilensky, 1981).

This argument can then be advanced a stage further by reference to the classic 'national efficiency' arguments in favour of at least some state welfare programmes of which education is currently (and yet again) the most debated example (see Chapters 2 and 3 for historic arguments relating to health care). For health care we have already noted the limitations of an oversimplified view of the relationship between health care and health standards (see Chapter 10). Nonetheless even those most well-known for putting medical care in a more modest place as a contributor to improved health standards, do not deny its contribution to good health (see for example, McKeown, 1976). Certainly there is abundant evidence that more affluent populations wish to spend more on health care. There is also equally abundant evidence that 'socialised medicine' (the NHS model) provides a most cost-effective means of delivering such health care. The example of Canada, where a switch to a universal and largely government-funded system led to a levelling off of health care costs by comparison with the increasingly competitive and commercial USA system, is a further example of this point (see for example, Timmins, 1988, p. 77). Indeed the NHS is now so cheap to run that it is difficult to avoid the conclusion that it is seriously underfinanced by the standards of equivalent industrial societies. It is the more market-orientated systems that have experienced greatest difficulties in cost-containment, the over-prescription of drugs and over-use of surgical intervention. There may be economic benefits in good health care (the health status of the labour force) but also a strong efficiency case for delivering that good health care through a universalist state system like the NHS, since

> the volume of expenditure being putatively siphoned away from wealth creation by expenditure on health care was considerably lower ... (in the UK) ... than elsewhere. (Harris, 1990, p. 180)

We can conclude this section by noting the significance of health care costs for small-firm bankruptcies in the USA and the powerful economic disincentive effects identified with residualism. Issues of economic well-being, like those of freedom and social well-being, do not necessarily diminish with a diminishing state involvement in health care.

The attempt from the radical right has been to seek to sustain a view in which there is a necessary inverse relationship between state expenditure on state welfare (like the NHS) and freedom, economic and social well-being. This view is seriously flawed because:

(a) there is a serious evidence problem (eg: social well-being);
(b) what evidence there is does not necessarily support this view (eg: economic well-being);
(c) the opposite point can be argued (and where appropriate, there is evidence to support this alternative view);
(d) it presumes there are no freedom, economic and social well-being issues associated with profit, competition, altruism, philanthropy and familial care as alternative means of providing health care for members of any community.

Conclusions

In reviewing the debates relating to universality and selectivity we are focusing on a long-standing and inevitable source of conflict; long-standing because many of the key elements of the conflict are discernible in nineteenth century debates about the role of the state in health care; inevitable because they reflect different philosophical and value systems; and whereas these differences may be resolved around the concept of some state intervention (the residual model of state welfare, see, Chapter 11) the implications of moving beyond the residual model are too significant to identify any really common ground.

What we can say with a degree of certainty is that there is a 'real debate' to be conducted around the themes identified in this chapter. In particular the anti-state welfare arguments associated with the radical right are highly contentious and less secure than they appear to be when presented by their keenest advocates. In many respects the well-founded, general case for markets does not translate well into a specific case for markets in health care. Most specifically the attractive conceptual simplicity of the cases for markets and the minimal state is in no way matched by the practical realities of their implications for health care.

A key element in the arguments is the right to health care. Rights to *minimal* health care may be operationalised through markets and the minimal state; rights to *optimal* health care are almost certainly impossible to achieve by these means. Anti-state welfare arguments should focus *less* on the illusory benefits of market-dominated health care and *more* on why it is appropriate that certain sections of the population should be permanently consigned to limited access to health care which is of low-quality; for there is compelling evidence that this must be the outcome of their preferred answers to the question of how health care should be provided. By the same token, rights should perhaps figure more significantly in pro-state welfare arguments; as we shall see in the following chapter they form one important strand of the debates relating to institutional and community care.

13
Community or institutional care?

The community is an euphemism for the world at large, in which the disadvantaged citizen is dumped and told to make out as best he can and not to return to be a burden on the state. It is treated by the state, in short, as a dustbin into which all but the most dramatically dangerous (and hence politically embarrassing) problems can be dropped in the hope they will remain largely invisible (Clarke, 1976, p. 235)

It is one of the most stubbornly persistent illusions in social policy studies that eventually the concept of community – as a basis of shared values – will resolve all our policy dilemmas. The very fact that this notion is cherished from left to right across the political spectrum makes it highly suspect. There is no unitary definition of community because, like the concept of equity, it is open to various interpretations. The idea that in a complex industrial society the notion of community could provide a basis for shared values (and hence for consistent social policies) is erroneous (Pinker, 1982, p. 241)

Introduction
The concept of community appears to be important in a number of areas of social policy. Children in care have been placed in community homes; they and other children have gone to community schools and may continue their education in community colleges. In the 1970s parts of some of Britain's cities were the subject of community development programmes modelled to some extent on the community action programmes pioneered in the USA in the late 1960s. Many local authorities and voluntary organizations have been employing community workers for some

time. There have been advocates of community social work and community policing.

None of this commitment to the 'community' label will surprise observers of health and health care in Britain. There is a tradition of community health care represented by community-based medical practitioners (GPs), pharmacists in high-street chemist shops and community-based nursing staff. The latter include long-established provision of health visiting, district nursing and domiciliary midwifery, plus the more recent introduction of community psychiatric and mental handicap nursing. Finally, there is the enormous volume of informal caring devoted to everything from the terminally ill and those with major disabling conditions, to the immense quantity of minor childhood ailments that are effectively contained and cared for within families. The latter is represented by the relatively unchanging statistics that indicates that the vast majority of reported illness is dealt with by community-based general practitioners as well as the role played by community-based nurses and pharmacists.

Since the establishment of the NHS there has also been a clear trend towards a different, more intensive use of non-community facilities for a wide-range of health problems (see for example, Chapter 5) while at the same time a considerable political consensus has been built up around the desirability of community care policies (Walker, 1983, p. 157). To some extent the latter may reflect the positive qualities with which both 'community' and 'care' are imbued, and the varied interpretations that can be placed upon 'community care'. In supporting 'community care', different groups and individuals may have been, and may still be, supporting different concepts of 'community care'. The most obvious distinction is that between care *in* the community and care *by* the community. The former has been characterised as 'concerned with the provision of care by *paid* social services workers *in* the community ... (rather) ... than *by* the community' (Walker, 1982a, p. 4, our emphasis). The latter is taken to refer to the 'provision of help, support and protection to others by lay members of societies acting in everyday domestic and occupational settings' (Abrams, 1977, p. 125). Whilst it may be impossible to envisage care in the community unsupported by care by the community, or vice versa, there is clearly potential for significantly different policies for community care to be developed around these concepts and a considerable potential for conflict. In particular, different policies for community care may have radically different implications for public expenditure – compare the resources required for maintaining small-scale but good quality institutional care alongside large-scale, good quality care *in* the community; and the resources required for the total abandonment of institutional care alongside a reliance on care *by* the community.

The case for the institution

By the mid-nineteenth century ... (the asylum and prison were) ... places of first resort. (Cohen, 1979, p. 609)

Part of the background to contemporary debates about the development of policies for community care is the development of policies for institutional care – most especially in the nineteenth century. Generally we can characterise the situation as one in which the appropriate response to a range of social needs and social problems was seen as investment in forms of specialised institutional care – prisons, industrial and reform schools, childrens homes and, as we noted in Chapter 1, new voluntary hospitals, the county asylums and the new Poor Law hospitals. These changes have been seen as sufficiently widespread to be categorised as a trend in the 'social organization of deviance' (Scull, 1979) and they have been linked to a number of factors.

Obvious structural factors include industrialisation and urbanization; one example would be the 'public health problem' (see Chapter 1); a further example would be the suggestion that the 'mentally and physically handicapped can more easily take some part in agricultural work than in the more demanding occupations characteristic of industrial society' (Parker, J., 1975, p. 20). Similarly the increases in the nineteenth century in the rates of 'known persons of unsound mind' per thousand population and 'the rate of insanity per ten thousand people' (see Jones, 1972, p. 356 and Scull, 1979, p. 225) might be attributed to the social and psychological stresses inextricably linked to the dramatic changes associated with industrialisation and urbanisation. This perspective fits in with a well-established thesis that developments in state welfare were in part a response to the social problems of an urban, industrial society (Wilensky and Lebeaux, 1965, p. 240). However it must also be noted that it was the economic growth associated with industrialism that afforded the resources to invest in the new institutions. If industrialism created 'new problems'; it also created the means to respond to these 'problems'.

Further structural themes have been advanced which relate the 'institutionalisation of social problems' to the operation of a capitalist market economy and especially the 'laissez-faire' ideology that dominated the British policy agenda for much of the nineteenth century (see Chapter 1). Specialist forms of institutional care are said to respond to identified needs and problems in a mode that could be seen to interfere least with the 'free play of market forces' – better to remove the disabled and destitute from their communities entirely, than to support them in their own homes and so distort the workings of the labour market (hence the principle of 'indoor relief', see Chapter 1). Meanwhile the investment in the new institutions could be seen as a tangible indication of the 'care', 'support' and 'training' provided by industrial capitalism.

Three other rather general themes can be identified. Firstly, the extent to which this new 'social organization of deviance' represented a rational-bureaucratic approach to 'social problems' – the 'scientific' identification and categorisation of separate groups (eg: the young offender from the adult offender, the mentally ill from the physically ill). Secondly, the extent to which this process was inextricably associated with the development of 'specialist bodies of knowledge' and the development of professions – most obviously in the development of specialist hospitals and especially in relation to the development of asylums and the asylum doctors (see for example, Abel-Smith, 1964, pp. 22–6; see also Scull, 1979). Thirdly, and certainly linked to professionalisation, the extent to which the process of institutionalisation developed its own inherent dynamic as the building of the institutions created a need for more institutions by formally identifying and establishing a 'new response' to a range of 'social problems'. This perspective does not necessarily contradict the idea that certain social problems may have become more significant with industrialisation and urbanization, but it does add the other dimension with which we have become increasingly familiar – the 'submerged iceberg' effect (see especially Chapters 5 and 10) in which previously unmet or differently met need is 're-directed' towards a new, or newly accessible, service.

Two other possibilities follow from the 'submerged iceberg' effect. One is the extent to which social and economic changes were constraining the ability of families and communities to sustain their caring roles – creating a new 'institutional population' for which care had to be provided. However this view may rest a little too heavily on overly attractive views of pre-industrial Britain. An alternative, at least for people with mental health problems, is that their needs were previously ignored or neglected in the late eighteenth and early nineteenth century when:

> (there) was no clear definition of what constitutes insanity, and certainly no recognition of the insane as a separate social class requiring a distinct form of treatment ... only a small proportion of the total number were recognised as being insane, and the majority were treated as though they were fully responsible for their actions. If their mental condition reduced them to penury, they came within the purview of the poor law, if it led them to break the criminal code they were judged by the penal law. If they wandered abroad from their legal place of settlement without means of support, they were involved in the rigours of the vagrancy laws ... (therefore) ... the person who was recognised as insane ... whether he was rich or poor ... was almost certainly to be confined, neglected, and intimidated, if not treated with open cruelty. (Jones, 1955, pp. 1–2).

The latter point also alerts us to what might be rather clumsily labelled as 'transinstitutionalisation' by which the 'new state institutions' (eg: the asylum) removed people from the 'old state institutions' (eg: the workhouse) (see Chapter 1). In addition, part of the growth of publicly-financed institutions (the county asylums) was replacing private provision ('private madhouses' and 'single lunatics' confined in ordinary houses). The growth of publicly-financed asylums should not be taken to represent simple increases in the institutionalisation of the mentally ill, but partly a transfer of individuals from other, possibly less satisfactory, forms of institutional confinement. Certainly the twin policies of creating infirmaries and seeking to eliminate outdoor relief played their part in increasing the institutionalisation of the sick during the nineteenth century (see Abel-Smith, 1964, p. 86).

This 'transinstitutionalisation' might on some criteria be deemed a form of 'progress', alerting us to a further and final perspective on the new institutions – that they did, in certain respects, improve the circumstances of some groups. Later policies for community care would be significantly hampered by, for example, the building of large institutions ten to twenty miles out in the countryside around London (see Maxwell, 1990) and these locations can easily be said to represent a 'social organization of deviance' that relocates social problems away from the public gaze ('out of sight, out of mind'). On the other hand these rural locations were also a response to the then current theories of disease (especially the miasmic theory). Furthermore whilst it may have been unfair to refer to 'palatial workhouse infirmaries' (see *British Medical Journal*, February 9th, 1884; quoted in Abel-Smith, 1964, p. 149), there is the case that 'infirmary treatment was often a considerable improvement on the normal housing conditions of the poorer classes' (Brand, 1965, p. 99); that the inmates were often better fed, better clad, better housed and better cared for than they were before their admission, and 'better than the great mass of working classes who earn their own living' (Abel-Smith, 1964, p. 64). Certainly some of the new institutions represented improvements in quality of care by comparison with what had gone before (see Abel-Smith, 1964, pp. 200–1) – 'rescuing' some of those they contained from the 'worse havens' of 'privatised institutional care' (see also Heywood, 1965, on baby-farming) or the 'ultimate safety-nets' of the nineteenth century prisons and workhouses. It is also probable that the 'batch living' of institutional life was a less unfamiliar and devaluing experience in the middle of the nineteenth century by comparison with the middle of the twentieth century. These new socially segregated, geographically-isolated institutions must not automatically be presumed to be obviously the wrong solution to a wrongly perceived problem, despite the late twentieth century epithet of 'warehousing'.

From institutional to community care

We will take policies for community care to refer to policies for certain categories of need, that make little or no use of large, socially segregated, geographically isolated institutions. Using this definition we can describe the last fifty years as representing a commitment to such policies – a trend away from services and policies based on 'the institution' to ones that place a major emphasis on 'community care'. For people with mental health problems, we can see a trend away from provision based exclusively on the 'mental hospital', with the development of a range of services including out-patient, and day-patient care, community nursing, social work support, day centres, hostels, and group homes. For elderly people, we can see a similar trend away from provision based on the workhouse, with the development of a range of services – health visiting, home help, care attendants, social work support, day centres, and 'sheltered housing'. Having made this general, and generally valid point, we should be wary of presuming that a wide range of social policies fit clearly and neatly into this pattern.

Firstly, the trend away from the institution-based services is reasonably clear, but it is not universal. Certain rather important events in life (birth and death) have tended to be 'institutionalised' with much greater proportions of births and deaths now occurring in hospitals rather than in the community (at home) – especially since the Cranbrook Report (1959) with regard to maternity cases.

Secondly, it is apparent that 'community care' is not a new phenomenon. As we noted above there are well-established 'community care' traditions in health care – for example, health visiting. The community-based tradition is also well-established in social care – for example, community-based child care workers.

Thirdly, recognisable 'community care' policies were developed in the nineteenth century, including the 'boarding-out' (fostering) of children in the care of both public authorities and voluntary organisations. Also some county asylums pioneered outpatient facilities in the later part of the nineteenth century (see Roberts, 1967). Some of these initiatives were in response to the perceived problems of institutional care. Dr Barnardo opposed 'anything approaching institutionalism ... (which) ... should be scrupulously avoided' (see Heywood, 1965).

Fourthly, some of these long-established initiatives in 'community care' initiatives were questioned on the grounds that:

> the boarding out of children was being pursued because its chief merit in the eyes of representatives of the ratepayers, was that it was cheap. (Heywood, 1965, p. 91)

Fifthly, the general and generalisable trend towards policies for community care conceals variations in their active pursuit for different categories of need. Such policies were clearly a priority for child care services following the publication of the Curtis Report (1946) and the passing of the Childrens Act, 1948 (see Heywood, 1965, and Packman, 1975). Such policies only became a priority for children and adults with learning difficulties following the publication of the White Paper, *Better Services for the Mentally Handicapped* in 1971 (DHSS, 1971b).

We should certainly not presume that we have just discovered either the virtues of 'community care' or the 'problems of institutionalism'. Nor should we presume that we are being unduly perceptive in noting the danger of community care policies being pursued for purely economic reasons.

Finally, we must not forget the obvious point that 'institutional care' and 'community care' represent two ends of a continuum. Policy and practice as advocated, enacted and interpreted has been, and continues to be, subject to variation not only by category of need but also by location (the latter sometimes, and sometimes not, justifiable by variations in local circumstances). In the context of this continuum, advocates of '100 per cent institutional care' or '100 per cent community care' have been in a minority; and the 'practical reality' has to date located different aspects of health care somewhere between the ends of the continuum throughout the twentieth century.

Community care and consensus

We can identify with a degree of certainty that firstly, a political and professional consensus was established around the desirability of 'community care policies'; and that secondly, throughout the existence of the NHS, there has been an increasingly widespread advocacy of, and requirement for, community-based policies in policy documents and legislation. The policy documents include the Curtis Report (1946) on childrens services, the community care plans of 1963 (Ministry of Health, 1963; see Chapter 5), and the 'Better Services' White Papers of 1971 and 1975 (DHSS, 1971b and DHSS, 1975b; see also Chapter 5). The legislation includes the Childrens Act, 1948; the Mental Health Act, 1959; the National Assistance Act, 1948; the National Assistance Amendment Act, 1962; the Health Services and Public Health Act, 1968; the Chronically Sick and Disabled Persons Act, 1970; the Mental Health Act, 1983; and the Health and Community Care Act, 1990. (For further examples, see Walker, 1982a, pp. 14–20 and Jones and others, 1983, Ch.6.)

However it may well be that this 'political consensus' reflected a lack of clarity about what community care means – in a clear parallel to Pinker's comment about the concept of community (see p. 269 above). This danger was recognised some time ago by Titmuss who commented that

> the aspirations of reformers are transmuted, by the touch of a phrase, into hard-won reality. What some hope will one day exist is suddenly thought by many to exist already. All kinds of wild and unlovely weeds are changed, by statutory magic and comforting appellation into the most attractive flowers that bloom not just in the spring but all year round. We are all familiar with that exotic hot-house climbing rose, 'The Welfare State', with its lovely hues of tender pink and blushing red, rampant and rampaging all over the place, often preventing people from 'standing on their feet' in their own gardens. And what of the everlasting cottage-garden trailer, 'Community Care'? Does it not conjure up a sense of warmth and human kindness, essentially personal and comforting. (Titmuss 1961, p. 104)

What Titmuss's comment alerts us to is the possibility of a vague, ill-defined concept of 'community care' commanding widespread support precisely because it is vague and ill-defined! Given Titmuss's critical comments, and the more clearly discernible commitment to policies of community care that has emerged in the post-war period, we obviously need to ask whether there was a well-founded rationale for such policies.

The case for community care

We can identify four inter-related themes which with varying emphases have made the case for policies of community care. These are:

(i)   the public burden case;
(ii)   the efficiency case;
(iii)   the needs case; and
(iv)   the rights case.

The *public burden* case has been simple and straightforward – it rests on our inability to afford to maintain and staff the large institutions. In particular it was noted that it was becoming increasingly difficult 'to staff isolated institutions in an age when few people are prepared to make a career in residential work' (Brown, 1977, p. 195; see also the Williams Report, 1967).

The *efficiency* case also concerns costs, but focuses on the relative costs of forms of care along the institutional / community care continuum. The following comparisons serve to illustrate the point but were preceded and followed by similar calculations (see for example, Boswell and Wingrove, (eds) 1973, Chapter 6 and the Audit Commission, 1986)

Table 3: Comparative costs – institutional and community care

The average cost of mental handicap hospital in-patient care:	£6000 pa
hostel place:	£1500 pa
day centre place:	£1200 pa

Source: DHSS, 1981c

The implication of these figures seemed clear. For the same budget, more people could be helped by using less-institutional settings. This became an especially powerful argument when it was complemented by the needs case.

The *needs* case can itself by sub-divided into four inter-related dimensions. Firstly there was the growing evidence of 'over-institutionalisation' with researchers consistently concluding that a substantial proportion of the existing 'institutional population' did not need to be placed in such institutions twenty-four hours a day, seven days a week, and (for some of the residents) for many weeks or even years. The early research produced quite dramatic figures – only 15 per cent of mental illness in-patients needed to be hospital in-patients (McKeown and others, 1958). In the 1960s, 1970s and early 1980s, various sources were still concluding that at least 30 per cent of elderly people, people with mental health problems and people with learning difficulties were located unnecessarily in forms of institutional care (see McKeown, 1967; Gilderdale, 1971; DHSS, 1972d; Durkin, 1972, p. 7; DHSS, 1981c).

This identification of 'over-institutionalisation' was itself related to changing (especially professional) perceptions of the needs of individuals who had traditionally been viewed as 'suitable cases for long-term institutional care'. This was especially related to developments in geriatric and psychiatric medical and nursing care (especially the so-called 'pharmacological revolution' (Jones, 1972 in the case of the latter; see also Martin, F.M., 1984, p. 2 and Jones, 1983, p. 226). For people with learning difficulties:

> the work done in the hospitals and elsewhere ... has demonstrated that even the severely handicapped have previously unrecognised capabilities for the development of manual and other skills and varying degrees of social independence if they receive the necessary stimulus and appropriate education and other forms of training. (DHSS, 1971b, p. 19)

Alongside this growing recognition of the potential for new forms of support, and the identification of 'overinstitutionalisation', was a growing concern as to whether the traditional institutions were an appropriate setting in which to meet the needs of their residents. Certain dimensions of this problem can be observed in Goffman's classic definition of the 'total institution' as a place where:

> all aspects of life are conducted in the same place and under the same single authority ... inmates typically live in the institution and have restricted contact with the world outside. (Goffman, 1961, pp. 17–18)

This 'restricted contact' with the outside world was seen as increasingly problematic now that many of the services identified their rehabilitative and/or curing roles, in addition to their traditional long-term caring roles. Traditional forms of institutional care had not facilitated 're-entry' into the wider community – indeed the barriers involved in the transition from the 'total institution' to 'normal society' were well recognised for a range of individuals previously living (and working) in, for example, the armed forces, childrens homes, mental hospitals, and prisons.

Finally the distinctive qualities of the 'total institution' were seen as not simply limiting the 'need-meeting' capacities of the services based there, but also of 'creating needs'. This argument was probably first used most effectively for the mental health services with the concept of 'institutional neurosis' (Barton, 1976) in which the adjustments made to the distinctive qualities of institutional life were seen to generate their own psychiatric (behaviourial) problems. Subsequently the 'dependency enhancing' effects of residential care for older people was noted (see for example, Walker, 1982b) and a dramatic TV documentary produced in the UN Year of the Disabled Person made a graphic case for the difficult and disturbing behaviour of young people with learning difficulties being a function of their institutional confinement rather than a rationale for that confinement (see *The Silent Minority* 1981). It can be seen that a particularly effective case for community care could be assembled around the twin themes of efficiency and needs. The final theme we can identify – and there is a sense in which it was perhaps the final theme to get on political and professional agendas – was the 'rights' case.

The *rights* case can itself be broken down into three linked themes. Firstly, and relating closely to the needs case, there are the disabling effects of institutional care noted above. If institutions do indeed 'create needs' and in certain respects 'disable' their residents, this is not just 'a problem for professionals' who might be presumed to be meeting needs and minimising dependency – although Illich has claimed that professionals themselves disable the lay person and deny individual autonomy. This 'disabling effect' can be seen as an affront to the rights of the individuals concerned. What is the justification for requiring those in need of care and support from the wider community to receive that support in 'disabling' institutional settings. The point was made with increasing force for the different groups who had been most subject to the 'institutionalisation of social problems' in previous eras.

There is no deliberate policy of punishment on the part of institutions but unfortunate side effects develop if a child is removed from the nuclear family and, although the policy is to care for the child ... the outcome is inevitably detrimental to the recipient. (Tutt, 1974, p. 48)

There is evidence in many cases of loss of contacts with relatives and friends without the substitution of social relations with fellow residents. There is the restriction of occupational activity and evidence of loneliness and apathy – by comparison with people of comparable age and physical condition outside. And quite apart from the deplorably low standards of amenities there is also the organizational rigidity of institutional life which inevitably creates severe problems of adjustment and integration for residents from diverse backgrounds. Many old people are dismayed at the interruption of a lifetime's routines, loss of contact with locality and family and reduction of privacy and identity. The closer a residential institution approximates in the scale, privacy and freedom of the private household, the greater the qualified expression of contentment. (Townsend, 1973, p. 218)

In ensuring that handicapped people are able to enjoy similar living standards as those enjoyed by non-handicapped members of the community the question becomes one of whether this can be accomplished in an isolated institutional setting. (Jaehnig, 1979, p. 9)

The second, and obviously linked dimension to the 'rights' case, was the growing awareness of, and concern for, the stigmatising effects of institutional care. This became more obvious when policies of rehabilitation were hampered by cases of discrimination against ex-long-stay hospital patients. More generally it could be seen to reflect the extent to which life in a traditional institutional setting was increasingly a devalued and devaluing experience. In his account of 'total institutions' Goffman contrasts 'batch living' with 'a meaningful domestic existence':

Total institutions are also incompatible with another crucial element of our society, the family. Family life is sometimes

> contrasted with solitary living, but in fact the more pertinent
> contrast is with batch living, for those who eat and sleep at
> work, with a group of fellow workers, can hardly sustain a
> meaningful domestic existence. (Goffman, 1961, pp. 21–2)

What is perhaps missing from Goffman's evocative phrasing, is
the sense of the social and economic changes that made this
contrast much more marked and poignant for individuals in
the latter half of the twentieth century by contrast with the
impoverished and impoverishing 'batch living' that was imposed
on many working-class households by the social and economic
conditions of nineteenth century Britain. This concern with the
'citizenship rights' dimension of the traditional institutional services was taken up most obviously in concepts of 'normalisation'
and 'social role valorisation' in services for people with learning
difficulties and the campaign to reform the Mental Health Act,
1959 (Gostin, 1975). Policies for community care become 'a move
to provide disadvantaged and disabled people with services in
settings which everyone in the community values, as a way of
establishing or re-establishing fulfilled lives' (Heginbotham, 1990,
p. 43).

The third dimension of the 'rights case' became a major political
issue from 1968 onwards with the first of a depressingly lengthy
series of enquiries into the neglect and ill-treatment of long-stay
residents of a variety of institutions – especially, but not exclusively, NHS hospitals (Martin, J.P., 1984; see Chapter 5). More
recently attention has focused again (see Curtis Report, 1946 and
also the Court Lees case) on the inadequacies of childrens homes
(see DoH, 1993b). Life in our traditional institutions was not only
probably disabling, and certainly devaluing; it was also potentially
dangerous.

When attempts were made to identify those factors that seem
to precipitate abuse and neglect the following characteristics were
noted:

poorly paid staff;
poorly trained staff;
overworked staff;
inadequate amenities; and
powerless inmates (see, for example, Beresford, 1978, p. 700).

In many respects these characteristics could serve as a description of many of the settings bequeathed from the 'institutionalisation of social problems'. Thus the concern with the disabling, devaluing and dangerous aspects of institutional life could serve as a basis for the right for a non-institutional life expressed simply but quite effectively as follows:

> all people should have the right to live within the community, contribute to it and benefit from it, and simply be a part of it, except in very rare circumstances. (Brown, 1977, p. 195)

Conflicts and community care

We have seen that a persuasive, and indeed quite powerful, case for community care could be assembled around the themes of efficiency, needs and rights. Yet despite this case, the history of community care policies has been problematic and controversial. This situation may be partly explained by some of the conflicts that can be identified with the policy.

Perhaps unsurprisingly one of the most enduring conflicts links the development of community care to our enduring theme of cost containment. In this instance the persuasiveness of part of the case for community care was perhaps counter-productive. The combination of the *efficiency* and *needs* cases suggested the potential to develop a more acceptable, accessible and effective set of services with limited additional expenditure, because of the savings that would accrue from redistributing resources from expensive and unnecessary institutional care, into cheaper, more effective and less institutional alternatives. There were a number of problems with this seemingly 'free lunch' in which everyone would benefit and there would be no losers.

Firstly, the scale of 'overinstitutionalisation' was such that the initial development of community-based alternatives often involved rather modest expenditure, given the limited dependency of the individuals who were diverted to non-institutional settings. This almost certainly exaggerated the 'cheapness' with which successful community care policies could be pursued with more dependent people. It is now possible to find examples where a 'community care package' is substantially more expensive than nursing home care (see for example, Stone, 1995, pp. 15–16).

Secondly, many calculations advanced as part of the efficiency case, underestimated the full range of services needed for successful community care policies (eg: building and planning regulations for access and mobility; labour regulations for discriminatory employment practices) and hence the costs of the latter. In many respects there is no excuse for such miscalculations since the point was made quite forcibly many years ago when it noted that to

> scatter the mentally ill in the community before we have made adequate provision for them is not a solution; in the long run not even for HM Treasury. Considered only in financial terms, any savings from fewer hospital inpatients may well be offset several times by more expenditure on the police forces, on prisons and on probation officers; more unemployment benefits masquerading as sickness benefit; more expenditure on drugs; more research to find out why crime is increasing. (Titmuss, 1961, p. 106)

Thirdly, it was in the nature of the 'total institution' that substantial savings from their reduced role would only accrue when they were completely replaced by a new continuum of community-based services. The 'efficiency savings' associated with community care are therefore significantly long-term rather than short-term. In the shorter-run the NHS might well be 'burdened' with sustaining a dual track of 'old fashioned institution-based provision' and the 'new community-based services'. Furthermore, the NHS was faced with the argument that current and capital expenditure on the traditional long-stay institutions should actually be increased to remedy the worse deficiencies identified in the 'scandals', and to provide for the increasingly dependent residents who remained in this setting. There was a failure to recognise the needs of the more dependent residents and the role played by their less disabled co-residents in caring for them; and hence the potentially profound implications of the transfer of the latter to the community. This may well have contributed to creating some of the factors that were to precipitate successive long-stay hospital 'scandals' as fewer staff coped with fewer, but more demanding long-stay patients.

Fourthly, it was consistently and widely-recognised that policies for community care were not facilitated by the various organizational and financial arrangements underpinning community care (see especially Chapter 6). There have never been effective mechanisms by which the efficiency gains that might accrue from a run-down of traditional institutions would be transferred to those health or social care services that were to be developed as part of policies for community care. In virtually all cases the resulting scenario has been that the traditional institutional provision has been eliminated too swiftly by comparison with the development of community-based alternatives. This was perhaps most marked in the mental health services. By 1975, when it had been expected that thirteen mental illness hospitals would be closed, only one large hospital had been closed in England and Wales (and that became a mental handicap hospital). But despite the very slow process of closing the old asylums, there was already evidence of discharged mental hospital patients left without help and:

> sensational stories of psychiatric hospitals dumping their patients in the streets are regularly cropping up in the national and local press. (See *New Society*, 22.7.76, p. 184; see, also Ball, 1972, p. 241)

At this time a key government document had to admit that 'by and large, the non-hospital resources are still minimal' (DHSS, 1975b. p. 14). Ten years later, academics were still searching for the evidence of significant shifts in resources towards community-based services (Walker, 1982, pp. 161–2); twenty years later, journalists were still suggesting that the mental health services 'in all major cities ... are in crisis' (Leading article, *The Guardian*, December 13th, 1993). The loss of acute hospital beds from London is perhaps the most recent example of this depressing scenario (see Chapter 9) with the Mental Health Task Force London Project concluding that patients with severe mental health illness were being discharged too early from some London hospitals because of bed shortages (MHTFLP, 1994).

For the moment it remains difficult to say with any degree of certainty whether the most recent health and community care reforms will resolve these long-standing concerns. There is no doubt that the organizational context of community care is both crucial and complex, involving as it does contributions from at least health care, social care, housing and social security agencies. The disaggregation of service provision in the quasi-markets for health and social care places a major burden on the service commissioners in providing the co-ordinated approach that will not otherwise emerge from a multiplicity of public, private and voluntary sector providers. The widespread sub-division of health care providers into hospital-based and community-based NHS Trusts may not be necessarily problematic, but does confirm some long-standing professional and organizational divisions. For the moment at least it is not reassuring that the Utting Report concluded that community care was 'dangerously fragmented, unco-ordinated and underfunded' (quoted in *The Independent*, 8/9/94, p. 6) and that the Davies Report into the death of Jonathan Newby should find that the 'network of health, social services and voluntary services were unplanned and disparate' (quoted in The Independent, 27/5/95, p. 3).

Most significantly, the potentially damaging split between health and social care budgets remains alongside a situation where, for example, who changes a patient's dressings following discharge from hospital might be a home care assistant (social care) or a district nurse (health care) – the outcome depending on where you live (Stone, 1995, p. 16). Perhaps the most bizarre consequence of this division is that it has somehow become possible to define long-term nursing care for older people as a non-NHS service – seemingly in contradiction to one of the fundamental guiding principles set out in the 1946 White Paper that a comprehensive health service 'must cover the whole field of medical advice and attention ... (and) ... must include ancillary services of nursing ... and of other things which ought to go with medical care' (Ministry of Health, 1944, p. 9). This situation takes on an even more surreal quality when it is remembered that the keenest advocates of the private sector recognise that the needs of the chronic sick should be 'financed by compulsory taxation' (Lees, 1976, p. 4).

Fifthly, the new commitment was to provide good quality community care. Whatever standards had been set by the new nineteenth century institutions, they were in many cases not providing good quality residential care by the second half of the twentieth century. Therefore the policy was not just about switching resources between different modes of service delivery but about significant changes in service standards and philosophy (eg: normalisation). The resources 'tied up' in old, poor-quality institutional care might not always be sufficient to develop new, high-quality community care.

Sixthly, community care services were not immune from the cost implications of demographic trends (see Chapter 5). Indeed larger numbers of elderly people were the major client group in terms of policies for community care and hence the phenomenon of needing more resources merely to sustain current standards and services was as marked for community care as for other aspects of health and social care (see for example, Heginbotham, 1990, pp. 46–7).

Seventh, and perhaps most significantly, the needs and rights cases for community care had been developed initially in relation to existing 'institutional populations'. However they were increasingly seen to have a wider significance; that is the needs and rights of those 'beyond the institution'. This was quite clearly expressed in the White Paper, *Better Services for the Mentally Handicapped* in 1971. It was this White Paper that proposed the first significant decline in the in-patient population for people with learning difficulties – the 1962 Hospital Plan had only proposed a decrease for mental illness in-patient beds and patients (see Chapter 5). But despite the policy for community care starting *only in 1971* with this White Paper, the same document noted that:

> about 80 per cent of severely handicapped children and 40 per cent of severely handicapped adults – and a higher proportion of the more mildly handicapped – live at home. (DHSS, 1971b, p. 4)

The message from this, and community based surveys on disability, was clear. If the 'institutionalisation of social problems' in the nineteenth century had indeed exposed a previously 'submerged iceberg' of unmet or differently met need, it was only a partial exposure. The inaccessibility and the stigma of institutional care may have contributed to this situation; but it also seems probable that despite the massive investment in institutional care it may in the end have been only marginal to the activities of the newly revealed and vast army of informal carers – a view that had already been partially confirmed by the research that indicated, for example, that most of the older people in residential care had limited access to informal carers – whether families or friends (see Townsend, 1973). If the needs and rights of those beyond the institutions were to be taken seriously it would require more resources than would be released through the recognition of the efficiency case for community care. Furthermore a new set of needs and rights now entered the equation – those of the informal carers. For it was reasonably clear that 'virtually no help' was available to those caring for other people at home (Brown, 1977, p. 199). Whilst the needs and rights of the latter were certainly not necessarily in conflict with those of the cared-for, they were not necessarily always compatible. So more accessible and acceptable community-based services will reveal more and more of a pre-viously 'submerged iceberg' of unrecognised and unmet need (Goodwin, 1989, p. 47) as service-providers become aware of those 'beyond the institutions' who had managed 'out there' by them-selves, or with support from informal carers. It is this, perhaps more than anything else, which sweeps away the 'free lunch' model of community care. Given uncertainties about the numbers and contributions of informal carers relating to various trends (for example, the scale and intensity of needs; separation, divorce and the reconstitution of families; the participation of women in the labour market) it seems the current and future resource implica-tions of 'good community care' are not such that they can be readily accommodated only through the resources still 'tied up' in traditional forms of institutional care.

Finally, in so far as the impact of a combination of cost-containment policies, and an unhelpful administrative infrastruc-ture contributed to widely perceived failings of 'community care', then perhaps the rights (and needs) of two other groups could be identified – the 'institutional' and the 'community' population. The dismantling of traditional institutional care with insufficient attention (or resources) committed to less institutional alterna-tives, has had its greatest impact on the most vulnerable and most dependent individuals. The generality, and indeed validity, of the arguments for community care can conceal variations in the circumstances of different client groups – children in care, people with learning difficulties, mentally ill people – and of individuals within these groups. It was clearly never part of the case for community care that all forms of residential care would be abandoned (the research on overinstitutionalisation was at times startling but never indicated that 100 per cent of those surveyed could be cared for in non-institutional settings). Yet at times local policies seem to have come close to this scenario. In these circumstances the rights and needs of the most dependent individuals are clearly at risk, raising questions of whether the right to a non-institutional life should be complemented by the 'right of asylum' (see Parry-Jones, 1987, p. 411) or the 'right to protection' if, as was noted many years ago:

> our society is increasingly unwilling to accept responsibility, socially and financially, for those who do not recover quickly and who do not conform to our expectations of medical productivity. (Titmuss, 1961, p. 108)

The right to long-term nursing care (as part of the NHS) may be another essential element in getting the balance 'right' between institutional and community care.

The rights of the wider community might also form part of the equation; whether certain behaviour can be adjudged sufficiently unacceptable to justify 'institutionalisation' continues to underpin ongoing debates – especially in relation to mental health legislation. Society is having to cope with the reversal of the nineteenth century institutional policy following a series of spectacular murders of citizens by recently released but inadequately cared for mentally ill people (see DHSS, 1988; Richie Report, 1994). In January 1995 the Blom-Cooper Report came to the conclusion that current arrangements (including the Mental Health Act, 1983) 'neither protects the public effectively, nor provides the care which seriously mentally disordered people need to have a more fulfilled and happier life' (Blom-Cooper and others, 1995). It is noticeable that subsequently (20 February, 1996) the Secretary of State, Stephen Dorrell, in a statement to the House of Commons, attempted to replace the phrase 'care in the community' with the term 'spectrum of care', re-emphasising the asylum at one end and the community at the other. The following month it was reported that there were currently 'about 400 health service enquiries into deaths involving care in the community cases' (*The Independent*, March 7th, 1996, p. 1).

The recent mental health cases may be seen as confirmation of an observations made twenty years ago (with regard to child care services) about the difficulty of regulating community-based provision (see Walton and Heywood, 1975, p. 173). They may also confirm the judgement and warning of the Social Services Committee ten years later that

> we do not wish to slow down the exodus from mental illness or mental handicap hospitals for its own sake, but we do look to see the same degree of Ministerial pressure, and the provision of the necessary resources, devoted to the creation of alternative services. Any fool can close a long-stay hospital: it takes more time and trouble to do it properly and compassionately. The Minister must ensure that mental illness or mental handicap hospital provision is not reduced without demonstrably adequate alternative services being provided beforehand both for those discharged from hospital and for those who would otherwise seek admission. (Social Services Committee, 1985, para.40)

Conclusions

Given our growing awareness of the limitations of institutional care in terms of the proportions of people with mental health problems, people with learning difficulties, and frail elderly people that the institutions actually care for, there may be some substance to the argument that, both the opening of new institutions in the nineteenth and early twentieth century, and the closure of such institutions in the final quarter of the twentieth century, represent rather marginal shifts in terms of both whether individual needs are being met, and how they are being met.

Nevertheless in terms of a restructuring of ideologies of, and resources for caring, both the 'institutionalisation of social problems' detectable in nineteenth century social policy, and the trend towards policies for community care discernible by the middle of the twentieth century, can be said to represent important changes. Our review of community care has highlighted three major themes. Firstly, that the *concept* of *community*, and its operational consequence, *care*, has been a highly valued idea for several decades, but has been unmatched by either a firm agreement on its meaning, or the economic support to give a reality to either its potential beneficiaries, its carers, or citizens at large. An early warning of this theme was given by Titmuss in 1961 (see Titmuss, 1968, Ch.9). Secondly, that the policy response to the concept has always lagged behind the political 'support' such a concept has engendered. Thirdly, the result of this gap between valued intention and policy response has been a distrust of the relocation of the populations of institutional care, the latter being seen as a nineteenth century reasoned response to the 'social problems' of the time, but unmatched by the same response required in a modern society. Thus, an ambiguous conceptual basis, an under-resourced policy and an ill-prepared citizenry have unintentionally combined to produce a lack of faith in what is assumed to be a widely shared commitment to supporting those with conditions requiring that very care summarised by the conceptual 'baggage' of community care.

The case for policies for community care – as we have defined those policies – can be well-founded on the needs and rights of a significant number of potentially vulnerable people of all ages. But there are other, and not necessarily complementary, needs and rights to be considered – especially of the informal carers and the wider community. There are, as ever, issues of costs, since there is no doubt that effective policies for community care require more resources than those released by the 'deinstitutionalisation of social problems'. We must conclude that policies for community care embrace a range of potential conflicts – including all those that have been generated by the organizational arrangements for health and social care, especially the associated problems of inter-professional non-co-operation and rivalry. These organizational arrangements and associated themes of professionalism, bureaucracy, managerialism and democracy are the subject of our next, penultimate, chapter.

14

Professionals or non-professionals?

The characteristic structure of welfare services in industrial societies was described many years ago as involving 'specialised bureaucratic agencies, professionally staffed' (Wilensky & Lebeaux, 1965, p. 230). 'Professional staffing' is certainly one of the distinctive characteristics of the organizational structure of health care and in Britain this structure has been a consistent source of conflict, most especially in relation to state involvement in health care since the latter part of the nineteenth century. Professional opposition to NHI focused more on financial and management arrangements than the principle of state regulated social insurance (see Chapter 2); professional support for radical health care reforms in the 1930s and early 1940s dissipated into fractious opposition to organizational details about the administrative arrangements for the new NHS (see Chapters 3 and 4).

The professional interest has been characterised as operating in certain directions, most notably in terms of the maximisation of individual and group autonomy and the minimisation of lay (including democratic) control (see Chapter 6). In addition to their general anti-democratic bias, the professions also stand accused of using their power and status to establish and maintain particular definitions of health and social needs, and particular responses to these needs (see Chapters 5 and 8).

> professionals ... tell you what you need ... they claim the powers to prescribe ... they not only advertise what is good, but ordain what is right. (Illich, 1978, p. 49)

There is also the well-documented conflict between professional and bureaucratic modes of work. When social policies are translated into bureaucratic health and social care delivery systems, the stage is set for a conflict between values based upon professional discretion and judgement, and bureaucratic rules based upon accountability and the responsibility for rationing scarce resources. As a result professionals are seen as posing particular problems for notions of accountability within state welfare. Their claims to individual and group autonomy (peer review) cut across conventional lines of accountability; the latter may be difficult enough to sustain in the context of a large state welfare organization like the NHS, without the added complication of a 'reliance on experts and professionalism' (Day and Klein, 1987, p. 2). Thus professionals are not readily susceptible to such regulation and scrutiny on behalf of the wider public interest, despite their employment status as public servants.

Professional power and organizational structures

The rapid advance of medical science and the increasing complexity of medical practice have outstripped the ability of the average local councillor to make informed decisions concerning the provision and management of medical services and too often policy is determined by local politics and personal factors. (BMA, Medical Planning Commission, 1942)

Professionals and professionalism appear as central issues in relation to health and community care. For the latter in particular there is a very lengthy history of failures to deliver the sort of professional collaboration to which service-users might feel reasonably entitled. This history is at least partially entangled in issues of professional power and the politics of policy-making.

Before the NHS a combination of local authorities and voluntary institutions were the key arbiters of the availability of health care resources. The outcome for the hospitals was a collection of independently managed institutions providing an arbitrary patchwork quilt of services of varying degrees of efficacy, separated and enclosed by financial, legal, medical, residential and occupational barriers and categories. This provided the basis for a powerful 'rational' case for restructuring health care in the UK (see Chapter 2). The establishment of the National Health Service, although associated with socialist aspirations represented by the absence of service-user charges and the twin goals of minimising inequalities in health and access to health care, has also been identified with the less ideological, more technical goal of a more efficiently managed health care system (see for example, Eckstein, 1958).

The organizational details of the new service proved to be controversial as the representatives of the medical profession sought to minimise lay control over their activities. This was most obviously represented in the resulting tripartite administrative structure, by the relative autonomy of the teaching hospitals, the proscribed role for local government, and the independent practitioner status of GPs. This political compromise on management and funding arrangements would be the subject of further conflict within the Service, between the Service and the politicians, and between the professionals, the politicians and the public.

The compromise also enabled most of the medical profession to distance themselves from local government when the NHS was established, and reinforced the isolation of the solo community-based general practitioner from local authority employed community nursing colleagues in domiciliary midwifery, district nursing and health visiting. The so-called 'Doctors' Charter' of 1966 allied to other changes, including increasing government expenditure on health centre construction, encouraged GPs to work together in group practices. When the Health Services and Public Health Act (1968) enabled local authorities to arrange cross-boundary visiting by their community nursing staff, the health centre-based primary health care team started to become a reality (see Chapter 5).

However, by the time this long-argued for, and long-heralded concept, was being put into practice, it had already been recognised for some time that effective community care required a collaborative enterprise between not just health professionals, but between health and social care personnel. This enterprise was clearly not facilitated by the separation of personnel and services between a tripartite NHS and local government (and within local government between district and county councils – and within the councils between different departments). But the costly and complex reorganizations of 1971 and 1974 did little to ameliorate this situation. The commitment to divide responsibilities between local authority social services departments and the new health authorities on a 'professional principle' (DHSS, 1970, p. 10, para.31; see also Chapter 6) established a new health and social care divide.

> At considerable expense, and with detailed arrangements much influenced by key professional groups, this lengthy restructuring process came to an end in 1974 with the success of policies for community care precariously dependent on the bridging of a health and social care divide more clearly delineated in administrative, financial and professional terms than at any stage in the history of post-war health and community care policies. (Carrier and Kendall, 1995, p. 17)

This new health and social care division was the subject of a series of critical reports in the 1980s from the House of Commons Social Services Committee, the Audit Commission and Sir Roy Griffiths. All commented upon the problems of the organizational and professional divisions which prevented a tailor-made service from being truly responsive to well-defined client needs (see Social Services Committee, 1985, para.96; Audit Commission, 1986, p. 3; and Griffiths, 1988, pp. 11–12, 14–16, 18, 23, 25 and 28). There appeared to be a wide-ranging consensus that the organizational arrangements which had to a degree been sought after by the health and social care professions, and the rationale for the existing divisions between those professions, were not providing the sort of services required.

Organizational trends and choices

> We tend to meet any new situation by reorganization and a wonderful method it can be for creating the illusion of progress, while causing confusion, inefficiency and demoralisation. (Gaius Petronious, 1st century AD)

> > The best laid scheme o' mice an' men
> > Gang oft a-gley.
> > (Robert Burns, To A Mouse)

Marx identified defective administration as one of the commonest explanations given for 'social problems' (see Pinker, 1971, p. 34) and it certainly appears that successive generations of politicians have seen organizational reform as a relevant response to problems. The administrative division of state welfare has been restructured on a number of occasions. Many have had an impact on the organization of health care, most obviously the Poor Law Amendment Act, 1834 (see Chapter 1), the Local Government Act, 1929 (see Chapter 2), the National Health Service Act, 1946 (see Chapters 3 and 4), the 'Seebohm' reorganization of personal social services and the subsequent (1974) NHS and local government reorganizations (see Chapter 6), the *Patients First* NHS reorganization (Chapter 7) and finally the health and community care reforms and the subsequent demise of regional health authorities (Chapters 7 and 8).

In so far as trends can be observed in the administrative restructuring of state welfare perhaps the most striking is the contrasting fortunes of local government before and after the Second World War. Before 1946 local government appeared to be mostly acquiring new welfare responsibilities, especially in the area of health and community care – for example, the asylums/ mental hospitals and other specialist hospitals (see Chapter 1), school health service, health visiting, domiciliary midwifery and the poor law medical services (see Chapter 2).

From 1946 onwards it became a net loser of services initially through its removal from the social security scheme (ie: public assistance) and its much diminished role in the new National Health Service (see Chapter 4). This process was virtually completed when the 1974 reorganization of the NHS ended local government responsibility for community health and school health services. In relation to health care the trend can be partially explained in terms of the 'anti-democratic' and 'anti-bureaucratic' biases of key professional groups (see for example, Brown, 1979, p. 30)

This centralising tendency was also evident in the role of non-state organizations as service providers. Once again the pre-war period saw a growing state involvement in health and other areas linked with a major role for non-state institutions as direct service providers (eg: the Friendly Societies and insurance companies, church schools, the voluntary hospitals). At the same time as the role of local government was diminished so a similar fate befell these organizations; the most significant change following the

Beveridge Report and the establishment of the NHS was the exclusion of Friendly Societies from any administrative responsibilities for health care or social security and the nationalisation of the voluntary hospitals. Subsequent trends saw the gradual disappearance of other voluntary sector providers.

The effect of this diminished role for local government and voluntary institutions combined with reorganizations of the personal social services, local government and the NHS, was to significantly decrease the number of agencies (including separate departments within organizations) concerned with service management and delivery. As Friendly Societies were followed by other voluntary organizations, so some hospital management committees, rural and urban district councils disappeared in advance of the 1974 local government and NHS reorganization, the latter removing separate Boards of Governors from most teaching hospitals. However few general trends are entirely straightforward. The self-employed GPs retained their status of independent contractors along with pharmacists, opticians and dentists. Their services continued to be delivered through a 'privatised' model (self-employed professionals and small businesses) throughout this period, whilst successive governments sought to revive and recast the role of housing associations some time before the Griffiths Report and related community care reforms re-asserted the potential role of non-state providers of social care.

NHS trust status has re-established an organizational unit whose number and appearance replicate features of the old hospital management committees and board of governors (see Chapters 7 and 8). Indeed earlier parallels might be found in the plethora of service providers that characterised areas of Victorian public administration before the local government reforms of the 1880s. Then it was possible to identify seven separate organizations concerned with public health matters at the local level – Water Commissioners, Commissioners of Sewers, Highway Surveyors, Poor Law Guardians, Select Vestries, Street Commissioners and Improvement Commissioners (see Fraser, 1973, p. 64). Whether a combination of 'internal markets' linked to 'contracting out' and 'privatisation' generate a similar number of service providers remains to be seen. For the moment, local government awaits a similar revival, and its decline as a service provider continues (eg:

grant-maintained ['opted-out'] schools and self-managed further and higher education institutions).

The history of state health care organizations can therefore be seen to have mirrored that of other state welfare activities (most obviously education). The trends may be accounted for in a variety of ways, but in terms of the key themes of this text they may provide further explanations for the some of the long-running conflicts surrounding organizational issues. Whilst organizational change may be pursued for a variety of wider political and economic motives, the range of organizational alternatives utilised in the history of state welfare is indicative of considerable potential for choice. Faced with a blank sheet of paper and the question of 'how best' to organise the 'administrative division of state welfare' (including therefore the NHS), the organizational reformer is faced with an intriguing array of inter-related choices many of which bring with them considerable potential for conflict and tension (Klein, 1995a, p. 148). These choices relate to *at least* the following:

(a) scale;
(b) hierarchies;
(c) dispersal and diversity;
(d) scope;
(e) divisions and categories;
(f) status;
(g) decisions; and
(h) complaints and redress.

We will examine each in turn to identify some of the conflicts inherent in these choices.

(a) Scale. There can be a basic commitment to some notion of optimum organizational size. One of the concerns about pre-war local government health services related to inappropriate size and boundaries (see Abel-Smith, 1964, p. 371 and Webster, 1988, p. 20). Some of the organizational changes of the 1960s and 1970s seem to have been predicated on assumptions about the 'economies of scale' that would flow from larger organizations, including for example the amalgamation of the Ministry of Health and Ministry of Social Security into the Department of Health and

Social Security (DHSS). Recent developments indicate a prefer-ence for smaller organizations; and indeed the DHSS has been reconstituted into its two predecessor departments. In both trends we can identify similar trends in (and almost certainly influences from) private sector organizations. The NHS was of course well known for being the largest civilian organization in the world often leading cost-conscious politicians to make the totally illogical observation that 'there must be scope for economies in an organ-ization that size'.

(b) Hierarchies. Here the crucial question for a service funded by central government revenues (like the NHS) is whether some less than central 'organizational layer' is needed and if so what form it should take. Health care has been managed and delivered at regional (RHBs and then RHAs), county (Health Departments before 1974, AHAs after 1974), city (county borough health departments before 1974), town (health department services devolved to district councils, mostly before 1959) parish (poor law authorities) and institutional (Boards of Governors) levels plus the distinctive 'health district' concept upon which HMCs, DMTs and DHAs have been based. One of the longest running debates concerned the necessity for regional authorities which were set to disappear in the First Green Paper (1968, see Chapter 6), survived into the 1990s (see Chapter 8), finally giving way to eight regional outposts in 1995 (see Chapter 9). Clearly opinions about the appropriate 'scale' of organizations will influence decisions regard-ing hierarchies.

(c) Dispersal and diversity. Given a hierarchy of some sort, at what points in the hierarchy will key decisions be taken? This is partly a question about the centralisation or decentralisation of power. It may be much influenced by other policy commitments. Can either 'territorial justice' in the allocation of health care resources or new priorities in health care be pursued effectively without a considerable degree of central direction? Does local independence and diversity make for a sensitive response to local variations in the pattern of health care needs or health services 'of uneven distribution and quality' (Webster, 1988, p. 20) and unac-ceptable disparities in, for example, the way local authorities charge people for social care (see for example, National Consumer

Council, 1995)? There has certainly been ostensible government support for a maximum delegation of power to local units of health care management for more than a quarter of a century. Some critics would certainly say that this may have gone too far given the well-publicised problems of some regional health authorities in buying and running computer systems (Public Accounts Committee, 1993).

District Management Teams (DMTs) within AHAs (1974–1981), Unit Management Teams within DHAs (1981–1991), and finally Directly Managed Units within DHAs (1991 to date), posed a further 'decentralisation and diversity' question regarding the degree of autonomy and discretion to be given to identifiable 'management units' within a 'local (health) authority' – a debate that can be paralleled in relation to the role of the divisional and area offices of local authority education, housing and social services departments. Of course how far local decision-making powers can be devolved will depend in part on the hierarchy adopted and the scale of organizations at different points in the hierarchy. There is also the crucial question of 'how real' is the devolution of power? Government claims of the institutional self-management and autonomy have been met with counter-claims of greater centralised control then ever before (see Jenkins, 1996 and Klein, 1995a, p. 215).

(d) Scope. For what should the organization be responsible? Should it be only hospitals (HMCs) or GP services (Executive Councils) or community health services (Local authority health departments) as with the original tripartite structure of the NHS? Alternatively perhaps hospital and community health services could come under one organization (the 1974 NHS reorganization) or one authority could have an overview of all health care needs (the DHA as health care purchaser since 1991). Given the problems of developing effective community care policies perhaps one organization should have overall responsibility for health and social care (The health and welfare authorities in Northern Ireland since 1974). It was clearly the view of the Sanitary Commission in 1869 that

> all powers requisite for the health of town and country should in every place be possessed by one responsible authority . . .

so that no one area shall be without such an authority or have more than one. (Quoted in Webster, 1988, p. 17)

This argument could be taken a stage further given the wide range of environmental factors impinging on health status (see Chapter 10); one organization should have an even broader overview of inter-related services. Given the otherwise inevitable problems of large scale organization perhaps this task should be undertaken at a local level. This of course can turn into the classic rationale for the tradition of 'generalist' or 'all-purpose' local government that was established in the UK following the late Victorian reforms which ended the plethora of overlapping, highly specialist organizations that had been established (eg: the Select Vestries and other public health bodies, see above). Local government was reasonably well-placed to take on this role for health and related issues by the 1930s (see Chapter 2) but as we noted other interests – including that of the medical profession – were less than enthusiastic about that seemingly 'rational response'.

Of course it is possible that the purchaser / provider split within the NHS provides an opportunity for reviving the role of local government as a purchaser (or commissioner) of health care for two reasons: Firstly, because local government would not become a direct employer of health professionals (who would work for the health care providers). Secondly, because unifying health care purchasing, commissioning and planning within local government does not present the same picture of potential 'organizational overload' previously associated with bringing the NHS into local government.

(e) Divisions and categories. Whether we opt to locate responsibility for all or some health care with 'generalist' local government or with 'specialist health' authorities issues of division and categories arise. For example 'generalist' local government may be subdivided into departments (education, health) that parallel the divisions between specialist authorities (Boards of Education, 1870–1906, Area Health Authorities, 1974–81). On what principles may services be divided or sub-divided.

Of considerable significance is the relationship between health and social care, and whether some attempt is made to contain health and social care within agency and organizational boundaries (eg: the old local authority health department) or whether it becomes the basis upon which boundaries are organised. One important decision in the history of post-war policies for community care was to adopt the 'professional principle' in allocating responsibilities and personnel to the health or personal social services in 1971 and 1974 thus reinforcing a health and social care divide that continued to hinder broader policy aims (see Chapters 6, 7, 8 and 13). One alternative model – basing service divisions on the needs of identifiable groups of service-users (eg: mental health and welfare services) was rejected despite receiving support from service user groups (see Heginbotham, 1990, pp. 52–5 for alternative organizational divisions).

The issue has assumed a further significance with a growing concern about the role of the NHS in meeting long term health care needs. The guidelines issued by the NHS Executive includes 'the expectation' that 'the significant majority of people who require continuing care in a nursing home setting are likely to have their needs met through social services' (NHS Executive, 1994, p. 2). It seems strange that what appears to be 'continuing nursing care' can be somehow defined as a responsibility of local authority social services departments rather than of a comprehensive NHS (see Ministry of Health, 1944, p. 9), especially since the allocation of services and personnel following the 1974 NHS reorganization means that the former are singularly ill-equipped to make judgements about the health care needs of those in longstay residential institutions. Indeed, for the moment at least, Social Services Departments seem to be having considerable difficulty maintaining standards in areas more cognate to their obvious expertise (ie: childrens homes; see, for example, DoH, 1993b).

A historical comparison with the Poor Law is not necessarily favourable to current practices in this regard when

> many of the medical staff of the poor law infirmaries gave the benefit of the doubt to patients whose medical needs were less urgent than their need for good food, warmth and social care. (Pinker, 1996)

It may be that an equally sensitive but contemporary blend of health and social care may require a recasting of current organizational divisions and categories – especially that between health and social care.

(f) Status. Given the history of health care in the UK and elsewhere (role of voluntary hospitals and Friendly Societies, see, Chapter 1) and government attempts to revive the 'agency model of welfare' (welfare pluralism), especially in relation to community care, the role of non-state organizations as service-providers remains an issue. To what extent should aspects of essentially state financed health care be delivered by (agents) organizations from outside the state administrative framework through various forms of 'contracting out'; and if such 'contracting out' is to be increased how do you manage the new regulatory regimes that it may require (see for example, Klein, 1995a, p. 160). A key role for 'privatised agencies' might of course be said to be an enduring feature of state health care given the crucial role of GPs since 1913 and their independent contractor relationship with first NHI and then continuing as 'an autonomous enclave within the NHS' (Klein, 1995a, p. 163).

There is a formal, 'legal status' dimension to this – government spokesmen taking pains to stress that 'opted out' schools and hospitals have not 'opted out' of the 'welfare state'. Nonetheless this organizational model parallels other reforms – eg: 'Next Step' agencies – and certainly complements forms of 'welfare pluralism' that give important service provider roles to voluntary and private sector organizations. Service delivery through a plethora of relatively autonomous budget-holders may bring benefits but health care historians may offer various notes of caution. Most obviously will we recreate contemporary equivalents of the voluntary hospitals improving their finances by 'farming out uneconomical long-stay cases to public institutions' (Eckstein, 1958, p. 147); the NHI approved society arrangements being dominated by a 'dozen huge societies' (Gilbert, 1970, p. 301); or the 'administrative chaos' (Hodgkinson, 1967, p. 669) prevalent before local government was reformed.

Of course what welfare pluralism may do is change the nature of our organizational choices and dilemmas since they are to some extent 'contracted out' to non-state organizations who will be left to resolve some issues of scale, hierarchy, and divisions for themselves. One opportunity certainly afforded by welfare plural-ism is the establishment of relatively manageable, combined, local health *and* social care purchasers / commissioners. It is difficult to conceive the position of those needing long-term care and those with serious mental health problems being worse served by that arrangement than the post-1974 health and social care divide.

(f) Decisions. Professionalism in health and social care implies that key decisions on the allocation of and access to resources, are based on, or even controlled by, professional discretion derived from their knowledge and expertise. This mode of decision-making we might characterise as individualised professional discretion.

The role of individualised professional discretion has attracted a wide range of critics. From the Left, the professions are represented as at least middle-class dominated and at worst as an integral part of systems of class dominance and inequalities. From the Right, the professions have conspired to escape the liberating forces of competitive free markets and thus sacrificed efficiency and consumer choice. Feminist perspectives cite the male domi-nance of the more prestigious professions and the role of these professions as part of the broader patriarchal nature of contem-porary society.

The recent policy agenda seems to reflect a deep rooted mistrust of public service professionalism. With *Working for Patients* (DoH, 1989a) and *Caring for People* (DoH, 1989b) came an advocacy for a new structure for welfare service 'independently managed, specialist units, professionally staffed' and disciplined by 'quasi-markets' and quantifiable targets for health and social care. This can be seen to represent the antithesis of what pro-fessional claims for high professional practice stand for. These claims are that professional judgements about client needs are often by their very nature unquantifiable; that quantification leads to performance league tables which become the dominant measure of success, thus devaluing the content of care; and that the introduction of a cash nexus into the relationship between the purchaser and provider can lead to a slippery slope in which professional judgements are 'bought and negotiated' rather than accepted as of right.

To what extent do the new reforms represent a *market* alternative to individualised professional discretion? There are a number of points to be noted in answer to that question. Firstly, what evidence we have of traditional professions (like medicine) being placed in more market-orientated contexts (eg: doctors in the USA) provides little or no evidence that their power or status is much diminished or that professional/client relations are much improved (judging by the volume of medical malpractice suits in the USA). Furthermore the financial remuneration of the professionals seems to be much enhanced in this market environment. Secondly, and more significantly, this scenario merely places professions in a different economic context. For market transactions to be a genuine alternative to individualised professional discretion, a decision currently taken by professionals (eg: access to prescription drugs) should be replaced by a straightforward consumer transaction (eg: the same drugs are bought over the counter at a shop with no professional controls exerted over the consumer). The obvious merit of this approach would be to dramatically diminish (and indeed even eliminate) professional controls over non-professionals, allied to the presumed virtues of competitive private markets – competition, choice and efficiency. However the extent to which health care markets can bring these virtues to the health care consumer are questionable (see Chapters 9 and 11).

It is possible to identify other alternatives to such individualised professional discretion in health and welfare and the most obvious is a *bureaucratic* approach – wherein decisions made by professionals are replaced by decisions taken by officials utilising a formal set of rules and regulations. The bureaucratic alternative can be identified with the advantages of a rule-based consistency of decision-making; if the rules and regulations are largely or wholly in the public domain then the bureaucratic approach looks a more effective guarantor of both the 'right to welfare' and the 'right to complain'.

On the other hand, bureaucracy has long been associated with 'rigidity', 'hostility to change' and the tendency to develop self-justifying routines. Commentators and consumers have little trouble in identifying this characteristic with social security bureaucracies, especially means-tested public assistance programmes. The resulting web of rigid rules is associated with claimant deterrence, rather than service-user entitlement. So welfare bureaucracies signify routines, rules, regulations, 'red-tape' and rigidity – a set of characteristics that seemed certain to militate against innovation, responding to new problems and the sensitive handling of human needs.

Welfare bureaucracy also implies a problem of inequalities in knowledge. The welfare bureaucrats know the rules and regulations which the non-expert consumer struggles to comprehend – a further factor to exclude the latter, even when some needs-based criteria defines them as eligible for services in cash or kind. Issues of inequalities in knowledge figure in another problem of bureaucracy – its anti-democratic bias. It is the officials of the bureaucracy who possess 'expert knowledge'. Can these bureaucracies and their expert, full-time officials be effectively controlled 'in the public interest' by the inexpert public representatives (councillors, MPs, Ministers).

Thus both professionalism and bureaucracy may be regarded as posing a rather similar problem for state welfare. They provide us with a situation where there are 'experts' whose knowledge is not widely shared, and where the control of these 'experts' pose considerable difficulties for the 'public representative'. The latter is presumably charged with ensuring state welfare develops in line with 'the public interest'. This conventional assumption of 'democratic control' may obviously be difficult to put into practice in the face of the power and influence of 'the expert'. The 'welfare consumer' may also find it difficult to challenge, complain about and change decisions made by 'experts' either in relation to what is done for a particular individual or decisions which affect a group of people (eg: changing the pattern of ante-natal care, closing down a local hospital).

Democratic procedures may also offer an alternative mode of decision-making about the meeting of needs. Public representatives might in these circumstances take decisions, for example, about the allocation of accommodation or school places, that could otherwise be seen as the purview of housing and education professionals. The democratic alternative can be identified with the traditional advantages claimed for representative democracy – that decisions will reflect 'the views of the community' and that the decision-makers are ultimately accountable to that 'community' through systems of election. Whatever the 'traditional virtues' of democracy and the role of elected public representatives, they have been largely absent from the NHS due to the limited role played by local government in health care since 1948, and especially since 1974. Elected public representatives were absent from this major public service, except in so far as mechanisms and formulas were in place for local government councillors to be nominated as public representatives. However with the introduction of 'quasi-markets' even this 'quasi-democracy' has disappeared.

The *managerial* alternative involves a transfer of power of key decision-making (especially about resources) to identified individuals who can be made simply and directly accountable through a managerial hierarchy to senior managers and (in state welfare) to public representatives. In the absence of other forms of potentially conflicting authority and controls (peer reviews, codes of ethics, rules and regulations) the manager has the potential, at a stroke, to resolve the problems of accountability associated with 'big government' and 'professionalism' – a way of making democracy work outside the context of parish, rural and urban district councils where the scale of activities precludes the democratic approach identified above.

The alternative of a managerial approach appears to have been extensively pursued – leading to the acronym NPM ('new public management') in the context of health and community care. For the NHS, the most significant event was the 'first Griffiths Report' and its recommendation that health authorities should identify general managers 'charged with the general management function and overall responsibility for management's performance in achieving objectives set by the Authority' (DHSS, 1983, pp. 11, 5). This was accepted by the Government, and from 1 April, 1984 the NHS abandoned a system of consensus team management – a form of managerial responsibility which had been based on a perceived need and demand for considerable professional autonomy (see Chapter 7).

For a number of key areas (eg: mental health) *judicial* modes of decision-making have always been an alternative. Decisions that might be taken by professionals are taken by courts or tribunals. A number of advantages have been claimed for this alternative most obviously in terms of the clearly defined rights of the individuals about whom decisions are being taken, public knowledge and scrutiny of these decisions, and associated virtues of taking note of the demands of 'natural justice' and due process'. A concern with the implications of extensive professional discretion seemed to be one factor influencing reform of mental health (and child care) legislation in a manner that has enhanced a judicial approach. The principal changes introduced by the Mental Health Act, 1983 were designed to improve the rights of patients or potential patients.

But if the judicial approach has a lengthy, if often overlooked welfare history (see Carrier and Kendall, 1992, pp. 67–71), it has not been short of critics and criticisms. In particular conventional court proceedings and 'legalistic approaches' to meeting needs have been questioned in terms of fairness, accessibility, costs, delays, and their adversarial nature (see for example, Carrier and Kendall, 1992, pp. 71–6).

Consumerism implies the empowerment of individual welfare service-users in non-market situations. Decisions that would be taken by professionals are at least subject to greater consumer influence or more radically are transferred to the service users (or their representatives). This has been advocated in a number of forms including consumer participation or representation within traditional or newly established advisory / decision-making forums (eg: School Boards of Governors, tenants groups) and the creation of quasi-markets (vouchers, parental choice of schools). These may be complemented by a general enhancement of welfare consumer rights. Its advantages seem clear in terms of enhanced individual freedom and control over activities which impinge on people's lives. The impact of consumerism seems most obvious and most dramatic in education policy, where it is presumed that parental choice of their children's schooling has been significantly enhanced, along with the position and influence of parent governors on school governing bodies. However aspects of consumerism have a lengthy history even in health care. For example, consumer representation might be regarded as more effective under the NHI Act of 1936 which fixed the membership of each Insurance Committee (the NHI equivalent of the FPC) at a minimum of twenty and maximum of forty, of whom three-fifths were *insured persons*, one-fifth members of county and county borough councils, and one-fifth medical representatives.

Voluntarism implies a reliance on philanthropy and mutual aid to deliver services that might otherwise be identified with the state and with professionals. It should not of course be taken to mean the substitution of 'incompetent amateurs' for 'skilled professionals'. There are well-established traditions of trained volunteers in health and social care (including many forms of counselling and advice work). An advocacy of voluntarism as an alternative to professionalism may identify a degree of 'overtraining' and 'elitism' with the latter. It may also reflect a degree of faith in personal commitment, and a lack of faith in cash and careerism as a basis for undertaking caring roles. The voluntary alternative combines the virtues of community involvement, freedom from the tyranny of wage- (and salary-) labour and an avoidance of the conspiratorial, power-seeking attributes of professionalism. However the extent to which successive governments' support for the voluntary sector has enhanced the role of voluntarism is not always easy to discern, given that the most well-known voluntary organizations are themselves the employers of significant numbers of paid and professionally qualified staff.

Finally the alternative of *informal caring* draws on the roles of families and communities. The greater contemporary significance of this community-based alternative has followed from a growing realisation of the volume of unmet needs with regard to, for example, people with physical disabilities, allied to the awareness of the vast army of informal carers (see Chapter 13). This alerts us to the presence of a mode of decision-making in which questions about the nature and extent of need are resolved informally by families and neighbours guided by the love and friendship they feel towards the individuals concerned. This approach embodies key qualities (tender loving care) absent from the necessarily socially distant professional approach (Ignatieff, 1984). It allows for the sort of personalised, and if necessary unconventional, approach with which professionals cannot, by definition, be associated.

A growing recognition of informal caring activity has led to attempts to reorder somewhat the perception of the professional role, most obviously through the Barclay Report (1982) where community social work was identified with enabling and supporting informal carers – an attempt to modify and qualify the role of professional social workers as 'front-line providers'. However, this approach was not supported by all members of the Committee (Pinker, 1982). Indeed while the 'community' is the focus of many contemporary care practices, it is nevertheless an idea that has attracted considerable criticism in terms of its components and operational difficulties. Even the family, once an unchallenged institution for the nurture of its members and the meeting of its lifetime needs, is no longer as stable an institution as it was once thought to be.

It is clear that our identifiable alternatives to professional decision-making come with their own set of potential problems. We may substitute for the discretion of professionals, the discretion of officials, magistrates, judges, councillors, the lay person (jury, voter, volunteer, informal carer) with no hint of a code of ethics to guide the latter. It is often difficult to fathom the basis of professional decision-making and the use of professional discretion. Nevertheless there is a community of professionals, often through regulatory bodies, which have as one of their key objectives, the monitoring of discretion in order to avoid abuse, inappropriate dispositions, and unethical behaviour. It is difficult to detect the same set of arrangements that govern the activities of bureaucratic officials, welfare managers, councillors, lay people and even magistrates and judges. We return to debate below.

(g) Complaints and Redress. One of the advantages of the judicial mode of decision making identified above, is that procedures for voicing complaints about decisions may be an integral part of the approach (ie: systems of appeal). Certainly the arguments relating to the significance and distinctive qualities of 'health care as a consumer good' (see Chapter 11) constitute part of the case for saying there should be adequate systems for responding to complaints about health care systems; and where appropriate offering redress to complainants. This was recognised when the introduction of NHI also saw the introduction of an NHI complaints system.

The organization of complaints procedures presents a further set of organizational choices and dilemmas. These include the remit of such procedures – this could include focusing on professional groups (eg: doctors, nurses, social workers), key components of state welfare (eg: health care, education), or perhaps service providers (eg: local government, NHS Trusts). There are then a set of well-known questions regarding issues of independence and formality, often resolved in favour of stages which start with internal, informal arrangements and conclude with independent, formal proceedings. All these issues have form part of quite a long-running debate about the adequacy of NHS complaints procedures.

A concern for patients views and a record of more critical patients was observed in the 1920s (see Abel-Smith, 1964, pp. 335–7); but a degree of insensitivity to health care users was said to be evident forty years later (Klein, 1995b, p. 306). Between these two dates, the introduction of the NHS completed the introduction of a somewhat complex array of means by which patients might voice their concerns, complaints, grumbles and grievances relating to the medical profession. In particular the continuing significance of the differences between hospital doctors and GPs represented by organizational and budgetary divisions (ie: the tripartite structure of the NHS) and employment status (ie: the independent contractor status of GPs) had led to the establishment of different complaints procedures for GP and hospital services – whilst it remained possible for certain cases to be the subject of court (eg: case of medical negligence) and/or professional disciplinary (ie: General Medical Council) proceedings. In 1973 the office of Health Service Commissioner was introduced. These arrangements were the subject of considerable and long-standing criticisms relating to their clarity, effectiveness, efficiency, fairness and perhaps, most significantly, their complexity (see for example, Klein, 1973; and Carrier and Kendall, 1990b).

All avenues of complaint – the Service's own arrangements, the Health Service Commissioner and the General Medical Council – experienced an increasing volume of complaints during the 1980s, an indication not so much that the NHS was deteriorating but rather that 'its rate of improvement did not match the rate at which expectations were increasing' (Klein, 1995b, p. 307). The NHS complaints procedures were the subject of a review by the Wilson Committee (Wilson Report, 1994). The key recommendation was that there should be a single system with similar features for handling all types of complaints about the NHS. Subsequently, the government agreed to act on the Wilson Committee recommendations, including extending the jurisdiction of the Health Service Commissioner to all complaints by, or on behalf of, NHS patients – including complaints about matters of clinical judgement (DoH, 1995).

Conclusions

The growth of contemporary professions has attracted a range of accounts. These extend from an essentially positive perspective identifying the functions and inevitability of professionalisation for industrial societies based upon the essential ethic of service to clients; to a more pejorative perspective which identifies the process of professionalisation with social exclusion, the aggregation of status, monopoly power and the mystification of knowledge.

Whatever judgement is made about these perspectives, and although professional expertise may not be the guarantee of the consistency and uniformity claimed by the professions themselves, nevertheless such expertise may generate more consistency of approach than a reliance on lay knowledge, public opinion, the common sense of the judiciary and the principles of politicians. Ombudsmen-like forms of redress may compensate the individual and judicial review may right an administrative wrong; but the absence of codes of ethics and acceptable professional practice must be a weakness in comparison to those safeguards in professional life. We can at least expect some uniformity and consistency of professional knowledge and expertise to be applied to common situations. Variability would have to be justified and defended to peers and tribunals; the bar of public opinion is notoriously arbitrary and not stable enough to provide a benchmark for meeting needs or redressing complaints.

We have already noted a number of fallacies associated with organizational reform (see Chapter 6). The 'single best solution' fallacy is well-illustrated by the different trends of (and fashions for) organizational formats and the range of organizational choices we have identified above. One conclusion is the necessity to protect professional expertise and skills in order to counter the problems associated with bureaucracy. Another conclusion is that we need those components of bureaucracy – guaranteed rights, consistency in the application of rules, justice between those with equal need in the allocation of resources – to provide parameters that can guide and where necessary constrain what could be an excess of professional discretion. In addition, the case may now be made and accepted that there is a role for the manager. Last, but by no means least, there is the case for a democratic context so professionals, bureaucracies and managers are subject to the control and accountability of the polity.

There are sources of conflict between, for example, professionalism and bureaucracy; professionalism and democracy; and professionalism and managerialism. Part One of this book provided a number of examples of those conflicts. Despite these conflicts the aim that emerges from our analysis is not one of identifying alternatives that may *supplant* professionalism in health care, but rather one of identifying alternatives that might in some respects *complement* professionalism in health care. The issue becomes one of the relative roles of professionalism, bureaucracy, managerialism and democracy in the NHS – most obviously because of the 'mutual dependence' of, for example, politicians and professionals, and managers and professionals (see for example, Klein, 1995a, p. 203 and Klein, 1995b, p. 324). This complements the idea that there are a 'plurality of often conflicting values that can be brought to any discussion of priorities in health care' (Klein, 1993, p. 310) – that there is no obvious set of principles, techniques or organizational arrangements to be discovered 'if only we were clever enough to find them'. What this debate also leads us to is the conclusion that organizational structures and organizational choices matter. There may be fundamental, and not always avoided, fallacies relating to so-called 'single-best solutions' and assumptions that organizational reform is 'the answer to everything'. However organizational change may be 'the answer to something'. We might, for example, follow Klein in trying to identify structures of decision-making that allow 'rational argument (in the sense of reasoned and open discussion) about priorities' (Klein, 1993, p. 310). We might, as a further example, follow a number of commentators in concluding that policies for community care in the UK would have been benefited from alternative organizational arrangements – especially ones that were less sensitive to professional sensibilities.

The latter point does of course remind us that there are problems with professionalism from the perspectives of politicians, planners and patients. On the other hand, some sort of commitment to a code of ethics and a 'service-ideal' might in the end offer one of the 'least-worst alternatives' available to a modern health care system. The same may also, in the end, be the case with the concept of a national health service. We will attempt to judge this in our final chapter.

15
Success or failure?

Introduction

Is it possible to understand and make a judgement in relation to the praise and blame heaped on the NHS by the professionals who deliver, the politicians who debate its legitimacy and the public who use the service? For the professionals, complicated questions of clinical and scientific expertise are now being placed alongside cost-effectiveness and efficiency as a measure of success or failure. For the politicians the level of resources and questions of failing to meet equitable standards of care within a national framework are a constant, potential source of conflict. For the user, the speed of entry into the system with the 'best possible' medical attention has tended to be the main concern. These issues have been perfect examples for critics of state welfare provision from both the Right and the Left, as well as from a myriad of pressure groups – including what Klein referred to as an 'unholy alliance' of Marxist sociologists, liberal economists and philosophical anarchists. All at times seem to be suggesting that the state 'has failed' to deliver the health care we might have expected or hoped for from the NHS.

Radical right and radical left (eg: Marxist) critics of state welfare share a number of common concerns. These include a perspective that identifies a fundamental conflict and contradiction between extensive state welfare activities (of which the NHS would be a prime example) and the operation of a modern industrial, capitalist economy. The radical right's 'public burden model of state welfare' features as a 'fiscal crisis' in a radical left critique – both identify important economic restraints on the growth of state welfare expenditure. In Marxist analysis this is a 'contradiction' since it is presumed that capitalist economies need such expenditure for economic, political and social purposes. For the radical right it is merely a 'conflict' since a much diminished state welfare sector allied to extensive non-state (especially private market) provision will actually meet needs more effectively than vast state welfare bureaucracies. We have reviewed this dimension of the radical right critique in Chapters 11 and 12. Our conclusion was that their case against the universalist / citizenship model of state welfare represented by the NHS was simply not adequate, especially in relation to the potential of non-state alternatives to state welfare to meet all the 'reasonable health care needs' of the population (see especially Chapter 11) and the potential of residual state health care targeted at vulnerable groups to provide them with 'reasonable quality health care' (see especially Chapter 12). Our conclusion re-aligns the radical critiques; neither the 'fiscal crisis' nor the 'public burden' are susceptible to 'easy resolution' since the 'radical right' prescription cannot be introduced by the painless expedient of substituting ostensibly better quality market-based health care provision for all, instead of the alleged poor quality of the NHS.

The radical right needs to re-invent some modern day version of the Poor Law medical service and the radical left needs to re-locate health care into a reasonably affluent but non-capitalist setting. Critics of the critiques might pose the question of whether these prescriptions can avoid the social and economic costs associated with either mid-nineteenth century Britain or the post-1945 command economies of Eastern Europe – given the status of the latter as amongst the nearest approximations to their conceptual preferences.

We return to the implications of some of these arguments below. For the moment we can proceed to identify the other common ground of radical left and right critiques of 'welfare states' in general, and the NHS in particular. Radical critics of the NHS are invariably clear about the limited impact of the NHS on health and health care. Beveridge's five 'giants' (see Chapter 3) still stalk the land, including 'Disease'. All this is unsurprising for the radical right given 'our mistake' of presuming to slay this particular giant with that singularly inappropriate weapon – governmental bureaucracy. More specifically, but significantly, health inequalities persist; this is unsurprising for the radical left since they are presumed to be inextricably linked with the capitalist mode of production and not amenable to amelioration through the superimposition of state welfare programmes. The NHS – along with the other components of the 'modern welfare state' (education, housing and social security policies) – had for all intents and purposes 'failed'. Indeed despite their association with the radical critics, these views were eventually to be described as the 'received wisdom' of 'social science accounts' of state welfare (see O'Higgins, 1983, p. 171).

Our Questions

In evaluating the idea that the NHS has failed we will focus on a series of questions. These are as follows.

1. Is there a tendency to 'overplay' the significance of changes in state intervention in health care? (eg: the establishment of the NHS)
2. Is there a tendency to 'underplay' what the NHS *has* achieved?
3. Is there a tendency to 'overplay' what the NHS *can* achieve?
4. Are 'unrealistic' criteria being used to judge 'failure' and 'success'?

We will pose each of these questions in turn, and suggest some issues for consideration and discussion under each question. In so doing we should point out that the questions are not 'self-contained categories'. They represent four ways to get into the question of the 'success' or 'failure' of the NHS. At various points the questions overlap with one another and bring us back to issues raised by following through a previous question.

1. 'Overplaying' the changes

In suggesting that there is a tendency to overplay the significance of changes in state welfare we do not wish to suggest that there is one 'correct' interpretation of the pre-World War One Liberal reforms and the post-World War Two Labour reforms in the UK. These reforms are clearly capable of sustaining a number of 'plausible accounts' of their nature, origins and impact.

For example, it is possible to develop an account of health care developments in Britain before the NHS which emphasises the continuity of services pre- and post-NHS, the modest qualities of the reforms that introduced the NHS, the pre-war and wartime consensus and its swift erosion in post-war Britain (see, for example, Chapter 4). We can extend this account by emphasising the limited opportunities that afforded themselves for 'planning for equity' in the British NHS given professional and political reservations about 'centralised planning' (see Chapter 5) and its 'politically compromised organizational structure' (see Chapters 4 and 6). This rather 'unexciting', even 'depressing', history might lead us to anticipate tangible but modest benefits from the NHS – a 'qualified success' with some inevitable 'failings'. This account might be complemented by cross-national comparisons identifying similar trends elsewhere (eg: the development of state social insurance schemes, see Chapter 2) and the relative success of other NHS type systems (eg: Sweden and social class inequalities in health).

The point here is that the British NHS may serve as an exemplar of a particular approach to health care (and state welfare generally). We have characterised this as the universalist / citizenship model of state welfare (see especially Chapters 4, 10 and 11). As such it might be taken to represent something of a 'social democratic' ideal. A more 'dramatic history' might focus on the NHS in the UK (eg: ignore Sweden); represent the creation of the NHS as in every way a radical departure from previous provision well-supported by complementary and radical reforms in education, housing and social security (eg: as part of the 'creation of the welfare state'); and present the operation of the NHS as commanding the full support of successive governments who have actively and consistently pursued all the egalitarian ideals associated with the Service (eg: the 'post-war consensus'). If the impact of the NHS on the health and health care needs of society can be demonstrated to be somewhat limited (eg: persistence of social class inequalities in health) in the rather favourable circumstances of our more 'dramatic history' then this may provide an opportunity to discredit the universalist / citizenship model of state welfare (in the form of the NHS) and indeed even the wider aspirations of the social democratic approach to state welfare. With so much going in its favour (eg: 'the post-war consensus') surely the Service would be an unqualified success; and if it has not been an unqualified success then surely the fundamental principles – universalist state welfare in a capitalist setting – are fatally flawed?

2. 'Underplaying' actual achievements

Whilst critiques of the NHS may have attained the status of a 'received wisdom', this hardly seems to settle the matter. Some time ago Kaim-Caudle (1977) introduced a different perspective on key statistics when he pointed out that if you use infant survival rates, rather than infant mortality rates, then class differentials have narrowed significantly. A wider ranging debate was provoked by the publication of the Black Report; this indicated that the statistical evidence for a 'failing NHS' were somewhat more contentious than had been anticipated in earlier debates (see Chapters 5 and 10). This discussion should perhaps be linked to wider debates about the validity and interpretation of 'official statistics' – especially crime statistics. For the purposes of our argument it is not necessary to 'resolve' any of the debates about health and health care statistics – merely to note that like all statistical data they do not necessarily and simply 'tell one story'. We can pursue some possible 'alternative stories' by asking further questions as follows:

(a) what about contingency and other forms of redistribution?
(b) what about the not readily quantifiable and non-quantifiable?
(c) does nothing else change?

(a) Contingency redistribution?

> it is the horizontal divisions of class, not the vertical divisions of ... (for example) ... region, which are the crucial breaks in British society by criteria of welfare, opportunity and influence ... there are not, in general, disabilities peculiar to coloured people ... the various services result in some narrowing of inequalities in real income ... but they reshuffle resources far more within classes – between earners and dependents, healthy people and the sick. (Westergaard and Resler, 1976 pp. 358, 176).

Social science debates are now such that the above quotation would be regarded as misplaced in its failure to recognise race and gender as important social divisions in society. However for health care (and other areas of state welfare) other crucial social divisions would include those based on age, disability, health status and location. It is interesting that the so-called 'horizontal redistributions' across such social divisions are reduced to a mere 'reshuf-fling of resources' in the quotation. Given firstly, the historical legacy of pre-NHS health services in the UK (see Chapters 1 and 2); and secondly, the cross-nationally observed phenomena of the division of professional service-users into 'interesting' and 'unin-teresting' cases (see Chapter 5) and thirdly, the concentration of 'elite health care institutions' in major urban centres, especially capital cities (see Chapter 9); then social divisions associated with health status (eg: those with chronic health problems) and location (eg: those in rural areas) assume a great significance in analyzing and evaluating health care. Indeed if state welfare activities are about some sort of redistribution of the command-over-resources over time, then redistribution between 'contingency' groups should be the most obvious effect of extensive state welfare activities (redistribution of resources from adults to children, from younger adults to older age groups, from people without disabili-ties to those with disabilities, and so on). Although the social divisions associated with these social contingencies can be linked to social class inequalities, this may not always be the case and where there are links such divisions are not necessarily secondary to class inequalities. For example, the usual assumptions about the relationship between social class and health status have been questioned (Stern, 1983).

Of course the NHS will not automatically be judged a 'success' when social divisions other than social class form the basis of the judgement. Nonetheless the flow of resources (related to sources of revenue and the location of expenditure) does indicate a redistribution of real income across these social divisions (eg: from men to women and from younger adults to older age groups). The point has been made that the middle-classes derived benefit from the introduction of the universalist NHS – thus moderating its supposed impact on social class inequalities. But the pre-NHS provision certainly made better provision for the working-class man in employment than it did for his wife, his children and his parents (see Chapter 2). This implies that the impact of the new service on other social divisions in society may have been much more significant than that identified in a traditional class-based analysis. Furthermore, although the perspective of 'middle-class benefit' may be valid, the middle classes will tend to make a more significant financial contribution to the NHS (via taxes) and there is anyway still a case for saying that the working-class are better off with the NHS than without it – a point to which we return below.

We would conclude by observing that the commonplace constructions of redistributions as 'vertical' and 'horizontal' reflect deep-seated assumptions that certain redistributions (eg: between social classes) are more significant than between other categories in the population (eg: between age groups). We would do well to remember that it is 'social scientists' who set up the tables and graphs that portray certain redistributions as 'vertical' and others as 'horizontal' and that apart from well-documented race and gender imbalances, children, old age pensioners, people with mental handicaps, people with physical disabilities and those with chronic health problems are not always well-represented in their ranks. We would argue that the so-called 'horizontal inequalities' (gender, race, age, physical and mental (dis)ability, location) are potentially very significant. Whilst this point has been made with increasing force and effectiveness for race and gender, it is not always voiced so effectively for the other divisions. Their introduction into evaluations of the NHS does not transform 'failures' to 'successes' , but it does generate a more complex and at times positive perspective on the Service's achievements.

(b) Not readily quantifiable and non-quantifiable?
The focus here is where empirical evidence is available, but is not readily susceptible to use for evaluative purposes. For example, the NHS may involve the provision of a service that has a very direct impact on the well-being of certain members of society (eg: hip replacements for elderly people) whose impact will not be reflected in the usual statistics (in this case morbidity and mortality statistics). With a concept as potentially broad as 'better health', and for a service as diverse as the National Health Service it is important to recognise the range of impacts that the latter might have on the former (see Chapter 10).

If forms of state welfare, like the NHS, are thought to have an impact on society, some of the possible effects may not lend themselves to a straightforward evaluation. Are there, for example, 'indicators that cannot be calculated', that are not counted in 'all the Blue Books and in all the publications of the

Central Statistical Office' (Titmuss, 1974, p. 150). Titmuss was referring to what he termed 'the texture of relationships between human beings' and some notion of 'social growth' (Titmuss, 1974, p. 150). For example, would certain forms of state welfare reduce or eliminate the

> sense of inferiority, pauperism, shame or stigma ... (associ- ated with) ... the use of a publicly provided services? (Titmuss, 1968, p. 129)

He suggested that this might be one outcome of the introduction of services like the NHS based on the universalist / citizenship model of state welfare (see Titmuss, 1974, p. 46). He also advanced a more significant thesis when he suggested that the way in which societies organise their 'health and welfare systems' may 'encourage or discourage the altruistic in man' (Titmuss, 1970, p. 225).

Of course Titmuss's views on these subjects may be contested. The crucial point is that he was directing our attention at the possible effects of state welfare which, if they are taking place, are of potential significance, but are not readily substantiated, or otherwise, by simple recourse to readily available quantifiable evidence. We do not wish to assert that the 'less-readily discerni- ble', the 'difficult' and 'impossible to measure' and the 'difficult to answer' *all* somehow conspire to support a positive interpretation of the NHS. However we would wish to identify three points. Firstly, that they can be seen as important elements in the universalist / citizenship model of state welfare and that state welfare delivered via this model – like the NHS -may have the potential to foster some sense of citizenship, or at least (and we might in the end regard this is as equally significant) diminish or not add to any sense of 'less than citizenship' (eg: stigmatised status) which may be the lot of certain groups and individuals in society. Secondly, that there is 'a lot there' – a substantial, diverse and diffused set of impacts on groups and individuals about which we are probably ill-equipped to make definitive judgements. If accepted, this in itself constitutes a case against those who may have plunged far to readily into making definitive and pejorative judgements that the NHS has failed. Thirdly, there are certainly strands in this 'less visible' and 'less measurable' impact of the

NHS where there is a case for coming to a more positive judgement on the impact of the Service in containing inequalities and enhancing citizenship.

(c) Nothing else changes?
This is an important question if it is asserted that because the fundamental inequalities in a society like the UK remain unchanged (eg: in health) then this constitutes an indication of the 'failure' of state welfare (eg: the NHS). There is an attractive, but misleading simplicity about this argument, although its limitations have been made clear on a number of occasions and some time ago; for example:

> if the effects of the welfare state on the actual distribution of wealth has been slight over a period of 50 years, this is not, of course, to say that without the welfare state the distribution of wealth might have become more unequal. (Barratt-Brown, 1971)

Changing or unchanging patterns of health status identified with individuals, groups and locations in a society do not occur in circumstances where the 'rest of society' remains unchanged.

> The emphasis today on 'welfare' and the 'benefits of welfare' often tends to obscure the fundamental fact that for many consumers the services used are not essentially benefits or increments to welfare at all; they represent partial compensations for disservices, for social costs and social insecurities which are the product of a rapidly changing urban-industrial society. (Titmuss, 1968, p. 133)

In terms of the debate about the impact of the NHS the idea can be most simply expressed by saying that the 'successes' of the Service can be cancelled out by the 'failings' of other social institutions or more generally by the effects of social and economic change in an industrial/capitalist society. There is a danger of writing off state welfare programmes such as the NHS as 'failures' because of the inegalitarian tendencies we associate with capitalism, industrialism and economic growth. Indeed from this perspective whilst we may be sad about the tenacity of inequalities and the tendency for economic change to generate new forms and patterns of inequality, we might take some satisfaction from the impact of the NHS if the pattern of health inequalities does remain unchanged, because the most likely alternative (in the absence of a universalist NHS) may be for them to widen – perhaps dramatically. In the UK the pattern of income inequalities changed little – apparently 'despite the welfare state'. But with the first post-war government (in the 1980s) that was manifestly uninterested in constraining income inequalities they increased quite sharply (Atkinson, 1996). Perhaps something of real value is achieved if we merely hold the existing pattern of inequalities!

3. 'Overplaying' potential achievements

The purpose of the NHS, Jennie Lee told the 20th anniversary Conference, was 'to ensure that everybody in the country irrespective of means, age, sex or occupation, should have equal opportunity to benefit from the best and most up-to-date medical and allied services available'. This objective, *which could hardly be described as extravagant*, has not been achieved. (George and Wilding, 1976, p. 106, our emphasis)

The overall duty of the Secretary of State, to provide a 'comprehensive' health service is *either absurd or meaningless*. No health care system can be comprehensive. (Brown, 1975, p. 160)

Perhaps one of the most important assumptions that will guide any evaluation of the 'successes' or 'failures' of any state welfare programme (the NHS) in any society (the UK), concerns what that state welfare programme can achieve, or more precisely what it might be reasonably expected to achieve given the 'right circumstances'. Our two quotations imply rather different assumptions. For Brown the aim of providing a 'comprehensive health service' is 'absurd or meaningless'. Yet this objective is considerably more straightforward than trying to combine it with the pursuit of equality of access and equity implied in George and Wilding's statement. Yet they describe their aim as 'hardly extravagant'. It is clear that George and Wilding on the one hand, and Brown on the other, have radically different ideas about what

we can reasonably expect of the NHS! We can explore the possible basis for such different ideas by looking at
(a) the concept of a 'social problem'; and
(b) the concept of 'finite resources'.

(a) Social problems
'Success' or 'failure' may be judged in part by reference to the persistence of particular social problems (homelessness, preventable disease and so on). For example, in the second of our quotations inequalities in access to health care persist with the implication that health care policies (which were presumed to do something about these inequalities) must have failed. But this judgement of health care policy is based on the worthy but harsh criteria by which success is equated with the elimination of certain social problems and the achievement of some sort of 'perfect/ complete equality'.

We have already drawn attention to the argument that state welfare may be more appropriately evaluated in terms of 'specific' rather than 'global' egalitarianism (see Chapter 11). A separate but related argument can be developed about the nature of social problems. The potentially 'inappropriate evaluation' involved here is that dynamic, 'subjective' social problems will be addressed as static and 'objective'. The significance of a failure to 'solve' such problems is then misread. For example, a set of social security programmes designed to eliminate 'subsistence poverty' are likely to appear remarkably unsuccessful in combating some form of 'relative deprivation'.

Whilst this argument has perhaps been most obviously recognised in relation to redefinitions of 'what constitutes poverty', 'social science' perspectives have identified the problematic nature of the concept of 'health' and 'illness' and the ways in which health care is socially constructed (see Chapter 10). For example the following statement seems to attribute a relatively straightforward, objective quality to routine measurements of service provision and the need for that service:

> services for the mentally ill have expanded in all advanced capitalist countries, but this must be set against the 'enormous rise in the prevalence of mental illness' [OECD, 1977, p. 41]. (Gough, 1979, p. 93)

But everything we know about long-term trends in mental health services and attitudes towards mental health problems would suggest that we will now record more 'mental health problems' than previously. For critics of 'professional imperialism' and 'bureaucratic aggrandizement' this may be further evidence that state welfare professionals and officials will generate statistics to justify their own existence. Nonetheless everything that we know about a range of social problems (of which the most obvious is probably child abuse) indicate that more accessible and approachable services will record more rather than fewer 'cases'. Indeed the clinical provenance in a range of studies of the 'submerged iceberg' of treatable medical conditions mean this phenomena is probably one element in the escalating costs of modern health care systems (see Chapters 5 and 10).

The persistence of certain 'health problems' or 'health care problems' may lead to justifiable criticism of the NHS. But the 'Giant' of 'Disease' recognisable to Beveridge and his contemporaries in the 1940s has been transmuted perhaps almost out of recognition by inter-related changes in attitudes, in medical science and in the demographic structure of society. There is no simple relationship between a better and more egalitarian health service and improvements in, and reductions in inequalities of, the 'health status' of individuals, communities or society as a whole; to assume otherwise is to disregard everything that has been said about the 'submerged iceberg of sickness', the relationship of definitions of sickness to their socio-cultural context, and the changing expectations of what health care systems can provide for patients.

(b) Finite resources

The so-called 'economic limits of state welfare' usually turn out to be 'political' or 'ideological' in origin rather than being clearly and unequivocally related to some 'real' resource constraints. Nonetheless, the world's resources are not infinite and anyway there may more immediate 'social limits to growth' (Hirsch, 1977) as well as more general limits posited by ecologists. Therefore any judgement of what a health service can reasonably achieve must take some account of the resources that might be available.

What is clear is that any evaluation of the 'social-problem' solving capacity of any state welfare programme is going to be significantly influenced by a set of underlying assumptions about the nature of 'social problems' and the 'resource implications' of solving such problems. These assumptions lead the writers to emphasise certain characteristics rather than others, to employ certain measures rather than others and so on. It is certainly possible to select certain 'characteristics' and 'measures' that emphasise 'failures' rather than 'successes'. Figure 5 illustrates this by reference to differing interpretations of key characteristics which then lend themselves to differing interpretations of what the NHS has or has not achieved.

Figure 5 NHS as 'success' or 'failure'

Characteristic	'The NHS has had some successes'	'The NHS has been a failure'
The nature of social problems are . . .	subjective, dynamic – difficult to solve	objective, static – easy to solve
The resource constraints on social welfare programmes are that . . .	there are 'real limits' to public welfare expenditure growth	there are only 'ideologically' motivated limits on public welfare expenditure
The general trends in an industrial society are of . . .	a changing pattern of inequalities, including greater inequalities in some circumstances	an unchanging pattern of inequalities
The significant social divisions in society are . . .	age, disability, gender, health, race, social class	social class (defined in terms of 'male breadwinner')

4. 'Unrealistic' criteria

By what criteria should we judge the NHS? Can we end up using criteria which lead us almost inevitably to a judgement that the service has 'failed'? There are certainly a range of criteria which can be deployed to judge the performance of the NHS. Four examples of such criteria are as follows:

(a) the 'Normative Model' comparison;
(b) the 'Policy Goal' comparison;

(c) The 'International / Contemporary' comparison; and
(d) The 'National / Historical' comparison.
We shall examine each briefly and indicate the varying judgements that they might generate.

(a) The 'Normative Model' comparison

This involves comparing outcomes of the 'real world' of the NHS with some 'ideal' model of an alternative to the NHS – a perfect version of the free market with complete consumer knowledge or a similar vision of a fair and egalitarian socialist society. This will always produce a *negative evaluation* of the 'working model' (the NHS) by comparison with the 'theoretical models' (free market medicine and socialist health care).

(b) The 'Policy Goal' comparison

This involves comparing the outcomes of, for example the NHS with its stated policy goals. This is clearly a valuable and instructive exercise in some respects, but does carry the inherent danger of always producing a *negative evaluation* because these goals have been defined in a somewhat inspirational or an overly ambitious manner. However we should note the conclusion that 'equity of access to the NHS ... has indeed been achieved' (Klein, 1995a, p. 224).

(c) The 'International/contemporary' comparison

Here the 'real world' of the NHS is compared with one or more other 'working' health care systems. There are well documented problems involved in such comparisons – trying to construct a 'World Series' of health care systems – and there are a number of criteria that could be deployed within this comparison. The latter might be how much freedom of choice for service users, or how good is the system at containing costs, or reducing territorial injustices in resource allocation, or eliminating inequalities in health; or some combination of these or other criteria. The resulting judgement on the NHS would depend on a number of factors including the features of a health care system that are most highly valued and the measures used. What is certain is that such comparisons could produce a *positive evaluation* of the NHS – perhaps especially in relation to cost containment! Certainly one recent comparative study was able to conclude that the predominantly publicly financed and publicly provided health care system in Britain appears close to allocating health care resources on the basis of 'equal treatment for equal need' and extracting payments in proportion to incomes. (Van Doorslaer, Wagstaff and Rutten, 1993, p. 256)

(d) The national/historical comparison

Here we compare the current NHS with its early years and perhaps with pre-NHS provision. This comparison is as fraught with difficulties as the international comparisons. In particular, technological changes make such historical comparisons very difficult – a problem to which we alluded in relation to the introduction of the internal market (see Chapter 8). What is certain is that such a comparison may once again produce a *positive evaluation* of the NHS.

The above does not exhaust the potential comparisons that might be drawn to form a judgement about whether the NHS has been a 'success' or a 'failure'. They are sufficient to make our point that different approaches can generate a range of judgements and in particular that some approaches will have 'judged a failure' as their almost inevitable outcome.

Conclusions

The National Health Service is the nearest Britain has ever come to institutionalising altruism. (Hennessey, 1992 p. 132)

Our final set of conclusions relate to what might be seen as the most enduring conflict of the period we have reviewed, especially over the last fifty years. How successful has been state intervention in health care and in particular is the concept of a national health service an appropriate one – has the NHS been a success or a failure?

All we can assert in response to that question is that there are no agreed upon criteria by which the success or failure of the NHS can be assessed, although we can, through the relevant social science literature, draw upon evidence relating to values across and within societies; comparative evidence to display similarities, differences and culturally specific forms of health care; and historical evidence.

We can certainly suggest that some attempt should be made to relate what is being achieved by the NHS in Britain today, to what was achieved in the past, and to what is achieved elsewhere. It is clearly instructive to relate the achievements of the NHS to its stated policy goals, even if it is clear that by the 'idealist' criteria as set out by Jennie Lee, the NHS has not been that successful. On the other hand if we set the current situation in historical perspective, it may be possible to claim more modest successes for the service. Inequalities in health and health care remain as major policy issues, but it can be argued that the situation is significantly 'less worse' than it was before the Service was established. Perhaps most pertinently some of the 'failings' of the NHS tend to look like 'successes' when the Service is looked at in an international context; for example, spatial inequalities are a profound problem for all 'health care systems' and have not been successfully combated by any existing health care system .

What perhaps we need is an intellectual equivalent of the emotional experience involved in the final scenes of Frank Capra's film *It's A Wonderful Life* (1946) in which George Bailey discovers what life would have been like if he had not lived. George Bailey's life had in some respects never quite worked out as he hoped – for example, he never got away from his home town of Bedford Falls. But Bedford Falls would have turned into a significantly different (and 'worse') place without his 'wonderful life' (ie: Pottersville).

So what would the situation be like without the NHS? This might be said to constitute the *key* but *unanswerable* question about any form of welfare – state or non-state. But although it cannot be answered in any definitive sense, it is susceptible to some comment and the production of some plausible answers. One set of answers might be derived from comparative analysis. What has been the effect of different models of state welfare in other societies – have they, for example, been markedly more or less 'successful' in solving 'health care problems'? Another set of answers may be derived from analyses of certain empirical evidence in one country. Welfare spending in general 'is notably more egalitarian than income distributed through the market' (O'Higgins, 1983, p. 181), and evidence for health care, especially the comparison with the USA, suggests health care spending through the NHS is more egalitarian than health care distributed through the market.

Perhaps in the end the judgement on the NHS would not be as positive as that on George Bailey. But drawing on international and historical comparisons; and making what we can of the non-state alternatives and the residual model of state welfare we might at least conclude that the NHS remains 'the least worst alternative' that any society might choose – indeed in many respects it may offer us our best hope of getting equity, effectiveness and efficiency in the allocation and utilisation of health care. It may compensate for diswelfares, even if it does not always enhance status and psychological well-being, which may only come through total individual self-sufficiency. It may not have the profound impact on inequalities hoped for by its founders, but it may significantly moderate the impact which economic inequalities would have on inequalities in health and health care, especially the latter where there would be a denial of applied knowledge in the health field to those unable to purchase it, even though this knowledge was collectively known. It may not convey the full sense of citizenship its founders hoped for, but it may at the very least limit the sense of non-citizenship that would otherwise be more pervasive for more vulnerable groups in our sort of society; in this way, and its impact on inequalities, the NHS may contribute to a more socially just society than we would have in its absence. Finally, and in contrast to the concerns of those who feared for the sense of community and professional commitment when a virtual state monopoly took over health care and displaced voluntary institutions, the NHS may have fostered levels of both individual altruism and standards of professional ethics that have eluded other health care systems both past and present. Judged against the 'real world' of 'real social institutions' in Britain and elsewhere there is much to be said in support of one judgement that the NHS is 'a striking success story' (Klein, 1995a, p. 226) and to concur with another judgement that the 'NHS was and remains one of the finest institutions ever built by anybody anywhere' (Hennessey, 1992, p. 144)

Postscript: A visionary gleam?

Whither is fled the visionary gleam?
Where is it now, the glory and the dream?
(Intimations of Immortality from Recollections of early
Childhood, Stanza IV, William Wordsworth, 1807)

The provision of high quality services is central to the
fundamental purpose of the NHS and spans a broad range of
existing NHS policies. The main elements can be defined as:
   the *effectiveness* of treatment, in terms of outcome for the
patient:
   the *skill, care and continuity* with which the service is
delivered;
   the *accessibility* of the service in terms of distance, time,
physical access, patient-friendliness, language and
understanding;
   the delivery of the service, covering the *physical environment* of care, and the *courtesy* and *efficiency* of the administrative arrangements.
(NHS Executive, 1997c, para.12, emphasis as original text)

Echoes of 1945?

As we completed the substantive chapters of this book, a General
Election was only a few months away. The likelihood of a Labour
government, ending an unbroken period of Conservative rule
since Mrs Thatcher won office in 1979, raised expectations of
changes in social policy. By the time of the election (1 May 1997),
the NHS internal market model had been in operation throughout
the 1990s, with constant criticism about a range of widely perceived problems – for example, lengthy waiting lists and times,

implicit rationing, community care deficiencies, costs of a bureaucracy, patients denied innovative treatment, and a two tier service based on fundholding and non-fundholding GPs. For at least some politicians, professionals and patients these problems could be partly if not wholly attributable to the Conservative government's public expenditure programme, its ideological objections to traditional models of public sector professionalism and planning, and its ideological preference for new public (sector) management in quasi-(internal) markets. We have attempted to identify the contribution of the latter innovations to contemporary problems above (see especially pp. 146–50 above) but clearly much of what we have written in this book indicates that these problems have a long history and have surfaced and resurfaced, especially in the half century that the state has been formally committed to establish and maintain an equitable, effective and efficient NHS (see especially pp. 192–8).

It was certainly presumed that a successful outcome for the Labour Party in the General Election would herald further changes in the funding, organization, and distribution of health care through the NHS. The landslide victory for Mr Blair and 'New Labour' on 1 May 1997, led immediately to policy reviews, and the question was raised as to whether or not the 'internal market' would remain the governing principle of the NHS. Indications of the new government's approach could be found in a number of publications and other pronouncements between 1 May and 9 December (when the first new White Paper on health issues was published).

Waiting for the White Papers

The new Government's view was clearly expressed by the Minister of State at the Department of Health (Alan Milburn). The previous Conservative government had 'left the NHS in a mess ... (with) ... record waiting lists . ... (There was) ... huge pressure on emergency hospital care ... (and) ... widespread hospital and health authority deficits (Milburn, 1997, p. 22). Action taken in advance of the first White Paper (*The New NHS*, Cm.3807) included claims of increased (in real terms) health funding, moving £100 million out of 'red tape' and into patient care, and of the largest new building programme in the history of the NHS (the latter through a continuing use of the reworked Private Sector Financial Initiative – PFI). The new government also signalled its interest in public health issues by appointing the first ever Minister for Public Health in England whose brief was identified by its first incumbent (Tessa Jowell) as working 'across government and across the department of health to ensure the causes ... (of ill-health) ... are identified, that strategies are identified and acted on'. This included ensuring that local authorities and health authorities 'abandon the old pointless territorial disputes' (see *Health Care Today*, October 1997, p. 24). This long-running theme of breaking down organizational barriers (see Chapters 6, 13 and 14, above) was also taken forward in one of the earliest initiatives of the new government. This came on 25 June 1997 at the NHS Confederation Annual Conference where the Secretary of State for Health (Frank Dobson) announced his intention to set up a number of Health Action Zones (HAZs). The purpose of HAZs was identified as bringing together all those contributing to the health of the local population – local authorities, community groups, the voluntary sector and local businesses in their work – to develop and implement a locally agreed strategy for improving the health of local people. Potential outcomes are ambitious and include hoped for improvements in the effectiveness, efficiency and responsiveness of services. Longer term achievements (over five to seven years) would include indications that the pattern of increasing health inequalities had been reversed. The other longer-term aspirations for HAZs indicated something of government thinking on the future of the NHS – a blurring of the distinction between secondary and primary care, co-operative and complementary commissioning procedures, more health care needs met outside traditional acute hospital settings, a public health dimension to the work of primary care teams with 'clinical effectiveness ... at the root of all that is done in the NHS'. It was proposed that there would be further rounds of HAZs; the 11 first-round HAZs were announced on March 31, 1998 (see NHS Executive, 1997d and *The Times*, 1/4/98, p. 2).

Also in June 1997, the Secretary of State announced an independent review of London's health needs to be carried out by a panel chaired by Sir Leslie Turnberg, then President of the Royal College of Physicians. This review had been promised by Chris

Smith when he was Shadow Health Secretary. Further pre-White Paper activity identified other themes in the new government's approach – especially the view that there were quite significant savings to be gained by eliminating the bureaucracy associated with the internal market and by reducing the number of health care providers – 16 mergers involving 30 NHS Trusts were said to be capable of yielding minimum net savings of £500,000 per merger (see *Health Care Today*, October 1997, p. 3). Clearly the new government was hoping to obtain additional resources for NHS patient care by releasing resources from changing NHS organizational arrangements – not a new idea of course! (see, especially, Chapters 6, 7 and 14, above). Certainly if anyone thought (rather naively given Labour's pre-election spending pledges) that there would be any scope for health authorities or NHS trusts to, in the words of the NHS Executive, 'relax their approach to achieving and maintaining financial balance, and improving value for money in the service', then they were obviously mistaken. The guidance issued on priorities and planning for 1998/89 stressed that

> rigorous and rapid action to improve cost-effectiveness and efficiency will be essential if the NHS is to achieve an acceptable balance between better patient care and financial stability. (NHS Executive, 1997a)

Meanwhile advice and comments on future directions came from a variety of sources. For example, Lord Philip Hunt (formerly Chief Executive of the NHS Confederation) expressed a widely held view that the NHS needed 'to find an effective mechanism for improving clinical outcomes and achieving greater consistency' and there was evidence also of both continuing support for GP and locality purchasing and for a more co-operative and collaborative approach than that associated with the competitive, internal market arrangements (see Abbott, 1997, p. 9–11).

The priorities and planning guidance published in September 1997 outlined a substantial agenda on health and health care including a Royal Commission on long-term care; White Papers on tobacco and replacing the internal market; and the development of a new and expanded public health strategy and a new Food Standards Agency. There would be new approaches to PFI, to NHS pay and to the *Patient's Charter* (plus a new long-term care charter). Public health issues and health inequalities were also identified as key areas for action (see NHS Executive, 1997c, para.1). The significance of information management and technology for the achievement of many of the government's objectives was also noted (NHS Executive,1997c, para.4). Reducing variations in access to and use of services was identified as an area where the NHS could make a significant contribution to the promotion of fairness and equity. This would involve action to reduce 'the most significant local avoidable health variations between different areas, social groups, ethnic groups, and men and women' (NHS Executive, 1997c, para.10). Areas identified for development including working 'to develop a leading role for primary care in commissioning and provision of health care' and ensuring that 'old people, adults with a physical or learning disability, children and other vulnerable people with continuing health care needs are enabled through the NHS contribution to their care, to live as independently as possible in their own homes or in homely settings in the community' (NHS Executive, 1997c, paras.29A and 29E). In the same month the new government indicated that the freeze in the overall public sector pay bill would remain in place for another year (see *The Times*, 13/9/97). Also in the same month the Under Secretary of State in the Department of Health (Paul Boateng) announced that plans to close the remaining thirty-five psychiatric hospitals would be halted while a new system is put in place to ensure that adequate alternative care in the community is available (see *The Times*, 13/9/97). At the time of writing we await details of the new system; of course something of the sort has been advocated for well over a quarter of a century so will be seen as long overdue in some quarters! (see Chapter 13, above).

Three other long-standing themes re-emerged in October 1997. Firstly, the BMA published a document indicating how the NHS could raise £10 billion per annum by charging patients including hotel charges for hospital beds, for GP consultations, for home visits by GPs plus increased prescription charges. However the BMA was not in favour of this approach, identifying some of the long-established objections to such a policy, most obviously that it would deter patients from seeking important help at an early stage so that costlier and more intensive care may need to be provided in the future when a simple condition develops into something more serious (BMA, 1997). Meanwhile others argued that we should continue the relatively modest reforms of the Thatcher/ Major era with private medicine, insurance, multiple forms of funding and self-provision playing a key role in Britain' health services (see, for example, Rees-Mogg, 1997) the point having already been made that if public finance remains the principal source of health care funding then 'the options for increasing the role of private funding should be honestly and openly explored' (Ham, 1997, p. 28).

Secondly, the Prime Minister predicted that the health service would be able to avoid its annual 'winter crisis' with the additional £300 million announced by the Chancellor of the Exchequer (this money was to come from the budgets of the Ministry of Defence and the Department of Trade and Industry). As ever doctors' leaders were unsure whether this would be sufficient (see *The Times*, 13/10/97 and Secretary of State for Health, 1997). Thirdly, long-standing concerns relating to community health care were voiced again. Mr.Dobson said he wanted to start breaking down the 'Berlin Wall' between health and social care, noting also that there were as many as six and seven thousand people in hospital who should not be there. Three areas for action were identified; firstly, local joint investment plans for continuing and community care; secondly, improving the content and process of multidisciplinary assessments; and finally 'the development of health and social care services for older people which focus on optimising independence through timely recuperation and rehabilitation opportunities' (see *The Times*, 13/10/97 and Secretary of State for Health, 1997). On the day that Frank Dobson wrote to health authorities informing them of the additional money to ease the pressures that lead to the NHS's frequent 'winter crises', the Audit Commission published another critical report on the balance between community and institutional care. As the Commission had graphically demonstrated over a decade earlier there remained perverse incentives within current arrangements. These included early discharge policies within NHS hospital services which could lead to inadequate rehabilitation and the transfer of patients to expensive nursing and residential care rather than back into their own homes – which is where they could go if time and facilities were made available for adequate recovery and rehabilitation within the NHS. Meanwhile the local authority social care service retained an incentive to place individuals in residential care where residents may contribute all or some of the costs from the sale of their own homes (Audit Commission, 1997).

Two equally long-standing issues resurfaced in November 1977. Firstly, the ever difficult 'politics of public health' generated a contentious issue when it was reported that the Government had 'reluctantly decided to abandon its plan to ban tobacco sponsorship of Formula One motor racing' (*The Times*, 5/11/97, p. 5). Secondly, came the news that hospital waiting lists were growing by 1000 patients per week, a clear indication that election pledges on this headline making issue are always problematic. Overall 1998/99 was identified as a 'transitional year' given the Government's commitment to replace the internal market with a 'new approach based on co-operation between all the players'. The four key themes were identified as promoting partnership; ensuring fairness; reducing bureaucracy and improving financial management (see NHS Executive, 1997a). Promoting partnership would involve 'an open and transparent approach to sharing information'; 'the involvement of local people, including users and carers ... (and hence) ... wide informal consultation'; and the development of longer-term agreements (NHS Executive, 1997b, paras.6, 10 and 13). The latter were seen as offering opportunities for greater involvement in the process by clinicians, users and carers. Ensuring fairness related to the concerns about financial equity between fundholding and non-fundholding GPs. Reducing bureaucracy focused particularly on multiple invoicing, unnecessary payment processes and variations in the information requirements of health care purchasers (NHS Executive, 1997b, paras 16, 17,18). Finally, four days before the publication of the long-awaited White Paper, the Secretary of State for Health announced the setting up of a Royal Commission charged with finding a fair and affordable way of funding long-term care for elderly people (see *The Times*, 5 December 1997, p. 8)

A watershed White Paper?

The Government has committed itself anew to the historical principle of the NHS: that if you are ill or injured there will be a national health service there to help; and access to it will be based on need and need alone – not on your ability to pay, or on who your GP happens to be or where you will live. (DoH, 1997, p. 5)

there will be a 'third way' of running the NHS – a system based on partnership and driven by performance. (DoH, 1997, p. 10, para.2.2)

The White Paper marks a watershed for the NHS. (DoH, 1997, p. 76)

This White Paper was originally scheduled for publication in the Autumn of 1997 (see NHS Executive, 1997a) but did not appear until 9 December 1997. It was said to be based on 'extensive discussions we have held with a wide range of NHS staff' (DoH, 1997, p. 11). Some of the key themes – commitment to fairness and quality, promoting partnership and co-operation, and the development of a leading role for primary care, were all clearly flagged up in early documents (see, especially, NHS Executive 1997c, para.2). Press leaks also indicated some of the major elements in advance of the publication of the White Paper (see, for example, *The Independent*, 12/11/97, 'Health spending power will switch to GPs', p. 1 and 'Under doctors' orders – where the NHS belongs', p. 20 and *The Times*, 26/11/97, 'Hospitals to publish costs league tables' and 4/12/97, 'GPs win control of NHS budget').

The Prime Minister's Foreword described the White Paper as a 'turning point for the NHS' (DoH, 1997, p. 2). A major aim was identified as replacing the 'misconceived' and 'divisive' internal market with 'integrated care' and a 'more collaborative approach' based on 'partnership and driven by performance' (see DoH, 1997, pp. 2, 10 and 12). The White Paper also proposed a further and significant organizational reform by which 'for the first time in the history of the NHS all the primary care professionals, who do the majority of prescribing, treating and referring, will have control over how resources are best used to benefit patients' (DoH, 1997, p. 37). This is what the pre-publication press leaks referred to as GPs winning control of NHS budgets. The changes proposed by the White Paper involve the establishment, throughout the NHS, of Primary Care Groups (PCGs) comprising all GPs in an area together with community nurses. The intention is for the new PCGs to succeed fundholding in April 1999 and that health authorities will, over time, relinquish the direct commissioning of services to the new PCGs 'as soon as they are able to take on this task' (DoH, 1997, p. 27). The intended outcome is that 'local doctors and nurses who best understand patients' needs, will shape local services' (DoH, 1997, p. 5). This is one crucial element in the 'third way' of running the NHS avoiding what the White Paper terms as the old 'stifling' top down centralised command and control systems of the 1970s and the 'wasteful grass roots free for all' of the 1980s (see DoH, 1997, pp. 10, 27).

In other respects there was a good deal of continuity with long-established aspirations for the NHS in what the Government included in the White Paper. The virtues of 'planning sensibly for change' were extolled and would be facilitated by 'scrapping annual contracts' (see DoH, 1997, pp. 15, 68). At least three of the six 'important principles' underlying the changes in the White Paper (see DoH, 1997, p. 11) – fair access, local responsibility and excellence – would not be unfamiliar to the authors of the seven 'objectives' for the NHS in the 1979 Royal Commission on the NHS – equality of entitlement, being responsive to local needs, and a high standard of service (see p. 226, above).

The first principle of a 'genuinely national service' with 'fair access to consistently high quality, prompt and accessible services' was to be achieved more effectively by abandoning the inherently unfair internal market, devising a national formula to set fair shares for the new PCGs and by developing new evidence-based National Service Frameworks to ensure consistent access to services across the country (see DoH, 1997, pp. 4, 13, 14, 18, 70). The new Frameworks would set out 'the patterns and levels of service which should be provided for patients with certain conditions' to ensure that patients 'will get greater consistency in the availability and quality of services, right across the NHS' (DoH, 1997, pp. 56, 57).

The second principle of making the delivery of health care a matter of local responsibility is pursued most obviously through the new PCGs. This commitment to local management has a long history – it was supported in most of the government papers that preceded the 1974 NHS reorganization (see, for example, p. 112, above). However it also draws on two by-products of the 'internal market' reforms – GP involvement in commissioning services and decentralising responsibility for operational management through NHS Trusts (see Chapters 7 and 8, above).

The third principle of 'excellence guaranteed to all patients' perhaps most obviously echoed previous aims for the Service (Bevan's 'universalising the best'). As with the renewed commitment to the principle of fairness, the government is hoping that working with the professions and representatives of users and carers to establish new, clearer, evidence-based National Service Frameworks will help ensure quality of care right across the country. In addition there will be 'explicit quality standards in local service agreements', a 'statutory duty for quality in NHS trusts', and a 'new system of clinical governance in NHS Trusts and primary care to ensure that clinical standards are met' (see DoH, 1997, pp. 18, 57). The new clinical governance arrangements will be complemented by a new Commission for Health Improvement (CHI) established 'to support the quality of clinical services at local level, and to tackle shortcomings'. This will be a statutory body 'at arm's length from Government' and is intended to 'offer an independent guarantee that local systems to monitor, assure and improve clinical quality are in place' (see DoH, 1997, pp. 18, 57–9). Finally, a new National Institute for Clinical Excellence (NICE) will be established which will produce and disseminate clinical guidelines based on relevant evidence of clinical and cost-effectiveness; associated clinical audit methodologies; and information on good practice in clinical audit (see DoH, 1997, p. 58).

Three other White Paper principles – efficiency, public confidence and partnership – do not find obvious parallels in the Royal Commission. The White Paper is explicit about the need for an efficient NHS – the Service 'has to make better use of its resources to ensure that it delivers better, more responsive services for patients everywhere' (DoH, 1997, p. 15). That efficiency did not feature in the Royal Commission's objectives was perhaps understandable given that their key conclusion was that the principles upon which the National Health Service was based seemed to be almost 'inherently efficient' by comparison with other health care systems. Here there is an element of continuity between the analysis of the Royal Commission and the new government, in so far as the new commitment to efficiency is to be met in part by the abandonment of the internal market which for many was seen as compromising the principles of the Service. In particular the White Paper identifies a number of 'internal market inefficiencies', for example the artificial budgetary divisions (emergency care, waiting list surgery and drug treatments) and the limitations of the existing Purchaser Efficiency Index (PEI). The PEI will be replaced in April 1999 by a new Performance Framework intended to focus on 'more rounded measures – health improvement, fairer access to services, better quality and outcomes of care and the views of patients – as well as real efficiency gains' (see DoH, 1997, pp. 11, 14, 20, 64–5.).

The Royal Commission of 1979 did not recommend any fundamental changes in what might be seen as the relatively undemocratic traditions of the NHS (see, for example, p. 296 and p. 307, above). The White Paper includes a commitment to 'a strong public voice in health and healthcare decision-making' with an expectation that health authorities will play a 'strong role in communicating with local people and ensuring public involvement in decision-making about the local health service' (DoH, 1997, p. 29). This is contrasted with the internal market which 'made it hard for local people to find out what their local hospital was planning' and allowed GP fundholders to 'make significant decisions without reference to the local community' (DoH, 1997, p. 11, 15).

The Royal Commission's objectives said nothing about partnership, but it would be fair to say that everyone is now more familiar with the obstructive and obdurate nature of the health and social care division put in place by the health and social service reorganizations of the 1970s (see, especially, pp. 113, 119, 135–8, 285, 295, above). The White Paper does indicate a renewed faith in the benefits of coterminosity with social services (DoH, 1997, p. 37), but there is now a commitment to breaking down organizational barriers and forging stronger links between the NHS and the local authorities. In particular 'there will be a new statutory duty of partnership placed on local NHS bodies to work together for the common good' which will be extended to Local Authorities by strengthening the existing requirements under the 1977 NHS Act (see DoH, 1997, pp. 11, 26).

The White Paper does include elements of continuity with health care before the inception of the NHS in 1948. The government reasserts a continuing faith in systems of professional self-regulation as 'an essential element in the delivery of quality patient services' (DoH, 1997, p. 59), although there is also a proposal to strengthen such systems (see DoH, 1997, pp. 56, 59). That most durable of 'social policy compromises', the independent contractor status of GPs also survives in the new NHS (see DoH, 1997, pp. 35, 40; see also, pp. 35, 74, 109, above). But the longest-running theme for not just the NHS, but for 'modern health care' (dating back at least to the end of the nineteenth century) is that of resources. On this topic there are two key elements in the White Paper. Firstly there is a commitment to raising 'spending in real terms every year' (see, for example, DoH, 1997, pp. 3, 8). Secondly, there is an analysis that seeks to expose the 'false dilemma' that the NHS cannot be maintained without 'huge increases in taxation, a move to charge-based services, or radical restrictions in patient care' (DoH, 1997, pp. 7, 8).

The White Paper contains a series of points in support of the contention that the basic principles of the NHS can be sustained without recourse to massive increases in taxation. The analysis reprises some of the arguments identified in Chapter 8 (see pp. 154–8, above). Firstly, there is the continuing widespread public support for the principles of the NHS; this implies that it should be politically feasible to deploy 'small' (as opposed to huge) 'increases in taxation' or further increase spending on the NHS by a redistribution of public expenditure from other services. Secondly, the potential for medical advances to achieve desired outcomes more cheaply (eg: more day surgery) is noted – a reminder that not all medical advances increase health care costs. Thirdly, there is the projected easing of demographic pressures (as the NHS has to respond to a much less dramatic increase in the number of people aged 85 years and over for the next decade).

The fourth point in the analysis is the potential to remedy the current 'uneven and unsystematic' take up of research findings on clinical and cost-effectiveness. The Government proposes to address the unjustifiable variations in the application of evidence on clinical and cost-effectiveness and the failure to share best practice in part by the two new national bodies – CHI and NICE – which will lead to 'rigorous assessment of clinical and cost-effective treatments and will ensure good practice is adopted locally' (DoH, 1997, p. 9). The CHI will 'support and oversee the quality of clinical governance and of clinical services' (DoH, 1997,

p. 56). The NICE will 'give a strong lead on clinical and cost-effectiveness, drawing up new guidelines and ensuring they reach all parts of the health service' (DoH, 1997, p. 18). There will be a national schedule of 'reference costs' which will 'itemise what individual treatments across the NHS cost'. NHS Trusts will be required to publish and benchmark their own costs on the same basis. The intention is to give Health Authorities, PCGs and the NHS Executive a 'strong lever with which to tackle inefficiency' (DoH, 1997, p. 19). The intended outcome is service and treatment based on the best evidence of 'what does and does not work and what provides best value for money' (clinical and cost-effectiveness) (DoH, 1997, p. 56).

The fifth point is the 'big gains in efficiency' (DoH, 1997, p. 9) to be derived from dismantling the internal market. Substantial savings (£1 billion over the lifetime of the current Parliament) are assumed from greater organizational efficiencies – cutting the number of commissioning bodies to as a few as 500; capping management costs with a combined Health Authority and PCG management cost envelope for each Health Authority area; and especially by eliminating what the White Paper refers to as the complex, time-consuming and wasteful bureaucracy of the internal market associated with administering competition – this includes fragmented decision-making, spiralling transaction costs, short-term and individual case contracting and the absence of strategic co-ordination (see DoH, 1997, pp. 2, 4, 8, 13, 14, 19, 22, 38, 72, 73, 74).

The sixth and final point is the 'better value for money' derived by aligning 'clinical and financial responsibility' for all professionals and in particular for teams of local GPs and community nurses working together in the new PCGs. These PCGs will be developed around 'natural communities' (taking account of the benefits of coterminosity with social services) and will typically serve about 100,000 patients. They will take 'responsibility for a single unified budget covering most aspects of care so they can get the best fit between resources and needs' (DoH, 1997, p. 19). The PCGs will be required to be representative of all GP practices in the Group, to promote integration in service planning, to have clear arrangements for public involvement, to promote the health of their local population, to commission health services for their population, monitor performance against service agreements, and to develop primary care and integrate it with other community health services (see DoH, 1997, pp. 18, 19, 34, 36, 37). The actual role of PCGs will vary from area to area as there will be four options for their responsibilities ranging from supporting and advising the Health Authority in commissioning care (Option 1) through taking formal, devolved responsibility for managing the budget for healthcare in their area, as part of the Health Authority (Option 2) to becoming established as free standing bodies accountable to the Health Authority for commissioning care (Option 3). All PCGs will begin at whatever point on the spectrum is appropriate for them, but will be expected to assume fuller responsibilities with an end-point in Option 4 – being established as free standing bodies accountable to the Health Authority for commissioning care and with added responsibility for the provision of community health services for their population. Existing, but 'more open', NHS Trusts will continue alongside, and will be accountable to, the evolving PCGs. Both sets of organizations will contribute to developing the Health Improvement Programmes. The Trusts will have a new stability through longer-term agreements although PCGs will still be able to change their local service agreement 'where NHS Trusts are failing to deliver'. It is clearly hoped that the latter will be infrequent given the 'new focus on quality' guaranteed in part through the clinical governance of Trusts, involving senior health professionals more closely in designing service agreements. The Trusts will also be accountable to Health Authorities and have a new statutory duty to work in partnership with other NHS organizations. The new openness of NHS Trusts will involve the obligation to publish details of their performance, including the costs of the treatments they offer (see DoH, 1997, pp. 45 46, 48, 49, 53).

Food safety – putting consumers first

From the plough to the plate, the ... (Food Standards) ... agency will put consumers first. It will have tough powers to make sure the high standards we are aiming for are met all the way from farms and shops, from restaurants and to our kitchen. (Sam Galbraith, Scottish Health Minister, quoted in *The Independent*, 15/1/98, p. 1)

The White Paper announcing the Food Standards Agency was published on 14 January 1998 (*Food Standards Agency – a force for change*, Cm.3830). The medical and agricultural consequences of the BSE crisis (and to a lesser extent the publicity surrounding *e coli*) are obviously part of the background to the establishment of what was described as 'one of the most powerful food watchdogs in Europe' (*The Independent*, 'Foul food: can the Government protect us from killer bugs?', 15/1/98, p. 1);. The new Agency will report to the Department of Health not the Ministry of Agriculture Food and Fisheries, and will be made up of a commission of twelve independent people backed up by advisory committees and several hundred civil servants. There was some disappointment that the Public Health Laboratory Service would not report directly to the new Agency, but the inclusion of advice and education on nutrition into the Agency's remit was seen as a recognition of food as a public health issue (see James, 1998, p. 416; see also pp. 207, above)

Equitable, rational and realistic – the future of London's health services

> we make proposals about how London's services can be planned equitably and rationally ... we believe ... our proposals are realistic and rational. (Turnberg Report, 1998, p. 1)

> The Government is determined to ensure that all Londoners have accessible top quality local services in GP practices, clinics and their own homes, supported by specialist advice, care and treatment in hospital and community settings; with accident, emergency and ambulance services capable of meeting foreseeable needs. (DoH, 1998a, p. 1)

The Turnberg Report (1998) was made available to the government on 18 November 1997 but was not published by the Government until 3 February 1998 (see, DoH 1998a). One of the most significant conclusions of the Review Panel was that 'there is no evidence that there are more acute beds available to Londoners than the England average'; indeed the Panel's interpretation was that 'London probably has fewer beds available to its population than the average' leading to the intention that the 'rationalisations being proposed should not result in losses of beds overall' (Turnberg Report, 1998, pp. 19, 1). This confirmed the views of those critics who suggested that the policy option of resolving the problems of London's health services by a reallocation of resources from existing hospital services was increasingly suspect (see pp. 186–7, above); and contrasted with the conclusions and recommendations of the Tomlinson Report (1992) and *Making London Better* (DoH, 1993a), that there was an over-provision of acute care in inner London (see pp. 181–4, above). The Review Panel's different conclusions derived from more reliable data; from referral patterns from outer London to inner London providers that were in the opposite direction to those predicted by Tomlinson (1992); and from primary and community care alternatives to inpatient hospital care not developing with the speed and quality assumed in the Kings Fund (1992a) and Tomlinson (1992) Reports. The Panel's recommendations on organizational arrangements complemented the themes of the *New NHS* White Paper (DoH, 1997) – accurate management information systems, good collaborative work, public health strategies as part of the planning agenda, improved local strategies for public consultation, groups of GPs commissioning services for populations of about 100,000, the centrality of close working with local authorities and the value of co-terminosity (see Turnberg Report, 1998, pp. 1–2). Long-standing concerns were expressed – 'general practice still lags behind the rest of the country and, in some ways, appears to be getting worse' – and long-standing priorities were re-affirmed as primary care, mental health and community health services (Turnberg Report, 1998, pp. 35, 1; see also pp. 171–2, above). Another long-standing agenda was also addressed by proposing not only that the two Thames Regional Offices should enhance their working relationship, but that the longer term aim should be 'a single London Regional Office' (Turnberg Report, 1998, p. 1; see also p. 168, above).

Given the consideration that there is not an excess of hospital beds in London, it was unsurprising that the Review Panel should call for a careful re-evaluation of existing proposals to close the Guy's Hospital Accident and Emergency Department; supported the case for a new hospital at Whitechapel ; and called for capital investment in the Whittington and Newham Hospitals. In terms of one of the highest profile elements in the debate about London's health care the Review Panel concluded that there was a 'continuing need for St.Bartholomew's Hospital to fulfil its service, teaching and research responsibilities' for several years yet, with a longer term future as a base for certain tertiary services (eg: cardiac and oncology services) (Turnberg Report, 1998, p. 77).

The government's response was to accept 'the recommendations in the Turnberg report' and to propose 'a programme to implement them'; this included building on 'the long-tradition of medical excellence at St. Bartholomew's Hospital' with a request that plans be developed for 'a specialist hospital providing cardiac and cancer services ... for implementation once the other changes in the East End have reduced the need for the wider range of services it now provides' (DoH, 1998a, pp. 1, 18). The public expenditure implications were estimated at £140 million over the lifetime of the current Parliament, with £30 million targeted on these services in 1998/99. The Government also accepted the case for capital developments in each of the five recommended sectors of London (North, South-East, South-West, West and East) at an estimated cost of over £800 million (DoH, 1998a, pp. 1–2).

Our Healthier Nation

The previous health strategy – *Health of the Nation* – included targets. But its vision for health was limited, mainly because of its reluctance to acknowledge the social, economic and environmental causes of ill-health. (DoH, 1998b, p. 57, para.4.12)

The Government recognises that the social causes of ill health and the inequalities that stem from them must be acknowledged and acted on. Connected problems require joined up solutions. This means tackling inequality which stems from poverty, poor housing, pollution, low educational standards, joblessness and low pay. Tackling inequalities generally is the best means of tackling health inequalities in particular. (DoH, 1998b, p. 12, para.1.12)

The Public Health Minister's role was identified as developing 'a coherent strategy for public health' seeking to 'systematically engage the many arms of Government in delivering better health for the whole nation by taking action to address the root causes of ill-health' (NHS Executive 1997c, para.5). This clear commitment to the inter-sectoral approach (see pp. 218–20 above) is also represented by the Cabinet Committee of Ministers from twelve different departments intended to support 'the co-ordination of health policy across Government' and the commitment to 'apply health impact assessments' to 'relevant key policies' (DoH, 1998b, pp. 31, 32). At the local level the Government proposes to place on local authorities a new duty to promote 'the economic, social and environmental well-being of their area' (DoH, 1998b, p. 44).

The consultative Green Paper on public health was originally scheduled for publication in Autumn 1997 (see NHS Executive, 1997c, para.8) but eventually appeared on 5 February 1998 (as *Our Healthier Nation*, DoH, 1998b). As with the previous White Paper, the Government claims to be pursuing another 'third way', this time between the 'old extremes of individual victim blaming on the one hand and nanny state social engineering on the other' (DoH, 1998b, p. 5). The latter comment is interesting since New Labour's interest in public health has sparked charges of the 'nanny state', pointing of course to one of the dilemmas of policies of illness prevention and health promotion (see pp. 217–18 above). The Minister for Public Health (Tessa Jowell) in an interview with *The Independent* was clearly sensitive to these criticisms noting that

> it is important that we go with the grain of public enthusiasm and don't turn people off by being overtly prescriptive, ambitious or intrusive. This is not about creating a nanny state but it is founded on the belief that people should be able to make grown-up choices on the basis of information they can trust. (*The Independent*, 5/1/98, p. 8)

Interestingly, the Government did not presume that the 'case for health' was self-evident and took the opportunity to elaborate on the 'overwhelming personal, social and economic case ... for improving our health' – that 'our own health and the health of our families and friends underpin our ability to enjoy life to the full' (the personal case); that everyone 'should have a fair chance of a long and healthy life' (the social case); and that to 'succeed in the modern world economy, the country's workforce must be healthy as well as highly skilled' (the economic case) (see DoH, 1998b, pp. 7, 9, 12, 14). Less surprising, given the critical comment on the previous *Health of the Nation* targets, was the commitment not just to improve the health of the population as a whole but also to narrow the health gap . In relation to the latter, the Government have established an independent enquiry into 'the evidence base for action to tackle inequalities in health' (see DoH, 1998b, pp. 5, 53; see also DoH, 1992).

Existing marked inequalities in health provide part of the rationale for identifying four priority areas in the Government's public health strategy for which 'realistic' but 'challenging' national targets will be set. The four priority areas are heart disease and stroke, accidents, cancer and mental health. These are 'significant causes of premature death and poor health' and 'there is much that can be done to prevent them or to treat them more effectively'. The implication is that the previous government's *Health of the Nation* targets may have dissipated energies by operating on 'too broad a front' (see DoH, 1998b, pp. 6, 56, 57; see also DoH, 1992)

There are specific additional resources associated with the Governments's public health strategy for Healthy Living Centres (£300 million from the National Lottery) and the Healthy Schools Initiative. But broader public policy measures – the Welfare to Work programme, the National Minimum Wage and an integrated transport policy – are clearly identified as essential to the 'New Public Health' (see DoH, 1998b, p. 29, para.3.5, p. 37, para.3.31 and p. 46, paras 3.61 and 3.63).

It is intended that the Consultation Paper will be followed by the publication of a White Paper on public health in the summer of 1998 (see NHS Executive, 1997c, para.8) and a comprehensive strategy on reducing smoking later in 1998 (see DoH, 1998b, p. 22). The latter will identify measures to reduce cigarette consumption as well as banning tobacco advertising (see *The Independent*, 5/1/98, p. 8).

Community care: pulling together at last?

We will end competition and replace it with a new duty of partnership so that local health services pull together rather than pull apart. (Frank Dobson quoted in *The Guardian* – 10/12/97)

I do not believe that greater control over the NHS budget by GPs will break down the 'Berlin Wall' between health and social services. This will only be eradicated when health and local authority budgets are merged. (Baroness Robson, House of Lords, 1997, Col.33)

The new government themes of partnership and collaboration would appear to have considerable potential in relation to policies for community care. The HAZ initiative is seen as offering opportunities to resolve the health and social care divide (see, for example, comments by Baroness Jay in the House of Lords debate on *The New NHS* White Paper, House of Lords, 1997, Col.34). A publication relatively early in the life of the new government recognised yet again that 'the effective delivery of community care requires co-ordinated provision of continuing health and social care services developed through partnerships between health, local authorities, housing, and other agencies' (NHS Executive, 1997c, Para.29E) and all three government ministers (Frank Dobson, Tessa Jowell and Paul Boateng) have made references to the need to break down the 'Berlin Wall' between health and social care.

In January 1998 a news report (in *The Daily Telegraph*) that care in the community was to be scrapped was denied by Frank Dobson on a BBC Radio 5 Live phone-in the next day. What the Minister did suggest however was that the line had been drawn in the wrong place.

I think they thought that virtually everybody could cope on their own. I think there was a feeling, as we approach the end of the twentieth century, people would be able to cope a bit better – but people who couldn't cope, couldn't cope ... we need to look at this right across the spectrum – from people who are just a bloody nuisance to people who may be a danger and against whom legal action needs to be taken (quoted in *The Independent*, 19/1/98, p. 8)

The following month the Parliamentary Under-Secretary of State with responsible for personal social services and community care (Paul Boateng) returned to the Ministerial theme of walls between health and social care. His optimistic view was that joint health and social care planning 'is beginning more and more to become a reality' and he indicated ongoing work, possibly leading to primary legislation in relation to the pooling of health and social care budgets (*Social Services Parliamentary Monitor*, February 24, 1998, p. 4). At the time of writing we are still waiting for further developments but the force and frequency of government statements promises more tangible action in this area.

Legislation, implementation, money and 'The Third Way'

Finally we should note that none of the White Papers have 'run the gauntlet' of the legislative process. The Labour Party has a substantial majority in the House of Commons but this has not prevented the medical profession seeking to oppose elements of previous health care reforms and effecting legislative details to a significant degree (see especially pp. 35–7 and pp. 77–9, above); and there is certainly a raft of legislative detail yet to come, including possible legislation on the pooling of health and social care budgets as we have noted above. The next stage – implementation – may also give 'a sharper edge to unresolved tensions in the White Paper' (Klein, 1998, p. 32).

In the 1998 Budget the Chancellor of the Exchequer announced an extra £500 million as part of a package of measures to reduce waiting lists and times. This brings the total amount of extra money allocated to health care in 1997/98 to £2 billion, and for the moment at least the *New NHS* White Paper commitment to raise expenditure on the NHS in real terms seems secure.

Finally the references in the *New NHS* and *Healthier Britain* White Papers to a 'third way' has begun to generate the inevitable debate about whether the new Government is developing its own distinctive approach to social policies. Some have already identified a consistent pattern around the themes of community, opportunity, responsibility and accountability (see Le Grand, 1998, pp. 26–7). This may indeed be the case, although the contrasts drawn with previous approaches in the *New NHS* White Paper are perhaps exaggerated. Problems of fragmented, unco-ordinated approaches to health care did not begin with the quasi- 'free for all of the 1980s' (see pp. 104–06, above) nor did 'stifling top down' approaches disappear with the ending of what is probably best labelled the quasi-'centralised command and control' of the 1970s (see pp. 128–29, above). It remains to be seen whether what we end up with over the next few years will be most appropriately labelled a quasi-'collaborative approach'.

Conclusions: there may be trouble ahead

The danger for Tony Blair is that the prejudices of old Labour will make a radical reform of the health service politically impossible. (Rees-Mogg, 1997)

if more money is not found, we are no longer going to be able to provide the comprehensive service the country has known for the last 50 years. (James Johnson, Chairman of the BMA consultants committee, *The Times*, 8/10/97)

People in developed countries rightly demand good health care. That demand can be met in a number of ways. Other countries may do it differently, but often more expensively, less fairly and with no appreciable improvement. The health of our economy depends on the health of the NHS and not just by ensuring a healthy workforce. The cost effectiveness of the NHS reduces the United Kingdom's tax burden to well below the European Union average, encouraging investment, and strengthening incentives to work and save. It also reduces the inflationary wage pressures seen in employer-based system such as Germany. A strong NHS means a competitive Britain. (Alan Milburn, Minister for Health, *The Times*, 26/11/97)

The arrival of a new Labour government generated a range of responses of what will, and what should, happen to the NHS over the next five to ten years. The Government seems committed to a set of principles not dissimilar from those on which the Service was based fifty years ago. For Londoners the evidence of commitment to these principles will have seemed direct and swift. The speed of announcing the London Review Panel after assuming office (General Election, 1 May 1997; Review announced 20 June 1997) and the complete acceptance of all the Panel's recommendations was an unusual event in British social policy. The challenge to the Kings Fund (1992a) and Tomlinson (1992) estimates of the number of acute beds required was quite direct, and the commitment to rebuild is an example of placing planning rather than the market at the centre of decision-making . The commitment of resources to support the recommendations removes a long-running political conflict between the London hospital community and the government of the day. The complete acceptance of every recommendation in the Strategic Review demonstrates quite clearly the combination of political power with an ideological commitment to an historically favoured public service.

The recommendations for London, accepted by the new Government, included organizational change in the form of the long-term aim of one strategic authority for London. Organizational change also featured in the *New NHS* White Paper (DoH 1997) and much of this has been well-received, in particular the 'sensible and welcome' process of bottom up evolution over five to ten years which eschews the 'immediate big-bang introduction of untested reforms' (see Dixon and Mays, 1997, p. 1640 and Glennerster and Le Grand, 1997). That the Government does not 'seek to enforce one model in every city, suburb and rural area' (Frank Dobson in the House of Commons debate on the *New NHS* White Paper, see House of Commons, 1997, Col.807) is a recognition that different arrangements might suit different parts of the country as the Royal Commission argued all those years ago (see p. 122, above). This includes a different set of arrangements for Scotland (see Secretary of State for Scotland, 1997) – although these did attract the criticism that they could represent a return to the old command and control approach (see Parston and McMahon, 1998, p. 213).

The gradualist introduction of PCGs has been supported given that they are seen as a 'sophisticated concept' that will need 'time to bed in'. Meanwhile concerns have been expressed about the interest, the time and the managerial capacity of all GPs in relation to the commissioning process (see, for example, *Daily Telegraph*, Editorial, 10/2/97; *The Independent*, Editorial, 12/11/97; and Lord Howe in the House of Lords debate on *The New NHS* White Paper, see House of Lords, 1997, Col.31). What these comments do indicate is that there are management needs and costs associated with the new PCGs (Dixon and Mays, 1997, p. 1640) which raises a series of inter-related issues. Firstly, whether the genuine concern with an overbureaucratic public service will result in shifting on to professional practitioners a bureaucratic burden, given the complications surrounding commissioning hospital and community services. Secondly, whether the intended significant downward pressure on management costs will limit the effectiveness of PCGs and health authorities to undertake their new roles in commissioning, planning, monitoring and regulating (Dixon and Mays, 1997, pp. 1639–40). Thirdly, whether there could be conflicts of interest associated with GPs acting as both commissioners and providers. With the latter there is the paradox that the service commissioning / service provider split is seen as worthy of retention for hospital services, but would seem to be abandoned for community health services as PCGs advance to the preferred Option 4 (see above). Fourthly, whether there is a tension between one the one hand, the new roles and the new institutions (HAZs, PCGs, NICE, CHI), and on the other hand, the intention to generate significant savings in the administrative and managerial costs of the NHS.

This of course brings us to the key question of resources and the hoped for contribution of cost savings linked to reduced bureaucracy and red-tape. For a start there is the cautionary observation that 'studies carried out in the US have generally shown that very little of expected savings have occurred' (*Health Care Today*, October 1997). 'Managers question £1bn savings target' was the headline on page 3 of the January 1998 issue of *Health Care Today*, echoing the concerns of others that the proposed savings are 'ambitious and will not of themselves provide the additional resources the NHS will need' (Ham, 1998b, p. 212). The Government's response must of course be that they are relying on more than administrative savings to provide more resources for services to patients. Indeed the *Healthier Nation* White Paper added to the *New NHS* White Paper arguments, by identifying the public health contribution to the resource problems of the NHS – 'by preventing avoidable illness we can concentrate resources on treating conditions which cannot yet be prevented' (DoH, 1998b, p. 4). However the Government would obviously be unwise to put too much faith in a contemporary version of the Beveridge assumption – in this case that moving towards a more effective and dependable NHS will somehow stem the increasing demands made upon the Service (see p. 58 and 92–5, above). The demographic position may be improving, but the Government may be making insufficient allowance for a countervailing increase in the public expectations of older people for whom the NHS has been a taken for granted element of their adult life, and who may be more aware of and less tolerant of, any form of age discrimination. The future provision of long-term nursing care for elderly people will obviously be of significance; it is clear that the authors of the 1944 White Paper did not intend this service to be marginalised within or excluded from the NHS (see Ministry of Health, 1944, p. 9; see also p. 286, above). Meanwhile in circumstances where we know that 'some disabilities remain more or less hidden' and that 32 per cent of men and 39 per cent of women who reported bladder problems had not sought advice from a health professional (see Calman, 1997, pp. 75, 69), it is apparent that the 'submerged iceberg of illness' continues and has the potential to confound all manner of calculations about future demand on the NHS – especially when the Government has raised expectations with references to 'prompt access to specialist services' and 'swift advice and treatment in local surgeries and health care' (DoH, 1997). The implication of a continuing complex relationship between health and the demand for health care, is that resource issues will remain the key political dimension of the NHS and that the outcome of the Government's Comprehensive Spending Review (due for completion in July 1998) may be one of the more significant events associated with the 50th birthday of the NHS.

Where at least the government can be confident, by comparison with the fears that dogged the early years of the Service (see, especially, pp. 80 and 92–5, above), is that it has in the NHS one of the most cost-effective health care systems since 'most European health economists agree that the best way to maintain control over spending is to have cash-limited budgets funded from taxes' (Maynard, 1998, p. 20). And with the ending of the GP's open-ended drug budget, all spending on the NHS will be capped for the first time. It is the operation of the Service within this cash-envelope that is likely to provide opportunities for the writing of future chapters identifying both conflict and continuity in the NHS. Indeed the potential for such conflict is perhaps recognised in the *New NHS* White Paper with the reference that 'it is clear that there are tough choices facing the NHS' (DoH, 1997, para.1.2). The Government has also recognised the problem of raising expectations with its ambitious public health agenda, since it is possible to target the more easily tackled health problems and end up widening health inequalities (see DoH, 1998b, pp. 56, 82).

Inevitably the new Government's reforms generate a range of questions. For example, the *New NHS* White Paper has a number of references to 'sanctions', 'reserve powers' and 'accountability'. This should produce administrative efficiency in which goals and performance targets are stated and measured for achievement. But given the statutory obligations of NHS Trusts, especially acute hospital trusts, to co-operate with other parts of the NHS to meet quality standards, at what stage will the threat to use the reserve powers become a reality? And what if – once the checks on quality are made and deficiencies are found – the professional response is that, with limited resources, the quality standards expected are impossible to achieve? There is certainly potential here for conflict between the government and the profession. Has the Government put too much faith in the benefits of information technology – perhaps a new version of the 'technocratic fallacy' (see p. 117, above)? Has the Government put more (and perhaps too much) power in the hands of professionals (Simon Hughes in the *New NHS* White Paper debate, see House of Commons, 1987, Col.803)? Has the Government 'too much belief in collaboration' (Glennerster and Le Grand, 1997) – what the Shadow Secretary of State referred to in the House of Commons debate as a 'touching old Labour faith in co-operation and good will' (John Maples, see House of Commons, 1987, Col.800) – perhaps a new version of the 'single best solution fallacy' (see p. 117 above)? Has the Government underestimated the difficulties in breaking down the barriers (the 'Berlin Wall') between health and social care – a 'statutory duty of partnership' could involve a 'shotgun marriage' rather than a 'professional meeting of minds' – perhaps a new version of the 'unitary' and 'organizational' fallacies (see pp. 116–17, above)? Will the transfer of power to GPs destabilise traditional professional working relationships, most obviously those between GPs and consultants (which do after all have a long, and at times problematic, history, see especially pp. 25–6 and pp. 77–9, above). Finally, and perhaps most significantly given its key role in *The New NHS*, is there a potential conflict between public and professional expectations and evidence-based health care? The NHS has been based on a combination of evidence-based medicine, ethical considerations, public expectations, and professional custom and practice – can we radically shift this balance without considerable conflict?

The Government may have struck a new balance between professionalism, bureaucracy, managerialism and accountability, but that will not of itself eliminate conflicts within the NHS. In particular, whatever administrative savings accrue over the next few years, the NHS will not be able to dispense with a bureaucracy based upon the need for accurate records, for the accountability of decision-makers for decision-making, to enable patients to seek redress in certain circumstances, for the assessment of the health needs of local populations, and for the delivery of a predictable level of health care. Without managerial and bureaucratic systems, professionals would be acting as lone entrepreneurs with responsibility but limited accountability (see Chapter 14, above).

Thus far the new government's initiatives on health and health care have been generally well received. The New NHS White Paper has been described as 'very positive', 'exciting', 'bold', 'brave' and 'imaginative', offering a vision for the future which is both 'radical' and 'right', promising an 'improvement in the fair delivery of health care' through 'empowering professionals, encouraging innovation, better informing the public, holding institutions to account through publication of standards' (see Editorial, *The Guardian*, 10/12/98 and Editorial, *The Times*, 10/12/97; Ham, 1998a, p. 2; Ham, 1998b, p. 212; see also the Director of Institute of Health Services Management and the Chief Executive of NHS Confederation quoted in *The Guardian* on 19/12/97). By contrast our commentary has assumed a somewhat cautionary tone which is perhaps inevitable given the historical perspective we have sought to introduce. In developing our historical perspective we have had occasion to use quotations from editorials in *The Times* to represent interesting contemporary perspectives on developments in health care. In this case *The Times* editorial concluded with the comment that the White Paper (*New NHS*) 'although admirable and imaginative, will not be the final word' (*The Times*, Editorial, 10/12/97). Given the lengthy history of conflicts and continuities we have sought to document we are equally confident that the current flurry of government documents on health and health care will not be 'the final word' from the government, the health care professions, the service users or the carers.

For the 'final words' in our text we offer our readers that section of the Prime Minister's speech to the Labour Party Conference that dealt with the NHS. It will provide you with one criteria (the policy goal option – see Chapter 15) by which to judge New Labour and the new NHS over the next few years. Mr Blair said the following:

> ... the same drive for reform applies to the NHS. I'm tired of hearing the NHS described as if it were a relic. It isn't. It was the greatest act of modernisation any Labour government has ever done. But my vision is not just to save the NHS, but make it better. The money will be there. I promise you that. This year. Every year. Millions saved from red tape, millions more into breast cancer treatment already under new Labour. The values will remain.
>
> From next April, the two-tier NHS of the Tories will go for good. And I tell you, I will never countenance an NHS that departs from its fundamental principle of health care based on need, not wealth.
>
> The hospitals will be built. Fourteen of them, the biggest hospital building programme in the history of the NHS. It will mean an extra £1.3 billion in 14 towns and cities; serving five million people. And as of today, it is 15.
>
> But money is not the only problem with health care in Britain. The NHS itself need modernisation and hard choices. We appointed the first Minister for Public Health because the health service should not lose millions every year because of avoidable illnesses like those from smoking. Barriers between GPs, social services and hospitals must be broken down.
>
> Hospitals cannot stand still. Increasingly, general hospitals will provide routine care, supported by specialist centres of excellence in treatment, research and education. GPs and

nurses will do more of what hospitals used to do, often working together on the same site in partnership with chemists, dentists, opticians and physiotherapists. New technology offers huge opportunities in the NHS and we haven't yet begun to seize them properly. We will get the money. But in return, I want reform.

From next April, there will be up to ten specially funded Health Action Zones set up in Britain. Their remit to experiment with new ideas in the way health care is delivered, so that patients get a better deal from their health services for the 21st century. The NHS was a beacon to the world in 1948. It will always be safe with us. I want it to be better with us. (as reported in *The Times*, 1/10/97)

Bibliography

Abbott, S. (1997) 'The Next Step', *NHS Magazine*, Autumn 1997, pp. 9–11, Leeds: NHS Executive

Abel-Smith, B. (1959) 'Trends in social policy: social security'. In Ginsberg, M. (ed.) (1958) *Law and Opinion in the Twentieth Century*, London: Stevens.

Abel-Smith, B. (1964) *The Hospitals 1800–1948: a study in social administration in England and Wales*, London: Heinemann.

Abel-Smith, B. (1971) 'The Politics of Health', *New Society*, 29 July 1971.

Abel-Smith, B. (1972) 'The History of Medical Care'. In Martin, E. W. (ed.) *Comparative Developments in Social Welfare*, London: Allen and Unwin.

Abel-Smith, B. (1976) *Value for money in health services*, London: Heinemann.

Abel-Smith, B. (1978) *National Health Service: the first thirty years*, London: HMSO.

Abel-Smith, B. (1990) 'The first forty years'. In Carrier, J. and Kendall, I. (eds) *Socialism and the NHS: Fabian Essays in Health Care*, Aldershott: Gower.

Abel-Smith, B. (1994) *An introduction to health: policy, planning and financing*, Harlow: Longman.

Abel-Smith, B. and Titmuss, R. M. (1956) *The Cost of the National Health Service* (National Institute of Economic and Social Research Occasional Papers 18) London: Cambridge University Press.

Abel-Smith, B. and Glennerster, H. (1995) 'Labour and the Tory health reforms', *Fabian Review*, Vol. 107, No. 3 (June 1995).

Abrams, P. (1977) 'Community Care: Some Research Problems and Priorities', *Policy and Politics*, No. 6, pp. 125–51.

Acheson Report (1988) Public Health in England, Cm. 289, London: HMSO.

Alford, R. (1975) *Health Care Politics: Ideological and Interest Group Barriers to Reform*, London: University of Chicago Press.

Allsop, J. (1984) *Health Policy and the National Health Service*, Harlow: Longman.

Allsop, J. (1995) *Health Policy and the NHS: Towards 2000* (2nd edition), London: Longman.

Anderson, M. (1980) *Approaches to the history of the western family, 1500–1914*, London: Macmillan.

Anderson, M. (1983) 'How much has the family changed?', *New Society*, 27 October 1983

Appleby, J. (1994) 'The Reformed National Health Service; A Commentary', *Social Policy and Administration*, Vol. 28, no. 4. pp. 345–57.

Arrow, K. (1963) 'Uncertainty and the Welfare Economics of Medical Care', *American Economic Review*, December 1963, Vol. LIII, No. 5, pp. 941–73.

Atkinson, A. B. (1996) *Incomes and the Welfare State*, Cambridge: Cambridge University Press.

Audit Commission (1986) *Making A Reality of Community Care*, London: HMSO.

Audit Commission (1992) *Lying in Wait: The use of medical beds in acute hospitals,* London: HMSO.

Audit Commission (1994) *Trusting in the Future: Towards an Audit Agenda for the NHS Providers*, London: HMSO.

Audit Commission, (1995) *A Price On Their Heads: measuring management costs in NHS Trusts*, London: HMSO.

Audit Commission (1997) The Coming of Age, London: HMSO

Ayers, G. (1971) *England's First State Hospitals and the Metropolitan Asylums Board 1867–1930*, London: Wellcome Institute of the History of Medicine.

Bacon, R. and Eltis, W. (1976) *Britain's Economic Problem: Too Few Producers*, London: Macmillan.

Baggott, R. (1994) *Health and Health Care in Britain*, Basingstoke: Macmillan.

Ball, D. (1972) 'Health'. *New Society*, 3 August 1972, p. 241.

Barclay Report, (1982) *Social workers: their role and tasks* (Chair: Peter Barclay), London: Bedford Square Press.

Barnett, C. (1986) *The Audit of War; The Illusion and Reality of Britain as a Great Nation*, London: Macmillan.

Barnett, C. (1995) *The Lost Victory: British Dreams, British realities 1945–50*, London: Macmillan.

Barr, A. and Logan, R. F. L. (1977) 'Policy alternatives for Resource Allocation', *The Lancet*, 7, May 1977, pp. 994–6.

Barratt Brown, M. (1971) 'The Welfare State in Britain'. In Miliband, R. and Saville, J. (eds) *The Socialist Register 1971*, London: The Merlin Press.

Bartlett, W. and Harrison, L. (1993) 'Quasi-markets and the National Health Service Reforms'. In Le Grand, J. and Bartlett, W. (eds) (1993) *Quasi-markets and social policy*, Basingstoke: Macmillan.

Barton, R. (1976) *Institutional Neurosis* (3rd edition), Bristol: J. Wright.

Bayley, H. (1995) *The Nation's Health*, London: Fabian Society.

Bean, P. and MacPherson, S. (eds) (1983) *Approaches to Welfare*, London: Routledge and Kegan Paul.

Beaver, M. W. (1973) 'Population, infant mortality and milk'. *Population Studies*, Vol XXVII, No. 2, July 1973, pp. 243–54.

Benzeval, M., Judge, K. and New, B. (1991) 'Health and Health Care in London', *Public Money and Management*, Spring, Vol II, No. 1, pp. 25–32.

Beresford, P. (1978) 'More Camberwells?' *New Society*, 21/28 December 1978, pp. 700–2.

Berlant, J. (1975) *Profession and monopoly: a study of medicine in the United States and Great Britain*, London: University of California Press.

Berlin, I. (1988) *Four Essays on Liberty*, Oxford: Oxford University Press.

Bevan, A. (1978) *In Place of Fear*, London: Quartet Books.

Beveridge Report (1942) *Social Insurance and Allied Services*, Cmd. 6404, London: HMSO.

Black Report (1980) *Inequalities in Health: Report of a Research Working Party*, London: DHSS.

Blom-Cooper, L. et al (1995) *The Falling Shadow: One Patient's Mental Health Care 1978–1993*, London: Duckworth.

BMA (1930) *Proposals for a General Medical Service for the Nation*, London: British Medical Association.

BMA (1938) *A General Medical Service for the Nation*, London: British Medical Association.

BMA (1942) *Medical Planning Commission*, London: British Medical Association.

BMA (1997) Options for funding the NHS, London: British Medical Association

BMLR (Butterworth's Medico-Legal Reports) (1992) London: Butterworths.

Booth, C. (1903) Life and Labour of the People in London, London: Macmillan

Booth, T. A. (1981) 'Collaboration Between The Health and Social Services: Part II, A Case Study of Joint Finance', *Policy and Politics*, Vol. 9, No. 2, pp. 205–26.

Bosanquet, N. (1989) 'An ailing state of National Health'. In Jowell, R., Witherspoon, S. and Brooke, L. (eds) (1989) *British Social Attitudes – The Fifth Report*, Aldershot: Gower.

Bosanquet, N. (1993), 'Interim Report: The National Health' in Jowell, R., Brook, L., Prior, G. and Taylor, B. (eds) (1993) *British Social Attitudes – The Ninth Report*, Aldershott: Dartmouth.

Boswell, D. and Wingrove, J. M. (eds) (1973) *The Handicapped Person in the Community*, London: Open University Press.

Boyson, R. (1971) *Down with the Poor; an analysis* of the failure of the 'welfare state', London: Churchill Press.

Brand, J. (1965) *Doctors and the State*, Baltimore: John Hopkins Press.

Brenton, M. and Ungerson, C. (1986) *Yearbook of Social Policy 1985–86*, London: Routledge and Kegan Paul.

Briggs, A. (1978) 'The achievements, failures and aspirations of the NHS', *New Society, 23.11.78, pp. 448–51.*

Bristowe, J. S. and Holmes, T. (1863) The Hospitals of England and Wales, Sixth Report of the Medical Officer of the Privy Council, London: P. S. King and Son.

British Hospitals Association (1937) *Report of the Voluntary Hospitals Commission* (Sankey Report), London: British Hospitals Association.

Brown, M. (1977) *An Introduction to Social Administration*, London: Hutchinsons

Brown, M. and Baldwin, S. (1978) *The Year Book of Social Policy in Britain 1977*, London: Routledge and Kegan Paul.

Brown, R. G. S. (1972) 'Reorganising the Health Service'. In Jones, K. (ed.) *The Yearbook of Social Policy in Britain 1971*, London: Routledge & Kegan Paul.

Brown, R. G. S. (1975) *The Management of Welfare: a study of British social service administration*, Glasgow: Collins.

Brown, R. G. S. (1979) *Reorganising the National Health Service*, Oxford: Basil Blackwell.

Bruce, M. (1961) *The Coming of the Welfare State*, London: Batsford.

Bull, D. (ed.) (1970) *Family Poverty*, London: Duckworth.

Burdett, H. (ed.) (1893) *Burdett's Hospital Annual and Year Book of Philanthropy*, London: The Scientific Press.

Burkitt, D. P. (1973) 'Diseases of modern economic development'. In Howe, G. M. and Loraine, J. A. (eds) (1973) *Environmental Medicine*, London: Heinemann.

Butler, J. R. and Vaile, M. (1984) *Health and Health Services: An introduction to Health Care in Britain*, London: Routledge and Kegan Paul.

Butterworth, E. and Holman, R. (eds) (1975) *Social Welfare in Modern Britain*, London: Fontana.

Buxton, M. (1976) *Health and Inequality*, Milton Keynes: Open University Press.

Buxton, M. and Klein, R. (1975), 'Distribution of hospital provision: Policy Themes and Resources Variations', *British Medical Journal*, 8/2/75 pp. 345–9.

Buxton, M. and Klein, R. (1978) *Allocating Health resources: a commentary on the Resource Allocation Working Party*, Royal Commission on NHS Research Paper, No. 3, London: HMSO.

Byrne, P. (ed) (1987) *Medicine in Contemporary Society*, London: Kings Fund.

Calder, A. (1971) *The People's War*, London: Granada.

Calman, K. (1997) 'On the state of the public health', *Health Trends*, Vol.29, No.3, pp. 67–79

Campbell, J. (1987) *Nye Bevan and the Mirage of British Socialism*, London: Weidenfeld and Nicholson.

Carr-Hill, R. (1987) 'The inequalities in health debate: a critical review of the issues', *Journal of Social Policy*, Vol. 16, pp. 509–42.

Carrier, J. (1978) 'Positive discrimination in the allocation of NHS resources'. In Brown, M. and Baldwin, S. (eds) (1978) *The Year Book of Social Policy in Britain 1977*, London: Routledge and Kegan Paul.

Carrier, J. (1980) 'London's health'. In Hall, P. (ed.) (1980) *A Radical Agenda for London*, London: Fabian Society.

Carrier, J. and Kendall, I. (1977) 'The Development of Welfare States: the production of plausible accounts', *Journal of Social Policy*, Vol. 6, Part 3 (July 1977), pp. 271–90.

Carrier, J. and Kendall, I. (1986) 'The Griffiths Report'. In Brenton, M. and Ungerson, C. (eds) (1986) *Yearbook of Social Policy 1985–86*, London: Routledge and Kegan Paul.

Carrier, J. and Kendall, I. (1990a) 'Working for patients?'. In Carrier, J. and Kendall, I. (eds) *Socialism and the NHS: Fabian essays in health care*, Aldershott: Gower.

Carrier, J. and Kendall, I. (1990b) *Medical negligence: complaints and compensations*, Aldershott: Gower.

Carrier, J. and Kendall, I. (1990c) 'At its best without equal'. In Carrier, J. and Kendall, I. (eds) *Socialism and the NHS: Fabian essays in health care*, Aldershott: Gower.

Carrier, J. and Kendall, I. (1992) 'Law and the social division of welfare', *International Journal of the Sociology of Law*, Vol. 20, pp. 61–87, London: Academic Press.

Carrier, J. and Kendall, I. (1995) 'Professionalism and inter-professionalism in health and community care: some theoretical issues' in Carrier, J., Owens, P. and Horder, J. (eds) (1995) *Interprofessional issues in Community and Primary Health Care*, London: Macmillan.

Carrier, J., Owens, P. and Horder, J. (eds) (1995) *Interprofessional issues in Community and Primary Health Care*, London: Macmillan.

Checkland, S. G and Checkland, E. O. A. (eds) (1974) *The Poor Law Report of 1834*, Harmondsworth: Pelican.

Chief Medical Officer (1995) *On The State of the Public Health 1994*, London: HMSO.

Clarke, M. (1976) 'Community as dustbin'. *New Society*, 29 July 1976, p. 235.

Cochrane, A. (1972) *Effectiveness and Efficiency: random reflections on health services*, London: Nuffield Provincial Hospitals Trust.

Cohen, S. (1979) 'Community Control – a new utopia'. *New Society*, 15 March 1979, pp. 609–11.

Cranbrook Report (1959) *Report of the Maternity Services Committee*, London: HMSO.

Crosland, C. A. R. (1956) *The Future of Socialism*, London: Jonathan Cape.

Crossman, R. (1969) *Paying for the Social Services*, London: Fabian Society.

CSO (Central Statistical Office) (1991) *Social Trends 21*, London: HMSO.

CSO (Central Statistical Office) (1995) *Economic Trends 495*, London: HMSO.

Curtis Report (1946) *Report on the Care of Children*, Cmnd.6922, London: HMSO.

Dawson Report (1920 *Interim Report on the future of the Medical and Allied Services*, Cmd. 693, London: HMSO.

Day, P. and Klein, R. (1987) *Accountabilities: five public services*, London: Tavistock.

DHSS (1970) *The Future Structure of the National Health Service*, (Second Green Paper), London: HMSO.

DHSS (1971a) *National Health Service Reorganization: Consultative Document*, London: HMSO.

DHSS (1971b) *Better Services for the Mentally Handicapped*, Cmnd.4683, London: HMSO.

DHSS (1972a) *Hospital Advisory Service: Annual Report*, London: HMSO.

DHSS (1972b) *National Health Service Reorganization: England* (Cmnd.5055), London: HMSO.

DHSS (1972c) *Management arrangements for the Reorganised National Health Service* (Grey Book), Report of the Management Study Steering Committee (Chairman: Sir Philip Rogers), London: HMSO.

DHSS (1972d) *Statistical and Report Series No. 3: Census of Mentally Handicapped patients in Hospitals in England and Wales 1970*, London: HMSO.

DHSS (1974) *Democracy in the NHS*, London: HMSO.

DHSS (1975a) *The First Interim Report of the Resource Allocation Working Party (RAWP)*, London: HMSO.

DHSS (1975b) *Better Services for the Mentally Ill* (Cmnd.6233), London: HMSO.

DHSS (1976a) *Priorities for Health and Personal Social Services in England: A Consultative Document*, London: HMSO.

DHSS (1976b) *The Final Report of the Resource Allocation Working Party (RAWP)*, *London: HMSO.*

DHSS (1976c) The NHS Planning System, London: HMSO.

DHSS (1976d) *Prevention and Health*, Cmnd.7047, London: HMSO.

DHSS (1977) *The Way Forward: Further Discussion of the Government's National Strategy*, London: HMSO.

DHSS (1978) *Prevention and Health: Everybody's Business*, Cmnd.247, London: HMSO.

DHSS (1979) *Patients First*, London: HMSO.

DHSS (1981a), *Growing Older*, Cmnd 8173, London: HMSO.

DHSS (1981b) *Consultative Document: Care in Action*, London: HMSO.

DHSS (1981c) *Consultative Document: Care in the Community*, London: HMSO.

DHSS (1983) *NHS Management Inquiry Report*, London: HMSO.

DHSS (1985) *Government Response to the Second Report of the Social Services Committee (Session 1984–85), Community Care with special reference to adult mentally ill and mentally handicapped people*, (Cmnd.9674), London: HMSO.

DHSS (1987) *Promoting Better Health – the government's programme for improving primary health care*, Cm 249, London: HMSO.

DHSS (1988) *Report of the Committee of Inquiry into the Care and Aftercare of Miss Sharon Campbell*, London: HMSO.

Dicey, A. V. (1930) *Law and Opinion in England*, London: Macmillan.

Dillner, L. (1993) 'London's specialist centres cut by half', *British Medical Journal*, Vol. 306, 24.6.93, pp. 1709–10.

Dixon, J. and Mays, N. (1997) 'New Labour, New NHS?', *British Medical Journal*, Vol.315, 20–27 December, 1997, p. 1639–40

Dixon, J. and Welch, H. G. (1991) 'Priority setting: lessons from Oregon', *The Lancet.*, Vol. 337, April 13, 1991, pp. 891–4.

DoH (1989a) *Working for Patients*, Cm.555, London: HMSO.

DoH (1989b) *Caring for People: Community Care in the Next Decade and Beyond*, (Cm.849), London: HMSO.

DoH (1990) *Community Care in the Next decade and beyond: Policy Guidance*, London: HMSO.

DoH (1992) *The Health of the Nation*, (Cm 1523), London: HMSO.

DoH (1993a) *Making London Better*, (Cm 2812), London: HMSO.

DoH (1993b) *Corporate Parents*, Heywood: Health Publications Unit.

DoH (1997), The New NHS, Cm.3807, London: Stationery Office

DoH (1998a), The Future of London's Health Services, London: Department of Health

DoH (1998b), Our Healthier Nation, London: HMSO

DoH/OPCS (1994) *Departmental Report: The Government's Expenditure Plans 1994–95 to 1996–97*, Cm 2512, London: HMSO.

DoH/OPCS (1995) *Departmental Report: The Government's Expenditure Plans 1995–96 to 1997–98*, Cm 2812, London: HMSO.

DoH (1995) *Acting on Complaints – The Government's Proposals in response to 'Being Heard', the report of a review committee on NHS complaints procedures*, March 1995, London: HMSO.

Doll, R. and Kinlen, L. J. (1972), 'Epidemiology as an aid to determining the causes of cancer', 49th Annual Report of the Cancer Research Campaign, London: Cancer Research Campaign.

Donaldson, L. (1993) 'Maintaining excellence: the preservation and development of specialist services' in Smith, J. (ed.) (1993) *London after Tomlinson – Reorganising Big City Medicine*, London: BMJ Publishing.

Donne, J. (1624) 'Meditation XVII'. In Abrams, M. H. (ed.) (1979) *The Norton Anthology of English Literature*, Volume One (4th edition), New York: Norton & Co.

Doyal, L. (1979) *The Political Economy of Health*, London: Pluto Press.

Draper, P., Grenhom, G. and Best, G. (1976) *The Organization of Health Care: A Critical View of the 1974 Reorganization of the National Health Service'. In Tuckett, D. (ed.) (1976) An Introduction to Medical Sociology*, London: Tavistock.

Dubos, R. (1959) *The Mirage of Health*, New York: Harper and Row.

Dunleavy, P. (1991) *Democracy, Bureaucracy and Public Choice*, Hemel Hempstead: Harvester.

Durkin, E. (1972) *Hostels for the Mentally Disordered*, London: Fabian Society.

Dworkin, R. (1978) *Taking Rights Seriously*, London: Duckworth.

Eckstein, H. (1955) 'The Politics of the British Medical Association', *Political Quarterly*, Vol XXVI, No. 4, pp. 345–59.

Eckstein, H. (1958) *The English Health Service: its origins, structure and achievements*, Cambridge (Mass.): Harvard University Press.

Emanuel, E. J. (1992) 'The Prescription', *New Republic*, 1/9/92. pp. 21–6.

Ensor, T. (1993) *Future Health Care Options: Funding Health Care*, London: Institute of Health Services Management.

Enthoven, A. C. (1985) *Reflections on the Management of the National Health Service*, London: Nuffield Provincial Hospitals Trust.

Evans, N. (1994) 'A Poisoned Chalice?, Personal Social Services Policy'. In Savage, S., Atkinson, R. and Robins, L. (eds) (1994) *Public Policy in Britain*, Basingstoke: Macmillan.

Expenditure Committee (1977) *Preventive Medicine*, Volume 1, Report, HC 169–i, London: HMSO.

Farrell, C. (1993) *Conflict and Change: Specialist Care in London*, London: Kings Fund.

Field, F. (1971) *Inequality in Britain*, London: Fontana.

Flowers Report (1980) *London Medical Education – A New Framework*, London: University of London.

Foot, M. (1975) *Aneurin Bevan 1945–1960, St. Albans: Paladin.*

Frankel, S. and West, R. (eds) (1993) Rationing and Rationality in the National Health Service: The Persistence of Waiting Lists, Basingstoke: Macmillan.

Fraser, D. (1973) *Evolution of the British Welfare State*, London: Macmillan.

Friedson, E. (1986) *Professional power: a study of the institutionalisation of formal knowledge*, Chicago: University of Chicago Press.

Fries, J. F. et al (1993) 'Reducing health care costs by reducing the need and demand for medical services', *The New England Journal of Medicine*, 29/7/93, Vol. 329, No. 5, pp. 321–4.

George, V. and Wilding, P. (1976) *Ideology and Social Welfare*, London: Routledge & Kegan Paul.

Gilbert, B. B. (1966) *Evolution of National Insurance in Great Britain*, London: Michael Joseph.

Gilbert, B. B. (1970) *British Social Policy 1914–1939*, London: Batsford.

Gilderdale, S. (1971) 'The feeble-minded in hospital', *New Society*, April 8th, 1971, p. 584.

Ginsberg, M. (ed.) (1959) *Law and Opinion in the Twentieth Century*, London: Stevens.

Glennerster, H. (ed.) (1982) *The Future of the Welfare State: Remaking Social Policy*, London: Heinemann.

Glennerster, H. (1995) *British Social Policy Since 1945*, Oxford: Blackwell.

Glennerster, H. Cohen, A. and Bovell, V. (1996) Alternatives to fundholding, Welfare State Programme No.123, London: STICERD

Glennerster, H. Matsaganis, M. and Owens, P. (1994) Implementing GP fundholding: wild card or winning hand?, Buckingham: Open University Press

Glennerster, H. and LeGrand, J. (1997) 'NHS is not dead yet', *The Guardian*, 10/12/97

Goffman, E. (1961) *Asylums: essays on the social situation of mental patients and other inmates*, London: Penguin.

Goodin, R. E. (1982) 'Freedom and the Welfare State: Theoretical Foundations', *Journal of Social Policy*, Vol. 11, Part, 2, April 1982, pp. 149–76.

Goodwin, S. (1989) 'Community Care for the Mentally Ill in England and Wales: Myths, Assumptions and Reality', *Journal of Social Policy*, January 1989, pp. 27–52.

Gostin, L. (1975) *A Human Condition: The Mental Health Act from 1959 to 1975*, Volume 1, London: MIND.

Gough, I. (1979) *The Political Economy of the Welfare State*, London, Macmillan.

Green, M. (1993) 'Clinical research'. In Smith, J. (ed.) (1993) *London after Tomlinson: Reorganising Big City Medicine*, London: BMJ Publishing.

Griffiths, R. (1988) *Agenda for Action, A Report to the Secretary of State for Social Services*, London: HMSO.

Guillebaud Report (1956) *Committee of Enquiry into the Cost of the National Health Service*, Cmnd.553, London: HMSO.

Hall, P. (1975) 'The development of health centres'. In Hall, P., Land, H., Parker, R. and Webb, A. (1975) *Change, Choice and Conflict in Social Policy*, London: Heinemann.

Hall, P. (ed.) (1980) *A Radical Agenda for London*, London: Fabian Society.

Hall, P., Land, H., Parker, R. and Webb, A. (1975) *Change, Choice and Conflict in Social Policy*, London: Heinemann.

Ham, C. (1992) *Health Policy in Britain: the politics and organization of the National Health Service* (3rd edition), Basingstoke: Macmillan.

Ham, C. (1994) 'Health Care; search for a vision'. *The Guardian*, 1.1.94

Ham, C. (1997) 'New British Labour Government: A turning point for NHS funding?', *LSE Health*, Vol.3, No.2, Summer 1997, pp. 27–28, London: LSE Health and European Health Policy Research Network

Ham, C. (1998a) 'Forward through fusion', *The Guardian*, 7 January 1998, p. 2

Ham, C. (1998b) 'Financing the NHS', *British Medical Journal*, Vol.316, pp. 212–213, 17 January

Ham, C., Robinson, R. and Benzeval, M. (1990) *Health Check*, London: Kings Fund Institute.

Harris, J. (1973) 'Food and fairness: the history of food subsidies', *New Society*, August 2, 1973, pp. 273–5.

Harris, J. (1977) *William Beveridge: A Biography*, Oxford: Oxford University Press.

Harris, J. (1979) 'Caring for the sick: a look back at the voluntary tradition', *New Society*, 9.9.79, pp. 287–90.

Harris, J. (1990) 'Enterprise and Welfare States: A Comparative Perspective', London: *Transactions of the Royal Historical Society*.

Harris, R. (ed.) (1965) *Freedom or Free for All? Essays in welfare, trade and choice*, London: Institute of Economic Affairs.

Harris, R. and Seldon, A. (1979) *Over-ruled on Welfare*, London: Institute of Economic Affairs.

Harrison, S. and Wistow, G. (1992) 'The Purchaser/Provider Split in English Health Care: towards explicit rationing', *Policy and Politics*, Vol. 20, No. 2, pp. 123–30.

HAS (Hospital Advisory Service) (1973) *National health Service: Annual Report of the Hospital Advisory Service*, London: HMSO.

Hayek, F. A. (1944) *The Road to Serfdom*, London: Routledge and Kegan Paul.

Hayek, F. A. (1976) *Law, Legislation and Liberty, Volume 2, The Mirage of Social Justice*, London: Routledge & Kegan Paul.

Healthcare 2000 (1995) UK Health and Healthcare Services Challenges and Policy Options, London: Healthcare 2000

Health Education Council (1987) *The Health Divide*, London: Health Education Council.

HEA (Health Education Authority) (1993) *The Smoking Epidemic, A Prescription for Change*, London: HEA.

Heginbotham, C. (1990) 'The future of community care'. In Carrier, J. and Kendall, I. (eds) *Socialism and the NHS: Fabian essays in health care*, Aldershott, Gower.

Heisler, H. (ed.) (1977) *Foundations of Social Administration*, London: Macmillan.

Hennessey, P. (1992) *Never Again: Britain 1945–51*, London: Jonathan Cape.

Heywood, J. (1965) *Children in Care: the development of the service for the deprived child*, (2nd.edition), London: Routledge and Kegan Paul.

Higgs, R. (1993) 'Human frailty should not be penalised'. *British Medical Journal*, Vol. 306, pp. 1047–50 (17 April 1993).

Hills, J. (1993) *The future of welfare: a guide to the debate*, York: Joseph Rowntree Foundation.

Hirsch, F. (1977) *Social Limits to Growth*, London: Routledge and Kegan Paul.

Hodgkinson, R. (1967) *The Origins of the National Health Service: The Medical Services of the New Poor Law 1834–1871*, London: The Wellcome Historical Medical Library.

Honigsbaum, F. (1979) *The Division in British Medicine: A History of the Separation of General Practice from Hospital Care 1911–1968*, London: Kogan Page.

Honigsbaum, F. (1989) *Health, Happiness and Security – the creation of the National Health Service*, London: Routledge.

House of Commons (1942) Official Report : Fifth Series : Parliamentary Debates 1941/1942, Vol. 383, London: HMSO.

House of Commons (1943) Offical Report : Fifth Series : Parliamentary Debates 1942/1943, Vol. 386, London: HMSO.

House of Commons (1946) Official Report (Fifth Series), Parliamentary Debates, 1945/46, Vol.422, London: HMSO

House of Commons (1985) Second Report from the Social Services Committee (Session 1984–85), Community Care with special reference to adult mentally ill and mentally handicapped people, Volume 1, London: HMSO.

House of Commons (1995a) *Parliamentary Debates* (Hansard), Vol. 257, No. 86, 5.4.95, London: HMSO.

House of Commons (1995b) *Parliamentary Debates* (Hansard), Vol. 259, No. 102, 10.5.95, London: HMSO.

House of Commons (1997) Official Report, Parliamentary Debates (Hansard), Vol.302, No.85, 9 December 1997, London: HMSO

House of Lords (1997), Official Report, Parliamentary Debates (Hansard), Vol.584, No.76, Tuesday, 9 December, 1997, London: HMSO

Howe, G. M. and Loraine, J. A. (eds) (1973) *Environmental Medicine*, London: Heinemann.

Humana, C. (1992) *World Human Rights Guide* (Third Edition), Oxford: Oxford University Press.

HSE (Health and Safety Executive) (1996) *Good Health in Good Business*, London: HSE.

Ignatieff, M. (1984) *The Needs of Strangers*, London: Chatto and Windus.

Illich, I. (1976) *Limits to Medicine : medical nemesis : the expropriation of health*, London: Boyars.

Illich, I. (1978) *The right to useful unemployment and its professional enemies*, London: Boyars.

Illsley, R. (1980) *Professional or Public Health?*, Rock Carling Lecture, London: Nuffield Provincial Hospitals Trust.

Illsley, R. (1986) 'Occupational class, selection and the production of inequalities in health', *Quarterly Journal of Social Affairs*, **2**, pp. 151–65.

Inner London Health Authorty Chief Executive [ILHACE] (1995) *Hospital Services for Londoners*, London: ILHACE.

Israel, S. and Teeling-Smith, G. (1967) 'The submerged iceberg of sickness in society'. *Social and Economic Administration*, Vol 1, No. 1, pp. 43–56.

It's A Wonderful Life (1946) RKO/Liberty Films (Director: Frank Capra)

Jacobson, B. (1993) 'Public health in Inner London' in Smith, J. (ed.) (1993) *London after Tomlinson: Reorganising Big City Medicine*, London: BMJ Publishing.

Jaehnig, W. (1979) *A family service for the mentally handicapped*, Fabian Tract 460, London: Fabian Society.

Jacobson, B., Smith, A. and Whitehead, M. (eds) (1991) *The Nation's Health – A Strategy for the 1990s*, A report from an Independent Multidisciplinary Committee, London: King Edwards Hospital Fund for London.

James, C. (1984) *Occupational Pensions: the failure of private pensions*, London: Fabian Society.

James, P. (1998) 'Food is a public health issue', *British Medical Journal*, 7 February 1998, Vol.316, p. 416

Jarman, B. (1981) *A Survey of Primary Care in London*, London: Royal College of General Practitioners.

Jarman, B. (1993) 'Is London Overbedded?', *British Medical Journal*, Vol. 306, pp. 979–82.

Jarman, B. (1994) 'The Crisis in London Medicine : How many hospital beds does the capital need?', Special University Lecture, London: University of London.

Jeffreys, M. and Sachs, H. (1983), *Rethinking general practice: dilemmas in primary medical care*, London: Tavistock.

Jenkins, P. (1963) 'Bevan's Fight with the BMA'. In Sissons, M. and French, P. (eds) (1963) *Age of Austerity*, London: Hodder and Stoughton.

Jenkins, S. (1996) *Accountable to None : the Tory Nationalisation of Britain*, London: Hamish Hamilton.

Jones, K. (1955) *Lunacy, Law and Conscience*, London: Routledge Kegan and Paul.

Jones, K. (1960) *Mental Health and Social Policy*, London: Routledge, Kegan and Paul.

Jones, K. (1972) *A History of the Mental Health Services*, London: Routlege, Kegan and Paul.

Jones, K. (ed.), (1972) *The Yearbook of Social Policy in Britain, 1971*, London: Routledge and Kegan Paul.

Jones, K. (ed.) (1974), *The Yearbook of Social Policy in Britain, 1972*, London: Routledge and Kegan Paul.

Jones, K. (ed.) (1975), *The Yearbook of Social Policy in Britain, 1974*, London: Routledge and Kegan Paul.

Jones, K. (1983) 'Services for the mentally ill: the death of a concept.' In Bean, P. and MacPherson, S. (eds) *Approaches to Welfare*, London: Routledge & Kegan Paul.

Jones, K. et al (1983) *Issues in Social Policy*, London: Routledge & Kegan Paul.

Jowell, R., Witherspoon, S. and Brook, L. (eds) (1989) *British Social Attitudes – The Fifth Report*, Aldershot: Gower.

Jowell, R., Brook, L., Prior, G and Taylor, B. (eds) (1993) *British Social Attitudes – The Ninth Report*, Aldershot: Dartmouth.

Jowell, T. (1993) 'Community care in London : The prospects' in Smith, J. (ed.) (1993) *London after Tomlinson: Reorganising Big City Medicine*, London: BMJ Publishing.

Judge, K. (1995) 'Income distribution and life expectancy: a critical appraisal', *British Medical Journal*, Vol 311, 11 November 1995, pp. 1282–5.

Kaim-Caudle, P. (1977) 'Inequality' in Heisler, H. *Foundation of Social Administration*, London: Macmillan.

Kennedy, I. and Grubb, A. (1994) *Medical Law : Text with Materials*, (2nd.edition), London: Butterworth.

Kings Fund (1987) *Planned Health Services for Inner London – Back to back planning*, London: Kings Edward Hospital Fund for London.

Kings Fund (1992a) *London Health Care 2010 – Changing the Future of Services in the Capital*, Kings Fund Commission on the Future of London's Acute Health Services, London: Kings Fund Initiative.

Kings Fund (1992b) *London Health Care 2010 – Review*, London: Kings Fund.

Kings Fund (1994) *London Monitor No.1*, London: Kings Fund.

Kings Fund (1995a) *London Monitor No.2*, London: Kings Fund.

Kings Fund (1995b) *Tackling Health Inequalities ; An Agenda for Action*, London: Kings Fund.

Klein, R. (1973) *Complaints against doctors*, London: Charles Knight.

Klein, R. (1976) 'The Politics of Redistribution', *British Medical Journal*, 9 October 1976, p. 893.

Klein, R. (1983) *The Politics of the National Health Service*, Harlow: Longman.

Klein, R. (1993) 'Dimensions of rationing : who should do what?', *British Medical Journal*, 9 October 1976, p. 893.

Klein, R. (1983) *The Politics of the National Health Service*, Harlow: Longman.

Klein, R. (1993) 'Dimensions of rationing : who should do what?', *British Medical Journal*, Vol. 307, 31 July 1993, pp. 309–11.

Klein, R. (1994) 'Can we restrict the health care menu?', *Health Policy*, **27**, pp. 103–12.

Klein, R. (1995a) *The New Politics of the NHS* (Third Edition), Harlow: Longman.

Klein, R. (1995b), 'Big Bang Health care Reform – Does It Work? : The Case of Britain's 1991 National Health Service reform', *Milbank Quarterly*, Vol. 73, No. 3, pp. 299–337.

Klein, R. (1998) 'Labour's Third Way: Solution or Delusion?', *Parliamentary Brief*, March 1998, p. 32

Laslett, P. (1965) *The World We Have Lost*, London: Methuen.

Last, J. M. (1963(, 'The iceberg: "Completing the Picture" in General Practice.' *The Lancet*, 6 July 1963, pp. 28–31.

Lawson, N. (1993) *The View From No. 11 : Memoirs of a Tory Radical*, London: Corgi.

Le Grand, J. (1998) 'The Third Way begins with Cora', *New Statesman*, 6 March 1998, pp. 26–7

Le Grand, J. and Bartlett, W. (eds) (1993) *Quasi-markets and social policy*, Basingstoke: Macmillan.

Leathard, A. (1990) *Health Care Provision: past, present and future*, London: Chapman and Hall.

Lee, K. and Mills, A. (1982) *Policy making and planning in the health sector*, London: Croom Helm.

Lees, D. (1961) 'Health Through Choice'. In Harris, R. (ed.) (1965) *Freedom or Free for All? Essays in welfare, trade and choice*, London: Institute of Economic Affairs.

Lees, D. (1976) 'Economics and non-economics of health services', *Three Banks Review*, July 1976.

Lindsey, A. (1962) *Socialised Medicine in England and Wales*, London: University of North Carolina Press.

LHPC (London Health Planning Consortium) (1980) *Acute Health Services in London*, London: HMSO.

LHPC (London Health Planning Consortium) (1981) *Primary Health Care for Inner London* (Chairman, Sir D. Acheson), (May 1981) London: HMSO.

LIG (London Implementation Group) (1993) *Speciality Reviews, Reports of Independent Reviews of Specialist Services in London: Cancer; Cardiac; Children; Neurosciences; Plastics and Burns; Renal*, (June 1993), London: HMSO.

London Advisory Group (1981) Reports (Chair: Sir John Habakkuk), London: DHSS.

Marmor, T. (1983) *Political Analysis and American Medical Care: Essays*, Cambridge: Cambridge University Press.

Marris, P. and Rein, M. (1972) *Dilemmas of Social Reform: poverty and community action in the United States*, London: Routledge & Kegan Paul.

Marshall, T. H. (1950) *Citizenship and Social Class*, Cambridge: Cambridge University Press.

Marshall, T. H. (1963) *Sociology at the Crossroads and other essays*, London: Heinemann.

Marshall, T. H. (1981) *The Right to Welfare and other essays*, London: Heinemann.

Martin, F. M. (1984) *Between the Acts: Community Mental Health Services 1959–1983*, London: Nuffield Provincial Hospitals Trust.

Martin, J. P. (1984) *Hospitals in Trouble*, London: Basil Blackwell.

Matthew, H. C. G. (1984) 'The Liberal Age (1851–1914)'. In Morgan, K. O. (ed.) *The Oxford Illustrated History of Britain*, Oxford: Oxford University Press.

Maynard, A. (1998) 'Injection of reality prescribed', *Times Higher Education Supplement*, January 30, 1998, p. 20

Maxwell, R. (1990) 'London's Health Services' *Christian Action Journal*, Special Edition, Autumn, 1990.

Maxwell, R. (1994) *What next for London's health care?* London: Kings Fund.

Mays, J., Forder, A. and Keidan, O. (eds) (1975) *Penelope Hall's Social Services of Modern England*, London: Routledge & Kegan Paul.

McKeown, T. (1967) 'Medical and Social Needs of Patients in Hospitals for the Mentally Subnormal'. *British Journal of Preventive and Social Medicine*, Vol 21, pp. 115–21.

McKeown, T. (1976), The Role of Medicine: Dream, Mirage or Nemesis?, Nuffield Provincial Hospitals Trust, London

McKeown, T. et al (1958) 'Institutional care of the Mentally Ill', *The Lancet* (March 29th, 1958)

Mechanic, D. (1976) *The Growth of Bureaucratic Medicine: An Inquiry into the Dynamics of Patient Behaviour and the Organization of Medical Care*, New York: John Wiley & Sons.

Mechanic, D. (1992) 'Professional judgement and the rationing of medical care', *University of Pennsylvania Law Review*, 140 (5), pp. 1543–72.

MHTFL (1994) Priorities for Action: a report by the Mental Health Task Force London Project, London: Mental Health Force Task Force London Project.

Milburn, A. 'For a healthier Britain', *Fabian Review*, Autumn/Winter 1997, p. 22, London: Fabian Society

Mill, J. S. (1859) *On Liberty*, London: J. M. Dent.

Ministry of Health (1921) Voluntary Hospitals Committee (Cave Committee), Final Report, Cmd.1335, London: HMSO.

Ministry of Health (1944) *A National Health Service*, Cmd.6502, London: HMSO.

Ministry of Health (1946) National Health Service Bill. Cmd.6761, London: HMSO.

Ministry of Health (1962) Hospital Plan for England and Wales (cmnd.1604), London: HMSO.

Ministry of Health (1963) Plans for Health and Welfare Services of the Local Authorities in England and Wales, Cmnd.1973, London: HMSO.

Ministry of Health (1963) Plans for Health and Welfare Services of the Local Authorities in England and Wales, Cmnd.1973, London: HMSO.

Ministry of Health (1968) *The Administrative Structure of the medical and related services in England and Wales*, (First Green Paper), London: HMSO.

Mittler, P. (1965) *Mental Health Services*, London: Fabian Society.

Mooney, G. (1992) *Economics, Medicine and Health care* (Second Edition), London: Harvester Wheatsheaf.

Morgan, K. O. (1984a) Editor's Foreword. In Morgan, K. O. (ed.) (1984) *The Oxford Illustrated History of Britain*, Oxford: Oxford University Press.

Morgan, K. O. (1984b) *Labour In Power 1945–1951*, Oxford: Clarendon Press.

Morris, J. N. et al (1953) 'Coronary Heart Disease and Physical Activity of Work'. *The Lancet*, Vol. 2, 21 November 1953, pp. 1053–7.

Muir-Gray, J. A. (1979) *Man Against Disease: Preventive Medicine*, Oxford: Oxford University Press.

Mumford, L. (1940) *The Culture of Cities*, London: Secker and Warburg.

Murray, C. (1990) *The Emerging British Underclass*, London: Institute of Economic Affairs.

Murphy, E. (1992) *London Views: Three essays on health care in the capital*, Working Party No. 5, London: Kings Fund London Acute Services Initiative.

National Audit Office (1987) *Use of Operating Theatres in the National Health Service*, HC 143, London: HMSO.

NCC (1995), Charging Consumers for Social Care, London: National Consumer Council

Newdick, C. (1995) *Who Should We Treat? Law, Patients and Resources in the NHS*, Oxford: Clarendon Press.

NHS Executive (1994) *NHS Responsibilities for meeting long term health care needs*, HSG (94), London: DoH.

NHS Executive (1993) Managing the New NHS: a background document, Leeds: Department of Health

NHS Executive (1997a) Letter: NHS Priorities and Planning Guidance, EL (97) 39, Leeds: Department of Health

NHS Executive (1997b) The Commissioning Process for 1998/99, Leeds: Department of Health

NHS Executive (1997c) Priorities and Planning Guidance for the NHS: 1998/99, Leeds: Department of Health

NHS Executive (1997d), Letter: Health Action Zones – Invitation to Bid, EL (97) 65, Leeds: Department of Health

Nicholls, G. (1854) *History of the English Poor Law*, London: King.

Oakley, A. (1984) *The Captured Womb*, Oxford: Blackwell.

OHE (1994) *Health Information and the Consumer*, London: Office of Health Economics.

O'Higgins, M. (1983) 'Issues of Redistribution in State Welfare Spending'. In Loney, M., Boswell, D. and Clarke, J. (eds) *Social Policy and Social Welfare*, Milton Keynes: Open University Press.

Packman, J. (1975) *The Child's Generation: Child Care Policy from Curtis to Houghton*, Oxford: Basil Blackwell.

Parker, J. (1965) *Local Health and Welfare Services*, London: Allen and Unwin.

Parker, J. (1975) *Social Policy and Citizenship*, London: Macmillan.

Parker, R. (1975) 'Social administration and scarcity'. In Butterworth, E. and Holman, R. (eds) (1975) *Social Welfare in Modern Britain*, London: Fontana.

Parker, R. (1976) 'Charging for the Social Services', *Journal of Social Policy*, Vol. 5, Part IV, October 1976, pp. 359–73.

Parston, G. and McMahon, L. (1998) 'A third way? England-yes Scotland-maybe', *British Medical Journal*, Vol.316, 17 January 1998, p. 213

Parry-Jones, W. L. (1987) 'Asylum for the mentally ill in historical perspective', *Bulletin of the Royal College of Psychiatrists*, pp. 407–10.

Paulus, I. (1974) *The Search for Pure Food: a sociology of legislation in Britain*, London: Martin Robertson.

Phillimore, P., Beattie, A. and Townsend, P. (1988) *Health and Deprivation: Inequality and the North*, London: Routledge.

Phillimore, P., Beattie, A. and Townsend, P. (1994) 'Widening inequality of health in northern England 1981–1991', *British Medical Journal*, 30 April 1994, Vol. 308, pp. 1125–8.

Phillips Report (1954) *Report of the Committee on the Economic and Financial problems of the Provision for Old Age*, Cmd.9333, London: HMSO.

Phillipson, C. (1990) 'A Policy for Health Care for Older People'. In Carrier, J. and Kendall, I. (eds) *Socialism and the NHS: Fabian Essays in Health Care*, Aldershott: Gower.

Piachaud, D. (1981) 'Peter Townsend and the Holy Grail', *New Society*, 10 September 1981, pp. 419–21.

Piachaud, D. (1987) 'Problems in the Definition and Measurement of Poverty', *Journal of Social Policy*, Vol. 16, Part 2 (April 1987), pp. 147–64.

Pinker, R. (1966) *English Hospital Statistics 1861–1938*, London: Heinemann.

Pinker, R. (1971) *Social Theory and Social Policy*, London: Heinemann.

Pinker, R. (1982) 'An Alternative View.' In Barclay Report *Social Workers and their Role and Tasks: the Report of a Working Party*, London: Bedford Square Press.

Pinker, R. (1996) 'A Celebration of Brian Abel-Smith's Work – The Hospitals 1800–1948; Public Lecture, London: London School of Economics.

Pollitt, C., Harrison, S., Hunter, D. J. and Marncoch, G. (1991) 'General Management in the NHS: The Initial Impact 1983–88', *Public Administration*, Vol. 69, Spring 1991, pp. 61–83.

Porritt Report (1962) *A Review of the Medical Services in Great Britain*, London: Social Assay.

Powell, M. (1992a) 'The geography of English hospital provision in the 1930s: the historical geography of heterodoxy', *Journal of Historical Geography*, **18**, 3, pp. 307–16.

Powell, M. (1992b) 'Hospital Provision before the National Health Service: A Geographical Study of the 1945 Hospital Surveys', London: The Society for the Social History of Medicine.

Power, C. (1994) 'Health and Social Inequality in Europe', *British Medical Journal*, 30 April 1994, Vol. 308, pp. 1153–6.

Powles, J. (1973) 'Science, Medicine and Man'. *Social Science and Medicine*, Vol. 1, pp. 1–30.

Public Accounts Committee (1993) Sixty Third Report: Wessex Regional Health Authority Regional Information Systems (December 1993), London: HMSO.

R v Cambridge Health Authority: exparte B., *The Times*, 10 March 1995.

Rawls, J. (1980) *A Theory of Justice* Oxford: Oxford University Press.

Rees-Mogg, W. (1997) 'Why the NHS is the sick man of Europe', *The Times*, 6/10/97

Rein, M. (1970) 'Problems in the Definition and Measurement of Poverty'. In Townsend, P. (ed.) *The Concept of Poverty*, London: Heinemann.

Ritchie Report (1994) *The Report of the Inquiry into the care and Treatment of Christopher Clunis* (Chair: Jean Ritchie), London: HMSO.

Robb, B. (ed.) (1967) *Sans Everything*, London: Nelson.

Roberts, N. (1967) *Mental Health and Mental Illness*, London: Routledge, Kegan and Paul.

Robinson, D. (1973) *Patients, Practitioners and Medical Care: aspects of medical sociology*, London: Heinemann.

Robinson, R. and Judge, K. (1987) *Public expenditure and the NHS: Trends and Prospects*, London: King's Fund Institute.

Robinson, R. and Le Grand, J. (eds), (1994) Evaluating the NHS Reforms, London: Kings Fund Institute

Rowntree, S. (1901) *Poverty: A Study of Town Life*, London: Macmillan & Co.

Royal Commission on the Law relating to Mental Illness and Mental Deficiency (1957) Report (Chair: Lord Percy of Newcastle), Cmnd.169, London: HMSO.

Royal Commission on Local Government in Greater London (1960) Report: Chair: Sir Edwin Herbert, Cmnd.1164, London: HMSO.

Royal Commission on Local Government in England (1969) Report, (Chair: The Rt.Hon. Lord Redcliffe Maud), Cmnd.4040, London: HMSO.

Royal Commission on Medical Education (1968) Report, (Chair: Lord Todd), Cmnd.3568, London: HMSO.

Royal Commission on National Health Insurance (1926) Report, Cmd.2596, London: HMSO.

Royal Commission on the NHS (1979) Report (Chair: Sir Alec Merrison), Cmnd.7615, London: HMSO.

Royal Commission on NHS Research Paper 1 (1978) *The Working of the National Health Service*, London: HMSO.

Royal Commission on the NHS (1979) Report, (Chair: Sir Alec Merrison), Cmnd.7615, London: HMSO.

Rumsey, H. (1856) *Essays on State Medicine*, London: John Churchill.

Ryan, J. with Thomas, F. (1980) *The Politics of Mental Handicap*, Harmondsworth: Penguin.

Ryan, W. (1971) *Blaming the Victim*, London: Orbach and Chambers.

Sand, R. (1935) *Health and Human Progess: an essay in sociological medicine*, London: Kegan Paul, Trench, Trubner & Co.

Savage, S., Atkinson, R. and Tobins, L. (1994) *Public Policy in Britain*, Basingstoke: Macmillan.

Savage, S. and Robins, L. (1990 *Public Policy under Thatcher*, Basingstoke: Macmillan.

Scammells, B. (1971) *Studies in Social Administration: Administration of Health and Welfare Services*, Manchester: Manchester University Press.

Scull, A. (1979) *Museums of Madness: the social organization of insanity in the nineteenth century*, London: Allen Lane.

Secretary of State for Health (1997), Letter to Chairs of Health Authorities, Trusts Chairs, Leaders of Councils: Additional Resources 1997/98 / Better Services for vulnerable people, 20 October 1997, London: Department of Health

Secretary of State for Scotland (1997), Designed to Care, Edinburgh: Stationery Office

Sedgwick, P. (1982) *Psycho-politics: Laing, Foucault, Goffman, Szasz and the future of mass psychiatry*, London: Harper Row.

Seebohm Report (1968) *Report of the Committee on Local Authority and Allied Personal Social Services*, Cmnd.3703, London: HMSO.

Seedhouse, D. (1986) *Health: The Foundations of Achievement*, Chichester: John Wiley and Sons.

Seedhouse, D. (1987) 'Does the National Health Service have a purpose'. In Bryne, P. (ed.) (1987) *Medicine in Contemporary Society*, London: Kings Fund.

Seedhouse, D. (1993) *Fortress NHS: a philosophical review of the National health service*, Chichester: Wiley.

Seldon, A. (1966) 'Which Way to Welfare?'. *Lloyds Bank Review*, No. 82, October 1966, pp. 34–48.

Shiu, M. (1993) 'Controversies in Treatment: Should smokers be offered coronary by-pass surgery? Refusing to treat smokers is unethical and dangerous precedent'. *British Medical Journal*, Vol. 306, pp. 1048–9 (17 April 1993).

Sidaway v Governors of Royal Bethlem Hospital [1985] 1 A11 ER 643.

Silent Minority (1981), Channel 4, London

Simey, T.S. and Simey, M.B. (1960) Charles Booth: Social Scientist, London: Oxford University Press

Sissons, M. and French, P. (eds) *Age of Austerity*, London: Hodder and Stoughton.

Smith, J. (1993) 'Introduction' in Smith, J. (ed.), 1993 *London After Tomlinson: Reorganising Big City Medicine*, London: BMJ Publishing.

Smith, J. (ed.) (1993) *London After Tomlinson: Reorganising Big City Medicine*, London: BMJ Publishing.

Smith, R. (1989) 'Words from the source: interview with Alan Enthoven', *British Medical Journal*, Vol. 298. 29 April 1989, pp. 1166–8.

Social Services Committee (1985) Second Report from the Social Services Committee (Session 1984–85), Community Care with special reference to adult mentally ill and mentally handicapped people, Volume 1, London: HMSO.

Social Services Committee (1988) *Resourcing the NHS: Short Term Issues*, Volume One, London: HMSO.

Social Services Committee (1989) *Fifth Report: Resourcing the NHS: the Government's White Paper: Working for Patients*, London: HMSO.

Stacey, M. (1988) *The Sociology of Health and Healing: a textbook*, London: Unwin Hyman.

Stark-Murray, D. (1971) *Why a National Health Service?* London: Pemberton Books.

Starr, P. (1982) *The social transformation of American medicine*, New York: Basic Books.

Stern, J. (1983) 'Social mobility and the interpretation of social class mortality differentials', *Journal of Social Policy*, Vol. 13, Part 1, January 1983, pp. 27–44.

Stevens, R. (1966) *Medical practice in Modern England – the impact of specialisation and state medicine*, New Haven: Yale University Press.

Stone, N. (1995) 'Community care and the limits of the market', *Fabian Review*, Vol. 107, No. 2, April 1995.

Sugden, R. (1982) 'Hard Luck Stories: the problem of the uninsured in a laissez-faire society', *Journal of Social Policy*, Volume 11, Part 2, April 1982, pp. 201–16.

Surtz, S. J. and Hexter, J. H. (eds) (1965) *The Complete Works of St. Thomas More*, Volume 4, London: Yale University Press. (Quote is from pp. 139–40.)

Szreter, S. (1988) 'The importance of social intervention in British mortality decline c.1850–1914: a reinterpretation of the role of public health', *Social History of Medicine*, Vol. 1, No. 1, pp. 1–37.

Tawney, R.H. (1964), Equality, London: George Allen and Unwin

Tawney, R. H. (1966) *The Radical Tradition: Twelve Essays on Politics, Education and Literature* (edited by R. Hinden), Harmondsworth: Penguin Books.

Thane, P. (1982) *The foundations of the welfare state*, Harlow: Longman.

Thatcher, M. (1993) *The Downing Street Years*, London: Harper Collins.

Thomas N. and Stoten B. (1974) 'The NHS and local government'. In Jones, K. (ed.) (1974) *The Yearbook of Social Policy in Britain*, 1973, London: Routledge and Kegan Paul.

Timmins, N. (1988) *Cash, Crisis and Cure: Guide to the NHS Debate*, London: Newspaper Publishing.

Timmins, N. (1995) *The Five Giants: A Biography of the Welfare State*, London: Harper Collins.

Titmuss, R. M. (1950) *The Problems of Social Policy*, London: HMSO.

Titmuss, R. M. (1961) 'Community care: Fact or Fiction'. In Titmuss, R. M. (1968) *Commitment to Welfare*, London: George Allen and Unwin.

Titmuss, R. M. (1963) *Essays on the Welfare State*, London: George Allen & Unwin.

Titmuss, R. M. (1968) *Commitment to Welfare*, London: George Allen and Unwin.

Titmuss, R. M. (1970) *The Gift Relationship*, London: George Allen and Unwin.

Titmuss, R. M. (1974) *Social Policy: An Introduction*, London: George Allen and Unwin.

Titmuss, R. M. (1987) *The Philosophy of Welfare*, London: Allen and Unwin.

Tomlinson Report (1992) *Report of the Inquiry into London's Health Service, Medical Education and Research*, London: HMSO.

Townsend, P. (1962) *The Last Refuge: a survey of residential institutions and homes for the aged in England and Wales*, London: Routledge & Kegan Paul.

Townsend, P. (1970) 'Foreword'. In Bull, D. (ed.) (1970) *Family Poverty*, London: Duckworth.

Townsend, P. (1968) *Social Services For All?* London: Fabian Society.

Townsend, P. (1973) *The Social Minority*, London: Allen Lane.

Treasury (1976) *Public Expenditure to 1979–80*, Cmnd.6393, London: HMSO.

Treasury (1977) *The Government's Expenditure Plans*, Cmnd.6721, London: HMSO.

Trombley, S. (1989) *Sir Frederick Treves: The Extra Ordinary Edwardian*, London: Routledge.

Tuckett, D. (ed.) (1976) *An Introduction to Medical Sociology*, London: Tavistock.

Tudor-Hart, J. (1971) 'The Inverse care Law', *The Lancet*, 27 February, pp. 405–12.

Turnberg, L. (1998) Health Services in London – A Strategic Review, London: Department of Health

Tutt, N. (1974), *Care or Custody: community homes and treatment of delinquency*, London: Darton, Longman and Todd.

Underwood, H. J. and Bailey, J. (1993) 'Coronary by-pass surgery should not be offered to smokers'. *British Medical Journal*, Vol. 306, pp. 1047–50 (17 April 1993).

Van Doorslaer, E., Wagstaff, A. and Rutten, F. (1993) *Equity in the Finance and Delivery of Health Care: An International Perspective*, Oxford: Oxford University Press.

Walker, A. (1982a) 'A Caring Community'. In Glennerster, H. (ed.) (1982) *The Future of the Welfare State: Remaking Social Policy*, London: Heinemann.

Walker, A. (1982b) 'Dependency and Old Age'. *Social Policy and Administration*, Vol. 16, No. 2, pp. 115–35.

Walker, A. (1983) *Community Care*, London: Macmillan.

Walton, R. and Heywood, M. (1975) 'Child Care, Culture and Social Services Departments'. In Jones, K. (ed.) *The Year Book of Social Policy in Britain 1974*, London: Routledge & Kegan Paul.

Watkin, B. (1978) *The National Health Service: The First Phase 1948–1974 and After*, London: George Allen and Unwin.

Weale, A. (1982) 'Freedom and the Welfare State: Introduction', *Journal of Social Policy*. Volume 11, Part 2, April 1982, pp. 145–8.

Webb, B. and S. (1910) *English Poor Law Policy*, London: Longman.

Webster, C. (1988) *The Health Services Since The War, Volume 1, Problems of Health Care, The NHS before 1957*, London: HMSO.

Webster, C. (1990) 'Conflict and Consensus: Explaining the British Health Service'. *Twentieth Century British History*, Vol. 1, pp. 115–51.

Webster, C. (1995) 'Local government and health care: the historical perspective', *British Medical Journal*, Vol. 310, 17, June 1995, pp. 1584–7.

Webster, C. (ed.) (1991) *Aneurin Bevan on the National Health Service*, Oxford: Wellcome Unit for the History of Medicine.

Westergaard, J. and Resler, H. (1976) Class in a Capitalist Society, Harmondsworth: Penguin

White, A. (1901) *Efficiency and Empire*, London: Methuen & Co.

WHO (1948) WHO Constitution, Offical Records, No. 2 (June (1948), Geneva: WHO.

WHO (1973) *Better Food for a Healthier World*, Geneva: WHO.

WHO (1977) *Health For All by the Year 2000*, Geneva: WHO.

WHO (1981) *Managerial Process for National Health Development: Guiding Principles*, Geneva: WHO.

WHO (1996) *Annual Report*, Geneva: WHO.

Wilding, P. (1982) *Professional power and social welfare*, London: Routledge & Kegan Paul.

Wilensky, H. and Lebeaux, C. (1965) *Industrial Society and Social Welfare*, New York: Free Press.

Wilensky, H. (1975) *The Welfare State and Equality: structural and ideological roots of public expenditures*, London: University of California Press.

Wilensky, H. (1981) 'Democractic Corporation, Consensus and Social Policy'. In *The Welfare State in Crisis: An account of the conference on Social Policies in the 1980s*, 20–23 October 1980, pp. 191–2, Paris: OECD.

Wilkinson, R. G. (1992) *Income Distribution and Life Expectancy*, *British Medical Journal*, Vol. 304, pp. 165–8 (18 January, 1992).

Wilkinson, R. G. (1995) 'Commentary: A reply to Ken Judge:

mistaken criticisms ignore overwhelming evidence'. *British Medical Journal*, Vol. 311, pp. 1285–7 (11 November 1995).

Willcocks, A. (1967) *The Creation of the National Health Service*, London: Routledge Kegan Paul.

Williams Report (1967) *Caring for People*, London: HMSO.

Wilson, N. (1938) *Public Health Services*, London: William Hodge.

Wilson Report (1994) *Being Heard: The report of a review committee on NHS complaints procedure*, (May 1994), London: HMSO.

Woodward, J. (1974) *To do the sick no harm: a study of the British voluntary hospital system to 1875*, London: Routledge and Kegan Paul.

Wordsworth, W. (1807), Intimations of Immortality from Recollections of Early Childhood (from Hutchinson,T (ed), The Poetical Works of William Wordsworth, London: Henry Frowde

Yates, J. (1987) *Why Are We Waiting?*, Oxford: Oxford University Press.

Young, F. G. (1968) 'The origin and development of the University of London with particular reference to medical education'. In Royal Commission on Medical Education (1968), Appendix 14.

Index